9.95

D0615620

"*An Odyssey with Animals* demonstrates that even someone who has held hard-line positions in the animal research/rights debate can offer a thoughtful perspective, and suggest points where compromise might be reached. This is one of the strengths of Morrison's book—the way his story becomes a journey of exploration, and the way that he not only solidifies some of his own opinions but also allows himself to be open to possible shifts. The book highlights how precious (and precarious) is the potential for change in the midst of conflict—both because it offers such resolution and because Morrison's perspective, along with his role in the history of this movement, is so valuable. Morrison's reputation as an outstanding researcher and his importance as one of the rare scientists willing to speak out on this issue will undoubtedly make *An Odyssey with Animals* a valued part of the continuing public discussion on animal research."

—*Deborah Blum, Professor of Journalism, University of Wisconsin-Madison, and author of* The Monkey Wars

"Here is the account of a spine-chilling journey through the world of animal use and the abuse of science. It is written by one whose rich experience, deep understanding, warm heart, and balanced mind qualify him beyond all others to tell the awesome tale. This is a splendid book."

—*Carl Cohen, Ph.D., Professor of Philosophy, University of Michigan*

"*An Odyssey with Animals* by Adrian Morrison does for the animal rights and welfare debate what Lance Armstrong's book accomplished for cancer; although bad things happen to good people, our response to personal adversity can be transcendent. *Odyssey* candidly describes how Morrison, a scientist, veterinarian, and community leader became the target of animal rights extremists, giving us a balanced corrective in which reason supplants rage, knowledge replaces superstition, and love trumps hate. *Odyssey* is accessible, entertaining, appalling, and inspiring."

—*Ralph Lydic, Ph.D., Bert La Du Professor of Anesthesiology, University of Michigan*

AN ODYSSEY WITH ANIMALS

A Veterinarian's Reflections on the Animal Rights & Welfare Debate

Adrian R. Morrison

OXFORD
UNIVERSITY PRESS

2009

OXFORD
UNIVERSITY PRESS

Oxford University Press, Inc., publishes works that further
Oxford University's objective of excellence
in research, scholarship, and education.

Oxford   New York
Auckland   Cape Town   Dar es Salaam   Hong Kong   Karachi
Kuala Lumpur   Madrid   Melbourne   Mexico City   Nairobi
New Delhi Shanghai Taipei   Toronto

With offices in
Argentina   Austria   Brazil Chile   Czech Republic   France   Greece
Guatemala   Hungary   Italy   Japan Poland   Portugal   Singapore
South Korea   Switzerland   Thailand   Turkey   Ukraine   Vietnam

Copyright © 2009, by Oxford University Press, Inc.

Published by Oxford University Press, Inc.
198 Madison Avenue, New York, New York 10016
www.oup.com
Oxford is a registered trademark of Oxford University Press

Library of Congress Cataloging-in-Publication Data

Morrison, Adrian R.
An odyssey with animals : a veterinarian's reflections on the animal rights & welfare debate / Adrian R.
Morrison.
p. cm.
Includes bibliographical references and index.
ISBN 978-0-19-537444-5
1. Medical sciences—Research—Moral and ethical aspects. 2. Biology—Research—Moral and ethical aspects.
3. Laboratory animals. 4. Animal experimentation. 5. Animal welfare—Moral and ethical aspects. I. Title.
R724.M845 2009
610.72—dc22   2008053834

1 3 5 7 9 8 6 4 2
Printed in the United States of America
on acid-free paper

To my wife Olive,
with love and appreciation,
as partial repayment on
a debt that can never
be fully repaid

Acknowledgments

The chance to thank friends and colleagues for their generous assistance as I wrote this book is the best part of all—after the Dedication. Much credit goes to them in this finished product; any errors of fact or interpretation are mine.

I begin with Jan Dizard and Buster. Each in his way—the former cerebral and the latter emotional—made fundamental contributions to the creation of this book. They set me on the right path after several years of fumbling in the dark.

I am very grateful that my friend David Dinges, editor-in-chief of the journal *SLEEP*, and past-president of the World Federation of Sleep Research and Sleep Medicine Societies, took time from his very busy schedule to write the Foreword. He has been one of my staunchest supporters through the years.

Only because of the dedicated and competent management of my laboratory (and of me) by my assistant of more than 40 years, Graziella Mann, could I have found the time to complete this book. We have had a great time together.

Also, the privilege of having the freedom to pursue my interests, wherever they might lie, is due to my position as a professor at the University of Pennsylvania. I cannot imagine a better life. Furthermore, the National Institutes of Health, the most generous medical institution in the world, has supported my scientific work, some described in this book, for more than 40 years.

I have often read tributes by authors to the publisher's editor, and now I know why they are so effusive. Sarah Harrington, a true professional, turned my manuscript into a book with her skillful edits and suggestions, not to mention her encouragement. I cannot thank her enough. In the same vein, I am grateful for the critical reviews by various anonymous reviewers, who in more than one instance saved me from myself.

For her skillful editorial work as a former textbook editor I am thankful to my friend from college years, Carole Hauser, who helped me in the early stages. My old friend and collaborator in my early years in neuroscience, Peter Hand, who also shared in some of the experiences recounted in Chapter 2, read the entire book for accuracy and grammar—yet one more collaboration between us. Also, two other friends, Michael and Debbie Decker, took the trouble to read an early draft of my manuscript and made some critical corrections and suggestions after I thought I was finished. Finally, Edgar H. Brenner, a good friend and colleague, was a big help.

The library staff of the School of Veterinary Medicine, Barbara Cavanaugh, Jason DeMedeiros, Catherine Hinton, and Daniel Lane, as well as Frank Campbell, who introduced me to the marvelous bibliographic tool RefWorks, were a huge help. Dan, in particular, did an incredible job in tracking down references. Nothing proved too obscure for him to find. The marvelous library system of the University of Pennsylvania was the key, of course. Also, the bibliographic service, RefWorks, was of considerable aid. Richard Castledine, Marc Christof, and Jay Lesseig of the RefWorks support staff were very patient with me as I constructed my bibliography.

I am also grateful that Andrew Skolnick, science and medical writer and photographer, offered to host on his Web site our article published in the now-defunct Web magazine, *HMS Beagle.*

Likewise, Jacquie Calnan of Americans for Medical Progress, Alice Ranaan of the American Physiological Society, Barbara Rich, formerly of the National Association for Biomedical Research, and Michael Stebbins of the Foundation for Biomedical Research were invaluable sources of information and advice. Patti Strand, founder and executive director of the National Animal Interest Alliance, taught me to see a number of animal-use issues more clearly than I had.

Experts in other areas were generous with their time and insights as well. On philosophical issues I could not have done without Lance Stell and Jerry Tannenbaum. Gary Althouse, Stanley Curtis, James Ferguson, David Galligan, Eric Gingerich, and Paul Thompson provided critical advice on agricultural issues. Frank Brennan and Bruce Overmeir helped me to understand behaviorism and what it contributed to our knowledge of brain function. Mark Duda,

Executive Director of Responsive Management, was very helpful in providing survey data on attitudes toward trapping.

I had the unusual experience and pleasure of writing three articles with a man I have met only through e-mails and one telephone call: Jack Botting, formerly a writer for the Research Defence Society. Also, his own articles on the history of medical advances dependent on animals published by the Research Defence Society were a great source of information for me. Finally, Jay Schulkin, a philosopher and neuroscientist as well as great friend, advised me and did his best to get me to write this book.

I also owe a great deal to my family and the close friends who stuck with me through a very dark period in 1990: Eileen Conner, the late Alan Epstein and Jay Lash, Graziella Mann, Richard Ross, Alan Rosenquist and daughter Ingrid, Larry Sanford, and the late James Sprague and Eliot Stellar. For his sound advice during the dark days, I am grateful to my former chairman, Leon Weiss. Chuck Newton, one of our associate deans, was also someone I leaned on.

In a more general way, there are individuals who have been vital to the development of my career. Fredrick Goodwin gave me a big boost when he entrusted me with the directorship of the Program for Animal Research Issues at the National Institute of Mental Health. Mortimer Mishkin of the National Institute of Mental Health has been a strong supporter of my public education efforts. That work has received financial support from The Grateful Dead through their Rex Foundation and from another foundation that prefers to remain anonymous.

Finally, for making me the scientist and the man that I am, I credit my professors: Robert Habel, and now unfortunately gone, William Chambers, Louis Flexner, Chan Nao Liu, James Sprague, and Eliot Stellar—and, of course, my parents.

Some passages in this book have been adapted from portions of essays published in *The American Biology Teacher, HMS Beagle, The Iowa State Veterinarian, Lab Animal, Missouri Medicine, Perspectives in Biology and Medicine*, and *Scientific American*, from chapters in books published by John Libbey, M.I.T. Press, and Transaction Publishers, and from columns I wrote as president for the National Animal Interest Alliance News.

Contents

XI

Foreword

*M*oral discourse and concern about the use of animals in biomedical research has evolved in parallel over the last half century with the use of public funds to support research on a vast array of biological mechanisms relevant to understanding healthy functions and eradicating conditions that cripple and kill many millions of humans globally. Rarely has the discourse on human–animal relationships achieved such a thoughtful and honest consideration as that offered by Professor Adrian R. Morrison. What is most remarkable about his principled perspectives on the relationships between animals and humans articulated in the chapters of this book is the absence of vitriol that would be expected of someone who was the target of people bent on assassinating his character, destroying his long and distinguished career as a scientist and teacher, intimidating him into silence, and persuading his family, friends, neighbors, and university community to withhold support for him. Yet, his personal odyssey into the more fundamental considerations of our moral obligations to animals was borne from just such an attack on him.

There is little doubt that the assault Adrian endured in 1990, which he describes in this book, was the result of his long history of writing and lecturing on biomedical research involving animals, in which he thoughtfully offered another view from those who assert that humans have no right to use animals for any purpose, including biomedical research. He did this while many in the academic community were cowed by the attacks he and other scientists endured. At a time when relatively few scientists, or even organizations representing them, were resisting the anti-science forces of the radical element in the animal rights and liberation movement, Adrian was standing up to them and becoming a visible target for their wrath and intimidation. Throughout this difficult time he behaved with quiet courage and dignity.

While the initial effects of the destruction of his office records and the subsequent campaign of intimidation visited upon him were apparently successful, these acts also awakened a sleeping giant, by raising awareness in the broader scientific community that what Adrian was being subjected to was an affront to biomedical science in general and to the public that supported such research. Within two years of the campaign of intimidation that he endured, Adrian was honored with the Scientific Freedom and Responsibility Award from the largest scientific society in the world—the American Association for the Advancement of Science. The award was given "for his dedicated promotion of the responsible use of animals in research and his courageous stand in the face of great personal risk against attempts to curtail animal research essential to public health."

Clearly, the value of biomedical research and the promise it holds for making life better for humankind must be weighted against the use of animals in such research. We can and should ponder the profoundly important moral issues of how humans and animals relate to each other in many areas, including research. In the pages that follow, Professor Morrison presents an informed and thoughtful analysis of human–animal interactions, arguing that when humans use animals, the use must be deemed realistically necessary, and when this criterion is met, humans have an obligation to care for the animals they use. The obligations of humans toward animals are profound, and no one articulates this with greater clarity and thoughtfulness than Adrian Morrison.

David F. Dinges, Ph.D.
Past-President, World Federation of
Sleep Research and Sleep Medicine Societies
and Editor-in Chief, *Sleep*

AN ODYSSEY WITH ANIMALS

Introduction

A very negative series of events in my life led to the writing of this book. Out of these experiences arose my desire to tell a story about the animal rights issue—a story that will go beyond the animal welfare debate of the past few decades to explore human beings' long-term and complex relationships with animals. This book examines how humans and animals are alike, how we differ, what we can learn from them, and how we can use them. It is also a story about those who seek to better the lot of animals under human control, a notion that any humane individual must support, but also about those who go well beyond the norms of civilized society in their efforts to blur the distinction between humans and the animals we use.

Here is a brief summary of how it all started (the full story is told in Chapter 2). The phone rang on Sunday morning, January 14, 1990 while I was sitting on my living room couch completing a paper on the use of animals in biomedical research. The paper was for a symposium on the use of animals in biomedical research, sponsored by the American Association for the Advancement of Science. The Associated Press had mistakenly called one of my sons to get my reaction to the news that the Animal Liberation Front (ALF) had broken into my laboratory at the University of Pennsylvania. My heart sank; I was well aware of the challenges some of my colleagues had faced after similar raids. When I arrived at the university, I found that the raid had focused on my office, which unknown individuals had trashed while ransacking my files and scrawling graffiti across the walls, signing them "ALF."

I was shocked but not surprised—indeed, surprised to be so shocked. During the previous decade, I had gained some notoriety within the "animal rights world" as an outspoken defender of the use of animals in conducting biomedical research and a supporter of the scientists who conducted it. Consequently, I had become increasingly vulnerable to unwanted attention from animal rights activists.

Nothing prepared me for the immediate barrage of media attention following the break-in. For instance, a negative article featuring me appeared in the March 6 issue of *The Village Voice*.[1] This article was later sent by the People for the Ethical Treatment of Animals (PeTA) to many households in my community. One of my neighbors gave me the packet that he had received in the mail to keep me posted. During this time my family and I received hate mail, along with death threats uttered over the telephone by unidentified persons. These continued for months, as did several other instances of overt intimidation.

After the dust had settled—this took a few years—I wondered how I could proceed with my work in the face of such overt hostility toward me and toward biomedical research itself. Believing that society should examine in a reflective, unemotional way, based on rational inquiry, how we should interact with animals in the modern world, I decided to take time away from my primary interest in sleep research to write this book. It is an expansion of a letter I wrote almost 20 years ago to the president of my university about academic freedom and integrity, and represents more than 15 years of study of the issues surrounding animal rights, animal welfare, and the human use of animals for a variety of purposes.

The animal-extremist movement's campaign against me was profoundly upsetting, but it has spurred me to reflect on my life's work and the animals that work has involved. It has also induced me to reflect on other common ways that people use animals—some of them acceptable and some reprehensible, according to my standards. I cannot be a completely dispassionate academic observer, though, because I was part of the debate for so many years and, for a while, deeply wounded by the actions of my ideological opponents. Nevertheless, I have strived to be honest and fair in my assessments. I hope I have succeeded.

I was inspired in part by Jan Dizard. Professor Dizard is a sociologist at Amherst College who introduced himself to me through his wonderful book, *Going Wild: Animal Rights, Animal Welfare and the Contested Meaning of Nature*.[2] He has since become a good friend. In *Going Wild*, he analyzed a proposal to cull the deer herd that threatened the waters of the Quabbin reservoir, which supplies the city of Boston. As usual when animals are deprived of natural predators, the deer had reproduced themselves well beyond the capacity of their forest home and were laying bare the forest floor as they browsed everything in sight, destroying the organic richness of the ecosystem. The result was increased flow of sediment into the reservoir.

Jan wrote a masterful, dispassionate analysis of the competing interests of three groups: the governmental authorities charged with managing the reservoir in a manner that would ensure a decent water supply, the hunters who saw game aplenty, and the animal rightists devoted to protecting the deer. It was more than his deft handling of the complexity of the situation that impressed me, though. He achieved this balance as a hunter himself, his quarry being upland game birds. At the time his book was published Jan was writing a column on hunting and fishing for the *Boston Globe*. My aim has been to emulate him in writing this book.

Now, more than 25 years after my introduction to the extreme end of the animal rights and liberation movement, I have a more measured, informed view of the issues. In the midst of the controversy I had become embroiled in, I forgot one very important thing: I love animals and do not enjoy harming them. After all, that is why I am a veterinarian. But through the years I have learned to separate the radical from the sensible regarding the improvement of animal welfare, and to appreciate that there can be honest disagreements about what "sensible" means. For instance, I can readily appreciate how people make children out of their pets, which brings me to Buster.

Buster is an ordinary, black and white, "tuxedo" cat we obtained in the spring of 2000 as a 2-month-old kitten through a friend's rescue service. He soon took to me, and I to him. Whenever I stopped walking while he was near me, he would lie on my feet to be petted before moving on. He often stood on my chest while I lay in bed, looking closely at me while purring right in front of my face. Now as an adult of 9 years he will still jump into the bed in the middle of the night and snuggle down to have his belly rubbed as we both drift off to sleep. When I have a bagel for breakfast, Buster joins me for his dollop of cream cheese on the edge of my plate. I can overlook that sometimes he's just dropped the bloody remains of a little carcass on the nearby doorstep before entering the dining area. That is his nature.

What goes on in Buster's mind, I will never know, but like many others, I sorely wish I did. I talk to him while he watches me working in the yard, but he never answers. Whenever I move elsewhere, he follows, but at a distance chosen by him. Then he climbs a tree, seemingly to show off. He comes down the drive to greet me when he hears a friend's car bringing me home, and he walks me down the drive in the morning. In his feline way, he may be fond of me, but it saddens me to know that I am engaging in uncritical anthropomorphizing, probably reading too much into his behavior. But with my children grown and with children of their own, I too need a new "child" to help keep me happy.

My relationship with Buster added to my desire to know more about our relationships with animals and to determine where and how we can draw a line between them and us—and why some people have difficulty drawing that line. Why can most of us humans see that we are different from animals in terms of our moral concerns, and so like them in other ways, while others cannot?

Many books have emerged as "animal rights" has become almost a household phrase. Prior to 1975, when the seminal animal rights book *Animal Liberation* appeared, 107 books and articles on animal welfare had been published, starting from ancient times. Of these, 13 appeared from 1970 to 1974, and only 9 were published during the immediately preceding several years. But between 1975 and 1988, an astonishing 225 new books and articles on animal rights issues appeared.[3] There have been many more since, and in many languages.

The watershed event, according to philosopher and animal liberation proponent Peter Singer[4] (Singer regards animal "rights" as a political construct, whereas "liberation" is a purer notion), was the publication of a collection of essays that Singer termed a "manifesto for animal liberation," and which he likened to the women's and black liberation movements. *Animals, Man and Morals* was published in 1971, and its editors, Stanley and Rosalind Godlovitch and John Harris, were postgraduates studying philosophy at Oxford when their book appeared. They set the tone of the movement with the concluding words of their preface:

> The authors have been very careful in seeing that the
> argumentation contained in this book is correct. Needless to
> say, should the reader himself find no fault in the positions
> he will find in these pages he is, as a rational being,
> committed to act in accordance with them. Should he fail to
> do this, he can only have been terribly misled since
> childhood about the nature of morality.[5]

My bookshelves confirm the fact that a vast literature in addition to this seminal work has accumulated over the past 30 years. They sag from the weight of the many books that would not have had a place there years ago, prior to my introduction to the animal rights and liberation movement. There are works on ethics, history and sociology of science, medical history, and branches of medical science beyond my own narrow field of sleep research. And then there are those rather specifically related to the issue: laboratory animal medicine, animal rights, agriculture, and hunting, to name but a few. Indeed, a book edited by Andrew Harnack, *Animal Rights: Opposing Viewpoints*,[6] is a remarkable collection of essays by various participants in the animal rights and welfare debate. That book delves into many of the same issues raised here. With all of these books on the subject, what more can I say? What can I add to this debate?

I submit that I can add the unique personal insights of one who first worked with animals as a boy on the farm, then as a student of biology, a veterinarian, and for nearly 50 years as a researcher investigating the workings of the brain. Approximately 30 of those years have also been spent explaining the accomplishments of biomedical research, defending its practitioners, and studying the animal rights and liberation movement and its philosophical underpinnings. My professional background and my veterinary training have provided me with extensive knowledge of animals and their uses. My personal background has obviously also helped to form my opinions on how animals may be appropriately used.

Thus, my hope is that this book is unique, written as it is by one with varied experiences associated with animals and the public debate over their rights and welfare. The ideas expressed here arise out of the ambivalence that I feel (indeed, that any humane individual most likely feels) having used animals for human benefit—and often to their detriment. My personal idiosyncrasies, by definition, will probably not match those of all readers, but I believe them to be within the norms of society at large. The central questions in this book, then, are the following: May one ethically and morally interfere in the lives of other species, to the point of harming and even killing them? When is the use of animals appropriate and when is it not? Are there good reasons to put humans into a special category that excludes other animals, while still recognizing our relatedness to them?

A note about terminology: there are those within the animal rights and welfare movement who believe that human life is worth no more than that of other animals. Some of these people damage property, threaten the lives of those who use animals, and even attempt to commit assault or murder in their effort to save animals. This subsection of the animal rights movement has been classified by the FBI as "one of today's most serious domestic terrorism threats."[7] They are extremists in the truest sense, and I refer to them as such in this book.

Others in the movement, such as those who condemn the fur industry, engage in stunts like parading naked with signs. Though extreme, these tactics do not, to my mind, constitute extremism—just activism. Unfortunately, there are others who damage stores, throw paint on fur coats, and release mink from farms to die in the wild. They would obviously fit into the first category: *extremists*.

Then there are those who gather in peaceful (and lawful) protest, or who contribute money to organizations engaged in some of the activities just described, often because they have been fooled by false claims of animal abuse or graphic photographs that have been doctored or taken out of context. Of course, overlaps among these groups are possible, if not likely. I would consider these members of the movement—those who object to animal use but who do not employ extreme measures themselves—to be *animal rights and welfare activists* (as opposed to extremists).

There are also those who use animals but are also involved in efforts to improve the treatment of them. These individuals comprise what I consider to be the *animal welfare movement*—whether they engage actively through contributions to local humane societies or other good works or simply share the beliefs of those who do. Certainly, I am a member of this group. We think animals have certain claims on us humans when they are under our control, including the right to decent care. Put another way, we believe that, as humans, we have a moral responsibility to treat these animals well.

This position is distinct from the aims of the *animal rights and liberation movement*, and here I think it is important to acknowledge the difference between animal rights and animal welfare. Those who belong to the animal rights group believe in severely limiting the way humans use animals, encouraging our removal from the animal world in many ways. Those who belong to the animal welfare group wish to improve animal health and welfare in a number of different contexts. I will expand on the subtle but important distinction between these two ideologies later in the book.

There are those in the animal welfare camp who object to the idea that many species are "renewable resources" that humans may justifiably use—hunting them for food is one example. I would place these people in the *extreme animal-welfare* category—those who aim to change drastically the way we use animals. On the other hand, I think that animals are a renewable resource and that ensuring animals' welfare while they are alive, and providing a humane death for a legitimate purpose, is our only charge.

It is my perception that recently, in the movement and associated literature, there has been a more noticeable shift toward use of an umbrella term, *animal protectionism*. I do not favor this designation because, though a noble-sounding banner, it could easily cloak an extremist fringe. As my story unfolds, I think you will be able to determine where you feel most comfortable within this spectrum.

Turning to the pages that follow, Chapter 1 begins with a bit of my earlier history with animals, so that readers will have some insight into the man who has written this book—an ordinary person thrust into extraordinary circumstances by chance. Then I discuss how society in general thinks about animals, and introduce those who object to any use of them whatsoever. Some of these individuals have views that are so strong that they wish to eliminate the boundary I believe exists between humans and animals. They would grant animals the same rights afforded humans in a free society, a notion with which I strenu-ously disagree. Among these people are those who promote or commit violence against animal users. I briefly discuss what we would lose as a society, were these people to have their way.

Chapter 2 draws on my personal experiences in several cases of animal rights extremism involving other scientists. It also expands on the brief sum-mary of my own problems to illustrate in more detail how some members of this movement can feel passionate enough about their beliefs that they will engage in dangerous, illegal acts, or indulge in false accusations against scientists.

The following chapter is a retrospective of my own scientific use of animals in biomedical research and the attending personal ethical dilemmas faced in the pursuit of my profession. Chapter 4 focuses on biomedical research in a larger context, and explores how science works in general. Included is a discus-sion of the regulations governing the use of animals in biomedical research and teaching, providing several examples of the contributions of animals to medical progress, and explaining the meaning of the term *animal model*. The chapter also includes a discussion of the use of animals in education.

Unfortunately, some members of the animal rights and liberation move-ment use misinformation to promote their cause, much of which originates from distortions of the value of animals for medical progress. Some of these distortions are put forth by medical professionals. A number of examples of such misrepresentations of medical history are offered in Chapter 5, in which I illustrate that the claims made against the usefulness of animals in biomedical research are simply false.

A history of the evolution of the animal welfare movement, with an empha-sis on their use by scientists in particular, is offered in Chapter 6. In Chapter 7, I examine what animals are, what they can do, and what they can know, leading up to discussion in the next chapter of what, in my opinion, we can do with and to them.

Chapter 8 considers contemporary animal use in a sociological and cultural context to demonstrate the challenges inherent in deciding how we should relate to animals. I consider a number of ways in which we use animals beyond biomedical research—in hunting, in modern agriculture, in bull fighting, in cock fighting, and in rodeos—arguing why some and not others are morally acceptable. I am certain that not all readers will agree with the positions I take in this chapter.

Finally, in Chapter 9, I examine the restrictions that a few philosophers would place on the human use of animals, and how these restrictions have formed the foundation of the modern animal rights and liberation movement. The chapter continues with an exploration of the origins of this movement, extending back to very early thoughts about human–animal interactions. I then defend the specialness of human life, acknowledging that all animals are worthy of respect and even awe at their special abilities.

The book concludes with an epilogue that reviews the issues raised, providing an argument against the notion of "benign neglect" of animals, a poor solution that inevitably follows from the extreme animal rights and liberation movement's perspective. Although the answers to questions posed in the book have often turned out to be ambiguous—in my opinion, there can be disagreement so long as there is no violence, implied or overt—I still believe there are distinct physical, moral, and philosophical boundaries between animals and humans that can be rationally defended, and should be.

Searching for the Boundary Between | 1
Animals and Humans

A s a boy I could never bring myself to kill an animal: I loved them. In fact, I had determined from an early age to pursue a career in veterinary medicine in order to take care of them. When the time came to enter veterinary school, my biggest worry was whether I would be able to do what was part of any veterinarian's duty: euthanizing animals to relieve their suffering. I had no way of knowing that as an adult I would find myself in the position of using animals in biomedical research in ways that often harmed them and resulted in their deaths. I have spent many years of my life doing what I shied away from as a boy. For more than forty years, with a bit of time out for clinical veterinary practice, I have studied the brain and the way it manages the transformations between sleep and wakefulness in the laboratory. Over the years these studies have involved many experimental surgeries under anesthesia and the killing of many cats and rats.

When I was eight, we moved to a farm in southeastern Pennsylvania where my father became a part-time farmer, raising chickens, goats, and pigs for our own food. We also enjoyed eating the game that one of my uncles shot on our land. I could not stomach the thought of killing anything. Dad chopped chickens' heads off and consigned me to plucking them, often alone at night in our cold, scary barn. I sometimes walked a muskrat trap line with a friend but could not set traps myself. My mother was a city girl and afraid of guns, so I shied away from them too (and still do). But I did not think then that the hunting and trapping practices of my friends and uncle were wrong, and nor do I think so now, as long as these practices are done for a worthwhile cause, such as having food on the table or supporting a living selling pelts—and done respectfully. Contrary to accusations often hurled at them, most people who harvest from nature are generally respectful of it and of the animals they hunt.

Having grown up on a farm, I feel acutely attuned to the ways in which our society's views toward animals have transformed since my boyhood. It turns out I am not alone. Richard W. Bulliet, a professor of history at Columbia University, wrote a penetrating book about the changing attitudes of humans toward animals from pre-history to the present in *Hunters, Herders, and Hamburgers: The Past and Future of Human–Animal Relationships*.[1] The book is a masterful compendium and analysis of the incorporation of originally wild animals into the human realm over thousands of years. Bulliet posits a period during which early humans recognized no difference between themselves and the various species around them, upon which they preyed, and received like attention in return. Our earliest relatives then reached a stage of "separation," at which point they theoretically—for this is prehistorical speculation— consciously saw themselves as something different. This period led into what Bulliet terms the "predomestic era": animals assumed some significance beyond a potential source of food. Think of the Paleolithic cave drawings and myths surrounding animals as they gradually became domesticated, leading into the period of what Bulliet labeled "domesticity." We began to control animals. They began to work for us "agriculturists."

According to Bulliet, my generation is the last to contain a majority of people with an attitude of "domesticity," in contrast to that of subsequent "post-domesticity" generations. Those who belong to Bulliet's domesticity category, like me, "consider daily contact with domestic animals (other than pets) a normal condition of life: in short, the farming existence of a bygone generation for most Americans, but contemporary reality for most of the developing world." The present "'postdomestic' people live far away, both physically and psychologically, from the animals that produce the food, fiber, and hides they depend on, and they never witness the births, sexual congress, and slaughter of these animals."[2] These postdomestics—and my suburban life has certainly been leading me in this direction—think of animals as more than just beings to be used by humans. The very active animal rights and liberation movement has arisen out of this postdomestic attitude, and in its extreme variant seeks to bring an end to any human relationship with animals.

Animals Are Important to Us

Discussion of our relationships with animals is timely, then, because animals clearly hold a great fascination for us even though modern life is moving us away from most of them. How can both humans and animals best fit in to our modern world? We can be greatly concerned for animal welfare, even to the extent of focusing more on their welfare than that of fellow human beings (in the case of some individuals).

Consider these examples. A taxi ran amok a few years ago in New York City, injuring among others a blind man and his dog. Both went to hospitals appropriate for them, and both, fortunately, recovered. Because the event made the newspapers, both received get-well cards and even money from sympathetic strangers, but the dog attracted by far the bulk of the attention.[3] More recently, a heinous act of cruelty took place in a community just north of Philadelphia. Three young men obtained a dog, a Dalmatian, and then proceeded to allow a fighting dog to use it as practice. Tying the Dalmatian to a tree with its mouth taped to suppress its screams, they then turned the fighting dog loose to tear into the pitiful creature. At their preliminary hearing, a crowd of 600 spectators outside the courthouse screamed for vengeance.[4]

These incidents reveal in a striking way the great hold that animals have over us, and affirm the concern of most people for their welfare. Most of us have pets that have meaning in our lives, as my description of Buster in the Introduction makes abundantly clear. If they fall ill or sustain injury, those who have the resources will expend extraordinary sums in veterinary fees and medicines to restore them to health. For those who are old or lonely, animals may provide a reason for living.

Other people use animals to make a living, but that does not mean they view animals strictly as commodities. For instance, my encounters with dairy cattle brought me to veterinary medicine. Walking among them and listening while milking them to the slow, steady "rump ... rump ... rump" of their teeth as they ground their food was one of the peaceful pleasures of a gentler time that I remember with nostalgia. In a herd that appeared so uniform to a casual observer, some cows had something extra special that earned them a name— Daisy, The Red Cow, Speckles. Some were favorites: one with unusually beautiful markings, or even the ever-present ornery cow that made a contest of getting her into her stanchion for milking twice every day. When the time came to send such a partner in work to slaughter, no good farmer rejoiced. These were my experiences more than 50 years ago, and I admit that the dairy industry has changed—most milking herds now are immense—but many of the people who work closely with dairy cows have not changed in their respect and appreciation for animals. Even in large agricultural operations this attitude is essential for the health and productivity of the animals.

We who use animals in research, who have to operate on them and ultimately kill them, do (and should) think seriously about how we use animals. At times we actually grieve if, for example, we have worked with an animal over many months and then must kill it to examine its brain. For instance, a company that makes medical devices to be implanted into humans recently created a lovely memorial park to honor the laboratory animals they use. I was invited to speak on the ethics of animal use in biomedical research at the park's dedication.

Think of the rodeo cowboy who respects the bull he cannot ride, and of the true hunter who may lower his gun rather than bring to earth a beautiful stag. Most farmers, hunters, fishermen, dog breeders, scientists, and other users of animals have a personal ethical code that governs their behavior. Of course, there are those within these professions who do not behave ethically, but this does not of necessity make that particular use of animals reprehensible in and of itself. Unfortunately, those not familiar with rural culture (Bulliet's postdomestic generation) may erroneously prejudge activities that they have never practiced or experienced; nonscientists, or nonbiomedical scientists for that matter, may likewise wrongly condemn research activities employing animals, not understanding the degree to which these scientists' health has resulted from the very research they might question.

The lives of humans have been intertwined irrevocably with animals for thousands of years. Even today, we humans depend on animals for enjoyment, and animals are important to our welfare—this compels us to be concerned with their welfare. Our own humanity depends on our humane treatment of animals; we diminish ourselves when we act otherwise. We are the only species that, when recognizing suffering in another being, seeks to alleviate it rather than take advantage of it. Not all of us are as considerate of animals as we should be, of course, because we humans are not perfect as a species. There are those who willfully abuse animals, and we are rightly angered by such wanton cruelty. We make laws to prevent and punish this behavior.

I would allege that all but the sadist is concerned about the welfare of animals. Yet, sadism is not required for animals to be harmed. Much abuse probably arises out of unconscionable laziness or woeful ignorance. With cruel indifference, a vacationer leaves a pet behind at a holiday site because the animal will not accommodate to that person's "real life." A family ignorant about dogs and the training they require rids itself of a behavioral problem by dropping the dog off at the local shelter, where, too often, it will be "put to sleep." A lover of cats collects so many of them that the welfare of all is threatened. In fact, the "pathological collecting" of animals, largely by lone, elderly women, is a public health problem and a mental health issue poorly understood and badly managed by community services, according to a study by veterinarian Gary Patronek.[5]

Adherents to a Cause

A new participant in these matters is now on the scene, however, one with a truly revolutionary idea: that all of our interactions with animals are morally wrong. The traditional concept of animal welfare contrasts sharply with that of the more radical animal rights and liberation movement. In the most extreme cases, those who adhere to the latter philosophy believe that even well-treated pets are victims of exploitation. Some people are so captured by the idea of animal rights and liberation as to be consumed by it, at least as revealed in the following quotes, gathered during a sociological study conducted a number of years ago by psychologist Harold Herzog:

> We recently annihilated the roaches here in our house. I will tell you this—before we resorted to that, I walked around for a week trying to telegraphically tell these roaches, "You have invaded my territory" and we are going to take drastic actions. In my fantasy, I was hoping that they would automatically disappear.
>
> My husband and I have lots of fights about it. I would really give anything to be active in animal-rights organizations like the Animal Liberation Front, and it really causes problems in my marriage. We have arguments about the animal-rights issue constantly.
>
> It definitely interferes with my social life. I won't go out with anyone who is not a vegetarian. It limits the pool of possible men.[6]

Herzog performed a qualitative survey, rather than adding up numbers in a quantitative survey, in order to dig deeply into the thoughts and motivations of a small number of animal rights adherents. He found that some individuals come to the movement having embraced the philosophical underpinnings, while others enter it after being greatly moved by pictures and tales of abuse. Some of those Herzog interviewed evidence the same attitudes of religious fundamentalists: they know they are right, and brook no opposing viewpoints.

One interviewee said, "I definitely have the sense that what I am doing is right, and if you argue with me I'm not going to listen because I am right."[7] I myself have encountered this attitude in words and in facial expressions of disgust with me. It seems that having been captivated by the idea of animal rights, some adherents become obsessed with the issue and troubled by the moral ambiguities of living in a world where there are other species with competing interests to consider. At the same time, Herzog found those whom he interviewed to be intelligent and articulate.

I can understand and sympathize with these sentiments to a point: casual harm or destruction of a living animal is wrong in my view. Yet I have done some very harmful things to animals in the belief that in a small but important way, I was advancing biomedical science and, therefore, human welfare, which is unabashedly where my allegiance ultimately lies.

The quotes above are mild, almost wistful statements, compared with those uttered by some leaders of the animal rights and liberation movement. At its extremist core, today's animal rights and liberation movement diametrically opposes Judeo-Christian teachings and Western thought that accord human beings a special place in nature, which is the necessary foundation for human rights. Consider this statement by an avowed and dynamic leader of the movement, Ingrid Newkirk, cofounder of People for the Ethical Treatment of Animals (PeTA):

> Animal liberationists do not separate out the *human*
> animal, so there is no rational basis for saying that a
> human being has special rights. A rat is a pig is a dog is a
> boy. They're all mammals [emphasis in original]. (Ingrid
> Newkirk, as cited in McCabe)[8]

Relatively few of us, I would wager, can agree totally with this statement, but the coffers of PeTA are overflowing with donations from sympathizers, so someone is in tune with them. Just as inexplicable to me are the words of Chris DeRose, speaking as the head of Last Chance for Animals:

> A life is a life. If the death of one rat cured all diseases, it
> wouldn't make any difference to me.[9]

Similarly expressing a view that diminishes the moral value of human life is this statement by Michael W. Fox, a veterinarian and former officer in the Humane Society of the United States (HSUS):

> The belief that all life is equal because of our planetary
> relations (both human and nonhuman) are sacred leads to

the inevitable conclusion that it is unethical to value one life
over any other. Thus the life of an ant and the life of my
child should be granted equal consideration.[10]

These statements are now almost two decades old and are often quoted, particularly Newkirk's; more disturbing is the ideology that has recently evolved from them. Jerry Vlasak, MD, a practicing trauma surgeon, stunned U.S. Senator James M. Inhofe (R-OK) at the October 26, 2005 Senate Committee on the Environment and Public Works hearing when he responded to a question by saying, "Non-human lives . . . are as precious as animal[sic] lives. At one time, racism and sexism and homophobism were prominent in our society. Today speciesism is prominent in our society. It is just as wrong as racism." When asked about a statement he made at an animal rights conference, "I don't think you'd have to kill—assassinate—too many [doctors involved with animal testing] . . . I think for 5 lives, 10 lives, 15 human lives, we could save a million, 2 million, 10 million non-human lives," Vlasak replied, "I said in that statement and I meant in that statement that people who are hurting animals and who will not stop when told to stop, one option would be to stop them using any means necessary and that was the context in which that statement was made." When Senator Inhofe asked whether his solution could truly include murder, Vlasak assured him that "that would be a morally justifiable solution to the problem."[11] Vlasak has also said that he is "not encouraging or calling for" violence, rather that "if by chance violence is used by those who fight for non-human sentient beings, or even if there are casualties, it must be looked at in perspective and in a historical context."[12]

Such thinking puzzles me, and I do not understand those who can justify destruction of property even into the millions of dollars—misanthropic acts that harm many of their fellow humans—let alone assassinations, all in the service of animal rights. As a scientist and a medical professional, I am even more perplexed by the work of other physicians who appear to willfully misrepresent the value of research using animals. But more about that in Chapter 5.

Developing a Response

Throughout history, humanity has associated with animals in ways that have benefited human beings. Animals have been hunted for food and clothing, accepted at our hearths for companionship, and brought into our fields to produce and provide food. As Bulliet pointed out, only during the latter two-thirds of the last century could most people begin to imagine living without animals as part of our daily lives. We were completely dependent on them. But as the twentieth century progressed, technological advances rendered animals' visible presence in our lives unnecessary. We can eat a steak without coming close to a living cow, or wear a wool sweater without having to shear any sheep. But now, according to some, we have no need, indeed no right, to interfere in animals' lives. This belief motivates the animal rights and liberation movement, which, as I have noted, follows the thinking of a small group of vocal philosophers.

The idea that we humans can live without using or interacting with animals in various ways is wrongheaded; but to a number of people in our society—a wealthy, developed society that can afford such notions—the idea rings true, for these people are members of the postdomestic generation. Less than 1 in 50 of us has a direct association with agriculture today, compared with 1 in 4 people in 1930 and 1 in 2 back in 1880.[13]

In addressing concerns about the use of animals in biomedical research, we must also consider the fact that in the developed West those younger than 50 comprise the healthiest population in history. For example, I wonder whether those born after 1950 can fully appreciate the hysteria of the U.S. polio epidemic. Today polio is virtually extinct, thanks to a vaccine that required extensive animal testing prior to use in humans. Also consider the following words of Oxford physician and pharmacologist, Sir William Paton, speaking of the time of his training in the 1930s:

> One no longer sees infants with ears streaming pus, school
> boys with facial impetigo, beards growing from heavily
> infected skin, faces pocked by smallpox or eroded by lupus,
> or heads and necks scarred from boils or suppurating
> glands. Drugs and a better diet have transformed haggard
> patients with peptic ulcers. The languid, characteristically
> brown-skinned case of Addison's disease of the adrenals; the
> pale, listless patients of chronic iron deficiency or pernicious
> anemia; and the cretin or, conversely, the young woman
> with "pop eyes" and overactive emotional behavior—due
> respectively to thyroid deficiency or excess—are all being
> treated. The soggy hulk of a patient in the edematous stage
> of chronic kidney disease is relieved by diuretics. As a result
> of polio vaccine and control of tuberculosis, we see few
> crippled children: as one walks behind a group of youngsters
> today, varied as ever in shape and size, the marvel is how
> straight their limbs and backs are. The chronic arthritics
> with their sticks are being replaced with septuagenarians
> swinging along on their plastic hips. The patients now are

rare that once one saw dying from an infected mastoid,
struggling for breath in the last stages of heart failure, or
dying from appendicitis, leukaemia, pneumonia, or bacterial
endocarditis.[14]

We can thank, in great part, the animals used in biomedical research for the
scientific advances that abolished these horrific conditions.

We who acknowledge the importance of animal use in modern society can
joust intellectually with philosophers, but we must be careful to keep in mind
biological reality and to challenge those philosophers of the animal rights and
liberation movement to do the same. All organisms struggle to stay alive,
including humans. Inherent in this struggle is the use of animals to our benefit.
Ethical proposals dealing with human use of animals in research or in a number
of other ways, for that matter, must consider our strong biological urge to stay
alive. Ignoring this biological urge, some philosophers have devised unrealistic
schemes for human life, as will be discussed later.

It is important to remember, too, that animals, depending on the species,
have benefited from their association with us—consider the relief from disease
provided by modern veterinary medicine. Although I personally think it is necessary to put humans first for the protection of our society, our ethical concern
must ultimately extend to all animals. We hold the fate of countless species in
our hands as we advance our material interests—by expanding housing into
once uninhabited woodlands, building new roads, drilling for oil, and making
other environmental intrusions (as well as in biomedical research). The fate of
the world, at least one hospitable to human life, depends on sensible and sensitive behavior on the part of humans.

Scientists in particular have a responsibility: they must reflect on ethics as
they pursue their profession. Van Rensselaer Potter, a Wisconsin professor of
oncology, proposed this notion in 1970, and was belittled for it initially. He
called his melding of ecology, medicine, and human values *bioethics*. Although
later given only a medical connotation, Potter's term encompassed a broader
view. He proposed the term "in order to emphasize the two most important
ingredients in achieving the new wisdom that is so desperately needed: biological knowledge and human values. . . . Man's survival may depend on ethics
based on biological knowledge, hence bioethics."[15] Potter's concept denotes an
imperative balance between the importance of scientific inquiry and the preservation of the very ethics that make us human. The remainder of this book is
an attempt to seek out and achieve this very balance.

and its sister organization, the Foundation for Biomedical Research (FBR), had combined incomes of roughly $3,000,000 per year over the same period (2005–2007).[2] AMP's income was less than $900,000 in 2007. My impression is that society in general has taken a greater interest in the welfare of animals, and these figures bear this out. People appear to be so interested in animals that they are willing to contribute time or money to organizations not necessarily working in the contributor's best health interests—PeTA in particular—and are less willing to support those that most definitely are. PeTA advertises heavily, and a variety of celebrities support the organization even though some have struggled with severe medical problems within their families.

Unfortunately, admirable concern for animal welfare has sometimes degenerated into actions and behaviors that endanger human society, and there are those within the most radical circles of the animal rights and liberation movement who would deprive other people of rights and freedom—in the most extreme cases, of their lives—for the sake of the cause. Many universities, research institutions, and individual scientists have been victimized by actions stemming from this attitude. Hostilities toward biomedical scientists have dramatic implications for society at large, for we depend on the work of scientists for important medical advances. In the following pages I will discuss several clashes between animal rights activists and biomedical scientists (including the nightmare I went through in 1990), and then demonstrate that the dangers to individual scientists and other animal users not only persist but are on the rise.

The Silver Spring Monkeys

My introduction to the animal rights movement came with the Silver Spring Monkey Case in November 1981. Dr. Edward Taub, a neuroscientist, was charged with cruelty to the monkeys used in his research. The ordeal dragged out for a decade and included two separate trials conducted by the State of Maryland—the first with a judge only, the second, a jury trial. It ended, essentially, with a set of final experiments in 1991 (which, incidentally, gave us new insights into the ability of the cerebral cortex to reorganize itself after removal of some of its normal connections).[3] In order to study movement of an arm devoid of sensory feedback, Taub cut the nerve fibers that bring all the sensory information (touch, pressure, sense of position, and pain) from the arm of a monkey into the spinal cord. He later trained the monkeys to use those "deafferented" (lacking in sensation) arms, even though the animals could readily use the good arm. From this experiment he learned that motivation, such as treats of food, worked well for monkeys (the success of positive motivation permitted him to abandon the electric-shock technique he had used earlier at another institute) and was critical in rehabilitation of the limb. Taub used this insight much later to train human victims of stroke to use their own "useless" arms, a magnificent advance in the treatment of the aftermath of a stroke.

Ugly is the best word to describe the deafferented arm of a monkey. There are sores and gnawed fingers; bones can break because the altered blood supply may deplete them of calcium. Bandages work on some monkeys and not on others, because some persist in tearing at the bandages, thereby damaging the arm further. Bandaging too tightly can lead to disaster, for the limb can swell, cutting off circulation, with gangrenous results (gangrene became the centerpiece in the most shameful episode in the whole Taub case, as I will relate later).

Taub was an ideal target for animal rights activists. In his work on monkeys he did experiments that to the untrained eye would appear disgusting; and he did these experiments in a small, isolated research laboratory without modern facilities. The Institute for Behavioral Research (IBR) was not associated with a major university.

In the summer of 1981, animal rights activist and PeTA cofounder Alex Pacheco appeared at Dr. Taub's laboratory as a student and asking to participate in Taub's research. Like most scientists, Taub was eager to welcome an interested student, particularly one willing to work as an unpaid volunteer, so he responded enthusiastically to the young man's desire to learn and took him on. While Taub was on vacation, Pacheco brought unauthorized individuals into the laboratory during closing hours. According to Taub's lawyer, Edgar H. Brenner, the two caretakers for Taub's laboratory were both curiously and unaccountably absent 7 of the 15 days prior to the eventual police raid, compared with one absence during the prior 423 days; as a result, the lab had not been properly maintained for those 7 days.[4] The visitors, who arrived at night during that period, photographed the animals with the arms I have just described, as well as the monkeys' cages—dirty from the absence of caretakers.[5] With this questionably incriminating evidence in hand, Pacheco notified the Montgomery County police that Taub was mistreating his monkeys. The police then raided the laboratory and confiscated the monkeys.

Here is what happened, in Taub's words:

> The search and seizure in my laboratory was planned well in
> advance to have maximum media coverage. . . . There was a
> virtual mob of media people. This can be arranged only with
> a great deal of prior effort. . . . A press release was prepared
> by PeTA in advance of the execution of the search warrant,

the period the animal was in the custody of the NIH. The prosecutor asserted repeatedly that the condition of Nero's arm was a consequence of infection of the bone, osteomyelitis. At a second trial in the summer of 1982, which did include a jury, this case of osteomyelitis was presented as convincing evidence of neglect in Taub's laboratory, since osteomyelitis is usually a longstanding condition. The prosecutor also convinced the jury that Taub had neglected Nero; they cleared Taub of charges of inadequate veterinary care of six of the monkeys but convicted him of neglecting Nero.

But it was not osteomyelitis that had caused the deterioration of Nero's arm. I later learned of the real reason after a visit to the Poolesville facility at the invitation of officials of the NIH. During my visit, a person I did not recognize surreptitiously pushed a previously withheld postmortem report into my hand as we were leaving and remarked, "Here, I think you'll find this interesting." I remember reading the report during a meeting later that day and blurting out, "Pete, we've just been handed a smoking gun." The report stated "evidence of necrosis" (gangrene) and nothing about osteomyelitis. The NIH had neglected to reveal its mistake to Taub. In spite of his warning that the reflex control of circulation in the arm was disturbed and that a bandage might induce problems in it, the veterinarians at the NIH had cut off circulation in the arm by bandaging it, thereby causing it to become gangrenous and necessitating amputation.

According to Edgar Brenner, Taub and his defense team did not know about the postmortem report conducted on the amputated arm, and its conclusion that the arm showed evidence of bandaging (a distinct impression on the skin) and of gangrene, but none of osteomyelitis. The prosecutor in Taub's case failed to reveal this report, before or during the trial. The NIH knew that there had been no bone infection, but Taub and his defense team did not. Taub's lawyer in the second trial quite appropriately objected to introduction of the report because he had not had a chance to review it before it was presented in court.[11]

Of course, I did not realize any of this at the time I testified for Taub. My purpose in being in the courthouse in Montgomery County, Maryland, was to defend a man besieged by many forces: the criminal justice system of the State of Maryland, the U.S. Government in the form of the NIH, and just about everybody who was reading and believing the negative writings of unsympathetic (and misinformed) journalists.[12]

Dr. Taub was very fortunate that Peter Hand and I agreed to testify—as were stroke victims and biomedical research in general, as it turned out. Moral support was what Taub desperately needed—something that would keep him going during those dark days (here I speak from bitter experience). The attitude of the larger scientific community was that Taub's was a small laboratory, just part of a relatively insignificant private institute. With both the police and NIH arrayed against him, Taub's was a difficult case to defend. Many of his colleagues found it expedient to not become involved. This would not be the last time that the urge to sacrifice a weak member of the group for the "good of the herd" would come into play.

Looking back, there was a certain irony to the trip Pete and I took to Poolesville, in that we were invited to observe how well the monkeys were living there. On our way back to the car, I asked Pete where he would choose to live if he were a monkey—in the NIH facility or in Taub's laboratory. He laughed because he knew what I was thinking. In Taub's facility, the monkeys had been facing each other, and the room had a warm, cozy atmosphere. At Poolesville the monkeys were in squeaky clean quarters, but they all faced a blank, concrete wall. In terms of enrichment of animal quarters, an issue I will address in Chapter 4, Taub's facility certainly had the edge, as the monkeys had a more interesting place to live.

Taub endured two administrative hearings in an attempt to restore his NIH funding, which had been revoked because of deficiencies in his laboratory. The first was before a Public Health Service Board where the NIH was represented by a lawyer and Taub, by Peter Hand and me. The second hearing took place at the highest level, the Department of Health and Human Services. It was hopeless. Taub's small institute could not afford to improve the caging, install a system for handling air, or make any of the numerous changes that the Public Health Service's (PHS) *Guide for the Care and Use of Laboratory Animals*[13] recommended for the monkeys' quarters. Furthermore, the NIH would not permit the use of his current grant funds to update the laboratory.

In November 1981, the Society for Neuroscience formed the Ad Hoc Committee on Animals in Research, which included Peter Hand and me, to look into the Taub situation. Incredibly, the largest neuroscience society in the world had never thought such a committee necessary until the Taub case broke, but when it did, there was much discussion on the subject in the Society for Neuroscience's newsletters over the years 1982–1984. The NIH committee formed in September 1981 and charged with investigating Taub's laboratory had concluded that the small institute (IBR) housing Taub's lab did not provide adequate veterinary care, did not have a properly constituted animal care committee, and did not have an adequate occupational health program. It also maintained that the facility required improvements to meet PHS and NIH standards, which the hearing boards affirmed. The ensuing to and fro arguments that appeared in the newsletter are too complicated to review here in detail. Taub did have an old facility that needed updating, but the cages he used were standard for the times. Although our committee urged scientists to be certain

and Cognitive Sciences (representing 18 national societies), and the Society for Neuroscience wrote their own joint letter to the editor[20] arguing that Singer had used "the credibility granted to him as a book reviewer for *Nature* to enshrine through repetition a distorted version of the case." The authors of the letter noted that Singer "glosses over the huge financial benefits PeTA has reaped by using the hapless primates as bait for a decade of direct-mail fund-raising." The authors likely felt compelled to add this last phrase because of Singer's statement that the Taub case had transformed PeTA "from a two-person [Newkirk and Pacheco] operation to the largest animal rights group in the world [in 1994], with 400,000 members, 70 employees and a budget of $10 million."[21]

Singer claimed that "Taub failed to provide basic veterinary care to the monkeys in his laboratory."[22] In another letter (also from the Federation of Behavioral, Psychological and Cognitive Scientists), psychologists Neal Miller and David Johnson refuted Singer's statement, quoting directly from the report of the Grant Appeals Board, which concluded, "In summary, the record does not support a conclusion that the monkeys were actually harmed by the lack of regular veterinary supervision, or that the condition of the monkeys showed inadequate veterinary care."[23]

Most importantly, Miller and Johnson observed that the decision of the Maryland Court of Appeals

> vindicated Taub on two grounds: his research (which addressed problems of stroke rehabilitation by creating in monkeys a comparable loss of sensory perception) fell within the state statute's exemption for "normal human activities to which the infliction of pain to an animal is purely incidental and unavoidable" and as federally funded research with regulated species, it was already subject to multiple federal regulations concerning humane animal care and use.[24]

Singer also argued in his *Nature* piece that in 1983 officials at the NIH had disagreed with the medical conclusions of Peter Hand and me, and had stated that "fractures, dislocations, lacerations, punctures, contusions, and abrasions with accompanying infection, acute and chronic inflammation, and necroses are not the inevitable consequences of deafferentation." As I have stated, Pete and I disagreed with the NIH statement for sound medical reasons. Besides Taub, we were the only people involved in the issue who had direct professional knowledge of the difficulties in maintaining monkeys with deafferentations of limbs. But the NIH veterinarians in charge of the monkeys soon learned for themselves the difficulties in treating these animals. (Both Pete and I later came to sympathize with these veterinarians, aware as we were of the challenges they faced.)

Singer went on to write in his review: "A decade later, one of these veterinarians [who had testified in Taub's favor] was appointed director of the Office of Animal Research Issues at the National Institute of Mental Health." The implication was that there was so little concern for animal welfare within the NIMH, a government agency, that someone like me would be appointed to such an important post.[25]

The book that Singer reviewed was Kathy Snow Guillermo's *Monkey Business: The Disturbing Case that Launched the Animal Rights Movement*,[26] and through his remarks on this book and the events it described, Singer took the opportunity to vilify Taub and his supporters. The second book Singer reviewed was Barbara Orlans's *In the Name of Science: Issues in Responsible Animal Experimentation.*[27] Orlans is associated with the Kennedy Center for Bioethics, having been a scientist and administrator at the NIH in earlier years. Her book recounts the efforts to bring better regulation of animal use in science. Singer rightly applauded her efforts, but failed to note that many scientists, including me, were reluctant to work with her at the time because they were already heavily engaged in simply holding the line against extremist attacks. In retrospect, I wish I could have felt free to pursue her ideas, because the system had to change.

What became of Edward Taub? After obtaining his position at the University of Alabama, he began to work in the field of rehabilitation medicine. He and his colleagues have since demonstrated that stroke victims can be trained to use an arm rendered "useless" by a stroke.[28,29] This is accomplished by restraining the normal arm and forcing the patient, through small increments of difficulty (a process known as "shaping") to employ the affected limb for various tasks until it becomes useful once more.[30] This new method, called constraint-induced movement therapy (CI therapy), is described by Kopp and colleagues as follows:

> CI therapy changes the contingencies of reinforcement
> (provides opportunities for reinforcement of use of the
> more-affected arm and aversive consequences for its nonuse
> by constraining the less-affected arm) so that the non-use
> of the more-affected arm learned in the acute and early
> sub-acute periods is counter-conditioned or lifted. Second,
> the consequent increase in more affected arm use, involving
> sustained and repeated practice of functional arm

videotapes depicting experiments on head injury in baboons. These tapes were somehow acquired by PeTA, which then edited the material into a video montage lasting less than 30 minutes. PeTA entitled the montage *Unnecessary Fuss*. The title was derived from a comment Gennarelli had made when speaking of the raid and publicity attendant to it: he had dismissed the clamor as an "unnecessary fuss."

Head injury can be brutal. Pictures of baboons with their heads fixed in a device that suddenly accelerates and decelerates for the purpose of slamming the soft, vulnerable brain against an unforgiving bony skull would make even a drill sergeant recoil. But those experiments had an important purpose, namely, to better understand exactly how the brain is damaged under controlled conditions, so that scientists can devise improved treatments for human brain injury.

Unfortunately, young laboratory workers were shown clowning around and misbehaving in other minor ways in front of the camera, with semi-comatose, helpless animals in their arms. This created an image of heartlessness that was exploited in *Unnecessary Fuss*, along with the use of various propaganda tricks. Though I do not fully excuse their actions, I recognize that these young technicians most likely were in need of the psychological relief sometimes provided by humor. Even when macabre, humor has a curative power. Humor helped me survive the difficult months that preceded my father's death as my family and I cared for him at home. Humor also allows surgeons to separate themselves psychologically from the patients they operate on, so that they can do their jobs safely and effectively.

The dean of my school at the time, Robert Marshak, and I are quoted in *Unnecessary Fuss*, even though we knew hardly anything of the Head Injury Research Laboratory until the time of the raid. A reporter at *The Philadelphia Inquirer* had asked me about sadism among scientists, a notion that I rejected, saying that I both respected and enjoyed animals. The reporter translated this sentiment into the fatuous expression: "I love animals. I enjoy them." In *Unnecessary Fuss*, these words, followed by my name, appear in white lettering on the screen just prior to injury of a baboon with a voice-over stating, "Dr. Morrison defends the practices of the Head Injury Laboratory." Fortunately, the NIH did not accept PeTA's major claim that the laboratory's research on animals was unnecessary and improper scientifically. Gennarelli's laboratory was awarded additional funds in 1993 by the NIH for similar studies on miniature pigs, after certain controls were instituted.

There are those at my institution (and quite likely others) who have unfortunately elected to use *Unnecessary Fuss*, which is replete with some clever misrepresentations, as a training film for scientists, the purpose being to demonstrate how *not* to run a research laboratory. In fact, the laboratory was poorly over-seen, and behaviors like smoking in the laboratory should never have been allowed. But my colleague Peter Hand discussed the film with the scientists, analyzed it, and after three viewings ferretted out many outright fabrications or cleverly worded misrepresentations (and which have nothing to do with the management of the lab). The animals *were* anesthetized with a dissociative anesthetic that a leading anesthesiologist at the university had approved, despite the film narrator's claim that no anesthesia was used (can you imagine trying to restrain an unanaesthetized baboon on a table with only its head fixed in a device?). A scene showing forceps being dropped on the floor and reused was from an autopsy and not a surgery, as was stated by the narrator. Also, the narrator commented that acid was spilled on an animal when in fact the scien-tist was joking—he had actually spilled physiological saline. The laboratory's grant application did refer to using anesthetics, contrary to a statement in the film claiming otherwise.[35] The case has been included in textbooks of bioethics. In criticizing the laboratory from an ethical standpoint, one book, *The Human Use of Animals: Case Studies in Ethical Choices,* failed to mention the critical problem that underlay the laboratory's work: human brain injury.[36]

It is true that a committee formed by the Office of Protection from Research Risks, NIH, consisting of a neurosurgeon, veterinary anesthesiologist, and veterinary pathologist, found several conditions within the lab to be at odds with the Public Health Service Animal Welfare Policy. These included a lack of anesthesia (a highly questionable conclusion, as noted below); inadequate supervision; poor training; inferior veterinary care (in this case the reference was to the lack of adequate record keeping and lack of direct veterinary input into the choice of anesthetics, analgesics, and tranquilizers,although it must be remembered that neurosurgeons were involved); unnecessary multiple injuries to single animals; humor; smoking; "statements in poor taste around animals;" and improper clothing. Actually, it took a year and the threat of a federal sub-poena to get PeTA to turn over the approximately 60 hours of videotapes from which *Unnecessary Fuss* had been abstracted.[37] The committee did not find fault with the scientific integrity of Gennarelli's experiments.[38]

A surprising voice dissented from key points in the NIH review and some of PeTA's claims in their film, the then–executive director of the Pennsylvania Society for the Protection Against Cruelty to Animals (SPCA), Erik Hendricks. He served on a university-constituted six-member commission that also reviewed the laboratory and which was "given total access to anything and anyone who had any connection with the laboratory." Hendricks published an article about *Unnecessary Fuss* in the PSPCA newsletter *Animaldom* that reveals an admirable rationality suggesting that a serious concern for animal welfare

to record the activity of individual nerve cells that play a role in regulating respiration. Then he determines how closely an individual neuron is linked to breathing by teaching the cat to hold its breath for an instant in order to observe whether the nerve cells stop firing for a moment. He achieves this end quite easily. The cat learns to associate a light puff of ammonia with the ringing of a bell. Before long, it holds its breath when the bell rings alone, a classic case of conditioning to a previously inconsequential stimulus. If the neuron stays active when the cat falls asleep, it cannot be linked tightly to breathing, but its activity might still be altered when the cat falls asleep. Or a cell may change its pattern of firing dramatically with both holding breath and with sleep. Through experiments like these, Orem is trying to identify which cells are for breathing associated with sleep and which ones are not. This system is complex and far from understood. Given the various serious problems of breathing occurring during sleep in humans (such as sleep apnea), Orem's studies assume medical significance for the future, but not immediately.

In some ways, Orem was a most unlikely target. His laboratory was in the middle of West Texas—far from the hotbeds of radical animal-rights indignation seemingly native to the East and West Coasts, far from the headquarters of PeTA, In Defense of Animals, and Last Chance for Animals. Orem is a superb (and caring) scientist working in an institution with a model program for animal care, one that was fully in compliance with the new government rules promulgated in 1985. Not only was he adhering strictly to the legal requirements, he went beyond them and in an interesting way: He employed a nurse and playmate for his cats, and three-legged Floyd, who had nothing to do with the experiments. Floyd was a pet.

With no exaggeration, Orem's laboratory was run perfectly, unlike those in the previous two cases, which occurred before enactment of laws in 1985 that changed the face of biomedical research. As we will learn, the attack also showed how vulnerable some administrators in government may become to outside intimidation.

Why did Orem merit such attention? Why was he chosen out of so many investigators in the field of animal-based research in the behemoth state of Texas? What qualities or circumstances make a scientist vulnerable to intimidation? To my mind, there are a few factors that increase a researcher's risk of coming to the attention of animal rightists. First, the scientist is studying a species with a high profile amongst activists and the public, such as cats, dogs, or one of the primates. Second, the researcher is studying the brain, which is not well understood by most people. Finally, the experiments are invasive, so that even accurate descriptions or pictures of them would be disturbing to lay persons. Essential also is the collusion of an "insider"—one or more individuals with enough knowledge of the research laboratory, access to the lab, and a willingness to break the law if necessary. The Texas Tech incident probably had all these elements, although no one involved in the break-in was ever identified. I have no theories on who that unknown "insider" (if there was one) may have been.

In their book, Lutherer and Simon write that just 3 days after the raid, "Ingrid Newkirk, cofounder and national director of PeTA, held a news conference" in Lubbock. "Persons who were not members of the press were excluded," and stolen items were displayed. Also "a doctored version of the stolen videotape was shown, accompanied by very misleading commentary by Newkirk." This version came from a videotape that Orem had made and shown earlier at a scientific meeting. "Newkirk claimed that PeTA had no involvement with the break-in and that the material had been left anonymously by members of the ALF (and received on a holiday)."[44] As a result of the furor stemming from statewide publicity, the university initiated an internal investigation. But there was more to come: a formal complaint by PeTA to the Office of Protection from Research Risks (OPRR; now the Office of Laboratory Animal Welfare) of the NIH led to an OPRR investigation of Orem's laboratory. Yet another investigation into the lab's conditions was launched. Orem's work was funded by the National Heart, Lung, and Blood Institute (NHLBI), one of the institutes of the NIH. In an unfortunate response to political pressure from Congress, the director of the NHLBI ordered an unprecedented simultaneous review, instead of waiting for the release of official findings from the OPRR. I was called on by the NHLBI to participate in this unorthodox review, which to my mind was unnecessary and somewhat suspect. Eventually, but with reservations, I agreed to take part in it.

Unlike the NIH team that investigated Taub in 1981, consisting of bureaucrats and laboratory-animal veterinarians and lacking entirely in practicing neuroscientists, the group assembled by the NHLBI had four working scientists schooled in the areas of Orem's research, and two officials of the Institute. I doubled as a veterinarian and a practicing scientist. Orem was offended that the investigation was even taking place, as well he should have been; we scientists felt that the NHLBI had wrongly succumbed to outside pressure. As it turned out, our committee found Orem's laboratory and the animal-care program at Texas Tech to be exemplary. The OPRR came to the same conclusion:

> OPRR concludes that there has been no substantive
> evidence presented or found that would support the
> contention of noncompliance with the PHS Policy on the
> part of Dr. Orem or the University. To the contrary,

She noted that "in schools, many programs that purport to be 'humane educa-tion' are in fact animal-rights propaganda, manipulating children's emotions to win them to a political movement."

Exactly 1 month after the controversy over the course had been made public, the Animal Liberation Front (ALF) staged their raid on my laboratory. Interestingly, instead of focusing on the alleged "cruelty" of my research on sleeping cats, the ALF made clear that I was being punished for defending Taub and Orem and speaking out against the movement's assault on biomedical research. The attack, I concluded, was one of vengeance; the aim of these extremists was to frighten me into silence.

That conclusion proved to have been justified because Ingrid Newkirk, national director of PeTA at the time and a major apologist for the ALF, was quoted in an article that appeared later in March in *The Village Voice*: "PeTA intends to use Morrison to persuade other vivisectors who were heartened by his strong stand on animal research that it doesn't pay off." The article went on: "Now the spotlight is on him, and what happens next will deter others who might want to follow in his footsteps."[50] According to that same article, stolen documents obtained in the raid revealed that I had written over 300 letters urging on colleagues, challenging misstatements by the media and certain poli-ticians, arguing against overly restrictive legislation, and probably more. Not having the letters myself, since they were stolen, I cannot confirm the accuracy of the article's claim.

Thankfully, there was no hesitation on the part of the president and provost of the University of Pennsylvania to issue a statement to the press deploring the raid. A press conference held a few days after "my" break-in was attended by university officials, a representative of the National Institute of Mental Health, and one from a patient organization known as the incurably ill For Animal Research (iiFAR); it was a cheering moment.

Nevertheless, I was hardly feeling jolly. The raid on my lab was frightening, mainly because of the attention focused on me—I had been the subject of numerous newspaper articles and newscasts. Fame is no fun when you know you are famous because someone hates you. Although a number of colleagues said they were right behind me, my interest was in having people beside me or, better yet, in front of me.

Many efforts were made to frighten and discredit me following the break-in. Two of the attempts to ruin my reputation were particularly despicable; fortu-nately, they were unsuccessful. PeTA contacted my neighbors with a mailing containing the *Village Voice* article and a letter presenting them with negative opinions about me dated May 8, 1990, and signed by a PeTA researcher. The letter referred among other things to a series of very negative articles on my contributions to science commissioned by the animal rights organization, the American Anti-Vivisection Society (AAVS), and was distributed widely. To the best of my knowledge, none of my neighbors took the articles seriously.

After receiving phoned death threats and hate mail, including an envelope opened by my secretary that contained a bloodstained condom allegedly tainted with HIV-infected blood, I went on the defense. Worried about my family's safety, I kept a baseball bat by the back door. I removed our mailbox from the end of the driveway, and changed my license plate number to make me less visible to those who might track me. Having been an amateur boxer during my veterinary school days, I even talked of hanging a heavy bag in the garage to get in shape. The last impulse seems silly now, but it was a measure of my concern: what might happen next?

Repeated victimization by unknown assailants is debilitating. It required a year to handle the situation with equanimity. Yet, fear was not the worst of it. The lack of immediate outspoken, local support in the early days from the veterinary school's administration (in contrast to the president and provost of my university, who had issued the statement supporting me) and all but a few friends, colleagues, and students—I received dozens of letters from friends and strangers from around the world—both angered and saddened me. That early silence was one of the worst aspects of the ordeal, and it took me several months to come to grips with what I then thought of as unforgivable abandonment by my colleagues. (John Orem suffered the same depressing lack of local support.) But eventually I came to understand their fear and to forgive them.

At the end of the year, I was somewhat redeemed by a statement, signed by hundreds of people at the University of Pennsylvania, that deplored the AAVS's attempt to destroy my scientific reputation. But not everyone in the university community treated me so well. Acting under the auspices of the School of Arts and Sciences Committee on Academic Freedom and Responsibility, three professors from the departments of chemistry, political science, and Romance languages ruled that the teacher of the Discovery Program course had had her academic freedom trammeled, because the university had cancelled her course. They mentioned my name specifically and clearly placed considerable responsibility for the course's cancellation on me, because I had complained so vigorously to my dean and the chief veterinarian at the Philadelphia Zoo, who in turn urged the university to drop the course.

Quasi-judicial committees at universities seem to have a penchant for egregious procedural errors: this committee fell into line. They listened to the teacher and the program director, and they read "clippings from the *Philadelphia Inquirer* and *The Daily Pennsylvanian*,"[51] apparently stimulated by the press release from the AAVS. The committee members also claimed to have read all

and should have been awarded knighthood for his service. In fact, when one resigns as director of that council, knighthood is a matter of course. But it appears that animal rightists' intimidation blocked the honor, as the government succumbed to extremists' pressure. A secret memo leaked in 2003 noted that Blakemore's "controversial work on vivisection" had prevented the granting of a knighthood that year.[59]

Reflecting back on the individuals discussed earlier, all are ethically conscious people concerned seriously with advancing knowledge necessary to medical progress—I count myself among them. We have devoted our lives to an endeavor that brings little in the way of fame or fortune. One researcher developed a technique that is revolutionizing stroke rehabilitation, and another, a neurosurgeon, who also saves lives every day by performing surgeries, has drastically improved the treatment of head injury. Regardless of whether certain individuals disagree with these researchers' use of animals, do the researchers deserve to have their lives and livelihoods threatened? Do their families deserve to live in fear of masked intruders and arson?

The violence has continued. The FBI lists ALF and their ecological equivalent, Earth Liberation Front (ELF), as the most active domestic terrorist threats in the United States today. John E. Lewis, deputy director of the FBI's Counterterrorism Division, said in testimony before the Senate Judiciary Committee on May 14, 2004:

> Domestic terrorism involves acts of violence that are a
> violation of the criminal laws of the United States or any
> state, committed by individuals or groups without any
> foreign direction, and appear to be intended to intimidate or
> coerce a civilian population, or influence the policy of a
> government by intimidation or coercion, and occur
> primarily within the territorial jurisdiction of the United
> States. . . .
>
> In recent years, the Animal Liberation Front and the
> Earth Liberation Front have become the most active
> criminal extremist elements in the United States. Despite the
> destructive aspects of ALF and ELF's operations, their stated
> operational philosophy discourages acts that harm "any
> animal, human and nonhuman." In general, the animal
> rights and environmental extremist movements have
> adhered to this mandate. Beginning in 2002, however, this
> operational philosophy has been overshadowed by an
> escalation in violent rhetoric and tactics, particularly within
> the animal rights movement. Individuals within the

movement have discussed actively targeting food producers, biomedical researchers, and even law enforcement with physical harm. But even more disturbing is the recent employment of improvised explosive devices against consumer product testing companies, accompanied by threats of more, larger bombings and even potential assassinations of researchers, corporate officers and employees.[60]

According to a report from the Foundation for Biomedical Research,[61] of 836 acts of terrorism in one form or another in the United States between 1981 and 2005, 90% have involved biomedical research. Furthermore, the report shows that those incidents have increased dramatically in the last 5 years. Since this particular foundation focuses mainly on biomedical research, it is likely that additional terrorist activity directed at agriculture, hunting, and other settings where animals are used is not included in that report, so the instances of extremism may be far higher in number. Millions of dollars in damage has been caused during this period, and this does not even begin to measure the losses resulting from the theft of valuable research animals and data, and the negative impact on researchers themselves.

Beyond the direct attacks on individuals and institutions, the movement has now targeted what they term "tertiary" institutions, such as those that provide financial support and services to animal-related enterprises.[62] Under duress, the Royal Bank of Scotland and various other financial institutions in the UK and the United States discontinued their association with Huntington Life Sciences, one of the largest companies providing services to pharmaceutical, agrochemical, and biotechnology enterprises.[63] In 2005, the New York Stock Exchange (NYSE), which had proudly stated its defiance of terrorism after the destruction of the Twin Towers in September 2001, asked Huntington to withdraw its already announced listing on the morning of the big event. The NYSE offered no explanation and refused comment. Given the amount of violence that Huntington had experienced—the CEO was clubbed on the head by an assailant in the UK who was ultimately arrested and jailed, for example[64]— it is not a reach to infer intimidation as the reason for the security exchange's action.[65]

What began with the Silver Spring monkeys in the summer of 1981 has grown to this: laboratories destroyed; researchers driven from their work; homes seriously damaged; and calls for assassinations —all in the interests of saving primarily rats and mice, at the expense of many sick people. There is a better way: support research that will eliminate or at least reduce the need for animals in the search for ways to advance medicine. That, of course, is only a dream, for now.

For example, as I relate in the next chapter, the pressure to ban totally the use of higher apes will negatively impact many humans hoping for relief from certain diseases.

Ignorance of the process of science probably underlies much of society's concern about what goes on in animal laboratories. This in turn leads to pressures for tightened control, for "alternatives" to using animals, for more "precision" so that animal lives are not "wasted." I have very clearly stated that I believe using animals wastefully is, in fact, cruel—if there should be an equally effective way to gain certain information other than using an animal, that would be the humane path to follow. But at the same time I know through long experience that research is an inherently wasteful activity, for researchers enter many blind alleys during the course of scientific inquiry. Nature is, in many ways, a maze; the beauty of pure research is that one may stumble across an answer to one riddle while studying an entirely different question.

For example, the late Neal Miller,[1] a towering figure in twentieth-century psychology, believed that students should appreciate the history behind their disciplines and that scientists had a responsibility to make such history accessible to them. So he wrote a prologue to a psychology textbook that summarized the important scholarship of Judith Swazey, who wrote about the complex development of the schizophrenia drug chlorpromazine. Miller compared the research that led ultimately to chlorpromazine to the assembling of a complex puzzle of many parts. It involved the study of the chemical structure of dyes, investigation of the fungus ergot, and one of its components, histamine, and then antihistamines. Further study of a blue dye effective against malaria led to the discovery of a new antihistamine that produced drowsiness. Ultimately, a medical treatment for schizophrenia emerged from this unplanned development of tranquilizers, but not without the additional help of psychologists in understanding how animals learn, and developing behavioral tests useful for examining drug effects.

Miller's effort led me to pledge to do the same service on behalf of my own scientific research.[2] As he said, it is important to describe the process of science as it is conducted by real people, in this case me and some of my colleagues, so that the public can better understand why a few of us have been so active in defending biomedical science and its practitioners. Nonscientists' lack of knowledge of this process—how scientists get their ideas and how seemingly haphazard the process can be—can render them vulnerable to manipulation by those who would misrepresent us. People must understand and appreciate the workings of scientific research if they are to legislate it wisely and agree to fund it.

Therefore, in this chapter, I will describe in some detail my own work over a period of more than 40 years. My aim is to illustrate how a single phenomenon or mystery can so grip a scientist that trying to understand it brings a purity to the effort that justifies the use of animals in research. I hope to convey the sense of wonder we scientists experience as seemingly unrelated pieces of information eventually merge, like streams or rivers into a larger body of water, into a new ocean of understanding of one single phenomenon. What has interested me enough to spend 40 years of my life studying sleep? Rapid eye movement (REM) sleep. As you read more about REM, I hope you will come to realize why I have been so driven to understand it.

Probing the Nature of REM

I have the Philadelphian's habit of jaywalking and the memory of one of my college swimming races to thank for an increased understanding of REM sleep. These unlikely sources set me on the road toward finding an explanation for the way various elements of REM group together in a comprehensible package.[3] I must admit, however, that it was a book on bird behavior that really provided the key to my success.

Before turning to bird watching, jaywalking, and swimming, though, I will offer an overview of sleep. Historically, sleep had always been seen as a quiet withdrawal from the world. The brain waves of sleep, recorded by means of electrodes stuck to the scalp and connected to a recording machine by way of wires, revealed a pattern of activity (called the electroencephalogram, or EEG) quite different from that observed when the subject was awake: the low-amplitude waves occurring at a high frequency as written out on recording paper were replaced by high-amplitude, low-frequency "lazy" waves. These low-frequency waves certainly fit the notion of sleep. That view of sleep changed dramatically, however, with the discovery of REM in 1953 by a graduate student, Eugene Aserinsky, and his professor, Nathanial Kleitman, at the University of Chicago.[4] Instead of the waveforms characteristic of sleep as it was known—we now call that phase non-REM—the EEG revealed a pattern essentially like that of wakefulness. They found that REM always appeared periodically after a length of time spent in non-REM.

The effect of their discovery was tremendous. Within 10 years a mob of scientists was puzzling over REM, and within 20 years their efforts led to the development of a new medical specialty: sleep disorders medicine.

Why did REM create such a flurry of activity? Quite simply, it provided a gateway to the study of dreams, for REM had two striking characteristics that made its detection easy and excited the imaginations of researchers. First, the brainwaves of a person in REM resembled those of a person who is awake, and second, the accompanying rapid, darting movements of the eyes, which gave REM its name, suggested that the sleeper was literally watching dream events. These two features allowed researchers to detect the occurrence of REM easily. So whenever the REM pattern occurred, the researcher could wake the sleeper and ask if he or she were dreaming and, if so, what the person remembered.

Dream researchers then made two exciting observations that dispelled a couple of long-held beliefs. The first discovery was that everyone dreams. There are no nondreamers—only those who do not recall their dreams in the morning. When these individuals are awakened during a bout of REM, they can and will report having dreamed. Those who do remember dreaming, but not necessarily every morning, still dream several times every night.

The second observation refuted the common belief that a dream does not occur in real time—that is, that a dream only *appears* to be long to the dreamer; in reality it is a fleeting event. To test this notion, researchers simply woke up sleepers after varying lengths of time spent in a REM period and asked them to report their dream. Those they woke up 5 minutes into REM gave a report that had significantly fewer words than reports from those aroused after 15 minutes of REM. The resulting finding was that a dream lasts as long as it seems to last, and dreamers are not being fooled by dreams that seem to occur in a flash.[5]

Observant dog owners had long noted that their dogs seemed to be dreaming when they yelped and howled and paddled their legs while asleep.[6] In fact, dogs, too, are in REM at that time. The whining and yelping that hunters thought were the result of dreams of the hunt are likely due to something less dramatic. Breathing is very irregular during REM—deep or shallow, fast or slow. At the same time, muscle twitches, which also cause the rapid eye and leg movements, occur all over the body, including in the throat. Although no scientist has bothered to study this, I think that the combination of unpredictable movements of throat muscles and the irregular flow of air to and from the lungs causes what sounds like the yelping of a hound, not dreams of chasing raccoons up trees. While sitting in our kitchen years ago I would often hear our Labrador retriever, asleep on the floor beside me, yelping like a hound during her irregular breathing in REM. I never heard her making such sounds while she was awake.[7] As for what dogs are dreaming about, who can say? A dog's dream is to a human's dream as a dog's thoughts are to a human's. How can we ever know? Nevertheless, I will explore animal "dreams" a bit later, as a remarkable phenomenon has recently given us some insight into them.

We know that in addition to humans, mammals have episodes of REM because a brain-wave pattern similar to ours appears periodically during their sleep. Indeed, scientists first observed another interesting feature of REM in animals (cats initially), not in people: paralysis of the muscles occurs, because the nerve cells (called *motor neurons*) in the spinal cord that induce them to contract are inhibited by higher brain centers. The movements previously mentioned merely break through the paralysis irregularly. So a person is normally paralyzed for several minutes about five times a night (assuming about 8 hours of sleep), because REM alternates with non-REM approximately every 90 minutes in people. In dogs and cats this sleep cycle is shorter: REM occurs every 25 minutes.

I entered the research picture in 1964, about 10 years after the discovery of REM. At that time, the paralysis of REM excited much interest, for it had been discovered only a few years earlier by the French researchers Michel Jouvet and Francois Michel.[8] In fact, their finding is an excellent example of how science progresses in unexpected ways. Jouvet and Michel were studying the startle reflex in cats, a basic response to noise that is experienced by everyone. In order to remove the influence of higher brain activity, or "thoughts," they separated the lower brain leading into the spinal cord from the higher brain and then recorded muscle contractions in the cat's neck after a loud noise.

In between experiments they continued to record the electrical activity of the muscles, which increases or decreases as muscles contract or relax. We are fortunate that they did, for a curious thing happened: periodically the muscle activity fell to zero. Perhaps Jouvet and Michel thought at first that their equipment was working improperly, always a concern for a researcher. But they observantly noted that the toes and whiskers twitched during this period, just as they do during REM, and reasoned that the lower part of the brain sufficed for REM to occur. By chance, Jouvet, one of the leading sleep researchers, happened upon a very important discovery because their follow-up research in normal cats revealed the same absence of muscle activity, usually referred to as *atonia*, during normal REM.

Althtough we are still not certain where in the brain excitatory activity originates, it irregularly overcomes the inhibition of the nerve cells (motor neurons) in the spinal cord and causes muscles to contract, resulting in the brief excitations of the motor neurons that induce twitches of muscles, including those that generate the rapid eye movements, interrupting the ongoing paralysis. Fortunately, the process of muscle inhibition does not occur in the heart muscle and involves the diaphragm only slightly,otherwise we would die. The muscles of the tongue and throat are also atonic (paralyzed) during REM, and hypotonic (less active than when awake) during non-REM sleep. This can impair breathing during sleep under various conditions. For example, too much fat around the throat when throat muscles are atonic or hypotonic may block the airway during sleep. This sleeping person will then struggle to breathe, awaken subliminally, and repeat the process throughout the night. The result is a very tired and miserable person with a strong tendency to fall asleep during the day. Like the drunken driver, this very sleepy driver is a great danger to himself (affected individuals are usually men over 40) and to society. This condition is known as obstructive sleep apnea (absence of breathing).

Yet paralysis during REM is really quite a sensible arrangement. Think of some of your dreams and imagine what kinds of trouble you would find yourself in if you were to act them out. In fact, there are those who do, again, the majority being older men. Mark Mahowald, a neurologist, and Carlos Schenk, a psychiatrist, reported in 1986 a series of cases in which patients had violent activity while they were dreaming.[9] Further tests in the hospital revealed that the movements could be correlated with the "actions" in their dreams. This strange condition was coined REM sleep behavior disorder (RBD). Fortunately (for patient and bed partner), Mahowald and Schenk found a medication that suppressed the violent behavior during REM. Neurological examinations of these patients revealed that about 50% of patients with this problem were normal while awake. Unfortunately, as the years have passed, many of these patients have developed one or another neurodegenerative disorder, such as Parkinson's disease. RBD has proven to be a harbinger of worse things to come for some of these patients.

A dream report of one of Mahowald and Schenk's patients is particularly striking. It well illustrates the "reality" of a dream and the great importance of paralysis during the dream state. This patient was 62 years of age and dreamt that he was playing football. As a running back, he had received the ball for a plunge through the line. He woke up as he crashed into a defensive lineman while struggling to gain some extra yards. Regrettably, the lineman proved to be his bedroom dresser. Even more regrettably, he was an old man in his pajamas with the only spectator being his horrified wife.

Mahowald and Schenk recognized RBD for what it is: a disturbance of REM (rather than epilepsy, as had been theorized), and they credited earlier experiments performed in cats with leading them to this recognition. First Jouvet[10] and then Henley and me[11] found that creating a bit of damage to the lower brain in a region called the pons eliminated the muscle atonia that usually occurs during REM, allowing the cats to exhibit various types of movements in a state we call REM without atonia. (To create a lesion, we heat a thin wire insulated except at its tip and introduce it into the brain to burn some of its insensitive tissue; the cat remains under surgical anesthesia throughout the procedure.) These behaviors can range from simple head lifting to walking practically normally. The amount of activity varies from cat to cat and, thus, from lesion to lesion. The degree of complexity of behavior depends on where and how much damage occurred. Always, though, the cat appears alert to the untutored eye, even if it can only partially raise itself. It will appear to search for something in front of it, orient its head in the direction of a nonexistent sound, pounce on imaginary prey, and jump as if startled, all without awakening.[12]

How do we know the animal is not awake? We can wake it up, and it then moves perfectly normally. That sounds like a silly answer, but really it says a lot. The cat is in a state from which it can easily be aroused, as in normal sleep, and not experiencing an epileptic fit, from which it could not be aroused. We perceive the change to wakefulness because the third eyelids of cats and other animals, which partially cover the eyes as they normally do in sleep, instantly retract. The animal will then blink if facing a bright light. Moreover, if the cat is standing on all fours in the state of REM without atonia, the cat will stand more erect when awakened and move gracefully, not awkwardly.

In the absence of this observable behavior, sleep researchers generally depend on recordings of brain and other types of activity of the body to study sleep. These include muscular contractions, rate and depth of respiration, brain and body temperature, and heart rate and blood pressure. The recordings measure amplified electrical activity generated by brain, heart, or muscle cells, which drives a pen back and forth over paper moving beneath it—much like the lie detector device often portrayed in movies and on cop shows.

The brain waves recorded on that paper are the result of the activity of many neurons that forms the EEG. The EEG takes different forms in wakefulness, in non-REM and REM, and in different disease states. It appears almost flat in deep coma, and contains many large "spikes" in epilepsy. More nonscientists may be familiar with the EKG, or electrocardiogram, which shows the patterns of electrical activity associated with the contractions of the heart. The principle is the same. Scientists are even able to record electrical activity painlessly from deep within the brain by means of very fine wires placed within or near single nerve cells. It is possible to take such recordings in a nonanesthetized animal (or human) because the brain itself does not sense pain when something cuts through it. Nature saw no need for a sense of pain in an organ already so well protected by a thick skull.

Insights from Bird Watching, Jaywalking, and Swimming

With this background on sleep research and a description of REM, I will now turn to the three seemingly unconnected activities—reading a book on bird behavior, jaywalking, and, swimming a 100-yard race—and how they contributed to my theory about the appearance of muscle paralysis during REM.

My first insight came after reading *The Herring Gull's World* by Nikko Tinbergen,[13] one of the world's leading ethologists (one who studies animal behavior under natural conditions). The book is a masterpiece, as is the research behind it. By means of careful, detailed observations of the birds' interactions with each other, other creatures, and objects in their surroundings, Tinbergen developed such insights that he seemed to crawl into the gull's mind. Much of what he found resulted from paying close attention to the gull's various postures and movements. Armed with such understanding, he explained why the birds behave as they do.

At the time I was reading *The Herring Gull's World*, my laboratory was studying the role that one portion of the brain, the cerebellum, might play in the control of posture, movement, and muscle tone during sleep. The cerebellum had long been known to be a regulator of all three during wakefulness. An inebriated person staggering down the street is a clear picture of someone with a damaged cerebellum. (Police have been known to mistakenly haul in more than one unfortunate person with cerebellar disease on charges of public drunkenness.)

When awake, cats with damage to the cerebellum act the same as people with the same damage—their posture, movements, and muscle tone are impaired. When they were sleeping, the cats' activity seemed unchanged from normal. In our laboratory, the pens of their EEGs traced rather unimaginative lines on the paper flowing beneath them. That may have been the end of it had I not been reading Tinbergen's book, which raised a question: what if we were to imitate Tinbergen and watch our cats with damage of their cerebellum while they are sleeping, rather than watching the pens? Would their behavior reveal something that our expensive recording machinery did not?

Now watching a cat sleep may seem as exciting as watching corn grow, and it usually is, but this time it was different. Just before the cat entered REM, a series of very slight jerks of the legs occurred, ceasing as the paralysis of REM took over. Inspired by Tinbergen's careful work, my colleagues and I were able to glean much information from these seemingly inconsequential movements.

First, these movements differed from cat to cat. In some cats the elbow flexed, and in others it extended. We reasoned that the cerebellum, which works to prevent movement from being too excessive in one direction or another (preventing "drunken" staggering back and forth), had been damaged in a way that allowed too much movement in one direction or the other, even in sleep. In fact, a cat that suddenly flexed its elbow just before REM also flexed it excessively when it was awake and walking. We reasoned that modulation by the undamaged cerebellum normally allows the muscles to settle smoothly into the atonic state of REM.

Again, that could have been the end of our findings. But the observant young veterinary student working with me, Bob Bowker, happened to drop his keys on the floor and then note that the same leg that jerked spontaneously just before REM also responded with the same movement in non-REM when the keys dropped. He also observed that one of the pens traced a big wave when the leg jerked in response to the noise. He may well have missed the wave if there had not been the accompanying leg jerk to signal when the noise occurred.

This simple observation gave us immediate insight into a prominent phenomenon of REM that many scientists had puzzled over, a waveform that appeared spontaneously in the same line traced by that pen just prior to and during an episode of REM, ceasing abruptly when the episode terminated. It also set me on the path to understanding much more about REM in general. That particular pen had traced the recording of electrical activity from a group of neurons in a brain structure called the lateral geniculate body, which normally transmits the information coming from the eye to the part of the cerebral cortex where vision is organized. We now know that nerve impulses generated in nerve cells in response to a noise can enhance the transfer of information through the lateral geniculate body on its way to the visual cortex.[14] This makes sense when we are awake and need visual acuity when something occurs that is signaled by a sound. But no one would have thought to record from the lateral geniculate body had there not been such great interest in the visual imagery of dreaming in those years.

To recapitulate, for about 1 minute prior to the beginning of REM, when a cat is asleep and obviously not looking at anything, one sees the same large waves (denoting a great deal of nerve cell activity) that Bob saw after noises, but occurring spontaneously every second or so. We now call them PGO waves, after sites in the brain where they were first studied—the G for the lateral geniculate body where the neurons from retina of the eye terminate;[15,16] the P for the pons, a part in the lower brain; and the O for the occipital, or back, portion of the cerebral cortex where vision is organized. PGO waves always herald the beginning of another period of REM.

Because PGO waves have assumed such importance in my scientific career, I never tire of anticipating their appearance. Indeed, their inevitability, an expression of nature's will, reminds me of the birth contractions I timed for my wife on five different occasions. PGO waves are associated with my scientific offspring just as surely as those contractions were connected with my children. Indeed, I can't help watching a cat or dog asleep anywhere without watching for the first muscle twitching that signals the onset of yet another REM period.

But unlike birth contractions, the normally spontaneous PGO wave could also be evoked by a sudden noise. We found that sounds also elicited PGO waves before and during REM in cats without cerebellar damage, in between those that occur spontaneously in great abundance as well as in non-REM. It took us a while to get to this point because we were still stuck on the idea that they were somehow linked with movement, a secondary response to the movement.[17]

A student was yet again the key to another breakthrough. I had assigned a particular reading to Penn undergraduate Peter Reiner, who was doing an independent study with me. In the article the author referred to a drug that created insomnia and also released PGO-like waves even during wakefulness. He had remarked that each time a wave appeared, the cat acted as if it had been startled.[18] I immediately ran down the hall to tell Bob what we had read and my conclusion: "We're startling our cats with noises, so REM with all its PGO waves must be a period when the brain is startling itself."

We had to admit that the spontaneous "startling" represented by PGO waves did not awaken cats, but then neither did our tones. Then we thought of the behavior of cats in REM without atonia. They, too, seemed to startle spontaneously, but more often they oriented (directed their attention) to nonexistent objects, and they did that throughout each episode of REM without atonia. Further studies convinced us that the amplitudes of PGO waves were a measure of the degree of alerting within the brain, although it was obviously below the threshold for behavioral arousal, i.e., awakening. Indeed, much later we found that during REM the amplitudes of PGO waves match the highest amplitudes observed as cats orient when they are awake.[19]

Thus, through the experimental trick of lifting the body out of paralysis, we showed in a striking way this fundamental feature of REM: "alertness" during sleep. This does not mean that one is more easily roused from REM than from non-REM, for much evidence points to the contrary. Rather, the point is that the behavior we observe in REM without atonia, added to the insights gained from recording PGO waves (not to mention the EEG), suggests that the REM brain most resembles the waking brain when an animal (including a person) is on high alert.

These observations point to one obvious conclusion: the paralysis of REM is secondary to the brain's highly "excited" condition because we can eliminate the paralysis and still REM appears. Although it is quite handy that we are paralyzed—just remember some of your dreams—it is not a prerequisite for REM to occur. The findings from RBD patients confirm this conclusion. Considering how similar these two obviously different states of being are, REM without atonia and the "alerted" brain during wakefulness, I was primed to pay close attention to my own reaction when something unexpected and "startling" happened. This brings us to jaywalking.

Commuters from Philadelphia's majestic 30th Street Railroad Station gather to walk to a major gateway to the University of Pennsylvania campus at 34th and Walnut Streets. There at a traffic light they must cross Walnut Street. Often, pedestrians cross Walnut before the light changes to green because, like them, the traffic tends to move in bunches, leaving the street empty of cars for a long enough period to cross safely. Pedestrians, most likely still in a group, will have calculated the distance between themselves and any oncoming vehicles and judged the street still safe to cross.

And what about the straggling jaywalker lagging a few yards behind that band, perhaps a professor lost in thought? He still has time to decide whether to go forward, but it is what happens just before he makes that decision that interests us. Just as a car enters his peripheral field of vision, he will sense a slight give in the knees or, if already walking, a slight "hitch" in his stride as the leg moving forward stops moving for a fraction of a second. I experienced this phenomenon not long after we had gained our insight into REM as a period when the brain acts as if it were continually receiving internally generated alerting signals. Having safely reached the other side of the street, I had a sudden flash of insight: the paralysis of REM depends on the brain's "alerting" just as the hesitation in movement does when we are awake, but in exaggerated form.

That exaggerated response to alerting can appear at times during wakefulness. An experience from long ago flooded my memory just as I reached the other side of Walnut, something that happened to me as a college swimmer during a 100-yard freestyle race. This event involves flurry of action that is over very quickly. In a 25-yard pool, the swimmers make three turns as efficiently as possible. In this particular race I was in the lead going into the final turn, so I was very excited, to put it mildly. But a very peculiar thing happened while completing the last turn: I stopped dead in the pool, unable to move a muscle. In the churning water surrounded by tumbling bodies I felt paralyzed, as if in a bad dream. (Actually, awareness of difficulty in moving appears in some dreams, which is quite likely the result of feedback information from the inhibited muscle-control system.) It could only have been a second or so, but by then everyone had left me behind. I came in dead last, and heartbroken. My coach tried to console me, saying my muscles must have tied up. Even then, I knew that tightened muscles had not stopped me; there was simply no muscle power. Something had overloaded my circuits and shorted their energy supply.

The brief paralysis brought on by the excitement of possibly winning a race was a gross exaggeration of what transpires when one is suddenly surprised (excited) by an unexpected stimulus. Thinking back on that moment, while standing at 34th and Walnut, it all came together. The atonia of REM is an inevitable consequence of the peculiar high level of excitement within the brain, peculiar because it actually occurs within sleep. And because REM will still occur without the atonia in our experimental animals and in people with RBD, the excitement generated within the brain during REM must not be dependent on the paralysis to keep an individual from awakening.

Why is the brain in REM in such an excited state? Someone who works only with people might answer that that this excitation is necessary for humans to dream. But that explanation doesn't work very well for animals. A strictly non-teleological explanation would be that various neurons rest at different times during sleep, and this can be said for many different classes of nerve cells, so that those neurons keeping the brain in a quiet state are not active in REM, allowing others to exhibit a pattern like alerting with the link to actual arousal blocked. In other words, we really do not know the explanation.

But the linkage between excitement and suppression of motor activity that seems to be shared by two grossly different behavioral states is an example of nature's parsimony and, therefore, efficiency. Why create two parallel systems when one (with some modifications, depending on the particular demand) will do? Males use the same organ for reproduction and urination, with obvious modifications according to use. The same muscles we employ to move us from one point to another serve to increase our body temperature by shivering when we are cold. The lungs, chest muscles, and diaphragm that participate in respiration also help us eliminate heat during panting. Our airway allows us to communicate as well.

Why not assume, then, that the nervous system evolved to allow an animal to react in an automatic manner when the brain is very excited? And why not use the same mechanism whenever running about willy-nilly would be disad-vantageous, such as when we are asleep? Patients with RBD can tell us about the disadvantage of not being paralyzed during REM. When we are awake, an unexpected stimulus is always potentially life threatening. To protect us, nature has installed a little "look-before-you-leap" program. There is always a brief moment of hesitation, orienting the head toward the stimulus and then a rapid assessment of the situation, before appropriate action is taken. This could be "run," "approach for closer inspection," or "dismiss as unimportant."[20] Recall that the appearance of the PGO wave in the lateral geniculate body represents an increase in visual acuity as information passes through that structure on the way to the visual cortex.[21]

Various factors come into play during the animal's assessment of surprising stimuli. For example, a prey animal must decide if the stimulus is a predator and, if so, how far away it is before deciding to flee or ignore it. Test this idea yourself: clap your hands loudly as your neighbor's cat is strolling by. I did this once while sitting with my wife on our front porch. A strange cat was walking in the lane 20 yards away, and I clapped loudly. The cat stopped, looked at us, and then ambled on. I looked at my wife, saying, "That's what we study." She replied, "It makes sense to me."

Very satisfying support for our ideas came from another sleep researcher, one of my best friends, Pier Luigi Parmeggiani, the director of the Institute of Human Physiology in Bologna, Italy. In his presence, an unplanned experiment turned out perfectly in a delightful way. It occurred during the fall semester of 1984, when I was in Bologna on sabbatical leave. Pier Luigi and I had discussed my ideas, and he had read a paper of mine that was soon to be published in a book we had coedited. So he was primed for the experiment.

In October we spent a week in Erice, a hilltop village on the southeastern coast of Sicily. An international school there offered various courses, one of which Pier Luigi lectured in while I tagged along. Erice was periodically bathed in dense fog throughout the day, giving it an eerie, medieval feel, just the place for a mystery to be solved. Actually, the intermittent fog was due to a line of clouds that sailed along at hilltop level, hugging the coast like a line of flying ghost ships. Periodically, one would dock at Erice and then move on, leaving her sunny once more.

To travel between Erice and the train station at Palermo we had to endure a hair-raising ride, at the mercy of one of the school's macho drivers. The trip from Palermo had been so outrageously dangerous—at one curve we simply went over the edge and down a bumpy dirt road until our only slightly cha-grined driver could stop—that I refused to make the return trip with the same driver. Our new driver proved moderately more sedate, but this did not inhibit him from bursting free of Erice's narrow streets at the exit arch doing some-thing like 50 miles per hour. Just as we emerged through the archway, a man nearing it on foot froze, looked toward the vehicle barreling toward him, and then leaped to the side. Seeing the sequence of actions by the startled villager, Pier Luigi turned to me with a big grin and sparkling eyes, exclaiming, "You are right, Adrian! You are right!" He was so spontaneous and so positive that I felt my idea had received the ultimate blessing.

So, in the brain there is an "automatic" connection made between high levels of excitation and a system that puts a clamp on physical action, however brief that clamp might be. And though I am speculating to a degree here, the peculiar characteristics of narcolepsy, addressed in the next chapter, have helped to convince me that I am right. Various situations or stimuli, like laugh-ter, fright, anger, or startle, induce those suffering from this sleep disorder to collapse suddenly, as I did during my race. Tragically for them, however, it hap-pens over and over again throughout the day. These bouts of paralysis, called cataplexy, often continue right into regular REM episodes accompanied by the usual paralysis or atonia. Rather than following the normal sequence—waking, to non-REM, to REM—the narcoleptic often shifts directly from waking into REM. In these peoples' brains, there must be an instability that allows abnormal switching between the two different modes of the excitement–motor suppression system.

With this, I shall leave standard sleep research to illustrate further how research ideas can pop into a scientist's mind. In this case we again have the activism of extremists within the animal rights and liberation movement to thank for an important scientific advance. When they targeted me, I picked up another research interest: posttraumatic stress disorder (PTSD). Those of World War II vintage learned the terms "shell shock" and "battle fatigue," which referred to a state of being overwhelmed by the horrors of combat. These days we speak of the psychiatrically defined PTSD. A single traumatic event, such as a rape, a mugging, or bad accident scene, even when one is only witness to the horror, can trigger a host of symptoms that can persist for months or years, among them flashbacks, bad dreams, and hyper vigilance. How remarkable that a single event can last as a memory, just like that of a high school graduation, or the birth of a child, but so negatively, and with so many unpleasant side effects. Clearly, fundamentally traumatic events sear a pattern into the brain— where in the brain, we would like to know.

My insight into where to look came from an event associated with the animal-rightists' intimidation campaign against me. On the Thursday morning after the ALF invaded my office in 1990, I woke up feeling rather jaunty after the low mood of the previous few days. I decided to go to the university early for breakfast at one of my favorite restaurants. I felt so good that I even put on a tie, usually reserved for special occasions.

So, spiffed up, I walked down the drive to pick up our morning newspaper. At that moment, two young women with very grim expressions stepped out from behind our high hedge and began taking my picture; after a few seconds they jumped back in their car and drove away. One of those pictures later showed up in *The Village Voice* as part of the article mentioned earlier.[22]

This episode dumped me right back into my funk and killed my appetite. But something else, something peculiar, happened as well. Several days after the incident, I realized that each morning I had been attentively looking through the front door or window to determine the location of my paper. I asked myself, "Why should I care exactly where they are throwing our paper? I never did before. This is silly." At the same time, I realized that the red and green lights on our answering machine were attracting my attention to an unusual degree— typically, I just ignored them. Then it hit me: I was hypervigilant (one of the symptoms of PTSD) from the extremists' raid on my lab and the subsequent invasion of my privacy at home a few days later while retrieving the newspaper. I could not keep myself from orienting, keeping close track of my surroundings. Once again, a personal experience gave me a research idea—this one stemming from a bit of anti-research activity.

Through my lab's current research and the last series of experiments of my career, my colleagues and I would like to contribute something significant to the problem of PTSD, a crippling condition that afflicts about 30% of those who have experienced a psychologically traumatic stressor. The symptom complex includes insomnia and repetitive, stereotypical anxiety dreams, as well as the intrusive recollections and flashbacks during wakefulness already described. The sleep disturbance in PTSD is often resistant to available pharmacological and psychotherapeutic interventions, and hypothesis-driven treatment trials are greatly needed.

To make progress we must understand where in the brain the terrible memories driving the symptoms of PTSD reside, and then how to prevent their taking up permanent residence. We may even seek to block the effect entirely. Even the mildest of aversive stimuli can be remembered and then disturb sleep, a phenomenon that is very useful for our research. In our current studies we can avoid truly damaging stimuli and still disturb sleep in a manner analogous to PTSD. Linking disturbing, rather than painful, shocks (equivalent to those little, annoying jolts one receives when touching a metal surface on a cold, dry day) with a series of a few tones will disrupt REM in rats for many days when we present only the tone, the conditioning stimulus. The rats will also freeze, another measure of their mental disturbance. (To my mind, this is an example of the conscientiousness of most biomedical scientists who work with animals. We did our best to perform these experiments without physically harming the rats. Though I do not particularly enjoy scaring them either, I feel assured that my treatment of them was as humane as possible given the nature of these experiments.[23,24]

How can we prevent the effects of disturbing memories and their impact on sleep? Currently we are focusing on the amygdala, a structure deep within the brain, where one can also record PGO waves associated with orienting. The amygdala contains the mechanisms that add emotional tone to novel or previously disturbing stimuli, as in the case of tones in our experiments. In other words, the amygdala is responsible for the emotional overtones that accompany memories, and then searing bad events into memory so that they may be re-called years after the event.[25] Injection of various chemicals into specific areas of the amygdala may interrupt that acquisition of a memory of the conditioning stimulus. Once identified, relevant drugs could then be tested to see if they would block the memory or even erase it after the fact. That is my dream, at least. I also feel encouraged to continue in this line of research by the many cases of PTSD my psychiatrist colleague at the Verterans Affairs hospital is now treating, resulting from the war in Iraq.

Just think how much human suffering extending over years could be eliminated if we could prevent the establishment of a memory trace of some awful experience. Is this a pipe dream? Perhaps, but we now know that early intervention after a stroke with certain drugs that prevent brain cell death can greatly reduce the severity of the victim's symptoms. This was previously thought impossible.[26] Early intervention of some kind may also prove effective against PTSD.

Does every scientist work the way I do—following up on ideas without knowing where they may lead, getting inspiration from everyday occurrences? Certainly not. Some single-mindedly plow ahead furrow by furrow, uncovering new findings that add up to a whole, not allowing themselves to be diverted from an established goal. Although I love to see such scientists work, I like to do many things at once, anticipating that they will eventually plop into place, which they sometimes do. The way scientists like me work really represents in a microcosm the way that science in general operates. Ideas spring from many sources, and an observation made during the course of an experiment in one field may be the key to an advance in another. The observations themselves may not be all that exciting, but something about them may stimulate a notion that leads a scientist in an entirely new direction. In the modern era of e-mail and Internet communication, one scientist's data can inspire and redirect the work of another scientist on the other side of the globe. Recall that Tinbergen's observations of gulls' movements—such an unlikely source—triggered an idea that led to a new way of thinking about PGO waves.

Making Choices

A budding scientist makes a very important choice at the beginning of his or her career: the research problem on which to spend a lifetime.[27] My choice was to study sleep, but it could just as easily have been another subject, for example, the problem of the central nervous system's refusal to regenerate when damaged. Short of death, the worst that can happen is the accident that destroys a person as we know them because of brain trauma, or that confines an active young girl to a wheelchair or worse because of a severed spinal cord. As neurosurgeon and researcher Wise Young wrote in *Science*, "Regeneration of injured brains and spinal cords is the Holy Grail for many neurobiologists."[28]

In the early 1960s, though, when beginning my career, the prospects for solving the problem of spinal cord and brain regeneration seemed nearly hopeless. No less than the Spanish genius who had mapped the entire central nervous system, Santiago Ramon y Cajal, had pronounced in his grand treatise in 1913: "In adult centres the nervous paths are something fixed, ended, immutable. Everything may die, nothing may be regenerated."[29] This idea was still dogma in 1960, so I turned away from that important issue even though some of my professors were engaged in trying to solve it. Back then we could only demonstrate, in mammals at least, minimal new growth after damage to the spinal cord.[30] Processes of nerve cells (axons) in the spinal cord were observed to "sprout" into an area in which other axons had degenerated because they had been severed from the cell body giving them life, and even this ability was disputed.[31] The difficulty in obtaining more extensive growth was that stimulus to growth seemed to be lacking while, at the same time, toxic substances and the physical barrier of scar tissue acted to impede extensive axonal outreach.

However, the intervening years have witnessed exciting progress in this area. Many brilliant people have entered the field, and significant advances in understanding have followed. In addition to gaining insights into mechanisms of sprouting and its variability in various central neural systems, scientists have revealed a much greater potential for regeneration and restoration of function than had been imagined previously. With appropriate manipulations, some central pathways have been induced to regenerate sufficiently to permit some centrally directed movements, although they fall well short of being adequate for "normal" functioning.[32] Scientists have responded to this challenge by Cajal: "It is for the science of the future to change, if possible, this harsh decree [lack of regeneration in the central nervous system]. Inspired with high ideals, it must work to impede or moderate the general decay of the neurones, to overcome the almost invincible rigidity of their connections, and to re-establish normal nerve paths, when disease has severed centres that were intimately associated."[33] Now Wise Young has been emboldened to say that "the possibility of effective regenerative therapies for human spinal cord injury is no longer a speculation but a realistic goal."[34]

Much has been learned of the cascade of chemical events initiated by trauma by replicating these events experimentally in animals.[35] Possessing such knowledge, scientists are learning when and how to intervene in clinical situations, and are developing drugs that can block or minimize pathological events. If irreversible damage has already occurred, in the case of a stroke, for example, the method of rehabilitation developed by the much-maligned Dr. Taub working with monkeys is proving to be very beneficial.[36]

To advance this area of research and others directed at unraveling the mysteries associated with regeneration of the nervous system or those associated with various degenerative disorders of the nervous system, or any other medical problems, human volunteers are ultimately required. Of course, such studies must be done under strict guidelines to minimize the risk to the person who volunteers. Nevertheless, these studies can require considerable time commitment and even some real discomfort. Clinical researchers sometimes have difficulties rounding up volunteers. It seems to me, then, that those who propose that biomedical research on animals is either scientifically suspect or ethically wrong should feel honor-bound to participate as test subjects in clinical studies as often as possible. For my own part, I have participated for several years as a normal subject in clinical studies related to Alzheimer's disease and Parkinson's disease. These studies required annual memory tests, invasive spinal taps, EEG recordings, MRIs, and PET scans. My volunteering for this study was in honor of the cats and rats I have used for experimentation for so many years.

Biomedical Research and Its Animals | 4

*E*arlier I offered Sir William Paton's description of the ills he saw as a young man training in medicine and that I remember seeing as a boy. We no longer worry about these problems in our Western society (although many persist in the Third World), thanks to biomedical research, and thanks to the animals we have used to solve them. Animals have benefited from this research as well, of course. What many people fail to consider is that their dogs, cats, horses, and other pets, as well as animals used for food, are protected from various diseases because of work done on fellow members of their species—both the basic research performed to unravel the causes, and the testing of vaccines and other medicines for safety and efficacy. This is yet another instance in which we humans decide what an animal will be: in this case, a pet or an experimental subject.

Veterinary medicine has progressed just as tremendously as medical knowledge of humans since I received my Doctor of Veterinary Medicine (DVM) degree in 1960. One simple example is the common vaccine against canine distemperand hepatitis. In my mind I can still see the large bottle containing what looked like mud from a river bottom that we injected into dogs in those days of the early 1960s. Now those vials are as tiny and the contents as pink as the vaccines given to my grandchildren, and the injections are far less painful than those administered long ago. Indeed, essentially anything physicians can do for humans we veterinarians can do for animals.

This chapter, however, focuses on the contributions that animals have made to the health and welfare of our own species. We owe a great debt to laboratory animals for advancing the health of humans, eliminating the problems Paton mentioned, despite some claims to the contrary, some of them from rather unexpected quarters. Those claims will be analyzed, and discarded, in Chapter 5.

How Is Research Conducted?

We should first clear up misunderstandings about the nature of animal research. One point of confusion is the frequent interchanging of "animal research" and "animal testing." People are thus led to believe that they are the same thing, but they are really quite different. Animal testing is used to test for the safety or the efficacy of a certain substance or procedure. When animal testing is conducted, the scientist already knows much about the mechanisms of action of a product, but wants to be sure that it will be useful and not cause harm to patients. Is a drug or other product found to be safe to use on an animal therefore likely (but not with 100% probability) to be safe to use on people? After drugs are shown to be safe and efficacious in animal trials, they are then tested on twice as many human beings before release to the marketplace. Even then, after millions of doses are administered to people, problems with the drug may emerge, such as an unexpected side effect. Therefore, animal testing, and testing on human volunteers, is an important step in the process of developing new medications and medical procedures, but it is by no means perfect in terms of predicting potential problems.

A possibly more contentious issue is consumer product testing on animals, particularly for cosmetics. Many cosmetics are advertised as cruelty-free, conveniently omitting mention of the fact that the substances used would have to have been tested on animals at some time in the past, as required by the U.S. Food and Drug Administration (FDA). I see no reason to develop a new cosmetic that uses some new substance that would require testing; this strikes me as unwarranted and unethical. Products used around the home are another matter. In this case, animal testing may be absolutely required, since consumers, small children in particular, might be harmed by an unknown product. Reduction in the number of animals used, or even their elimination, in the testing of one product or another has the most chance of success because the purpose is quite clear: to eliminate the danger of harming living tissue, human or animal. Progress is being made on this score, I am happy to say.

Wonderful will be the day that we no longer need to use animals in a way that does them harm, or we are able to replace them completely in testing.

That day is some distance in the future. Nonetheless, considerable advances are being made in replacing animals with membranes from eggs, tissue culture, and the like for some product safety testing. If a substance damages simple tissue, then the answer is clear: be wary of that product because it may be harmful.

But in research, virtually every major advance in medicine has resulted, directly or indirectly, from research performed with animals. The contributions of animal research to public health cannot be overestimated. Consider the following examples: tetanus and oral polio vaccines, treatments for rabies and anthrax, cardiac catheterization, insulin treatments for diabetes, development of anticoagulants and antibiotics, open heart surgery, organ transplants, lithium, and other treatments for major mental disorders.

All scientific research is either basic or applied, whether it be in the field of chemistry, physics, or biology. Basic research is most like taking a step into the unknown; findings and results can be unpredictable. In biomedical research, the basic researcher seeks to understand a biological phenomenon for the sake of understanding it, not in an attempt to solve a specific problem. The good scientist, one with proper training, does not focus on trivial matters, though. He or she has developed a hypothesis and employs basic research in order to try to disprove it, the essence of good science. Nonetheless, basic research is the very first step toward solving a clinical problem, often without a specific disease in mind, because so many bits of information from varied and often improbable sources will ultimately come together to provide a solution to a diseased condition. In other words, good and successful basic research will usually end up solving a problem that the researcher did not originally intend to solve.

Applied research is different. It is conducted in much closer proximity to the clinical problem, and is an attempt to understand the mechanism underlying a particular condition or problem. In applied medical research, scientists seek to determine "what went wrong" in the body. For instance, researchers may seek to understand the mechanisms underlying a particular form of cancer, when certain cells multiply out of control, and how to stop their advance. Or they may know what the problem is, but must find a technique, device, or medicine that will fix the problem. For example, the creation of a new hip to replace one damaged by the ravages of age requires the introduction of materials foreign to the body. These materials must be implanted in animals first to determine whether the body will react badly to them. In both cases animals are required at some stage in the process. Many insights can be gained from work done using test tubes and tissue cultures or even modeling phenomena with computers, as well as using human volunteers. But for full understanding, whole animals are absolutely necessary and could not ethically be replaced with human beings. The species of animal may vary, and in some cases researchers may use a fish rather than a mammal, but an intact living being it must be.

To help the reader understand just how basic research and applied research fit into the picture, I will turn first to a remarkable survey illustrating how far removed from a particular clinical condition basic research can be and still lead to a major advance. I will follow that story with a real-life example of applied research—how one surgeon sought to keep his surgical patients from dying from malnutrition.

A Magnificent Study

We can thank Julius Comroe, a physiologist, and Robert Dripps, an anesthesiologist, both from the University of Pennsylvania, for showing us the sheer volume of basic research that might precede a major medical advance, and how many disparate fields this research can originate from.[1] Comroe and Dripps undertook a massive study to demonstrate the very broad base of fundamental research that underlies a particular discovery in medicine.[2] Extensive basic research from seemingly unrelated fields led to the studies examined here that can be defined as "applied." The fields Comroe and Dripps chose were cardiovascular and pulmonary diseases because of their own extensive knowledge of these areas, and because such diseases are annually responsible for more than half of the deaths in the United States.

The Comroe and Dripps report appeared in *Science* in 1976, just after Peter Singer had published the first edition of *Animal Liberation* in 1975. This timing was ironic because Comroe and Dripps's aim was not to defend biomedical research from attacks by the animal rights and liberation movement, but to provide a more than anecdotal report on the value of basic research in the advancement of medicine. In the 1960s, the idea of targeted, clinically oriented research (in effect, the opposite of basic research) was much in vogue in governmental circles, and Comroe and Dripps were concerned that such exclusive focus was harmful to medical progress. They enlisted a host of experts to help them determine the discoveries throughout history that led to medicine's most important clinical advances.

To get an idea of how much work and how many people are behind each of our medical and surgical marvels, I will describe the Comroe and Dripps study in detail. Some of these advances involved procedures and techniques that are so commonplace now that many of us may forget just how groundbreaking they were at the time of their introduction.

Comroe and Dripps proceeded as follows: they first asked 40 physicians to name the advances they judged most important to their patients. Comroe and Dripps then divided the lists according to whether they related to cardiovascular or pulmonary diseases and sent each list to approximately 50 specialists in each field. These physicians were asked to vote on the list they received and to add anything they believed had been omitted. In this way, Comroe and Dripps compiled a list of the top 10 clinical advances in cardiovascular and pulmonary medicine and surgery in the previous 30 years. Consider that they reported the results of their study in 1973, and then marvel at how many treatments we now regard as commonplace originated after the end of World War II. Here is the final list:

1. Cardiac surgery (including open-heart repair of congenital defects and replacement of diseased valves)
2. Vascular surgery (including repair or bypass of obstruction or other lesions in the aorta and coronary, cerebral, renal, and limb arteries)
3. Drug treatment of hypertension
4. Medical treatment of coronary insufficiency (myocardial ischemia)
5. Cardiac resuscitation and pacing in patients with cardiac arrest, slow hearts, or serious arrhythmias
6. Oral diuretics (in treatment of patients with congestive heart failure or hypertension)
7. Cardiovascular and respiratory intensive care units (including those for postoperative care, coronary care, respiratory failure, and disorders of the newborn)
8. Chemotherapy and antibiotics (including prevention of acute rheumatic fever and treatment of tuberculosis, pneumonia, and cardiovascular syphilis)
9. New diagnostic methods (for earlier and more accurate diagnosis of disease of cardiovascular and pulmonary–respiratory systems)
10. Prevention of poliomyelitis (especially of respiratory paralysis due to polio)

What lay behind these practically miraculous achievements that we regard now almost as natural rights? What questions had to be answered before someone benefited from each advance? Who were the researchers seeking the answers? Were they aware of where their research was leading?

To answer these questions, Comroe and Dripps had to determine the essential bodies of knowledge that had to evolve before each of the 10 advances helped a single patient. For this they turned to 140 additional consultants, 70 being practicing physicians. Among the others were 37 basic medical scientists and 33 engineers, science administrators, and science writers.

To illustrate what constitutes "a body of knowledge," consider a few of the 25 bodies of knowledge that had to be mastered before the first successful open-heart operation with complete cardiopulmonary bypass could be performed by John Gibbon in 1954. (This has particular meaning to me because my younger brother underwent that operation only 8 years later, in 1962, so that a hole between his two ventricles could be closed.) Some of the insights and techniques that Gibbon depended on included electrocardiography, cardiac catheterization, blood groups and typing, management of heart failure, asepsis, anesthesia and neuromuscular blocking agents, anticoagulants, pump-oxygenator, elective cardiac arrest, relief of postoperative pain, recording and warning systems for intensive care, diagnosis and management of circulatory failure, and management of infection.

Comroe and Dripps made special note of their including management of infection with antibiotics in their list, because we take them so much for granted that we forget that they, too, had to be discovered. Lewis Thomas, the noted medical essayist, elaborates on this point:

> Everyone forgets how long and hard the work must be
> before the really important applications become applicable.
> The great contemporary achievement of modern medicine
> is the technology for controlling and preventing bacterial
> infection, but this did not fall into our laps with the
> appearance of penicillin and the sulfonamides. It had its
> beginnings in the final quarter of the last [nineteenth]
> century, and decades of the most painstaking and
> demanding research were required before the etiology of
> pneumonia, scarlet fever, meningitis and the rest could be
> worked out. Generations of energetic and imaginative
> investigators exhausted their whole lives on the problem.
> It overlooks a staggering amount of basic research to say
> that modern medicine began with the era of antibiotics.[3]

The efforts of Comroe and Dripps are staggering as well. Having learned from their consultants that the 10 most important clinical advances in cardiovascular and pulmonary medicine and surgery depended on a total of 137 bodies of knowledge, they then examined about 4,000 articles and, out of them, identified approximately 2,500 articles that they deemed essential for the development of one or more of the 137 bodies of knowledge. They arranged these articles in chronological order wherever they fit in the 137 categories, and again, with the aid of consultants, selected 500 for detailed examination.

Comroe and Dripps did much more to ensure that governmental agencies bent on directing resources toward only the "practical" ventures recognized that theirs was "a painstaking scholarly review" and that their conclusions did not depend on "the imperfect memories of a group of scientists at a cocktail party." With their chronological lists they could show "that scientific advance requires far more than that reported by the discoverer or by those who wrote key articles essential for his discovery." This, of course, was Thomas's point regarding antibiotics.

Comroe and Dripps's chronology of discoveries in the development of electrocardiography clearly illustrates this point, and in a delightful way. Their chronology begins with the era B.C. and reference to the ancients for recognizing the early manifestations of electricity in such things as electric fish and rubbed amber. But their first two key articles were reports of discoveries made in the eighteenth century in Philadelphia and Bologna, the two cities central to my own scientific work. In 1752, Benjamin Franklin announced that he had proved the identity of lightning and electricity. Galvani, working in Bologna, published articles in 1786 and in 1791 discussing the concept of animal electricity and describing how discharge from the electricity caused heart muscle to contract. Nearly a century of work passed before the description in 1880 of the first EKG in an intact animal, a frog. Seven years later, a famous physiologist of the late 1800s, Augustus Waller, described the use of EKG in humans. In all, Comroe and Dripps and their many consultants identified 46 events and selected 12 of them as key in the long evolution from the primitive medicine of the ancients to the refinements accompanying cardiac catheterization in 1967. Even this monumental effort, they cautioned, presents "only a small fraction of the good, original research that helped to move us away from complete ignorance toward full knowledge."

Most relevant to a number of the issues discussed in this book is the pair's finding that 41% of the studies central to future clinical advances were conducted simply to understand biological phenomena; they were not clinically oriented. Those that they categorized as "clinically oriented" achieved that distinction in rather generous fashion, for the authors needed only to have mentioned briefly an interest in a particular disease, and the research could have been performed on anything from animals to subcellular particles.

The question is, would animal rightists have denounced these basic experiments at the time as irrelevant and wasteful of animal lives, just as they denounce basic research that uses animals today? Would governmental bureaucrats have been skeptical of these experiments' value? To my mind, the monumental study by Comroe and Dripps, undertaken to counteract foolish governmental policy four decades ago, simultaneously offers an effective rebuttal to the shortsighted claims of the animal rights and liberation movement.

Now, over 30 years after publication of the Comroe and Dripps study, policymakers governing medical science are repeating history, directing congressional efforts to focus biomedical research on "practical" results through "translational research." Bruce Alberts, editor of *Science* and former president of the National Academy of Sciences, recently argued, "With so many mysteries remaining about the incredibly sophisticated chemistry of life, it is certain that future medical breakthroughs will depend to a substantial extent on research on organisms that are much smaller and easier to investigate than ourselves." He added, "For this reason, an overemphasis on 'translational' biomedical research (which focuses on a particular disease) would be counterproductive, even for those who only care about disease prevention and cures."[4] Such research is, of course, but one tool among others, including research on standard laboratory animals, that leads to understanding of the basic mechanisms underlying disease.

An Immediate Life Saver

To continue with our description of research, I now turn to a major medical advance—a perfect example of applied research that has saved thousands of lives. It involved a good friend from my college days, Stanley Dudrick, M.D. Stan and I parted ways when I left Franklin and Marshall College in Lancaster, Pennsylvania, to attend veterinary school at Cornell University in Ithaca, New York. Upon returning to the Philadelphia area and to the University of Pennsylvania in 1961 to study neuroscience, I met Stan again in front of the Penn medical school. He was just embarking on a career in surgery as an intern.

When Stan was a medical student, his mentors Isidore Ravdin and Jonathon Rhoads, two great surgeons, had impressed upon him the importance of adequate nutrition in the care of postsurgical patients. In November 1961, three patients entrusted to Stan's care died after a long period of inpatient treatment. As Rhodes explained to a distraught Stan, they had all died of severe malnutrition.[5]

Surgeons at that time encountered many problems in safely administering sufficient nutrients to patients who could not or would not eat enough to stay alive. Prevention of death by malnutrition following a successful surgical treatment was not easy. A number of obstacles had to be overcome in order to provide adequate nutrition via a peripheral vein. There was an upper limit to the amount of fluid that a patient could tolerate intravenously each day.

Nutritional solutions had to be osmotic with bodily fluids to reduce damage to vessel linings and blood cells. Each substance could supply just so many calories, and the rate at which the nutrients could be metabolized had to be considered. The physicochemical properties of the materials used to inject nutrients had to be determined to minimize such problems as phlebitis and thrombosis. The ready, commercial availability of the various substances had to be established. A regimen of strict asepsis from beginning to end had to be followed. And, of course, the cost of the entire enterprise was a last important factor.

As Stan relates, "It was essential to overcome decades of written or verbal expressions by prominent physicians and scientists that total parenteral nutrition [nutrition through means other than by eating food, such as through an IV] was either impossible, or at best, improbable and impractical. Some evidence to the contrary had to be generated if prejudices were to be neutralized and if widespread clinical acceptance was eventually to occur."[6] Stan and his colleagues tried out methods on critically ill adults who would have otherwise died. Not only did patients have to be kept alive, but supplemental nutrients had to be added to provide the energy for healing, which led to creation of the term "parenteral hyperalimentation" by Dr. Rhoads.

These surgeons realized what an important achievement it would be to have sufficient control over parenteral nutrition: a baby unable to eat normally could be kept alive and actually grow. Initial studies in puppies were unsuccessful because researchers could not get enough nutrients into their subjects by using the standard technique of injecting into a peripheral vein. So Stan and his colleagues decided to introduce a catheter that would be left in a large-diameter vein near the heart of beagle puppies, which allowed them to introduce the maximum amount of fluid that an 8- to 10-week-old puppy could tolerate in a day. They made the fluid 30% hypertonic (a solution that has a much higher concentration of substances than the blood normally carries) so that they could introduce more nutrients. The large vein allowed the solution to be diluted rapidly, reducing the chance of damage to the lining of the vein. The results were irrefutable. "The two longest-term animals were fed for 235 and 255 days while they more than tripled their body weights and developed comparably to their control litter mates."[7]

The knowledge that Stan and his colleagues gained, through a process that included more problems to solve than briefly sketched here, allowed these surgeons to keep alive a 3-week-old infant dying from malnutrition due to the absence of essentially all of her small intestine. She lived for 22 months, but died as a result of complications from many interventions. Still, this was a major step toward the success of parenteral hyperalimentation, thanks in part to beagle puppies and a little girl. Sick adult humans also contributed mightily to the development of the techniques and substances infused to keep them alive.

Further Medical Advances Dependent on Animals

There are other medical advances, however, in which the use of human volunteers would have been impossible, not to mention unethical. Michael Festing,[8] an English toxicologist who is also the father of the current executive director of the UK's Research Defence Society, has summarized three cases illustrating this point: the making of a rabies vaccine, chemotherapy for syphilis, and the creation of a useful form of penicillin.

Rabies

Pasteur used dogs to develop a rabies vaccine. He induced the disease by injecting the virus into the dogs' brains. Then he created a vaccine using spinal cords from infected rabbits. Developing his technique over a 5-year period, Pasteur successfully prevented rabies in 50 dogs. When presented with a boy who had been bitten by a rabid dog, he vaccinated the boy at the parents' insistence and the child survived. From that point, he prevented the appearance of the disease in all but 1 of the first 350 people vaccinated (the individual who died did not receive treatment until 37 days after the bite).

Given the estimate at the time that between 40% and 80% of those bitten by a rabid animal would die, Pasteur's record was incredibly good, and the dog model was clinically validated in humans. Without his long experience with his vaccine given to dogs infected in his laboratory, how could Pasteur have been sure of the efficacy of his vaccine? If the vaccine were given to a person that had been bitten, the subsequent lack of symptoms might have been due to the vaccine's effectiveness or simply due to that person not developing the disease. On the other hand, if a person were given the vaccine and then developed rabies, it could have been because the vaccine was ineffective or because the vaccine itself had produced the disease. Without his prior knowledge that the vaccine successfully prevented rabies in dogs, Pasteur could not have been sure of his results in people.

Chemotherapy for Syphilis

In the second case, Festing illustrates the logistical problem, not to mention the ethical considerations, of developing a treatment for syphilis before the advent of penicillin. Paul Ehrlich, a German Nobel Laureate working at the turn of the twentieth century, reasoned that certain arsenic compounds might be effective against the spirochete that causes syphilis. Later, a colleague managed to infect rabbits, and Erlich screened the infected animals with hundreds of arsenical compounds (the basis of chemotherapy) and found *one* that proved effective. How could this have been done with infected humans? "The sheer logistics of working out dose levels, medical histories and treatment regimens for hundreds of syphilitic patients presumably at various stages of the disease, with no prior suggestion that any of the drugs were effective, would have made the research impossible."[9]

Penicillin

After Alexander Fleming discovered that the mold killed bacteria, Ernst Chain, a German-born Englishman, and Howard Florey, an Australian, succeeded in purifying penicillin to inject it safely into mice. In discussing this third example, Festing[10] quotes Peter Medawar's[11] description of the first experiment, which involved eight mice that had received a huge dose of streptococcal bacteria, four of them also receiving doses of penicillin. The four controls (the mice that did not get the penicillin) died; three of the four treated were fine; but the fourth died after 2 days. "They [the experimenters] all recognized that this was a momentous occasion. Animal experiments on a much larger scale soon made it clear that penicillin was indeed of great potential importance." Festing adds that in this case it might have been possible to inject the substance that killed bacteria directly into humans, bypassing trials on mice, but how were the experimenters to know that what was lethal to bacteria might not have been lethal or at least toxic to people as well? Determining which fractions of the "mould juice" would effectively kill bacteria in a Petri dish during the purification process also proved invaluable. So two animal models, bacteria and mice, advanced our knowledge, and both were indispensable in the process of developing penicillin for human use.

Diseases of Mice and Men

There is now a claim that the sophistication of medicine has surpassed obvious similarities in the anatomical structures of animals and humans—hearts or hip joints of dogs and people, for example. This line of reasoning holds that medicine as a science has now progressed to the point where differences on a genetic level between animals and people will render laboratory animals obsolete. How could the genetic makeup of a mouse be comparable to that of a human being?

In fact, there are a surprising number of diseases that result from a gene mutation that appears in both people and laboratory mice, not to mention other species. Muriel Davisson,[12] director of Genetic Resources at the famous Jackson Laboratory in Bar Harbor, Maine, has presented a "short" list of more than 40 such diseases, including defective genes associated with congenital goiter, pituitary hormone deficiency, morbid obesity with hypogonadism, and microphthalmia (tiny eyes).

For years the Jackson Laboratory has run a program to identify the occurrence of spontaneous genetic mutations within their very large mouse colony. They produce more than 3 million mice each year. Researchers are trained to look for promising defects that might be exploited to study the intricacies of a disorder, and animal-care technicians look for anything unusual as they perform routine maintenance of the colonies. These "oddballs" are then screened for possible introduction to an intricate breeding program that will eventually yield the defective gene or genes responsible for a particular disorder. Such identifications guide researchers studying the respective human genetic disorders.

The first groups of these mutant mice were identified and maintained in the 1930s, so the lab has a long and successful history of finding comparable defects in human beings. According to Davisson,

> Because mice have close metabolic and internal anatomical
> similarities to humans, mutant genes in mice frequently
> produce syndromes similar to human internal conditions.
> For example, the mouse eye and inner ear are almost
> identical in structure to the human eye and ear, and many
> mouse models closely resemble human deafness disorders
> and ocular disorders.... Importantly, the protein coding
> sequence of DNA is 85 to 95% conserved between the mouse
> and human genome. This genomic conservation provides
> additional evidence of potential benefits to be gained from
> using mouse models of human diseases.[13]

Even fruit flies, which share about 60% of the genes associated with human diseases, are proving useful in studying the mechanisms underlying human diseases, including the pathophysiology of Alzheimer's disease.[14]

Narcolepsy in Dogs

In my own field of sleep research, the recognition of altered genes in two species, dogs and mice, led to the dramatic discovery of a great decrease in number of a specific group of nerve cells in the brains of people suffering from narco-lepsy.[15] Narcolepsy afflicts about .05% of our population. People with narcolepsy are miserably sleepy all the time (think of that "gritty" feeling you get when you have not slept for a long time). As we know now, these patients also suffer from cataplexy, sudden attacks of muscle weakness that can extend to total paralysis in exciting situations, such as laughing at a joke or swinging a bat in a softball game. Generally, a person with narcolepsy will gradually sink to the ground during a cataplectic attack, and may be fully conscious or go into REM.

As I mentioned in the previous chapter, narcoleptics often experience direct entrance into REM instead of spending time in a preceding period of non-REM, when there is only relaxation of the muscles, as is the normal case. They may experience hallucinations while going to sleep, and upon awakening such patients can remain paralyzed, a condition known as sleep paralysis (normal individuals may occasionally have such an experience, even several times, so it is nothing to worry about in these instances). These symptoms point to insta-bility in the switching from one state to another: wakefulness to non-REM to REM and then back again to wakefulness. Really, it is a marvel that normally these transitions occur so easily without a hitch, considering all the nerve cells that must change their activity at just the right moment.

But step away from the science briefly and think of suffering an attack while sitting in the bathtub or driving a car. Appreciate the danger and inconvenience these individuals face in addition to the misery of always being sleepy. Furthermore, because physicians received little training in sleep mechanisms until recently (sleep disorders medicine only arrived on the scene about 30 years ago), many patients suffered the indignity of being diagnosed with some form of psychosis, and were treated accordingly. As yet, we have only medicines that ease narcolepsy symptoms; we cannot cure the illness nor alleviate all of its symp-toms. But that will soon change, thanks to very recent discoveries in animals.

For about 30 years, psychiatrist William Dement and his associates at Stanford studied dogs with naturally occurring narcolepsy. They first received a dog from a local veterinarian, for animals with narcolepsy occasionally show up at a veterinarian's office (with instances of sudden collapses in place reported by their owners), and not just dogs. Two of my colleagues and I studied a mare with signs of the cataplexy (moderate to severe muscle weakness) of narcolepsy.[16] Dement and his associates found that a number of dog breeds can suffer from narcolepsy, but the Stanford group found that of all breeds, a strain of Doberman pinschers bred true for the disorder. Signs of the narcolepsy appear in these dogs when they are about 4 months old, which somewhat parallels the time of appearance in many narcoleptic humans, adolescence. Dogs cannot report hal-lucinations, of course, but they do have sleep-onset REM and very dramatically demonstrate cataplectic attacks when excited.

A simple test can quantify the severity of the symptoms in each animal. A line of attractive food pellets are placed on the floor equidistant from each other, then the dog is released to go after the food. A normal animal will move right along, gobbling up the pellets rather rapidly, as can be imagined. Narcoleptic Dobermans, by contrast, struggle to get to the pellets because their overexcited brains cause them to collapse repeatedly in place as they move from pellet to pellet. The time it takes them to reach the end of the line, if they ever do, is much longer than that for normal dogs. The Stanford scientists named the test the Food-Elicited Cataplexy Test, or FECT.

In the late 1990s a finding revolutionized the study of narcolepsy and brought real hope for an effective treatment.[17] Two chemical substances called peptides were discovered within a small group of cells in a region of the brain known as the hypothalamus. The peptides have since been labeled hypocretins, or orexins. Two groups of scientists, one based in Palo Alto at Stanford and the other in Dallas, reported within a month of each other in 1999 that sleep alterations of narcolepsy were connected to defects in the genes associated with these substances.

Interestingly, the Dallas group was searching for genes that might be associated with weight control, which is also centered in the hypothalamus. Narcolepsy was far from their minds. They were studying alterations in feeding activity by looking at the effects of removing the relevant genes on feeding. To do this, the Dallas team created a "knockout" mouse, (one that lacks a specific gene being studied by researchers), and observed its feeding patterns. They found a reduction in food intake but not a dramatic loss in weight. Determined to study the feeding behavior further, they then used infrared video observations to watch the behavior of the mice in their active dark period. What they saw was striking: the mice periodically ceased movement and fell over. The researchers interpreted this behavior as a cataplectic attack.

At the same time, the dog watchers at Stanford with a specific interest in narcolepsy found, after a search lasting many years, a mutated gene for one of the hypocretins in affected dogs that altered the functioning of the hypocretin system. The hypocretin cells were then studied anatomically and found to extend their processes to various cell groups associated with sleep organization. Damage to this system removes the normally well-controlled transitions between states of wakefulness and sleep. Just 1 year after hypocretin burst onto the scene, two groups (the same one at Stanford and another that included scientists from UCLA, Michigan, and Pittsburgh) published papers reporting a tremendous loss of hypocretin-containing neurons in the brains of narcoleptics.[18]

Now the search is on for a drug that will replace the hypocretin absent or diminished in the brains of narcoleptics. The good news is that injection of hypocretin into narcoleptic dogs every other day holds cataplexy in abeyance for up to 6 days[19] and it improves cognitive performance in sleep-deprived monkeys.[20] Of course, much remains to be done before an effective drug for people will arrive on the market, but only 8 years ago at this writing we were nowhere in this search.

Genetic Similarity Between Human and Animal Diseases

We also have animal research to thank for the successes of enzyme replacement therapies, available for Gaucher's disease for over a decade, and expanding quickly for other diseases and inborn errors of metabolism, such as Hurler syndrome and Fabry disease. These disorders all result from the accumulation of toxic products in cells, including nerve cells, due to metabolic malfunctions in intracellular bodies called lysosomes. Mental retardation and early death are common features of several of these inherited conditions.[21]

Transgenic mice, those with a foreign gene inserted into their genome so that they express the symptoms of a specific human disease, have played an instrumental role in testing these therapies prior to human trials.[22] Also, a variety of species, including cats and dogs, have naturally occurring, homologous (meaning exactly the same) lysosomal diseases found in people, so study in these two species will eventually contribute to the welfare of multiple species. Although mice can be easily bred and economically housed, larger animals, such as dogs and cats, have several advantages over mice as research subjects: they have heterogeneous genetic backgrounds, and size and longevity that permit surgical manipulations; imaging and physiological measurements are suitable in them for determining the long-term effects of enzyme replacement therapies; and, in time, they are candidates for gene therapy, in which a normal gene is inserted into the genome to replace a defective gene. Because of the accumulation of clinical data on dogs and cats that is so similar to data obtained from human patients, they are an excellent model of the human patients who will ultimately benefit from this research.[23]

Animals and Behavioral Research

Behavioral research, which incorporates research on the brain, is probably the least understood (by the public) and most maligned (by animal rightists) branch of biomedical science. That may be why Peter Singer focused so heavily on behavioral research in *Animal Liberation*, which I will discuss further in Chapter 9. Although much of this disapproval probably stems from a lack of understanding of the field and its history, behavioral research does carry a special burden. As the argument goes, how could the much smaller brains of animals be used to study the workings and afflictions of the complex human brain? And if they can, does this not make animals too close in nature to us humans to permit their study? The latter is an ethical question to be discussed in the final chapter of this book. The answer to the first question is complicated and will be addressed after a brief tour of the central nervous system.

We start with the spinal cord, where the ultimate regulation of movement and the beginnings of sensation reside. My cat, Buster, and I both flinch and yowl or curse at a sudden painful stimulus, and our legs both jerk in response to a tap on the patellar tendon of the knee. The spinal organization of the neurons responsible for these activities is the same in cats as it is in humans.

Moving forward into the lowest part of the brain, in both Buster and me the same neurons control basic bodily functions, such as regulation of breathing, heart rate, and vomiting. Farther forward reside the nerve cells that regulate the behaviors of sleep and wakefulness, which are identical in humans and other mammals, and where dysfunction results in similar problems, such as the narcolepsy just described and REM sleep behavior disorder. In this brain region in all mammals are found the neurons containing the neurotransmitter dopamine, which degenerate in Parkinson's disease.

At the base of the cerebral hemispheres is the almond-shaped amygdala, where mechanisms leading to fear and anxiety in people and animals operate. Monkeys and rats have contributed much to our understanding of the amygdala. The overlying cerebral cortex is where all of us mammals analyze the sensations coming from the skin, muscles and joints via the spinal cord, or eyes and ears in the cases of vision and hearing.

Where we depart from our animal brethren is in the great development of the front part of our cerebral cortex, the frontal lobes, and the greater proportion of cerebral tissue, called association areas, which integrate the information obtained from the regions that directly receive sensory information. These latter regions are called the primary sensory and motor areas because they receive simple, pure sensations and direct the movements of the body. It is within the frontal lobes that we humans mull over the past, prepare for the future, and reflect on its implications. Animals do not have this last capability in particular, as far as we can discern. Animals prepare for the future in a limited, instinct-driven way: Think of squirrels gathering and burying nuts for the winter. How much they mull this action over is open to question.

To return to behavioral research and its use of animals, behaviorists changed psychology from a discipline that used almost exclusively "introspective techniques aimed at trying to isolate the elements of consciousness to the broader study of behavior, including verbal behavior," according to the late psychologist, Neal Miller. At the end of the nineteenth century, "the theory of evolution caused a search for behavioral similarities between animals and people and led to many uncontrolled anecdotal reports of highly intelligent actions of animals, such as opening gates, as if they understood the mechanisms of the latches."[24] The reasoning was that if animals evolved with bodies similar to ours that their thinking would be like ours.

A leading scientist of the developing field of psychology, Edward Thorndike,[25] sought a simpler solution and demonstrated that slightly hungry kittens would learn to pull a string that released them from a cage, allowing them to obtain highly desirable food, such as fish. At first the kittens did all sorts of irrelevant things, only occasionally chancing upon the string that released them. After successive trials the rewards occurred more frequently until the kittens only pulled the string. Learning required two things: motivation (hunger) and a reward (food). Thus Thorndike performed the first systematic study of animal learning, concluding that animals learn by trial and error reinforced by either reward or punishment. The process of learning according to him involved the formation of connections within the brain, and humans are the most evolved animal because they form the most connections. Consciousness in animals did not enter into Thorndike's work; he studied behavior, not consciousness.

B. F. Skinner and his students[26] refined Thorndike's methods and provided us with a number of insights, or what might be called "laws" of learning. For example, performance can be gradually improved by rewarding increasingly closer approximations of the desired response, and an appropriate schedule of reinforcement will maintain a high level of performance without requiring reward on every trial. The experiments of Thorndike and Skinner are examples of instrumental conditioning in which some type of overt response is required of the subject: Thorndike's hungry kittens had to learn that pulling a string (the instrumental response) would open their cage.

In addition to Skinner, the Russian physiologist and Nobel Laureate Ivan Pavlov[27] is probably one of the scientists associated with the study of behavior who is best known to the general public. He used another type of experiment with dogs that required no overt response. In this situation, a conditioning stimulus, such as a tone, is linked closely in time with an unconditioned stimulus, such as food. A conditioned response (salivation, in this case) is then measured when only the tone is presented. Pavlov's work taught us basic principles of learning: that immediate reinforcement (such as reward with a bit of food) with the unconditioned stimulus was more effective than delayed reinforcements; that a conditioned response to one stimulus will generalize to another, similar stimuli; and that favorable responses in non-reinforced trials will gradually cease or extinguish. Pavlov's type of conditioning is known as classical conditioning.

Having spent a year in the early 1970s in Warsaw, Poland, working under the direction of Pavlov's most famous student, the late professor Jerzy Konorski, who was the director of the Nencki Institute of Experimental Biology of the Polish Academy of Sciences, I know that dogs suffer not a whit in such experiments. Indeed, in Warsaw they enjoyed loving care from a retired Polish cavalry veterinary assistant who had experienced the fighting in World War II.

Much of the knowledge about how animals and humans learn, derived from the work of Thorndike, Skinner, Pavlov and others, is now commonplace. (Remember the reinforcing property of a dollar for every "A" on the report card?) This branch of psychology came to be known as Behaviorism, and asserted that scientists could only scientifically study what animals did, not what they were thinking. The Behaviorists did not deny that animals had internal mental states, but rather that we did not have the ability to measure them or to use these states as evidence for causality of actions. This school of thought has been ridiculed by at least one philosopher, Bernard Rollin,[28] who did not acknowledge that the laws of behavior discovered by the Behaviorists led to our understanding of how associations between events are organized in the brain and how understanding of these laws has advanced human welfare, as I shall now describe.

Subsequent students of behavior, called physiological psychologists, used the principles developed by earlier Behaviorists like Pavlov and Skinner to advance our understanding of addiction and its treatment. This is but one example of how Behaviorism has benefited modern medicine.[29] True, physiological psychologists have been interested in mechanisms underlying various bodily functions, such as eating and sleep and not the mind, and my recent work seeking to understand PTSD would fall into this category. But scientists are now feeling more secure delving into the properties of the mind, within the field of cognitive neuroscience.[30]

Consider additional contributions of the early behavioral researchers to human welfare that have been maligned by uniformed critics. Using the principles of classical conditioning discovered by Pavlov, O. Hobart Mowrer[31] developed a device very useful in curing chronic enuresis (urinary incontinence, or bedwetting) in children. A bell rings at the first appearance of moisture on a pad, immediately waking the child so that he or she can go to the bathroom. This is deemed the best method, a truly marvelous relief for those suffering from this embarrassing problem.

Neal Miller[32] describes other achievements based on the principles of classical and instrumental conditioning. For example, pigeons, whose vision is much keener than that of humans, have been trained to find colored life rafts floating in the ocean, and do so at a success rate of 85% compared to the 50% success rate achieved by helicopter pilots. A severely malnourished

9-month-old boy with ruminative vomiting (persistent vomiting with chewing of the vomitus) that was life threatening because of the resultant malnourishment showed remarkable improvement after just 13 days of conditioned avoidance training, as Miller demonstrates in a before-and-after picture in his article. By monitoring throat movements, researchers determined the pattern of sucking that preceded vomiting. On the third day of observation they administered a mild electric shock via an electrode attached to the subject's leg. On the sixth day of this treatment regimen, the child stopped the vomiting and rapidly became a happy, playful, normal little boy.

Also recall Edward Taub's achievement in finding a rehabilitative treatment for stroke using instrumental conditioning in his deafferented monkeys, who performed a task with their impaired arms to earn a food reward.[33,34] Finally, behavioral research, using the principles of learning, also directly helped wild animals that would otherwise have been exterminated because of their destructive effects on crops or on domestic animals. Learned taste aversion, which involves inducing nausea by treating the desired object (such as grass for Canada geese), will result in avoidance behavior, obviating the need for killing.[35]

How Animal Use in Research Is Regulated

By now you may be wondering whether anyone is keeping tabs on what scientists are doing in their laboratories. At the outset I want to make it absolutely clear that the following description of how biomedical research is conducted would not have been the same if given prior to 1985. Back then, in most institutions, only the individual scientist made decisions in the laboratory, and his or her personal standards ruled. Governmental guidelines set forth were just that: guidelines. Laboratory animal veterinarians often had no power and could even be barred from the laboratory by a scientist who thought that he or she knew better. Without a doubt there were abuses—and these have been well publicized—from the mishandling of the animals, and because insufficient thought was given to the planning of experiments, and experimenters lacked training in medical and surgical procedures. In my experience, most of the experimenters were no different from the "man on the street" in their concern for animals. As a result of changes made in 1985, the rules of research conducted with animals in the United States caught up to those of the United Kingdom, which has long regulated biomedical research very closely in the care given to animals used in research. Not only have we improved their physical care but we now conduct much more carefully planned experiments. I confess it is shocking to look back on the situation prior to 1985.

For the most part, the resistance to change in the early 1980s, mine included, was not because scientists were not concerned about the welfare of laboratory animals. Rather, we were resistant to the possibility of a burgeoning bureaucracy. To a certain extent that did occur, but overall, the changed environment in which we do our experiments today is for the better. Also, in the heat of the battle against those who were seriously misleading the public about the value and necessity of the use of animals in research, it was sometimes difficult to discern between those who wanted only better treatment of animals and those who wanted to block our work entirely. I freely admit that I made a number of mistakes in this regard. So focused was I on the unconscionable attacks on various researchers and the validity of biomedical research in general that I sometimes turned away the true welfarists. I needed time to resolve the latter problem.

The climate changed when two largely overlapping laws were enacted in 1985 to govern researchers' use of animals. They are administered by two federal agencies, the Department of Agriculture (USDA) and the Public Health Service (PHS), a branch of the Department of Health and Human Services, the major source of research funding for many scientists. Both laws require researchers to prepare a detailed protocol of the research proposed, answering such questions as the purpose of the research, its prospects for advancing knowledge that will benefit humanity (and animals), procedures for alleviating or eliminating pain in laboratory animals, doses of drugs and their anticipated effects, steps taken to minimize the number of animals to be used, and even whether animals are necessary to answer the scientific questions posed. These requirements were inspired by an influential book published by two British scientists, William Russell and Rex Burch.[36] They proposed that in the interests of laboratory animal welfare, scientists should adhere to the rule of the 3 R's: reduction (in numbers used), refinement (of experimental techniques to eliminate or reduce pain), and replacement (with alternative approaches when available).

An institutional animal care and use committee (IACUC), located at the researcher's institution but enabled by the two laws mentioned earlier to render decisions independently, reviews each protocol and approves or rejects it. It has been my experience that the proposal is almost always returned for fine-tuning before final approval, so there is no rubber-stamping. And "independently" means just that: the IACUC answers to no one at the institution, not even the president of the university. These committees are, in fact, acting as agents of the federal government.

The IACUC must include a veterinarian with knowledge of laboratory animal medicine, a researcher, a nonscientist, and someone not associated with the institution. This last person is often from the clergy or a local humane society. Of course, at large institutions the number of members far exceeds that required by law in order to deal with a huge number of protocol proposals. The PHS requires that the IACUC inspect all rooms where animals are used within its institution every 6 months, but the USDA also has its own veterinary inspectors who make unannounced visits.[37]

At my institution (the University of Pennsylvania) the protocol consists of 23 pages, in which researchers must summarize their project in lay terms, describe the procedures to be used and surgical methods in great detail, justify the need for using animals and the numbers required in statistical terms, outline the steps taken to avoid pain or alleviate it, and describe the method of euthanasia. There are also questions concerning where the procedures are performed and where the animals will be housed. Other questions specific to various procedures are answered when relevant. Also, every 3 years researchers must take a 90-minute test on all the regulations and proper procedures for working with animals. Those without formal training in experimental procedures must have hands-on training before they can work with animals in an experimental setting. I cannot think of a better system for ensuring animal welfare in the laboratory.

In addition to other requirements for the conduct of research established by law in 1985, researchers are obliged to prove that they have searched the scientific literature and can state with reasonable certainty that they are not performing needlessly duplicative research and that they cannot do the research without the use of animals. This is a time-consuming requirement instituted in response to claims from the animal rights and liberation movement that much research was unnecessarily repetitive and wasteful of animal lives. What serious scientist would want to conduct research already done by another scientist, except to perform the initial, essential replication of a new finding? What granting agency hampered by limited dollars would want to fund hacks? What experienced researcher is not already cognizant of the important literature in his or her field?

In my own case, how would I study sleep mechanisms if not in sleeping animals? Naïveté is easily determined by grant-reviewing bodies, and dishonest and lazy scientists are quickly weeded out by the system. As for advances in strictly technical skills involving anesthesia, analgesia, and surgical techniques, laboratory animal veterinarians are there to oversee us.

Somewhat surprisingly, the USDA does not concern itself with the use of rats, mice, and birds, even though rats and mice constitute the bulk of the animals used in research today. (That proportion can only be expected to grow as more and more genes are discovered in mice that are homologous with those involved with human disease.) How can this be? The simple answer is money. After the revised Animal Welfare Act came into force in 1985, the secretary of agriculture ruled that the department did not have the financial resources to regulate the use of species of great public concern, such as primates, dogs, and cats, while also bearing the burden of controlling the use of rats and mice. Instead, the Public Health Service regulates the use of these species through its mechanisms, and 90% of the rats and mice used in laboratories are subjects in studies financed by the Public Health Service via grants from the NIH. While it is true that the remaining 10% of rats and mice used in experiments are not regulated by any government agency, should we believe that those 10% are horribly mistreated, just because a USDA inspector does not drop by now and then? I hope not, but we must balance such concerns with the tremendous burden on the USDA were the agency to inspect all of the records involving millions of rodents. USDA resources are stretched thin as it is, so I think the secretary's decision was prudent.

Another mechanism that ensures proper care of laboratory animals, including rats and mice, is the evaluation of an institution's facilities and the welfare of its animals by the Association for Assessment and Accreditation of Laboratory Animal Care International, commonly referred to as AAALAC. The organization's executive director, John Miller, DVM,[38] estimated that 90% or more of all animals used in research, teaching, and testing in the United States reside in facilities accredited by AAALAC. Miller's estimate is derived from the following figures: 99 of the top 100 NIH awardee institutions' programs are accredited by the AAALAC, as are over 80% of the second 100, all members of PhRMA (pharmaceutical manufacturers), all major biotechnical companies, and all major producers of laboratory animals.

Institutions voluntarily seek the AAALAC seal of approval, though it is not easily obtained. The institution must first prepare an extensive and detailed description of all aspects of its animal care and use program. After that is approved by AAALAC, members of the organization's Council on Accreditation (both veterinarians and research scientists) visit the institution to perform a rigorous evaluation of the facilities and all aspects of the animal use oversight program. They report their findings to the full AAALAC Council, which then awards full accreditation or a provisionary status (deferral or probation) while minor deficiencies are corrected. This process is repeated every 3 years, with a different team of expert peer evaluators conducting the on-site evaluation. Any changes to the program and any serious adverse events must be reported to the AAALAC in an annual report. Based on my own participation in a couple of site visits, I can confirm that they are quite rigorous.

My belief is that the ultimate safeguard for animals is not oversight by committee or federal regulation. Instead, the single most crucial element in ensuring the welfare of laboratory animals is the scientist conducting the research. This person alone knows with absolute certainty whether an animal is being properly handled and whether the experiment is worthy of animal use. Only the scientist responsible for the research knows whether every other person working in the laboratory truly has the proper training and is caring for the animals in a humane and safe manner. A laboratory veterinarian of my acquaintance, Ronald Banks, has proposed that such thinking falls into the category of a fourth "R" that he would add to the 3 R's of Russell and Burch: responsibility.

The changes in regulations have brought relative evenness to the quality of animal care in laboratories and oversight of experiments over the past few years. Like all human endeavors, biomedical research will never be perfect; honest mistakes will be made. And, unfortunately, there will always be those who will try to cut corners or circumvent the law. But universities are firmly committed to conducting high-quality research in a responsible manner so that such behavior never goes on for very long. Furthermore, institutions stand to lose too much money in federal funding and private donations to brook any nonsense carried out by individual scientists. I now feel sanguine that, in general, we are doing a very good job at ensuring the humane treatment of laboratory animals—as well as we fallible humans can.

It is important not to take these last remarks to mean that cruelty and disregard for animal welfare was rampant in laboratories in decades past, brought under control only after the establishment of legally binding regulations. Although there were certainly abuses, scientists are generally ordinary and caring people who share with nonscientists a concern about the welfare of animals. The vast majority of them consider it their responsibility to provide good care to their animals and to cooperate with governmental regulation, and this attitude has not changed since the new laws were instituted. This personal concern is perhaps the most important factor in ensuring proper care and use of animals in biomedical research. Without it, governmental regulation of animal research could not be as protective of the animals as it is.

When asked and required to do better, we as a scientific community complied readily. A revolution was not required; the new system of controls was instituted rather smoothly. When speaking about the excesses of the animal rights and liberation movement, I am often challenged by the question, "Isn't it true that the animal-rights and liberation movement has revealed some serious problems in laboratories and caused improvements to be made?" My reply is in the affirmative. I have seen careless scientists make mistakes, and seen those with insufficient knowledge of veterinary care make poor choices, but never have I encountered a scientist who took delight in harming animals.

Why Scientists Conduct Research on Animals

I have asked myself how I could have done injurious experiments over the years, and my answer is that I am interested in science and in acquiring useful knowledge. Knowing that the experiments I have conducted have helped in the understanding of REM sleep behavior disorder has certainly eased my mind. Without realizing it through those years, I was close to being engaged in "translational research," the new emphasis on projects that will bring research results more quickly to the bedside. Researchers seeking federal funding have always been required to write about how the receipt of an NIH grant would benefit humanity, so that all the basic research supported by that body will eventually be translated into something "useful." For instance, I hope that the work my colleagues and I are now doing will provide some answers for treating PTSD.

Ultimately, though, it is the curiosity of our species that drives me to continue with my work, despite its heavy toll on the research animals I use. Consider these words of H. L. Mencken, with which I readily identify. The basic scientist is most assuredly his model:

> The value the world sets upon motives is often grossly unjust
> and inaccurate. Consider, for example, two of them: mere
> insatiable curiosity and the desire to do good. The latter is
> put high above the former, and yet it is the former that
> moves one of the most useful men the human race has yet
> produced: the scientific investigator. What actually urges
> him on is not some brummagem idea of Service, but a
> boundless, almost pathological thirst to penetrate the
> unknown, to uncover the secret, to find out what has not
> been found out before. His prototype is not the liberator
> releasing slaves, the Good Samaritan lifting up the fallen, but
> a dog sniffing tremendously at an infinite series of rat-holes.[39]

Mencken recognized that we are a very curious species, and that the scientist is perhaps the most curious of all. With our exceptional human brains we have made wonderful use of that curiosity to benefit both humans and animals; no other species has this capability. To me, ceasing to explore nature in every way possible would be an arrogant rejection of evolutionary forces and a denial of our unique abilities as humans. Further, abandoning those who still look to biomedical research to relieve their suffering would be irresponsible. Consider those who have or will suffer paralyzing damage to the spinal cord.

Each year, approximately 10,000 Americans will be condemned to spending their lives in wheelchairs or worse as a consequence of spinal cord injury.[40] Only continuing biomedical research will tell us why the central nervous system does not regenerate, allowing us to solve this problem.

Animal Happiness and Well-Being

Changing attitudes toward animals promise to bring more problems to biomedical researchers, according to lawyer and bioethicist Jerry Tannenbaum. Tannenbaum, the author of *Veterinary Medical Ethics*[41] and an acknowledged sensible thinker, warns that the traditional view of handling animals correctly, "animal welfare," is giving way to a new view of our duties to research animals, ensuring their "happiness," and to a new term, "animal wellbeing." The result is what he calls a "paradigm shift." In addition to ensuring that the animals in our charge are free from pain, hunger, thirst and filth, all of which a responsible scientist takes for granted, we are enjoined to ensure their "happiness." The problem is that this new view of what is necessary in the laboratory "is neither motivated by nor susceptible to factual verification. With very little empirical evidence about what kinds of pleasures animals of various species are capable of experiencing, it is assumed that the vast majority of animals used in research are capable of varied and exquisite pleasure."[42]

Despite the challenges inherent in ensuring the happiness of research animals, scientists have done their best to meet these new requirements. Improvements in the welfare of laboratory animals that came in 1985 with the Animal Welfare Act, administered by the USDA, required provision of exercise for dogs and the psychological well-being of nonhuman primates.[43] I remember the consternation in the research community as scientists and facility managers began to consider the costs involved and, on the science side, just what "psychological well-being of nonhuman primates" meant. I recall more than one person remarking, "We don't even know how to provide for the psychological wellbeing of our own species."

Despite this uncertainty, however, scientists got to work trying to figure out how to improve the care of their animals. One lesson learned has to do with the housing of monkeys: formerly individually housed monkeys are no longer abruptly grouped together for socializing without attention paid to who might beat up on whom, to put it simply. A lot of careful observation following various trials at enriching the lives of primates has been required to meet the mandate.[44]

Much work has also gone into the development of enrichment strategies for other species; whole books are devoted to this important issue. These studies have been conducted to determine what is actually good for animals, based on knowledge acquired about their biological and behavioral needs,in contrast to what scientists and veterinarians might think is good. A balance must be maintained between the needs of an experiment and the welfare of the animal. Without doubt, the one may interfere with the other, but this is not always the case. One instance in which synergy is found is when monkeys are asked to solve problems while researchers record the activity of particular neurons associated with the problem. Some monkeys will actually jump into the testing chair for the excitement of doing something different and new.[45]

Animal Needs and Human Needs

Tannenbaum sees this shift toward consideration of animal happiness as a dangerous one. He argues that "animal research will become more expensive, and more troublesome and difficult for IACUCs to approve. These factors will lead to reduced amounts of research. Eventually, if research animals come to be viewed as our friends—and as worthy of happiness and happy lives as we are—animal research will stop. This is precisely what animal activists who promote the emerging approach want."[46]

Tannenbaum's statement is a bold one, and one I believe he made to warn us of the danger of forgetting why we are doing biomedical research. Knowing him as I do, he is concerned about animal welfare, but worries how new information on animal preferences obtained scientifically, as shown possible by, among others, the British ethologist Marion Stamp Dawkins,[47] will be used by animal rightists. (I will offer further discussion of her achievements in Chapter 8.) How will IACUC and USDA inspectors balance animal preferences with the aims of a research project? USDA inspectors need have no training in research and can be exacting in their assessments of facilities, which adds to the threat of a creeping bureaucracy that may have nothing to contribute to animal welfare. Finally, and most importantly, there is the concern that many people who are not actually engaged in research may fail to realize that research depends on creativity as much as art does, and that creativity does not flourish in a climate of fear or one of pedantic overregulation. Both can impact medical progress in an unhealthy way.[48]

Education

Not all of my time is spent in the research laboratory; I am also a teacher, primarily of first-year veterinary students. Although I am a neuroscientist and have spent a lot of my professional life studying sleep mechanisms, most of my teaching time has been spent in the gross anatomy laboratory instructing students engaged in the dissection of various species in preparation for their careers as veterinarians. Many years ago, I also taught in the human dissection laboratory. I have loved anatomy since my comparative anatomy course in college, and more than 50 years later have not yet tired of seeing the beauty of the body as it is gradually revealed during the course of the dissection.

Regrettably, this anatomy training is becoming more difficult to deliver thanks to animal-rightist efforts to establish ordinances that constrict the supply of animals from pounds. These activists appear to prefer that animals be euthanized in the pound rather than serve a lasting purpose, which of course results in the deaths of even more animals. My view is that animals can serve as food for the mind as well as for the body as long as they are treated with care and respect, whether they are alive or dead. The National Association of Biology Teachers (NABT) agrees with me. Their guidelines state:

> "NABT encourages teachers to be approachable and
> responsive to substantive student objections to dissection
> and to provide appropriate lessons for those students. At the
> same time, NABT urges teachers to be aware that
> alternatives to dissection have their limitations. NABT
> supports the use of these materials as adjuncts to the
> educational process but not as exclusive replacements for
> the use of actual organisms."[49]

One popular view is that dissection is appropriate and acceptable for those in preparation for a medical profession, but for pre-college students it is improper since they do not require that training for their careers.[50] This notion has been advocated strenuously by organizations that propose to lead children away from such educational classroom activities.[51] I could not disagree more. Certainly, one must make allowances for squeamishness or well-considered ethical objections, but to argue that dissection is irrelevant in today's society is shortsighted and dead wrong in my opinion. One of my biology teacher friends told me that in her experience, many of the initially reluctant middle-school children in her classes were eventually drawn to the excitement of the exercise. Further, since when are children of this age expected to have already chosen a career path? It is entirely reasonable to surmise that participation in an effective and educational anatomy lesson incorporating dissection will encourage fledgling veterinarians or physicians to pursue these studies. Of course, it may do just the reverse with other students.

Nevertheless, our bodies are surprisingly similar to those of many of the animals that students might dissect, as I will describe in Chapter 7. And all people are better served by knowing as much about their bodies as possible. This enables us to follow a doctor's instructions and to keep tabs on the condition of various parts of our anatomy independently of medical advice.

Some argue that dissecting animal bodies is old-fashioned and must give way in the curriculum to advanced areas like molecular biology.[52] I agree that biology courses should introduce high school students to all areas of the science, including molecular biology. But to assume that dissecting an animal is less of an intellectual exercise than studying genetics, for example, would confuse the minute with the profound. Comparing the structure of different classes of animals leads one to understand better the great organizing theory of biology: evolution. Some claim that the labeling of parts—as if that were the sum total of a well-taught course—can be done just as well using charts and models or, better yet, computers. These arguments reveal a lack of appreciation of what the study of organismic biology can accomplish and how dissection contributes to that aim.[53]

Intelligently planned and performed dissections of fetal pigs or animal parts from a butcher, for example, allow students to involve themselves directly in exploring nature. In contrast, punching keys to "dissect" via computer is too far removed from reality to permit a real appreciation for animals as constructed; this would represent the antithesis of active learning. "Real material is truly interactive; 'interaction' with a computer keyboard is a trivial use of the term, and completely unrelated to the genuine interaction of touching an earthworm crop and gizzard, petting a gerbil, or holding a harmless snake," writes Richard Schrock, a professor of science teaching and editor of *The Kansas Biology Teacher*.[54] By comparing dissections in the classroom, students will observe that all of the specimens may not follow the textbook's description, thus demonstrating the principle of biological variation. This can lead to discussions of why some individuals contract a certain disease and why some do not, or why medicines work for some and not for others. Unfortunately, the influence of the animal rights and liberation movement on children has been powerful, so that there has been controversy as well as legal action over requiring children to participate in dissections, permitting them to learn through alternative means.[55] My own view continues to be that there is nothing like the real thing, and Schrock makes this point quite forcefully:

> Real labwork has real consequences. When students have
> successfully mastered a procedure or technique, they know
> they can really do it in the real world. When they click

through a simulation, they have merely completed an
artificial game. Real labwork increases involvement. In an
age of contrived media, students recognize the potential for
distortion. They want to test their own blood types, not
conduct an educational exercise. When given a choice
between observing a preserved human fetus from a medical
school or an identical plastic model, they focus solely on the
fetus—what they were like at one time and what at one time
had the potential to become one of them. *Science is universal
because it is based in real labwork* [my emphasis].[56]

Of course, observing live animals and learning their habits or particular
needs is important too. Keeping a guinea pig in the classroom introduces children to the idea of responsibility for beings under our control, as do field trips
to farms and zoos. Science fair projects that are not in any way detrimental to
the welfare of the animals can teach something of the process of science.

This year I advised a precocious sixth-grader on his science fair project.
He disliked the idea of declawing cats (as do I, except in special circumstances)
and wanted to prove that a normal cat could manage various obstacles better
than one without its claws. He had to understand that scoring the abilities of
various cats alone would introduce the bane of all researchers: experimenter
bias. So he was able to learn the importance of having a rater blind to the conditions, even though he had to do the experiment on his own. This one boy,
at least, will come to appreciate why the principle of objectivity is so important
in science—particularly medical science, such as when new pharmaceutical
drugs are tested for safety and efficacy prior to public use. But perhaps more
importantly, this young man has been given the opportunity to appreciate the
process of science, and the excitement that can come from asking a question
and answering it in a laboratory. It was my pleasure to learn that he won first
prize for his project as well as the prize for animal welfare offered by the
Women's Humane Society. I have confidence that he will grow up to be the sort
of inquisitive and informed citizen that our society so desperately needs.

Controversy over the use of animals in education extends even into professional schools where knowing the intricacies of bodies is more immediately
important: veterinary and medical schools. Many medical schools have phased
out the use of live animals for teaching physiological principles and surgical
manipulations, for several reasons: they are expensive; students object; and
certain animal rights organizations, such as the Physician's Committee for
Responsible Medicine (PCRM), which is associated with PeTa and has a very
low percentage of members who are actually physicians,[57,58] are a continual

annoyance, lobbying for elimination of animal use.[59] Other schools, such as Johns Hopkins University, the University of Wisconsin, and the Uniformed Services Medical School in Bethesda, maintain that live animals contribute significantly to learning.[60]

Although a host of studies listed on the Web site of HSUS show that test scores are equivalent or even better at various educational levels for those who have used cadavers or computer simulations instead of live animals, nothing quite matches dealing with unanticipated spurting blood in teaching surgical skills. It is a matter of choice, it would seem. My view is that if a live pig is to be used and its treatment is humane while alive, then eating it after slaughter and euthanizing it after the class amount to the same thing: food for the body or food for the mind.

Using animals to learn in veterinary schools presents a problem for our students. Their aim in coming to veterinary school is to heal animals. They face the problem of designating what an animal is to be: something to cure or something to learn from. It is the same problem I faced with cats through much of my career: pet one at home and perform experimental surgery on another in my laboratory. I am glad I no longer need to make the choice.

The choice is made easier for our students as they learn surgical principles in the required portion of our curriculum. First, they practice techniques on artificial devices, and then they have the experience of anesthetizing a dog from a local animal control organization, spaying it, and then caring for it. Then they hold what amounts to a fair to advertise their animal for adoption. Some of the dogs are returned to the shelter from which they came, with the promise that they will be adopted out and not euthanized. Likewise, ponies used in the large-animal surgery elective are found homes. This procedure is a vast improvement over what I had to do during my training. We performed a couple of major operations, a splenectomy on a dog and then another invasive procedure from which it recovered each time, and then euthanized it, a heartless procedure, even though we gave the animal postoperative care.

A Personal Philosophy

Whether the reader agrees with the foregoing discussions or not, I hope that I have at least demonstrated that I have thought much about my particular way of harming animals, even though I firmly believe it to be important and justifiable when thinking of my fellow human beings, whose suffering I most empathize with.[61] I must confess here that whenever I see a disabled, disfigured, or mentally impaired child, I feel great anger toward those who would block biomedical research.

But the invasiveness of vivisection is not something I prefer or participate in without reflection. Because I did experimental surgery on cats, I went through a soul-searching every few months, asking myself whether I really wanted to continue working on cats (we've had up to four of them at a time as pets over the years) or other animals for that matter. The answer was always "yes," because from my knowledge of medical history I knew that medicine cannot progress without animal experimentation and that such basic research leads ultimately to unforeseen benefits. I held that conversation with myself through the years while walking to the university from my commuter rail station. I no longer work on cats and am glad, although rats are cute little fellows, too. I mentioned these thoughts to my dear friend and professor, Jim Sprague (a member of the National Academy of Sciences for his basic work on vision in cats), during one of our frequent lunchtime conversations shortly before his death at 88. He told me that the day he retired from the lab when he was 70 he said to himself, *"Now I won't ever have to kill a cat again."*

Fudging the Data | 5

nly if we agreed that any experiment done on animals could also be performed using people could we then dispense with using laboratory animals. Certainly this would nullify the charge against biomedical researchers that results obtained using rats, mice, and other animals are invalid because rats, mice, and other animals are not human. Also, various spokespersons for the animal-extremist movement have used the logically unanswerable claim that biomedical researchers can not know whether they might have done without animals to advance medicine because they have not tried. In a debate in *Scientific American*, Jack Botting, a medical historian who wrote extensively on the achievements of medical scientists for the Research Defence Society, and I challenged two of these individuals, physicians Neal Barnard and Stephen Kaufman, to design an ethical experiment that would provide significant new data about mechanisms underlying a disease process in humans without using animals at some stage, and to be the first "mouse" to test a new drug for safety.[1] As far as I know, they have yet to accept the challenge.

Arguments against the necessity and even the usefulness of animal-based research abound in the animal rights literature. Epidemiology, tissue cultures, autopsies, and computers are offered as potential substitutes. All of these are useful and widely used tools, and any number of scientists that use animals will also employ one or more of these techniques in their work. But to claim that such alternatives could replace all studies on living organisms is naive. Moreover, if animals are not genetically close enough to humans to yield valid and useful results, how could a thin layer of cells in a Petri dish suffice? These suggestions are irresponsible, for they can lead unwary people with a natural and compassionate concern for animals to contribute time and money to a cause actually working against their best interests by attempting to put a stop to humane, life-saving biomedical research.

The nonscientist political leaders and philosophers of the movement may make uninformed claims against the value of animals to the advancement of medical science, but they are not the most culpable of wrongdoing. Rather, medical professionals who speak for the movement bear most of the responsibility for misleading people about the value of animals in research. Although extremists have attacked biomedical research through harassment, intimidation, and serious property destruction, medically trained individuals have engaged in another form of aggression against biomedical research using animals: misrepresentations of medical history. These physicians and veterinarians may be likened to the laboratory worker who changes numbers in the laboratory's notebook to make the results of an experiment look better than they actually are—"fudging" the data, in other words.[2]

The Nature of Honest Scientific Disagreement

Scientists frequently disagree on a variety of topics—hypotheses, acceptable experimental techniques, each other's data, even interpretations of the same data. This ongoing debate is healthy because it forces scientists to probe further into a phenomenon or refine their approach to a problem. My favorite story of how scientists can disagree in a fundamental, but honest, way comes from my own field of neuroscience and involves the basic unit of the nervous system, the neuron, or nerve cell, and the greatest scientific award of all for biomedical researchers, the Nobel Prize in Medicine or Physiology. This story also emphasizes how difficult it is to arrive clearly and cleanly at a fundamental understanding of anything in biology.

Camillo Golgi and Ramon Santiago y Cajal shared the Nobel Prize in Physiology or Medicine in 1906 for their studies of the microscopic structure of the nervous system. Golgi, an Italian professor, had developed a method of staining individual nerve cells with silver in a way that revealed the full extent of their very long processes, and used it to describe various types of cells. Cajal, who began his scientific career as a Spanish provincial physician, used Golgi's method to describe in extraordinary detail the microscopic characteristics of the entire brain. But each held to diametrically opposed views of how the myriad cells connected with one another—as a grand net, or reticulum, in which each neuron blended into another, or as separate entities that only contacted other neurons.

Cajal interpreted what he saw using Golgi's technique as demonstrating that separate neurons transmitted information from one to another in one direction at a region called a synapse. To his eyes, the synapse contained a space that completely separated the two neurons. But Golgi viewed the nervous system as a continuous net, as did many other "reticularists" of that era, and he held that view until the end of his life. Only the high level of resolution provided by the electron microscope in the 1950s finally laid the reticular theory to rest. Thus, these two men shared science's top prize while disagreeing at the most fundamental level.[3]

More recently, two physiologists also won the Nobel Prize in Medicine or Physiology, but at different times, having debated for many years the nature of the communication between two nerve cells. Sir Henry Dale, who received his Nobel Prize in 1936, held that that one neuron, called the presynaptic element, induced a change in the activity of a second neuron, the postsynaptic element, through the secretion of a chemical. By contrast, Sir John Eccles, the winner in 1963, saw the communication as purely electrical and vigorously challenged the chemical neurotransmission theory. Ultimately, *The War of the Soups and the Sparks* (a book recounting their debates over many years) ended in victory for the "soups," those who believed that transmission occurred via release of a chemical (a neurotransmitter).[4]

A further example illustrates how difficult it is to gain acceptance of a novel idea, as Stan Dudrick found in trying to introduce hyperalimentation, and demonstrates that scientists can disagree in fundamental ways without fudging the data. Arvid Carlsson, a Nobel Laureate himself in 2000, notes in his review of the soups-and-sparks war that he too had to struggle to gain acceptance of his discoveries of certain transmitters in the brain. Ironically, among the doubters was Dale, who had had to fight hard to gain acceptance of his own views regarding chemical transmission in the peripheral nervous system.[5]

Disagreements such as these follow an informal set of rules in which it is assumed that the contestants, such as Cajal and Golgi or Dale and Eccles, are honestly engaged even though biases may cloud their minds. Admittedly, now and then a renegade scientist fabricates data, but this is rare. His or her purpose is usually personal aggrandizement, plain and simple. Fortunately, the ways of science will ultimately expose dishonest scientists. No scientific claim can obtain general acceptance until independent laboratories replicate the findings. Rather than repeating experiments uselessly, a charge often made by those opposed to animal-based research, scientists must independently verify that a new finding is truly valid.

Misrepresentations by Medical Professionals

Here we must consider the animal-rightist claims of those who really should know better, the medically trained. Medical or scientific training, or training as a scholar in a nonscientific field, confers a high level of authority to statements made on intellectual matters. With that authority comes a responsibility to speak and act with integrity. Several medical professionals with ties to the animal rights and liberation movement seem to be either ignorant of the process of science or, for various reasons, unwilling to oppose the views of extremists that animals are not necessary for biomedical research. A third possibility is that the medical professionals whose work is discussed below truly believe that animal research has not contributed to medical progress. Naturally, I am at a loss to explain such views.

How did their training allow these individuals to escape any understanding of the process of science? To be generous, one reason might be the didactic nature of medical education. Little time is available for a professor to lecture on the history of the development of current treatments, so a physician might be able to finish his or her training with little appreciation for the intricacies of scientific discovery. (We have the same problem in veterinary medical education.) Furthermore, a literature search using the online database known as Medline (which catalogs scientific and biomedical bibliographic information for over 7,000 publications and includes about 11 million records) revealed no evidence that the individuals whose work is discussed in this chapter were experienced in truly basic animal-based research designed to uncover principles that might be applied to human medical problems. It is not unreasonable to conclude that these critics of animal experimentation are not equipped to appreciate the uncertainties, difficulties, and rewards of such research.

But ignorance of the challenges of basic biomedical research does not excuse certain methods employed by these medical professionals. They pervert the scientific discourse in which most biomedical scientists, veterinarians, physicians, and other health professionals engage. Some of their writings cite legitimate scientists out of context, and construct statements out of larger passages that distort the author's original meaning. These individuals even cite works that actually are contrary to their arguments. I can only assume that they hope to add credibility to their cause by quoting respectable researchers without regard to the real meaning of those researchers' words.

Ray and Jean Greek

Ray Greek, a physician (an anesthesiologist), and Jean, a veterinarian (a derma-tologist), begin their book, *Sacred Cows and Golden Geese*, with a remarkable anecdote. While they were students of medicine and veterinary medicine, their respective coursework led them to believe that their patients, human and animal, were too different in their diseases and reactions to medicines to warrant the use of animals to advance human medicine.[6]

Certainly, my experience has been quite different, for the activities and rela-tionships at the veterinary school where I have spent my professional career at the University of Pennsylvania with other professions are based on the concept of comparative medicine—One Medicine; Many Species—as we tout in our brochures. Our view is that we can learn about disease and its cures in all species by working together. In fact, it was a famous Philadelphia physician and signer of the Declaration of Independence, Benjamin Rush, who urged the establish-ment of a school of veterinary medicine at the University of Pennsylvania.[7] Several of my contemporaries in our clinics did quite a bit of their residency training at the Hospital of the University of Pennsylvania because they were studying in the early days of developing specialties in veterinary medical prac-tice, around 1960. Our Section of Comparative Medical Genetics studies a number of genetic diseases in animals that model the human conditions quite nicely.[8] Further, Dr. Charles Cornelius,[9] the former dean of the College of Veterinary Medicine in Davis, California, has listed about 350 diseases that humans and animals share wholly or in considerable part, rabies being a perfect example. And the list continues to grow.

The Greeks emphasize in their book that they are not interested in animal rights but only in demonstrating that using animals in research endangers human health. In their words, "the animal model harms people." Nevertheless, they acknowledge help from a variety of organizations associated with the animal rights and liberation movement, such as the American-Antivivisection Society, the Medical Research Modernization Committee, and the Physicians Committee for Responsible Medicine. But as Michael Festing has stated, "The Siren song of Ray and Jean Greek is highly seductive to those who campaign against the use of animals in research. If all models are scientifically invalid, their use could be banned immediately. Unfortunately, the Greeks are wrong."[10]

The Greeks present the same distortions of medical history as those pre-sented by other individuals discussed in this chapter. Their effort consists of an entire book that ranges over many areas of medicine. *Sacred Cows and Golden Geese* is full of myths, twisting of meanings, and illogic, as exemplified in the book's introduction. Although the book's argument is that animals differ too much from humans to be useful in research, the Greeks cite the problem of mad cow disease as a warning against using animal parts in restorative surgery. Eating the meat of such cows can result in the passing of altered prions (proteins that can "infect" cells and damage them) to humans, which leads to brain degeneration. How can this be possible, we must ask, if animals are so different from humans?

As for myths, especially those handed from one animal rights publication to another, the Greeks claim that penicillin kills guinea pigs. They proceed to ignore or downgrade the literature establishing the fact that penicillin is very effective in other laboratory species, that early adverse effects on guinea pigs were due to impurities in the penicillin administered, and that in later experiments some guinea pigs died after administration of a certain strain of penicillin containing a dangerous bacterium. The bacteria interacted fatally with the microscopic organisms naturally found in the herbivorous guinea pig's ample gut, thereby upsetting their digestive tracts.[11] Other examples of distortion and selective quoting abound in the book.

In the chapter on cancer research the Greeks include a quote from Nobel Laureate Renato Dulbecco: "If we wish to understand human cancer, the [research] effort should be made in humans because genetic control seems to be different in different species."[12] This statement followed a familiar premise by the Greeks: "Each creature has different physiologic and pharmacological responses."[13] In an earlier part of the article containing Dulbecco's statement, however, Dulbecco described the developments from studying cancers by different methods in various species that led him to the following conclusion:

> We are at a turning point (in 1986) in the study of tumor virology and cancer in general. If we wish to learn more about cancer, we must now concentrate on the cellular genome. We are back to where cancer research started, but the situation is drastically different because we have new knowledge and crucial tools, such as DNA cloning.

He went on to suggest a strategy that included sequencing the human genome and performing "cancer research with cells in culture or in *immunodeficient mice* [my emphasis]."[14] In other words, as any scientist would tell the Greeks, we will use the most appropriate method(s) at this stage of our knowledge to solve this particular problem.

In another chapter, "The Pathetic Illusion of Designer Drugs," the Greeks argue that inconsistencies in experiments with various species delayed introduction of cyclosporin and FK506 (tacromilus) as immunosuppressive antirejection agents. These are life-saving medications used in transplant patients and others with autoimmune disease. The same mystifying claim appeared in a letter they wrote to the editor of the *Journal of the American Medical Association*.[15] My friend Charles Nicoll of the University of California at Berkeley doubted the Greeks' claim and wrote to Sir Roy Calne in England, the author of one of the studies discussed by them. Sir Roy responded with an unpublished letter to the editor, which he has given me permission to quote here:

> I wish to point out that Dr. Ray Greek's letter in the Feb 9th issue of *JAMA*, re the Medical News and Perspectives article, takes out of context quotes from the literature, and this results in the distorted view of the relationship of animal experiments to progress in medicine. As any reasonably educated person knows, virtually every effective medicament and surgical procedure available in modern medicine only reaches the clinic because of preliminary investigations in animals. In particular, if cyclosporin had first been used in man it would never have been licensed because of its nephrotoxicity in man, whereas it wasn't nephrotoxic in animals and we would have lost the chance to use this extremely valuable drug. As far as FK506 and our own work is concerned, the fact that this agent was toxic in some of our animal experiments but not in others was an important observation that led to a cautious approach to dosage in the clinic and again the availability of an extremely valuable immunosuppressive agent.

Based on the number of references listed at the back of *Sacred Cows and Golden Geese* (949—some of them titles from the animal rights literature), the book seems scholarly on the surface. But legitimate works were disingenuously cited in the book to bolster an argument even if the author of that work would not support the Greeks' overall point of view. For example, they refer to an article by the late Paul Beeson, a distinguished professor of medicine at several universities including Yale and Oxford, to support the notion that animals played no role in the development of drugs for high blood pressure. Beeson made no such claim, but rather found it "interesting to note that three of the four major classes of hypertensive drugs now in use were not known to affect blood pressure until they were given to patients for other indications."[16] In other words, medical science forges ahead on many fronts, benefitting from the observations of alert physicians treating their patients in addition to the experimental work stemming from laboratory research. The occurrence of one medical advance made without the direct contribution of animal research does not negate the value of all research conducted with animals. (Actually, Beeson criticized Brandon Reines, a veterinarian whose work is discussed below, for "citing a statement of mine that seems to align me with the antivivisection movement."[17])

Furthermore, Beeson's 1980 paper was actually arguing the importance of creating an environment that would attract additional young clinician–scientists, obviously needed for their special insights. (I say essentially the same thing to my students: "Keep your eyes open and your mind clear because you may discover something important that was under everyone's nose.") As such, Beeson's comments were taken out of context to support the entirely unrelated argument made by the Greeks that animals stand in the way of medical progress. Furthermore, in his article in which he presented some of the challenges inherent in clinical research, Beeson noted the difficulty of knowing how a particular disease might begin, because patients come to a doctor only after a disease has progressed, adding that "only when it is possible to devise an animal model of the disorder under study is the clinical scientist able to investigate the early phases of a process."[18]

Another reference misused by the Greeks to support the case against a role for animal research in the development of antihypertensive drugs is Julius Comroe's *Exploring the Heart*,[19] a delightful but scholarly history of the experimentation that led to achievements in cardiovascular medicine and surgery. The Greeks quote a statement made by a scientist in Comroe's book: "We did not assess the activity of chlorothiazide in hypertensive animals prior to clinical trial."[20] Comroe reveals, however, that the scientist, Karl Beyer, had a long history of research in renal physiology in animals, first working to find a way to retain penicillin in the body, which later led him and others to the development of diuretics. He was convinced that "the substance worth developing was one that would eliminate sodium, chloride, and of course water, but not bicarbonate." His chemist colleagues created a number of substances similar to sulfanilamide, each of which had to be tested in animals for their diuretic effect. One of the most promising substances was altered chemically and "chlorothiazide (Diuril) was born."[21]

Beyer's conviction that a diuretic would be beneficial in the treatment of hypertension was clearly backed up by years of work in renal physiology in animals, so the Greeks' quotation is misleading. Beyer moved directly to patients (which would be impossible today) because of his long experience and strong hunch—not because the use of animals was unnecessary for the development of Diuril.

Another statement lifted out of context is the following: "The experiments are suggestive but not very conclusive. But if you are convinced the operation will work, I am convinced I know how to do it."[22] This was surgeon Alfred Blalock's response to Dr. Helen Taussig's request that he operate on one of her desperately ill "blue babies." The Greeks quoted Blalock's isolated statement and interpreted it as proving that "Blalock's animal experimentation was a flop."[23]

Taussig's little patients were blue because they were cyanotic, the scientific term for a bluish cast to the skin. This appearance results from low oxygen levels in the circulating blood. Oxygen in the blood corpuscles reddens the skin. The abnormal condition results from various developmental anomalies of the heart and the large vessels coming from it, such as narrowed pulmonary arteries that reduce the flow of arterial blood to the lungs where oxygen is transferred to it. Among the "inconclusive experiments" of Blalock and his super technician, Vivian Thomas, were those in which they had been trying to create cyanotic dogs for further studies on the benefits of a shunt they had devised. The shunt would bring additional blood to the lungs from an artery normally going only to the arm, the subclavian artery.

But Dr. Taussig had a little patient who could not wait for additional animal experiments to prove the efficacy of the shunt. So Blalock proceeded, actually guided by Thomas, who had done most of their experiments in dogs in an attempt to develop methods for anastomosing (suturing together) arteries.[24] They were not yet certain, without further testing on dogs, of the physiological effects the shunt from the subclavian to the pulmonary artery would have when a surge of blood entered a cyanotic human infant's lungs. This is why Blalock thought his experiments were not yet conclusive. The effect was wonderful for the child: "Her condition was considerably better than it had been before the operation."[25] Again, the Greeks' attempt to force the conclusion that animals cannot contribute to new advances in human medicine does not reconcile with the facts. Would any surgeon attempt such a drastic operation without considerable practice in suturing arteries together in animals, a new technique at the time? Blalock's team had already mastered this, thanks to their practice on dogs.

The tactic employed by the Greeks, as well as by the other writers discussed below, appears to be to search for statements in various research reports that, when isolated and quoted out of context, cast a dim light on the relevance of animal use to advancing human medicine. Some quoted scientists who can be contacted and are willing to respond to the misuse of their words, such as Sir Roy Calne, inevitably set the record straight. The Greeks have created the illusion of scholarship by scattering little lectures on basic topics in biology throughout their book. Of course, the knowledge offered in these sections depends on information gleaned from animal experiments. It is often true that final adjustments must be made in technique, apparatus, and dosage when the results of research are finally applied to humans, but this fact cannot be used to negate the value of the preceding work done with animals.

Neal Barnard, Stephen Kaufman, and Scientific American

In 1997, Jack Botting and I[26] engaged two physicians, Neal Barnard and Stephen Kaufman,[27] in an ill-conceived "debate" arranged for the pages of *Scientific American*. Kaufman is associated with the Medical Research Modernization Committee, which is devoted to pointing out deficiencies in various experiments employing animals. Barnard has long been associated with PeTA as the president of the Physicians Committee for Responsible Medicine (PCRM), which, as stated earlier, has a tiny percentage of members who are actually physicians. PCRM has received funding from PeTA, and in 1990 the AMA House of Delegates condemned Barnard for his misleading statements about biomedical research.[28]

In preparation for the *Scientific American* debate, each "team" drafted a presentation arguing its point of view, which was sent to the opposing team. But the material by Barnard and Kaufman was full of misrepresentations, and there was no way for the readers of *Scientific American* to know this. Botting and I pointed out Barnard and Kaufman's distortions to the editor of the magazine after receiving a draft of their presentation and analyzing their arguments, urging the editor to reconsider the wisdom of conducting such a debate. The editor's response was that the use of animals in research is an important societal issue and the debate should go on as planned. This was true, but two issues were involved, one ethical, and one scientific. How were lay readers to know that an ethical belief—and not scientific fact—may have been driving one set of authors to grossly misrepresent medical history? Even the average medical scientist could have been fooled by Barnard and Kaufman's misstatements, since not all scientists are familiar with the historical details of medical discoveries.

Our other concern was that *Scientific American* would provide the animal rights and liberation movement with a "legitimate" reference for all time.[29] With no chance for a rebuttal in the magazine, Botting and I presented our counterarguments to Barnard and Kaufman's claims in other venues.[30,31] If we had used our analysis of the rough draft we had been given by the magazine for our own side of the debate, we would have used up our allotted words without giving readers an accurate history.

For one of their falsifications, Barnard and Kaufman used an essay by Mayo Clinic neurologist David Wiebers and associates, published in the journal *Stroke*, to support their claim that studying humans exclusively was the course to follow in learning about the causes and course of stroke. While it was true that Wiebers and his coauthors had cautioned that "an *over-reliance* [my emphasis] upon such (animal) models may impede rather than advance scientific progress in the treatment of the disease," they also concluded with the following:

> Although the use of animals will continue to contribute substantially to research in stroke for the foreseeable future, the greatest potential lies in the study of molecular mechanisms in the pathophysiology of ischemia and the variables that affect extension and reversibility of the territory of ischemic injury. *There is also no current alternative to animal studies of safety and effect in the screening of agents that may benefit patients with stroke* [my emphasis]. Ultimately, however, the answers to many of our questions regarding the underlying pathophysiology and treatment of stroke do not lie with continued attempts to model the human situation perfectly in animals, but rather with the development of techniques to enable the study of more basic metabolism, pathophysiology, and anatomical imaging detail in living humans.[32]

One can wholeheartedly agree with this hope for the future. Clearly, though, the Wiebers group understood that animal models, though not perfect replicas of human systems, are necessary.

Among other claims, Barnard and Kaufman argued in their article in *Scientific American* that animal testing would not have prevented the horrendous birth defects caused by thalidomide, writing that "most animal species used in laboratories do not develop the kind of limb defects seen after thalidomide exposure; only rabbits and some primates do."[33] The implication was that scientists would have missed the defects if they had not been working with rabbits and some primates. Would this not be sufficient warning? Moreover, some form of congenital deformity does appear in rats, mice, and hamsters, which Barnard and Kaufman neglected to mention.[34] In fact, it was because thalidomide had been inadequately tested in Europe that an alert FDA official, Dr. Frances Kelsey, prevented its sale in the United States. Her action was validated by independent investigations in Europe by pediatrician Helen Taussig.[35]

These and other manipulations of legitimate scientists' writings peppered Barnard and Kaufman's article for *Scientific American*. One misquoted scientist,

Dr. David Salsburg, even wrote to complain to the magazine that his words had been taken out of context:

> My 1982 article, [cited to show the inadequacy of animal testing], was an evaluation of a specific biological assay for carcinogenicity that fails to meet the minimum standards of good scientific design. Just because some people do foolish things with animals is no reason to believe that all experiments using animals are worthless. The science of pharmacology has brought great understanding to the study of life, much of it through animal research and testing.[36]

Brandon Reines

Brandon Reines is a veterinarian who has specialized in advancing the thesis that significant medical advances are primarily due to observations made on human patients. I have already acknowledged that keen observations by clinicians have been invaluable in advancing our understanding of disease. Unfortunately, Reines also uses the same tactic of selective quoting that I have just discussed. For example, he relates the story of the developer of the bubble oxygenator used in heart–lung bypass as follows: "Lillihei himself says, 'We were feeling our way along as far as flow was concerned …. Then we got more experience with our heart–lung machine and it worked for all sizes of people.'" Reines concludes: "Thus, Dr. Lillihei and his associates made the heart–lung machine safe and effective during the course of practice on actual patients —not from studies on healthy laboratory animals."[37] What do those ellipsis points mask? "For patients whom we thought were too big for those first of our bubble oxygenator heart–lung machines, we used dogs' lungs. About fifteen times in all." The long paragraph by Lillihei continues by describing procedures for cleaning the dogs' lungs, and then leads into the words after the ellipsis points.[38]

In reviews published by the American Anti-Vivisection Society, Reines[39] discusses other aspects of cardiovascular research as well as the discovery of insulin and developments in chemotherapy for cancer, all the while consistently discounting contributions from animal-based research and, at times, emphasizing that such experiments were counterproductive. Ernest Verhetsel, an elderly gentleman with whom I corresponded for many years, thoroughly examined Reines's efforts in his book, *They Threaten Your Health*. In checking the accuracy of Reines' writings, Verhetsel went to the trouble of corresponding with some of the scientists quoted by him. In essence, their answers were the same: Reines had told only half the story. For example, in response to a summary statement by Reines that animal testing had never been and never would be of any use in preventing human cancer induced by chemical carcinogens, the scientist quoted, David Salsburg again, had this to say to Verhetsel:

> Unfortunately, no one can control the use of his scientific papers in the hands of those who have no real interest in determining the truth but are only looking for a club with which to beat their opponents. . . . What I know of cancer research depends very heavily upon animals. . . In fact, one of the most exciting new areas deals with drugs now being developed that would keep cancer from spreading or metastasizing in the body. It will be impossible to develop these new drugs without the use of mice in large numbers.[40]

Another example of Reines's misrepresentation of another scientist's work to argue against the use of animals in research is Dr. S. E. Salmon's work with in vitro non-animal models in cancer research. Reines offers this as proof that these models were preferable to animal research. Dr. Salmon also wrote to Verhetsel. "While I have personally worked extensively on in vitro models for cancer research and felt that they are very important, in my opinion, they never will completely replace animal models, as we always want to see that a finding made in the test tube applies also in vivo in animals without dangerous toxicity. To do otherwise would often prove very dangerous to humans."[41]

We leave Reines with just one more example. Michael Bliss, a historian at the University of Toronto, wrote a wonderful book about the events leading to the discovery of insulin. He opened *The Story of Insulin* with these beautiful words: "The discovery of insulin at the University of Toronto in 1921–22 was one of the most dramatic events in the history of the treatment of disease." He added, with absolutely no exaggeration, "Those who watched the first starved, sometimes comatose, diabetics receive insulin and return to life saw one of the general miracles of modern medicine. They were present at the closest approach to the resurrection of the body that our secular society can achieve."[42]

The story is more complex than this; however, Reines,[43] rather than reviewing history accurately, made a distorted case against animal research by claiming that animals, primarily dogs, were not essential in the discovery of insulin. Charles Nicoll and Sharon Russell, scientists working at the University of

California at Berkeley, asked Bliss for his reaction to Reines's version of the events:

> Reines's interpretation of my work is thoroughly distorted,
> wrong-headed and silly. I informed him of this several years
> ago when I first read his mindless writings on the subject. . . .
> Insulin would not have been isolated, at Toronto or
> anywhere else, without the sacrifice of thousands of dogs.
> These dogs made it possible for millions of humans to live.[44]

Bliss also sent a reply toVerhetsel:

> I was appalled at the distortion of my work in the pamphlet
> and have written both to Mr. Reines and the American
> Anti-vivisection Society protesting their unethical, distorted
> use of my material in a cause with which I entirely disagree.
> I believe that my book, *The Discovery of Insulin*, shows
> the absolute necessity for animal experimentation in the
> work that produced that momentous breakthrough.
> Thousands of dogs had to be sacrificed. When the research
> succeeded, thanks in substantial part to that sacrifice,
> millions of human lives were saved. Anti-vivisectionists who
> use my research to try to support their cases are either
> ignorantly or deliberately misunderstanding it. I cannot
> condemn their efforts too strongly.[45]

How Can They Do It?

For years the fundamental question raised by all of this "data fudging" has puzzled me. How could these medically trained professionals make such outrageous claims about biomedical research, and state them repeatedly? They are neither stupid nor mad, in my opinion. What they are is committed. They are "true believers." I am forced to conclude that they are proponents of the worldview that categorizes animals along with human minority groups that have been marginalized and oppressed in the past—much in keeping with the thinking expressed in Peter Singer's *Animal Liberation*. (Recall, though, that the Greeks are careful to point out that they do not subscribe to animal rights, so their motives in misstating medical history remain a mystery.) True, there is probably not a person alive who has not manipulated the truth in some minor way to advance an argument, but I refer here to individuals apparently so captured by their beliefs that they have gone well beyond mere manipulation.

Belief in an idea can be powerful enough to drive individuals to do, say, or write anything in its defense. So it is with those who deny the scientific value of animal research. The denials are even more surprising when they arise from people who have benefited from higher education in science or medicine.

Why not just ignore these medically trained individuals who distort the record? After all, their claims are ridiculous. Unfortunately, this is not a debate in which people like myself have the luxury of remaining silent, allowing animal rightists to manipulate those who are not savvy to their tactics. Proper public education on the subject is imperative. Those misrepresenting biomedical research show up on college campuses and in popular literature with claims not easily answered or even understood by those unprepared. *Scientific American* certainly revealed itself to be ill prepared to deal with their message.

Despite all that I have written, I do not want to give the impression that I lump all animal lovers—even those with what I deem to be extreme viewpoints—into the category of fervently anti-research, denial-stricken, true believers. Recall those who were part of the study conducted by Hal Herzog, whose responses to his survey were quoted in Chapter 1. They were painfully concerned about animals, and I respect their concern even though I consider their views to be at the extreme end of the animal welfare spectrum.

I vividly remember a middle-aged woman who was in the audience during a friendly discussion I participated in with Gary Francione, a published animal rights abolitionist.[46] The discussion was part of a night course given at a local medical school. Her face expressed anguish as I talked about my research using cats. During the question-and-answer period, she (sincerely, I believe) offered herself as a research subject instead of the cats. Somewhat taken aback, I passed on to other comments and questions. But after the session I went to her and told her I could honestly empathize with her, trying to console her.

I have often remarked that I understand many of the people who follow the animal rights and liberation movement. They love animals, and so do I. Many of them have been misled, though, into thinking that animals have been completely unnecessary in achieving the health they enjoy, and this has led them to support financially organizations that promote such ideas. I submit that it is the inability of the most extreme members of the animal rights movement to understand me and other biomedical researchers, and what we do, that will continue to prevent our two opposing groups from seeing eye to eye.

The History of Modern Animal | 6
Rights Activism

*T*he beliefs of the extreme end of the modern animal rights and liberation movement, that we simply cannot use animals for any purpose, differ from more traditional notions of animal welfare that have existed from antiquity. In the Western world, for example, Jews and Christians are enjoined by the Bible to eschew cruelty to animals, but they are still permitted to use them. Animals were too integral a part of ordinary life in Bulliet's[1] domestic society for the views of the modern animal rights and liberation movement, which has arisen in the postdomestic society, to gain a foothold. Even moral philosophers had reasoned that a quick death, such as one provided by a slaughterhouse, was justified because animals could not foresee their ends. The idea that death itself might be harmful to an animal, robbing it of the opportunity to live a fuller life, belongs to more modern thinkers.

Compared to contemporary treatment, animals in the past were used quite ruthlessly in all spheres. James Turner, a historian at the University of Massachusetts, puts it bluntly in his study of animal usage by Victorians. Throughout history, "beasts have been feared, loved, beaten, caressed, starved, stuffed, and ignored."[2] Given the common (and accurate) picture of present-day England as a land of animal lovers and a leader in regulating the welfare of laboratory animals, as well as the fount of the modern animal rights and liberation movement and its accompanying viciousness, I was astounded to read the following in Harvard historian Harriet Ritvo's book, *The Animal Estate: The English and Other Creatures in the Victorian Age*, about England at the beginning of the nineteenth century: "Those who deplored the mistreatment of animals agreed that the English were especially inclined to inflict it."[3] But by the end of the century the English were paragons of virtue.

What happened in the intervening years? The establishment of the Society for the Prevention of Cruelty to Animals (SPCA) in 1824, the addition of "Royal" by Queen Victoria in 1840, was a major event. MP Richard Martin provided an impetus with his 1824 bill "'to prevent cruel and improper treatment of Cattle' (interpreted broadly to include most farm and draft animals, but not bulls [referring to bull baiting I presume] or pets)."[4] Martin thought that the SPCA could capitalize on the sea change in attitudes toward animals that he believed his bill had instigated. The advance in new thinking about protecting animal welfare met resistance, however. Martin's attempts to abolish dogfighting and bull baiting as well as to protect dogs, cats, and monkeys elicited ridiculing comment, such as, "the next step will be to protect flies and beetles."[5] Those who were pressing humane concerns were on the offensive, while those who wished to continue using animals simply reacted, much as we see today.

For example, the Puritan Protectorate in England banned "cock fighting and cock throwing (a sport in which spectators threw stones at tethered birds)" in 1654.[6] A concern then and later was the degradation this sport brought to the perpetrators. While I generally disagree with the tactics of animal rights activists, I did find myself in agreement with their campaign during the 1990s to stop the annual live-pigeon shoot in a small Pennsylvania town. It was a moneymaking way to get rid of what many people considered to be pests. Skeet shooting with living pigeons, rather than with clay discs, was obviously harmful to the pigeons, but just as bad, the event degraded the people participating, particularly the young boys running around wringing the necks of wounded birds. Although this event was seen as a way of life in this small town, eventually bad publicity resulted in the end of the festival. Unfortunately, the practice continues in some private shooting clubs.[7]

Vivisection in the Raw

Historically, *vivisection*, a term common throughout the centuries but somewhat overshadowed by the emphasis on animal rights today, on animals without anesthesia was a matter of course. As early as 450 B.C. experiments were performed in Greece to demonstrate that the optic nerve was necessary for vision. Imagine cutting the optic nerve running from the eyeball without anesthesia!

Nevertheless, horrible as it was, simply tying the animal down, cutting it, and performing the experiment provided us with insight into a variety of functions of the body, insight that eventually led to current knowledge. Remember, though, that surgery on humans was not a treat, either. Adequate anesthesia for humans undergoing surgery did not arrive until 1850, and even then it was not necessarily safe or even available everywhere.[8]

The famous Roman physician Galen, who did not like to work on primates because their grimaces were too human-like, was troubled by the aesthetics of the situation, not the fact that his subject could be suffering. In keeping with the Stoic philosophy, only humans were endowed with reason, so "the animal's lack of a rational soul meant it had no personality or rights."[9] According to Roman law, animals were mere objects, and they often paid a terrible price for their lower status.

Such experimentation, horrible to contemplate now, continued through the centuries, although not without objection from some quarters of society. Some of the objections raised in the past have a familiar ring today. For example, in the early seventeenth century a physician to kings, Jean Riolan Jr., argued against the newly discovered lymphatic, rather than venous, absorption of food for two reasons: the anatomy of animals and humans differed, and results obtained from a stressed animal were unreliable.[10] The findings that lymphatics draining the gut carry absorbed nutrients into the circulatory system have held up quite well, although ultimately the nutrients do enter the venous system via the great veins entering the heart, together with blood from the entire body. Riolan was concerned that animals and humans were too different in structure for the dissection of animals to be of any use. We encounter the same objections from some contemporary physicians, but unlike the physicians discussed in the preceding chapter, Riolan was advancing his own opinion on the basis of knowledge of the day.

Along with the resistance from some physicians, moral objections to vivisection were creeping in as well in the seventeenth and eighteenth centuries.[11] Vivisection was sometimes discussed in ways recognizable today. A Swiss physician who was criticized for toxicological experiments—by this time the term *vivisection* stood for all animal experimentation, not just cutting—had this to say when accused of cruelty: "The argument of cruelty is put forward by some men, who themselves do not hesitate to fill their stomach with beef, veal, lamb, and fish almost every day."[12]

Squeamishness about certain experiments probably entered the picture more than once. For example, Robert Hooke, a well-known "natural philosopher," wrote to Robert Boyle, another famous scientist of the seventeenth century, that he could not perform a particular experiment because of the pain it caused to animals.

Unfortunately, the study of the functions of the body, physiology, necessitates that the research subject be living. We have seen that such study began on animals in antiquity, but the emergence of physiology as a medical discipline was a ninteenth-century phenomenon. Its establishment as an experimental science in the service of medicine required time and met opposition from two quarters: the strongly anti-vivisectionist element of the humane movement, and medicine itself. French basic scientists, who with their German counterparts had taken the lead in physiological experimentation, had to overcome the opposition of clinicians who were in charge in the medical establishment. These clinicians had strong beliefs about what was important for the advancement of medical knowledge: anatomical studies and vitalism, which is the belief in vital forces of the body that cannot be reduced to simple mechanisms. The science of experimental physiology eventually proved itself as the way to understand what disease does to the body.

There were many scientists in Europe who contributed to the development of this new critical discipline, but Claude Bernard emerges as one of the principle figures in this area, for two reasons. First, he was undoubtedly a brilliant scientist. He led in establishing the principles of experimentation, greatly advanced our understanding of the roles of the pancreas and liver in digestion, and laid the groundwork for understanding the self-regulation of vital internal processes, referred to now as homeostasis.[13] Second, together with René Descartes, Bernard is a favorite whipping boy of those who wish to remind the world how terrible biomedical scientists are—never mind that Bernard and Descartes were creatures of the nineteenth and seventeenth centuries, respectively, and that biomedical research is now conducted with humane methods. Given that physiological experiments require that the subject be alive—and we have already seen what that meant in the days before the development of adequate anesthesia—Bernard's experiments were surely brutal. Imagine studying the various internal organs as he did without anesthesia.

Vivisection—A Special Case

The chapter titled "A Measure of Compassion" in Ritvo's *The Animal Estate* contains a litany of cruelties to agricultural animals and other beasts of burden in England, acts arising out of frustration in getting a task done or out of crass ignorance. The RSPCA had enforcement powers, and they found themselves intervening in some horrendous cases. The great majority involved carthorses, which were naturally very numerous in the 1800s. To encourage their movement, various brutal instruments were used, from the obvious sticks and whips to shovels, chains, pitchforks, and even knives. One enterprising soul lit a bunch of straw and held it under the poor beast's "tender parts." Sheep and oxen that could not keep up with the flock or herd suffered similar abuse. Eliminating such cruelty was considered a way to improve the moral level of the society as much as it was to protect the animals.

Vivisection, however, obtained something of a bye from the RSPCA, because "higher" levels of society were its practitioners, rather than the "lowly" drovers who abused their draft animals. As Ritvo notes, "An incontestably respectable activity that required subjecting animals to pain challenged the social categories that underlay the RSPCA's interpretation of cruelty."[14] English scientists had not employed vivisection to any degree through the first half of the century, but by the 1860s they realized that French and German scientists were pursuing the most promising research by experimenting on animals, so their emphasis changed. With the increase in animal use for both research and teaching, the humane movement could no longer turn a blind eye to the activity of members in the "higher reaches" of society.

Compared to today's animal rightists, the English anti-vivisectionists of the nineteenth century presented little threat to medical research because the life-saving medical benefits obtained with experimentation marginalized them. Indeed, according to Ritvo, "the discovery of the diphtheria antitoxin in 1894, which promised to save thousands of lives each year, was a decisive blow,"[15] although Turner has noted that antibacterial treatment still had some way to go in acceptance by the medical establishment as well as the public.[16]

Activists for humane treatment of animals worked to ban vivisection and thought that the testimony they gave before the Royal Commission on the Practice of Subjecting Live Animals to Experiments for Scientific Purposes would produce that result. The physiologists and their supporters were eventually vindicated, however, with passage of the Cruelty to Animals Act of 1876. Instead of banning vivisection, the dream of the humane-movement activists, the act provided for a licensing system that permitted licensed scientists in licensed facilities to pursue their research on specifically licensed projects with government oversight. Although the anti-vivisectionists felt betrayed, the law was really a huge advance and stood the test of time for over a century, making the United Kingdom the world's leader in best research practices.

While scientists in the United States received little oversight until 1985, British scientists had had a rigorous system for protecting research animals for more than a century. The procedures for regulating research in the United States, described in Chapter 4, which took some getting used to, had already been around for a very long time in England. My hat goes off to those scientists.

American Anti-Vivisectionism

My focus in this chapter has been on England for two reasons. First, England led the way in the Western world in bringing high standards to laboratory animal research and in other fields as well. Second, it has also led the way in the area of animal-rights extremism. What was the situation in the United States during this same period?

Given my view that the term *animal protection*, as it is used today, can mask some rather nefarious activities that strike me as attacks on humanity rather than protection of animals, it is well to note that there was a distinction between animal protection societies and anti-vivisection societies in the United States around the turn of the twentieth century.[17] Animal protection societies, exemplified by the American Humane Association, founded in 1877, sought regulation of experiments in medical schools and laboratories as well as abolition of vivisection demonstrations in public schools. Henry Bergh, a wealthy New Yorker, founded the American Society for the Prevention of Cruelty to Animals (ASPCA) in 1866 and worked hard to eliminate vivisection on animals, although the society devoted most of its efforts to protecting animals in general use. The first American society devoted to anti-vivisectionism was The American Anti-Vivisection Society (AAVS) in 1883. Many more organizations, such as the New England Anti-Vivisection Society (1895), also still prominent today, soon followed.

Although anti-vivisection societies in the earlier part of the twentieth century were quite vigorous in protesting the use of humans in experimentation as well as animal vivisection, the 1970s brought a blurring of the boundary between humans and animals by thinkers to be discussed in Chapter 9, who inspired the modern animal rights and liberation movement—some even dismissing the principle of the sanctity of human life.[18] Nazi Germany's views of human beings, described later, will illustrate the dangers associated with such a stance.

As described in Chapter 1, Bulliet[19] has proposed the concept of domestic and postdomestic societies, which have differing attitudes toward animals. The views of postdomestic society, possessed by those born after World War II, have spawned a dedicated and sometimes violent cadre of individuals that have "elevated ignorance about the natural world almost to the level of a philosophical principle." Richard Conniff, a devoted environmentalist writing in *Audubon Magazine*, gave that description of the animal-rightist attitude in a humorous but nevertheless serious article on a controversy over fur sales in Aspen, Colorado.[20] In his view, activists within the postdomestic generations do not know how to interact with the animal world in a realistic way because, to a large extent, they are removed from nature by urban or suburban living and are anything but realistic about our relations with animals beyond pet-keeping. As agriculture became increasingly efficient and productive, the move from the farm to cities removed more and more people from the fields, woods, and experiences like those of my own childhood. In 1880 half of the U.S. population derived a living from agriculture; now, 1 in 50 Americans do.[21]

Those captured by the ideas of today's animal rights and liberation movement, far more divorced from the rural world than their nineteenth-century forbearers, do not accept, for example, the need to accept responsibility for managing wildlife populations by means of trapping. As Conniff wrote, they view trappers as "slack-jawed Neanderthals" when, in fact, the trappers he knows "are hopelessly retrograde, caught up in all the unfashionable minutiae of animal behavior, diet, habitat, and seasonal change. Like many farmers, the better ones actually love the animals they kill—and this obviously isn't the abstract love, the passion for the helpless victim, of most animal rights activists."[22] They set traps appropriately sized for their prey, run their trap lines frequently, and quickly dispatch the animal they have caught. The method, frequently a blow to the head, sounds awful, but it is quick, without the prolonged suffering that nature might eventually impose. Once more, trappers and others of us who love the wild know that nature is not kind in the deaths she imposes. We tend to forget that wild animals do not go gently into the night, as when starving deer die in March after a hard winter (described in Chapter 8).

The controversy over a proposed deer cull to protect the forest surrounding the Quabbin reservoir in Massachusetts, discussed in the Introduction, further exemplifies how far today's animal rights movement has diverged from its beginnings in both the United States and the United Kingdom. Without predators to keep their population in check, deer were merrily eating their way through the vital under-story of the Quabbin forest. In Philadelphia, deer were destroying the beautiful Wissahickon Valley in a similar manner; yet in both instances, activists were only interested in one species, ignoring all the others endangered by the destruction caused by browsing deer. Activists proved themselves a nuisance in trying to block a necessary cull. This new view of animals is distinct from that of years past, when people were concerned about animal cruelty while still using animals in a variety of ways.

A *LIFE* magazine exposé of a supplier of dogs for research also helped initiate the modern wave of concern for animals. The exposé was, in a way, the culmination of increasing concern for animals in the 1950s, which followed a half-century of relative quiescence and resulted from activities of the newly created Humane Society of the United States (HSUS), which had split off from the "sedate" American Humane Association in 1954. This story galvanized society into action, leading to the passage of the first Animal Welfare Act in 1966, long overdue in my opinion. It required the licensing of dealers and registering of laboratories, and established standards for laboratory animal care.[23]

Another shift was also taking place, as Fred Goodwin, then-director of the National Institute of Mental Health, noted: "There began to evolve in the mid-60's, a kind of demoralization or nihilism concerning the human condition; in the USA part of this shift reflected a post-Vietnam, post-Watergate mistrust of society's establishments and institutions."[24] Peter Singer, in the preface to the 1990 second edition of his book, *Animal Liberation*, also remarked that the time had been ripe in 1975 for acceptance of his thesis stated then: "No book can achieve anything unless it strikes a chord in its readers. The liberation movements of the Sixties had made Animal Liberation an obvious next step."[25]

Bulliet's postdomestic society had arrived. Whatever the reasons, many healthy individuals, already protected from numerous awful diseases as a result of the animal research of the past, were moved to embrace this philosophical outlook on human–animal relationships in the latter 1970s. Nevertheless, there was still much room for improvement in our treatment of animals, whatever one might think of the philosophical underpinnings of the movement.

One of the first actions that directly opposed biomedical research was led in 1976 by Henry Spira (now deceased) against scientists doing basic research into the neurological bases of sexual behavior. This research was being conducted on cats at the American Museum of Natural history in New York City, and was funded by the NIH.[26] Spira had been a very active protester against corrupt labor unions and knew the value of direct action to advance a cause, in contrast to the educational efforts being practiced by traditional animal welfare organizations. A cat lover as well, he had been inspired by a course taught by Peter Singer at New York University. Spira managed to convince at least one scientist "to support the claim that the research had no scientific legitimacy or demonstrable practical value." Members of Congress were outraged. In fact, the scientist, Lester Aronson, had had his laboratory inspected and approved by various governmental agencies and the museum, and his work had been reviewed and judged of high merit and scientific value by NIH review panels.[27] Yet, the museum caved in to the protest, and Aronson's funding agency gave him weak support. The laboratory closed with Aronson's retirement 1 year after the beginning of the protests.[28] It was a triumph of ignorance and sentiment over science.

Obviously this was not the last time that a scientist or an administration did not withstand the brute force brought against biomedical research by animal rights activists. Dr. Michiko Okamoto, who was conducting drug addiction research a decade later at Cornell University and was financially supported by the National Institute on Drug Abuse (NIDA), had attracted the attention of an organization called Trans-Species Unlimited. Dr. Okamoto's studies were on barbiturate addiction and withdrawal, and her results were commonly referred to in pharmacology textbooks. When Trans-Species Unlimited began to target Dr. Okamoto's work and her institution, Cornell issued a statement that her cat experiments were coming to an end. The activists claimed victory but soon learned that Okamoto had received funding for 3 more years of study on cats. Because of Cornell's cowardly compliance with the activists' demands, Dr. Okamoto was forced to return the grant.[29]

As chairman of the Society for Neuroscience's Committee on Animals in Research, I tried to help her resist the pressures she clearly felt from Cornell's medical school administration, even writing to Cornell's president in Ithaca and to a neighbor who served on its board of trustees—all to no avail. Her work was very highly regarded. Science lost in two ways as a result of Cornell's maneuver: future data were lost, and an extremist organization brought a great university, one of my alma maters, to its knees.

As animal rights actions became more radical, particularly in the area of biomedical research, marked by the release of animals from laboratories, destruction of laboratories, and harassment of scientists, it was only natural that research-protection groups would emerge. The current major players are the National Association for Biomedical Research (NABR) and its sister organization, the Foundation for Biomedical Research (FBR), organized in the early 1980s; Americans for Medical Progress (AMP), founded in 1992; and various state organizations, such as the Pennsylvania Society for Biomedical Research, all founded in those two decades. Members in Pennsylvania have been particularly active in educating children on the importance of biomedical research for their future health. Also, several individuals with serious illnesses, quite understandably angered at attacks on biomedical research, founded a now defunct organization called the incurably ill For Animal Research (iiFAR). To speak for other user groups, a dog breeder, Patti Strand, founded the National Animal Interest Alliance (NAIA) in 1992. I was a founding board member as well as president of NAIA for several years, in addition to serving on the board of AMP and as vice-president of my own state organization, the Pennsylvania Society for Biomedical Research.

Remarkably, these organizations are quite underfunded in comparison with the major players contesting the use of animals, as noted in Chapter 2. The reason, it would seem, is that simple claims of abuse or pictures, accurate or not, elicit great sympathy and monetary donations. Meanwhile, educational materials provided by the research-support organizations do not have the same appeal.

A further development in the late 1970s was the increasing emphasis on developing alternatives to using animals in product-safety testing in particular. Again, Henry Spira was a key figure. Using the same tactics he had employed against the American Museum of Natural History, he persuaded the cosmetics giant Revlon to contribute a large sum of money to find alternatives to the Draize test, in which materials were dropped into the eyes of restrained rabbits to determine if they would be irritating. Over the next few years, other companies followed suit and ceased the testing of cosmetics. In 1981, The Center for Alternatives to Animal Testing was established at Johns Hopkins University, with funding from many major companies that used animals, to find ways to reduce the number of animals used in product-safety testing and in biomedical research. The companies realized that reducing animal use had both an economic and humane effect: nobody makes money buying animals and caring for them in lieu of non-animal methods. Quite honestly, because we were under siege from extremists aiming to shut down biomedical research, a number of scientists, including me, were initailly skeptical of the alternatives movement. With time to catch our breath, however, that skepticism vanished, at least for me. I now strongly support the notion that alternatives to animal testing can help reduce the number of animals needed by these industries, so long as a total, bureaucratic ban on all animal use is not the result.

Also greeted cautiously was the founding of the Scientists Center for Animal Welfare (SCAW) in 1978 by F. Barbara Orlans, formerly a scientist at the NIH and now at the Kennedy Center of Ethics. Many of us were suspicious of SCAW at the time; in the context of being bombarded by animal rights accusations we were unable to see wisdom staring us in the face. Within a few short years, though, during my tenure as chair of the Committee on Animals in Research of the Society for Neuroscience from 1987 to 1990, I worked actively with the new head of SCAW, Lee Krulisch, speaking at some of the conferences the organization held on developing better practices in the use of animals and in overseeing their use. As something of a grand finale to my association with SCAW, I delivered the keynote address, "Thinking about Animals: A Personal Odyssey," at one of their conferences in September 2006.[30]

Descartes and Darwin: Two Key Figures in the Animal Rights Debate

In attacking biomedical research, spokespersons of the animal rights and liberation movement often employ the seventeenth-century ideas of René Descartes, implying that modern researchers share the French philosopher's views. Descartes proposed that both humans and animals could be compared to machines, or automata, subject to the laws of mechanics.[31] But speech and a rational soul elevated humans, leaving animals without the benefit of reason—truly rendering them machines, albeit fashioned by the hands of God. This idea left animals vulnerable to human use; Descartes argued that they could not reason, so they could not experience the "same" pain as humans do, and their expressions of pain were just external manifestations without the *mental* sensations. Some scientists of the day used Descartes' view that animals were like machines to justify their experiments—some avidly to the point of deliberate cruelty—even though Descartes did not argue that animals felt no sensation of pain, just that they did not think about it.

Descartes is excoriated in the animal rights literature for regarding animals as mere machines without feelings and, therefore, acceptable subjects for experimentation. His own writings tell a different story, according to bioethicist Jerry Tannenbaum, who wrote in answer to my request for insights into the real Descartes:

> He believed strongly that animals not only feel pain but experience many emotions. His last great book, *The Passions of the Soul*, discusses this to some extent. Like many after him, he could not envisage the complex thoughts of humans that are dependent on language. He thought that animals are indeed machines, in the sense that their behavior is completely determined by physical forces, with no free will while believing they are machines that have certain sensations and can experience certain emotions. Some who claim to have read Descartes believe he denied all feeling or sensation to animals. He did not. But he did think they are automata, or at least that we have no scientific evidence to believe otherwise. I wonder what he would say about some of the non-human great apes if he knew what we know now. He died too early (in his early 50s) to be able to write more on animal mentality. I wonder if he would have turned to the ethical implications of his work. He owned a dog that he loved.[32]

In a letter to Henry More on February 6, 1649, Descartes had this to say:

> But though I regard it as established that we cannot prove there is any thought in animals, I do not think it can be proved there is none, since the human mind does not reach into their thoughts. But when I investigate what is most

probable in this manner, I see no argument for animals
having thoughts except this one: Because they have eyes,
ears, tongues and other sense-organs like ours, it seems
likely that they have sensations like us; and since thought is
included in our mode of sensation, similar thought seems
attributable to them.[33]

In the next chapter I will explore how animals might "think" without words—
always a puzzle for me.

Jumping to the present, scientists have been depicted as Cartesians (disciples
of Descartes) in the animal-rightists' writings, although that charge seems to have
faded away recently. Modern laboratory care has been an effective response,
although really only in recent years have we been paying sufficient attention to
analgesia (pain relief) and anesthesia for laboratory animals.

Even in the eighteenth century the Cartesian view of a "beast-machine" gradually lost favor, in part because of the objections of well-known literati, such as the
poet Alexander Pope and, later, Samuel Johnson.[34] Pope had a friend and neighbor, the Reverend Stephen Haley, who did experiments on blood circulation and
pressure on dogs. Pope expressed concern to another friend, asking how we knew
we had the right to kill creatures so close to us, even if doing so might be of some
use to humans, a rather familiar refrain to us in the present. Johnson was strongly
against the cruelty of vivisection—and it was without doubt terribly cruel, as were
the operations performed on people—also believing vivisection to be morally
harmful to people. He inserted a refrain still heard today that "he did not believe
'that by living dissections any discovery has been made by which a single malady
is more easily cured.'"[35] Given that little was cured in those days, it was not a bold
statement. Ironically, that challenge has been reissued today, when many ailments
can be cured, but certainly not with information gained from just one experiment.
We could never satisfy Singer's standard that "if a single experiment could cure a
disease like leukemia, that experiment would be justifiable."[36]

In 1859 Charles Darwin published *The Origin of Species*, a work that has
been used by animal rightists in their quest to protect animals from human
use.[37] A variety of the commonly quoted modern writers dealing with ethics
and animals, such as Michael A. Fox,[38] Michael W. Fox,[39] Mary Midgely,[40] James
Rachels,[41] and Peter Singer,[42] credit Darwin with introducing the idea that evolution sealed our kinship with animals. For example, Singer has claimed that
"intellectually the Darwinian revolution was genuinely revolutionary. Human
beings now knew they were not the special creation of God, made in the divine
image and set apart from animals; on the contrary human beings came to realize that they were animals themselves."[43]

Darwin was not *that* revolutionary, however. His important contribution, providing an explanation for the mechanism of evolution, natural selection, added a key element to the idea that animals had evolved over time and that we are all brothers and sisters under the skin. But this idea extends back centuries to Plutarch and Lucretius and colleagues. The concept of the Great Chain of Being that linked animals with humans (though not necessarily stipulating that they were brothers under the skin) and even angels and God along in a continuum, with neighbors in the chain sharing at least one attribute, had been around for centuries in Western thought, originating with the Neoplatonists.[44] And such pre-Darwinian naturalist luminaries as Leibniz, Goethe, Saint-Hilaire, and Erasmus Darwin (Charles's grandfather) contributed as much toward the diminution of anthropocentrism as did Charles Darwin.[45]

Despite what some modern animal rights activists suggest today, Darwin's theories did not necessarily provoke in all people a greater sensitivity toward animals. For historical figures such as Leo Tolstoy and George Bernard Shaw, it was quite the opposite. According to Rod Preece, a Canadian professor of political philosophy and a writer on human–animal relations, "for Tolstoy, Darwinism destroyed the ideal of love for fellow creatures that abounded in primitive *Christianity* [my emphasis]," and "[George Bernard] Shaw did not see Darwinism as an appropriate basis for his own extensive animal sensibilities."[46]

Darwin is sometimes portrayed in the modern animal rights literature as having opposed animal experimentation. In fact, as Preece relates, "Darwin's own animal sensibilities oscillated between a deep caring for his fellow creatures and a far deeper caring for his own intellectual discipline . . . Animals mattered. Knowledge mattered more."[47] The record shows that he was leery of strong versions of England's 1876 Cruelty to Animals Act; Darwin pushed for weaker proposals and was not satisfied with compromises in the law. He was very much a proponent of solid basic research that was independent of immediate medical benefit, but at the same time an opponent of experiments conducted for "damnable and detestable curiosity,"[48] a sentiment shared by most of us today. If that curiosity lacks a strong scientific foundation, we should not harm animals simply to satisfy it. Indeed, the oversight of IACUCs is designed to prevent such abuse.

The Movement Today

As part of the paradigm shift in our consideration of animals, a true oddity of the past is finding its way into the present: the concept that animals be considered equal to humans under the law. Consider first these astounding examples from the past: "When in 1679 a London woman swung at Tyburn for bestiality, her canine partner in crime suffered the same punishment on the same grounds." So begins Ritvo's history in *The Animal Estate*.[49] Further, in Germany household animals provided support for their master's claims of a burglary by appearing in court if the master was not available. In Shakespeare's *The Merchant of Venice* a wolf's hanging for killing a human was mentioned so casually that one can conclude such punishments were commonplace.

Then, in the nineteenth century, the status of animals changed dramatically: They became property and were no longer "equal" under the law, at least as far as punishment for crimes was concerned. Ritvo offers an almost mystical reason for this shift in relationships: with movement into a more scientific age, nature no longer held magical powers that even animals were believed to wield. Humans became their masters; the dominated animals became property. Animals could no longer be held responsible for their "crimes," although a dangerous beast would have been killed then just as it would today to protect the public good.

Curiously, we now see a move backward, although some see it as representing forward thinking. Various efforts have been made recently to shift the status of animals from that of property, where they were placed in the nineteenth century, to a level approaching human equals under the law. In a number of cities, beginning in Boulder, Colorado, and now in 12 others, as well as in Windsor, Ontario, and in the entire state of Rhode Island as of August 4, 2004, owners of pets are now considered "guardians" of their animals.[50] These governments have put their citizenry in the position of manning pooper-scoopers for animals they no longer own (theoretically) and that bear no responsibility for their actions. Some would say that this effort is really designed to change our attitudes toward animals in the direction of animal rights beyond the basic rights that decent people accord them: the "right" to humane care, but a right without responsibilities, obviously. The Great Ape Project,[51] presented in the next chapter, might be considered in the same vein, for it seeks to accord apes rights beyond what is considered usual when animals are our immediate responsibility—that is, clean and adequate housing suitable for the species, food, and water.

At least 13 bar associations now have new animal-law sections and at least 50 schools offer courses on animal law. When I was in school, we were told that an animal was worth what the owner paid for it: $5 for a dog rescued from a shelter or millions for a racehorse. If an owner/guardian can sue for mental anguish, then a veterinarian's insurance premium would force veterinary fees beyond the reach of many owner/guardians, the net result being a decrease in animal welfare. This is not just a veterinarian's lugubrious fantasy; it has been reality over the past several years:

> As part of a divorce settlement, a judge orders a Colorado man to pay $140 per month in "pet support" for the family dog.
>
> In Seattle, a judge awards $45,000 to the woman whose 12-year-old cat was mauled to death by a neighbor's dog. The amount included $30,000 for the pet's special value, and $15,000 for emotional distress. The cat's owner said her animal's death left her with sleep disturbances, panic attacks, and depression.
>
> In Nashville, the owners of "Gizmo," a 16-year-old Yorkshire terrier killed last year when he was allegedly kicked like a football, are asking a civil court to award them $200,000 in damages. After the incident occurred, local police arrested two men, who were charged with cruelty to animals (a misdemeanor) and felony vandalism, a charge that could carry two to 12 years in prison.[52]

Charlotte Lacroix, a veterinarian and a lawyer, recently discussed in a lecture at my school the implications of the move to change the legal status of pets. "Under the 'guardianship' model, to require that pet owners always act in the best interests of their pets, regardless of the costs, goes beyond what most pet owners would want. So if the majority of society views pets as 'best friends' as opposed to children, then laws requiring owners to act in the capacity of guardian go too far."[53] Her view, and mine, is that we need to strengthen animal cruelty statutes. Dr. Lacroix added,

> There's no question in my mind that animals are not cars, but there's also no question in my mind that animals are not necessarily akin to children. They don't have the same needs, the same interests, nor are they humans with the same roles in society, etc. . . . Are we going to make them children overnight just by changing terminology, or instead maybe continue to strengthen the animal cruelty statutes by imposing additional obligations on pet owners and enforcing such laws before proposing new legal paradigms?[54]

We should not turn the law on its head without considerable debate. I believe that the purpose of this new proposal to change the status of animals is simply to release them from our control and, ultimately, limit drastically our use of them in various ways, including biomedical research—a dramatic paradigm shift that would not be in the best interests of humans. Indeed, it would not be in the best interests of animals. Just consider what veterinary bills for your dog or cat would be if veterinarians were forced to carry liability insurance with high premiums. Would the pet continue to go to the vet as often as it should?

But a word on the term *pet* used throughout this book. According to Stephan Zawistowski of the ASPCA, it likely is derived from the French word for "small," which is *petit*. I think he is correct when he writes in his excellent book, *Companion Animals*, that *pet* can have a pejorative connotation and that *companion animal* "reflects accurately the sense of companionship that people share with the animals that live with them."[55] Indeed, Buster is my buddy, even though I own him, to a certain degree.

Nazi Germany and the United States: Disturbing Forms of Vivisection in Recent Times

I close this chapter with examples of why concern for animals that is pushed to the extreme can be a real danger to humanity. Maintaining a moral separation between humans and animals that still recognizes the worth and wonder of animal life is extremely important, to my way of thinking. These examples take place in Nazi Germany, and in the early to to mid-twentieth century in the United States.

In early twentieth-century Germany, Hitler and his followers demonstrated what can happen when the love of animals becomes so perverted as to displace concern for other humans. Grotesquely, the Nazis were very concerned about vivisection on animals and actually banned it in Bavaria and Prussia. They eventually permitted some experimentation, but in a climate of heavy regulation. Under Hitler, a particularly degenerate case of animal love had emerged, although that love was secondary to an extreme hatred of certain groups of humans. In a brilliant analysis, Arnold Arluke and Boria Sax reflect on the bizarre behavior of protecting animals while subjecting humans to the most atrocious barbarisms imaginable.[56]

The Nazis extended and distorted historic romantic views of the German people. They romanticized animal instinct, believing that it brought humans closer to a more natural life, rebelling against culture and intellectualism. In elevating animals, particularly the fearless, aggressive predator, the Nazis reasoned that compassion toward humans (at least certain humans) was a weakness.

Indeed, animals were elevated to the sacred. The Nazis built on ideas such as those of the zoologist, Ernst Haeckel, writing around the turn of the century, who "attacked religion, primarily Christianity, for putting man above animals and nature, and for isolating man from nature and creating contempt for animals. Haekel believed that man and animals had the same natural as well as moral status and that much of human morality stemmed from animals."[57] This view was shared by Darwin and more modern scientists, as discussed in Chapter 7. But in extending Haeckel's ideas, the Nazis did not regard animals as property that humans could do with as they wished: "meat eating became a symbol of the decay of other civilizations; and vegetarianism became a symbol of the new, pure civilization that was to be Germany's future."[58] According to the late nineteenth-century composer, Richard Wagner, animal blood corrupted humans and the Germanic people had become contaminated by breeding with lesser peoples. Somehow, in Hitler's mind all of this translated into non-Aryans being lower than animals. The Nazis glorified the pig, indicating that for Nordic peoples "the pig occupies the first place and is the first among the domestic animals," and made a slam against Jews: "The Semites do not understand the pig, they reject the pig."[59,]

When it came to biology, the Nazis took a holistic approach and viewed the Jew as being behind a more mechanistic science. The vivisector was both "evil and Jewish" according to Wagner, who provided some of the underpinnings of the Nazis' philosophy. Wagner had, in fact, urged the destruction of laboratories and removal of vivisectors.

The Nazis, of course, carried the idea of racial purity to a hideous extreme. According to Arluke and Sax,

> the Nazi notion of race in many ways assumed the symbolic
> significance usually associated with species; the new
> phylogenetic hierarchy could locate certain "races" below
> animals. The danger and pollution normally thought to be
> posed by animals to humans was replaced with other
> "races." The Germans were the highest "species," above all
> other life; some "higher" animals; however, could be placed
> above other races or "sub-humans" in the "natural"
> hierarchy.[60]

The Nazi leaders' love of animals and concern for their protection allowed them to be "humane" while committing the most barbaric crimes against their fellow humans (although these were essentially and conveniently no longer of the same species). "The Holocaust itself may have depended on this unique cultural conception of what it meant to be human in relation to animals."[61]

This idea is reminiscent of the attitude toward African Americans and Native Americans during some dark periods in U.S. history. Beyond the practices of racial segregation in the United States prior to the Civil Rights Act of 1964, there occurred other detestable crimes against people: harmful experimentation on humans of all races, without their understanding the seriousness of what they had agreed to or not agreed to, as Susan Lederer describes *in Subjected to Science: Human Experimentation in the United States before the Second World War* in horrid detail.[62] Orphans, who were not given a choice about their participation, were favorite subjects. The various procedures applied to them make one cringe when reading this history. For example, in the early 1900s, tuberculin tests to diagnose the presence of tuberculosis were conducted on 160 children under 8 years old; all but 26 were orphans. Three different tests involved injections into muscle or skin or instillation into the eye. Diana Belais of the New York Anti-Vivisection Society, who was campaigning against the use of children in nontherapeutic experiments, wrote of those undergoing the last test, "the little children would lie in their beds moaning all night from the pain in their eyes. . . . They kept their little hands pressed over their eyes, unable to sleep from the sensations they had to undergo."[63]

Infamous as well is the Tuskegee Syphilis Study and the consequent deliberate withholding of effective treatment from uneducated African-American volunteers long after penicillin was found to be an effective treatment.[64] The study began in 1932 under the auspices of the U.S. Public Health Service and continued until 1972, when an outcry was raised. The result was passage of the National Research Act, enacted in 1974, which mandated informed consent and oversight by institutional review boards. This brought an end to unregulated human experimentation, which, if not a conscious governmental effort to eliminate an entire class of human beings as part of an evil ideology, was at least forgetful of the concept of the sanctity of human life.

The previous discussion of vivisection on humans illustrates how dangerous abandoning that concept can be.

Exploring the Nature of Animals | 7

*I*n previous chapters, I have described the issues and events that led to my devoting a considerable part of my professional career to debating the modern animal rights issue. I have also explored the historical developments that led to the current proliferation of extremism within the movement. This chapter considers what seems to lie behind it all: a very human desire to relate to the animals from which we emerged. Some of us are clearly less inclined to distinguish ourselves from animals, but nearly all of us have an intense interest in them. (Ironically, the individual who has perhaps driven the debate more than any other, Peter Singer, does not base his arguments on a particular love for nor interest in animals).

To begin, I would like to explore the nature of animals, including their cognitive abilities. My focus will be on mammals, the animals closest to us on the evolutionary tree. In "higher" animals (such as primates, dogs, and cats), academic interest has been largely focused on intellectual capacities: how and how much they can learn, what they remember, and how well they can communicate with humans. In studies on communication, most of the scientific community's attention has quite naturally focused on primates, especially chimpanzees. These apes are our closest relatives genetically and are obviously highly intelligent, so it is only natural for us humans to want to know just how much they understand beyond the simple commands we might give to a dog.

The fundamental question to address in the context of this book is, what differences exist between humans and animals that justify human use of animals for our benefit? The anatomical differences between us and other mammals in particular are surprisingly minor, even when it comes to the mammalian brain. True, we humans are not covered by a thick coat of hair, nor do we walk on all fours or have a tail. But we do suckle our young and have at least some hair, these being the defining features of mammals. Our bodies are certainly closer in substance to that of other mammals than they are to a tissue culture or a computer (the flawed substitutes offered by those who argue that animals are too different from humans to yield useful results in the study of disease). Our bodies are so similar that we share at least 300 diseases with various mammals according to Cornelius's survey, which was published nearly 40 years ago.[1]

The structures, features, and abilities that we see when we look at a chimpanzee, a dog, a horse, a giraffe, a mouse, or any other mammal are the results of millions of years of specializations that have allowed all creatures to fit the myriad ecological niches in which they survive. We share the same body plan with most mammals, but structures or functions may distort the appearance of that plan according to a given species' need. For example, the horse's long leg with only one toe nevertheless has the same bones that we have in one of our toes. The bones lengthen closer to the toe, however, and various muscles distally (farther from the body) are less bulky. This lightens the horse's leg, thereby increasing the length and speed of its swing in running away from predators. The giraffe's very long neck, which permits the animal to browse leaves high in a tree, looks very different from ours, yet it has the same number of bones as in our necks. The racing dogs that run so many miles so eagerly over the Arctic snow are far more efficient than humans in converting fats to energy, which enables their canine feats of endurance. Through arduous training, long-distance runners also convert those same fats to energy, just less efficiently. Right down to the level of the gene we share similarities with mice, thus scientists can identify defective mouse genes that enable them to find analogous genes in humans. This feat is leading to tremendous advances in medicine, as discussed in Chapter 4.

In light of these examples, it is easy to dismiss the claims that animals are too distant from us physically to be useful in research that advances human medicine. But what may give any humane person pause is the undeniable fact that animals also share with humans the capacity to feel pain and suffering. Peter Singer has based his philosophical opposition to animal experimentation on this simple but very important point. His position will be considered in greater detail in the last chapter. For now I will confine the discussion to the nature of pain and explore how animals and humans experience it.

Pain in Humans and Animals

Once when I stubbed my toe in the dark and then inadvertently stepped on Buster's tail, we emitted a respective loud "Ouch! [bleep], [bleep]!" and "Rrooww!" I have no difficulty in believing that we both experienced a similar sensation of discomfort, although what Buster thought about it I do not know. As animals, our reactions to potentially or actually harmful stimuli are universal, which speaks to their survival value. The verbalization of our pain likely evolved to warn our nearby companions of possible danger. Although we might wish that we did not have to experience pain, without a system that alerts us to noxious stimuli our lives would be constantly in danger and our life spans measurably shorter.[2]

Pain is a sensation that we perceive. It is a complex phenomenon; often when people speak of pain, they use terms like "pain nerve cells" or "pain fibers" in the spinal cord and brain. More properly, we should speak of *nociceptive pathways* (coming from the word "noxious"), which begin with receptors somewhere in the body that respond to noxious, or tissue-damaging, stimuli. The "toe-stubbing" detectors get us out of danger as rapidly as possible and are thus protective. If we have chronic pain that we cannot avoid, we seek relief by changing positions to protect the part that is hurting, or by not moving it, which promotes healing. Of course, pain can go on and on, becoming a major threat to our well-being. All of these aspects of pain make it incumbent upon human beings to avoid or minimize it in the animals we use—whether they are pets, farm animals, or research subjects. In biomedical research, we are legally required and morally obligated to inflict as little pain as possible.

At the same time, we must study pain mechanisms in animals to provide relief for ourselves, which presents difficult choices at times. Studies of acute pain in animals usually can be made easily bearable by allowing the animal to escape the pain when it becomes too uncomfortable; simply allowing the animal to move its tail or paw away from the source of the pain does the trick. The study of chronic pain does not permit that solution, so these studies can and should only be undertaken to understand how to provide relief for real human chronic pain.

The "pain system" is not simple, however; the way in which we experience pain varies with the circumstances. Consider this incredible story from a combat scene:

> He was a raw recruit from Parris Island, taking a beachhead
> in the Pacific. He was scared to death. Heavy enemy fire was
> killing his buddies all around him. When a shell burst

nearby, he felt an excruciating pain and the sensation of
blood pouring down his leg. There was a call for a
corpsman, and he was carried to a medical station, where
doctors discovered he had indeed been hit—on his canteen.
They sent him back out. More shells, more bombs.
Suddenly, he felt a sharp pain on his head, hit the sand,
rolled over, and ran his hand across his forehead. Sure
enough, there was blood. Again they carried him to the
medical station. The doctor took some tweezers, picked out
a few fragments of metal from his face, slapped on some
adhesive bandages and sent him back to fight once more.
By then, almost his entire company had been wiped out.
For the third time, a shell burst near him. It tore off his leg.
He did not feel a thing.[3]

Thus, not only tissue damage determines how we perceive pain. Past experience, our emotional state, the context and nature of the injury—all of these can affect how our brains process pain. Counterintuitively, some general anesthetics working to block consciousness of pain during surgery may at the same time activate peripheral nociceptors, leading to more postsurgical pain in combination with the tissue damage induced by the surgery.[4] Also, anticipation of pain seems to make the experience worse. Systems within the higher regions of the brain can influence what type of pain we experience, or whether we experience it at all. This can have real survival value: a gazelle may be hurting like the devil for some reason, but put that hurt aside when its brain directs it to run away from a charging cheetah. Stress and fear have analgesic (pain relieving) effects. For example, how many times have you heard or read about a professional athlete who played on in a game after an injury, not even thinking about the injury until after the game as over?

Rats exhibit a learned analgesia when confronted with cats or shocks paired with tones. Exposure to aversive stimuli will also induce analgesia in people.[5] Experiments in animals have shown what is going on in the brain in such situations: stimulation of a group of neurons in an area of the rat brain called the midbrain will suppress pain (measured by how high the temperature of a metal plate, on which the rat's tail rests, can rise before the rat whisks its tail off). Interestingly, sensitivity to touch and pressure is unaffected.[6] Stimulation of the same brain region in humans will also suppress pain. The neurons stimulated have receptors that are also stimulated by morphine, and morphine injected on the cells has powerful analgesic effects. As a result of these findings, morphine-like substances called endogenous opiates were discovered in the brain. The activation of these systems by the higher brain areas, put into motion in the situations described above (confrontation with a predator or presentation with a tone previously associated with a shock), provides natural analgesia.

With this explanation I do not aim to dismiss the issue of pain in animals, especially those used in experiments, as inconsequential. My point is that pain is a complex phenomenon, and that it may mean something different to animals than it does to humans. Sometimes the pain experienced by animals might not be as bad as it seems. For example, I have had two abdominal operations that caused me severe pain. My reactions are instructive. After surgery, I found any stretching of my abdomen while moving, coughing, or laughing excruciatingly painful, so I avoided such movements. Relief brought by the administration of a narcotic every 4 hours was heavenly. In light of this experience, watching a dog bouncing around directly after a spay operation has always puzzled me. I can only conclude that she is not thinking very far into the future, as I did lying in my hospital bed thinking of the pain to be experienced (and thereby only making it worse). We humans might add a layer of thought to our pain that animals may not. In fact, when preoperative anxiety in humans is high, postoperative pain is greater.[7] If an animal is handled with care and gently anesthetized—and this is easily done—how could its cognitive processes before surgery affect the degree of pain felt later?

Another example of animals and humans handling pain differently comes from an extraordinary report, offered by philosopher and cognitive scientist Daniel Dennett, from animal-cognition researcher Marc Hauser, about one of our closer animal relatives. Male Rhesus monkeys fight so ferociously during mating season that a winner may bite off a testis of the vanquished monkey, only to have the latter lick his wound and walk away, and then be seen mating a couple of days later. I would be (figuratively) licking my wound many days longer, and cannot imagine I would have much interest in pursuing the mating game for quite some time. As Dennett puts it, "the mind reels to think of it."[8]

Consequently, I find it hard to believe that a laboratory rat with an injured paw sits around thinking about how the pain is going to be just as bad the next day, agonizing over it as we humans would. At the same time, I would like to provide that rat with pain relief if possible, giving it the benefit of the doubt.

The Critical Difference: Animal Cognition

This brings us to the problem of animal cognition. Cognition is a vast and rapidly moving field. While I am hardly an expert in this realm of neuroscience, I can provide some general insights necessary to the question of what justifies our use and even harming of animals that can think to varying degrees.

What, then, is the thinking capacity of animals? In fact, it is considerable. Is there a clear divide, however, between humans and animals that permits our use of animals? Our questions about the thinking capacity of animals have answers based on science, but the ethical issue underlying the second question, that of a clear divide permitting our use of them, overshadows the science, at least in the minds of those involved in the animal rights and liberation movement. For those of us outside that movement the ethical answer concerning our uses of animals is more ambiguous, as the next chapter will illustrate. The ethical positions underlying the movement will be presented in the last chapter.

No scientific evidence refutes the generally accepted idea that we differ mentally in one crucial way: our ability as humans to reflect on our future, and to anticipate our eventual death. If animals had these cognitive abilities, I personally could not use them in ways that would lead to their deaths; certainly, my research career would be over. At the same time, I am unmoved by the idea that in killing animals, when we do it with thought and not carelessly, we deprive them of some ill-defined pleasures in the future that are ethically significant.

Nevertheless, both animals and humans can suffer in this life in ways that transcend mere immediate physical pain brought on by such conditions as extreme heat or cold, starvation, or the prolonged pain induced by a serious wound or an unrepaired broken leg. I am thinking of the suffering that is mental or emotional, particularly that which may go on for the duration of our lives. Although I believe animals can suffer beyond just the physical realm—the anecdotal reports of dogs grieving after their master's death come readily to mind, such as the famous Greyfriar's Bobby who lived around his master's grave for 14 years[9]—there is still a gulf between us and them. Consider the following example: an intelligent young teenager receives a severe blow to the head in a car crash that transforms him from a boy with a bright future into one that must be fed, clothed, and wheeled around by grieving parents for the rest of their lives. Could an animal match these parents' suffering? The capability of experiencing such grief cognitively for the duration of our lives, not to mention the suffering of the patient, is one of the things that I believe separates us from other animals.

This thought was brought home to me a few years ago by a review of a television documentary on the fate of boys from the 1965 graduating class of a Philadelphia high school who were sent to Vietnam. Their class reportedly contributed more of its members to that war than any other. As the father of four sons who were spared the risk of participation in that awful conflict by little more than a decade, tears welled in my eyes as I read the words of a mother spoken nearly 30 years after her son's death: "I pray every night. . . . Let me dream of him. Let me see his face."[10] To me this is suffering of a very high order.

There is no evidence that animals dream at such a high, psychic level. Indeed, the only evidence of observable animal "dreaming" I know of is that of the cats exhibiting REM without atonia, described in Chapter 3. The behaviors observed are rather mundane. People suffering from the strange sleep disturbance called REM sleep behavior disorder (RBD) exhibit complex behaviors that correlate closely with the dreams they later report when awakened.[11] If we can accept that the behavior one observes in the experimental cats is reflecting their dreams, then their "dream life"—and waking life?—is not very imaginative.[12] I have watched hundreds of episodes of REM without atonia. The cat gets up, walks clumsily, and looks around as if it were orienting, yet does not awaken. If the brain damage is in a specific place, the sleeping and dreaming cat may pounce on a "mouse." In other words, in their dreams, cats do exactly what they spend their waking hours doing when they are not eating, grooming, or copulating, which are periods when they are not particularly attentive. So the behavior we see during REM without atonia may well be responses to some of the pictures the cats have filed away in their minds, but not complex thoughts. In this case we have a "window on the sleeping brain" of a cat, just as clinicians do in the case of RBD patients.[13] The "scene" of RBD patients is far more complex and is bolstered by verbal reports consistent with the behaviors observed.

The implication, then, is that there is something crucially different, and much more sophisticated and nuanced, in the way we think, compared to thinking in animals. Of course, this is not easy to determine and is the stuff of much debate. Clive Wynne, a psychologist who examined the question of thinking in animals in his aptly titled book, *Do Animals Think?*,[14] came up with a graphic way of explaining the differences and similarities between animals and humans. Picture each species as a sandwich consisting of three layers. In the middle there is a center layer that is the same from species to species. This middle layer is "like us" (in other words, like us humans) in that, like animals, we all can learn new things and solve problems, although at differing levels of sophistication. Wynne's middle layer is covered in each species by two layers of "not like us." The bottom layer of the sandwich represents each species' unique sensory world and their abilities to operate in it: the smell-filled world of dogs, the sonar world of bats, and the electric and magnetic sensory worlds of some fish, to give a few examples. Then there is the crucial layer topping off Wynne's sandwich. Here we differ from animals mightily: we have language; we think about thinking; we have a concept of ourselves and can look far into the future; we can fear death coming days, weeks, months, and years in the future. Compare a condemned prisoner facing the death penalty with a steer in a feedlot nonchalantly stuffing himself with grain shortly before his trip to the abattoir. The prisoner can think about death even in the abstract—he can *anticipate* suffering and his eventual demise. We have no evidence that a steer or any other animal can do this outside the immediate environment where the smell of blood or sounds of agitated animals probably activate age-old responses that have evolved to warn of danger.

How can we be really sure of this difference between a condemned prisoner and a feedlot steer? There is no evidence that the steer contemplates the abstract concept of death—but is there solid evidence that it does not? Posed another way, how do we know with assurance what *anyone* else is thinking, let alone other species? Philosophers have argued about this problem for ages, so it will not be solved here. All organisms evolved to fit into their particular niches, and humans have developed a capacity to think in the abstract. "The mind is no exception to the facts of natural selection; it makes as little sense to expect that other species should share the uniquely human thought processes of the human mind as it would to expect that we should share an elephant's trunk or a zebra's stripes," writes Steven Budiansky, the author of several popular but well-argued books on various aspects of animal life.[15] Nevertheless, our thinking abilities did not spring de novo from unformed clay. As Franz de Waal, a noted ethologist and zoologist at the Yerkes Regional Primate Research Center at Emory University, aptly put it, "While it is true that animals are not humans, it is equally true that humans are animals."[16]

In Darwin's view, "a moral being is one who is capable of reflecting on his past actions and their motives—of approving of some and disapproving of others; and the fact that man is the one being who certainly deserves this designation, is the greatest of all distinctions between him and the lower animals."[17] There is no evolutionary continuity here in the strictest sense: there is a clear divide between humans and other animals. Nevertheless, even though animals cannot decide what a moral course of action would be in a particular situation, Darwin did recognize that our own moral sense must have had its early beginnings in nonhuman brains:

> The following proposition seems to me in high degree
> probable – namely, that any animal whatever, endowed with
> well-marked social instincts, the parental and filial affections
> being here included, would inevitably acquire a moral sense
> or conscience, as soon as its intellectual powers had become
> as well, or nearly as well developed, as in man.[18]

In the intervening years since this statement, many researchers have explored Darwin's proposition, even relating various behaviors observed in nonprimate species to the Ten Commandments, at least those not referring to a duty to God.[19,20]

de Waal,[21] who has studied human-like behaviors among chimpanzees and bonobos, has also offered evidence of roots of moral behavior in his apes and asks why evolution might cease at the point of developing moral behavior in primates—why can we not find a connection with animals in terms of rudimentary "moral" behaviors? Nevertheless, philosopher Phillip Kitcher adds an important caveat: chimpanzees are wantons, "vulnerable to whichever impulse happens to be dominant at a particular moment."[22] He then speculates that early in hominid evolution, language must have helped us to codify social norms, such as the Ten Commandments, that can put a brake on impulsive behavior for the common good. Animals have no such language.

Marc Hauser[23] seconds Kitcher's speculation and has summed up things nicely, noting that animals "experience emotions that motivate morally relevant actions" and "are endowed with several, if not all of the core principles of action that underlie the infant's initial state," but they are "remarkably impulsive, exhibiting little control in the face of temptation" and cannot delay "gratification in the context of helping another at a personal cost." The Congressional Medal of Honor would be out of their grasp, for animals do not act unselfishly in this sense. Their survival depends on looking out for Number 1. An obvious exception to this conclusion, though, is a mother's defense of its offspring in danger, whether the mother is a rat or a human.

Before continuing to explore the minds of animals, however, it is wise to heed the following advice from Gordon Burghardt: "Let us retain an open-minded delight in animal abilities, a respect for what they *may* be experiencing, and a balance between skepticism and incredulity. And we must not forget, nor ignore, the use, or misuse, to which our findings will be put in the growing debate on the treatment of our fellow creatures."[24]

Burghardt's request relates well to the evolution of my thinking on the animal rights controversy that has consumed so much of my career. Each of us has to decide what he or she finds acceptable in using animals of certain (or uncertain?) capability, and we must recognize that there can be honest disagreement. Those possibilities will be considered in the next chapter. Where one can draw a firm line of unabashed disagreement is when one's own position is represented untruthfully. The issue of the usefulness of biomedical research comes readily to mind in this context.

But to what extent might an animal think complex thoughts? A good starting point (a favorite in any discussion of animal cognition) is Clever Hans, the famous horse of the early 1900s that exhibited an extraordinary ability to solve arithmetic problems. Paradoxically, the story of Clever Hans has been used to argue against the idea that animals think, which is not my purpose here. Hans could add, subtract, multiply, and divide when his trainer presented him with problems of varying difficulty. Hans tapped out his answer with his forefoot. He did as well with difficult problems as he did with simple ones. Even strangers could present him with a problem, and Hans would respond correctly. But he fooled everyone—or, more appropriately perhaps, everyone was fooled. In 1907, psychologist Oscar Pfungt demonstrated what Hans was doing: the horse detected minute cues that his questioners unconsciously gave when Hans reached the right answer. Pfungt devised a very simple test: keep the questioner out of Hans's view. Hans failed the test every time. The explanation is simple: as prey animals on the open plains, horses evolved with an extraordinary sensitivity to visual cues. As a result of this evolutionary history, Hans could detect a slight change in body language of the questioner that escaped the notice of his examiners.[25]

Some thinkers reject all possibility of complexity in animal thinking because of past errors made in attributing *too much* sophistication to an animal's cognitive abilities. Donald Griffin and other strong proponents of thinking ability in animals have attacked this total denial as a return to the attitude of the Behaviorists, who would not acknowledge anything as subjective as thinking as they quantified the behavior of animals because thoughts could not be measured, discussed more fully in Chapter 4. But as Budiansky points out,

> No scientist ever suggested that Clever Hans hadn't *learned*. He certainly had learned. He just hadn't learned what the quick-to-anthropomorphize humans *thought* he had learned. The reason that most behavioral researchers reject anthropomorphism [interpreting animal actions as if they demonstrated human-like thought processes] is precisely because it offers a pat explanation that lets researchers off the hook from probing deeper for alternative explanations or confounding variables. Imputing reason and understanding seemed to explain Clever Han's behavior perfectly; why look further? [26]

Budiansky might be right in this particular case, but anthropomorphizing, carefully done, can help a scientist "enter" an animal's mind. Inferring something about an animal's mental state would be what Burghardt[27] would call "critical anthropomorphism." This can be done by a scientist who designs experiments on the basis of knowledge of an animal's natural history and normal behavior. Modern behavioral researchers, myself included, do not shy away from this trick, although at the beginning of my career there was strong pressure to avoid doing so. For example, we think of what might disturb our sleep and then put a rat in a similar situation that we assume makes it experience fear at some level, such as hearing a tone that earlier had been paired with an unpleasant electrical shock. Certainly, a hunter, an amateur ethologist really, tries to place himself in the mind of a deer he is stalking, even if he not aware he is anthropomorphizing, asking, "What would I do now if I were that deer—head for water or seek out browse? Where, then, should I lie in wait?"

de Waal[28] characterized "this use of [critical] anthropomorphism as a means to get at the truth, rather than as end in itself" to separate this tool from the uncritical anthropomorphism one can find in the popular literature. He gives an example of the latter, taken from *The Hidden Life of Dogs*.[29] Faced with a gang of dogs, author Marshall Thomas says her own dog's eyes exhibited "no anger, no fear, no threat, no show of aggression, just clarity and overwhelming determination." "Determination" and probably "clarity" are the uncritical part of Thomas's observation.

But what does go through an animal's mind as it performs some complicated task? How can a being think without assigning words during the task? Deaf and blind from a disease at 19 months of age, Helen Keller's human brain contained the elements for thoughts and speech that eventually emerge in children in all societies.[30] The gifted teacher, Anne Sullivan Macy, exploited these elements, enabling Helen to enter the world of speech, ultimately becoming a passionate public speaker on various social issues.[31] Helen Keller's (and our) brain organization is simply wanting in animals.

It is difficult for me to imagine life completely without reflective thought with words. Thus, Buster and I walk in the garden thinking in quite different ways, but not always. Upon reflection, we humans do go through life doing many things and even looking at various objects around us without deep thought. I can see the trees and shrubs in the garden as we walk and not name them as such in my mind. They obviously register at a certain level in my brain because my eyes' retinas capture the images, but just as a background to whatever is really on my mind. Should a bird or a dog suddenly appear, both Buster and I would hesitate if we were moving and turn our heads toward the intruder. In such a situation we are both at the mercy of the orienting reflex, discussed in Chapter 3. Buster and I do not need to decide deliberately to stop, turn our heads, and look at the dog or the bird; this happens instinctively with both of us. How we think of that intruder is at the crux of the matter: how were we each conscious of that intruder?

As I struggled to understand what we mean by "consciousness," I found the writings of Björn Merker, a Swedish neuroscientist with training in psychology from M.I.T. and a long interest in brain mechanisms of consciousness, very useful. He writes, "To the extent that any percept, simple or sophisticated, is experienced, it is conscious, and similarly for any feeling, even if vague, or any impulse to action, however inchoate. This agrees well with the type of dictionary definition that renders consciousness as 'the state or activity that is characterized by sensation, emotion, volition or thought.'"[32] And, further: "Accordingly, to see, hear, to feel or otherwise to experience something is to be conscious, irrespective of whether in addition one is aware that one is seeing, hearing, etc." Merker then added,

> Additional awareness, in reflective consciousness or
> self-consciousness, is one of many contents of consciousness
> available to creatures with sophisticated cognitive capacities
> [such as humans]. . . . However. . . even in their case it is
> present only intermittingly, in a kind of time-sharing with
> more immediate, unreflective experience. To dwell in the
> latter is not to fall unconscious, but to be unselfconsciously
> conscious. Reflective awareness is thus more akin to a
> luxury of consciousness on the part of certain big-brained
> species, and not its defining property [consciousness].[33]

It is this last capacity that I suspect the average layperson understands to be "consciousness."

To understand more about how Buster might think without language, I turn to Temple Grandin,[34] who opened my eyes to a real possibility, if not a probability: animals may think in pictures or smells or other stimuli that humans cannot perceive. Their "vocabulary" differs from ours, but is no less useful in many situations and can even surpass ours in usefulness. If you want to know who has visited the house in your absence, you would do well to have the olfactory acuity of a dog.

Temple Grandin is a remarkable woman. A professor of animal science at Colorado State with a Ph.D. in animal science from the University of Illinois, Grandin has a form of autism known as Asperger's syndrome. She sees the world in a way that most people do not, for she relies on pictures more than words in order to function in life. While most people generalize everything that they perceive to a degree that removes sharpness of detail from their surroundings, Grandin says she is like animals—acutely attuned to tiny details that can mean life or death for an animal.

She has used this special ability to carve out an important role: she is famous for designing slaughterhouses that enable animals to move through chutes without becoming upset. How does she do it? She observes "obvious" details in their environment that would spook an animal, but that animal handlers overlook—a windmill suddenly turning in a breeze, contrasts between darkness and bright sunlight, and many other details to which animals are attuned as if their lives depended on them. In fact, that is the case, for animals' lives do depend on attending to details, particularly in the wild. Those who do not are left behind by evolution, prevented from passing their substandard inattentive genes on to the next generation. Think of Clever Hans, who fooled audiences for years with his mathematical abilities. Animals must always be attentive to the world around them because for animals in the wild, life is always dangerous. Either they are eaten as prey because they have not been attentive enough or they go hungry as predators, for the same reason. Eating, avoiding being eaten, and resting, with time out for procreation, is an animal's life until it dies—frequently not gently, and absent any of the palliative medical care we provide our domestic animals. Of course, humans experience a more sophisticated, varied life.

Giorgio Vallortigara, a cognitive neuroscientist from the University of Trento, Italy, and several colleagues from other universities have taken issue with some of Grandin's conclusions about animal minds, in an excellent review of cognitive abilities of birds.[35] Germane to the hypothesis presented by Grandin, that animals depend on fine details rather than the bigger picture, they argue that there is varied evidence that animals operate in a world of global contexts as well as specific details. For example, food-storing birds are extraordinary in their ability to remember numerous food caches. One of these, Clark's nutcracker, can remember thousands of food caches it has stored.

In a sidebar to the article, Grandin responded:

> I think the basic disagreement between the authors and me
> arises from the concept of details—specifically how details
> are perceived by humans, who think in language, compared
> with animals, who think in sensory-based data. Since
> animals do not have verbal language, they have to store
> memories as pictures, sounds, or other sensory impressions.
> Sensory-based information by its very nature is more
> detailed than word-based memories.[36]

As a sleep researcher, I know well that individuals can perform complex acts without being aware of what they are doing, and then have no memory of their actions later on. We say in these instances that the individual is in a "dissociated" state, with a brain directing complex acts while the individual is totally unaware of his or her actions. A man in Canada drove 40 miles while in this state and killed his mother-in-law with no apparent motive. He was known to be very close to her, and relatives so testified. A jury acquitted him. A similar situation resulted in a life sentence in Texas, even though the situation was comparable and certainly believable to me and to the expert witness for the defense, the eminent sleep researcher Rosalind Cartwright.[37] Is this what it is like to be Buster when on the prowl? Is he in a dissociated state, not thinking in some fashion about what he is doing?

Of course not, Donald Griffin would argue. Griffin is a leading researcher on echolocation in bats and the pioneering proponent of the idea that animals are not mindless creatures. "The customary view of animals always living in a state comparable to that of human sleepwalkers is a sort of negative dogmatism. We know far too little to judge with confidence when animals are or are not conscious, and it is just as difficult to disprove as to prove that a particular animal is thinking consciously."[38]

I agree with Griffin if "consciousness" is used in Merker's sense, but the possibility that an animal can think to any degree approaching a human's complex thoughts without putting thoughts into words is just inconceivable to me. Griffin, perhaps without realizing it, illustrated this point in expressing the concern that too many people point to the Clever Hans story as a way of rejecting the idea of animal cognition. Griffin says, "What has been almost totally overlooked is the real possibility that Clever Hans was consciously thinking something simple but directly relevant to his situation—perhaps something like, 'I must tap my foot when that man nods his head.'"[39] Note, however, that Griffin had to put human words into Hans's head to make his point. Hans's brain had all the information that "told" him that a movement on the part of the experimenter would lead to a treat if he stopped "counting." This he had learned over time, but he had no words to express his brain's state. It was at a level of consciousness that could not reach ours without language. Merker's generous definition of "consciousness" seems to cover this behavior.

Griffin has amassed many examples of fascinating behaviors that he believes demonstrate that animals, from fireflies to whales to apes, engage in conscious behavior. How can they be thinking without words, though? Certainly the brain activity of animals measured by a variety of means is similar to that of humans. For example, the EEG that reveals the various stages of sleep and wakefulness in a cat, as described in Chapter 3, is quite similar to that of humans in comparable stages. This is not surprising, for the microscopic structure of human and mammalian brains, the arrangements of neurons in particular patterns, for example, is identical in various regions. It is the massive increase in key parts of the brain, particularly the frontal lobes, and not necessarily the absolute size that makes the difference.

I think that sensory patterns in animals' worlds, a là Temple Grandin, must combine with memories of a host of situations common to their environments that form "thoughts." It is the idea of thoughts without words that seems to be the sticking point between the various philosophers and scientists arrayed on either side of the divide: conscious animals versus unconscious animals, and their definition of "consciouness." Through words we learn about the future and the past, either from books or through talking with others. Animals can't benefit from bull sessions.

To better understand some of the workings of memory, my laboratory is studying the effect on rats' sleep of a mild aversive stimulus (five shocks to the foot, comparable to touching something metal on a cold, dry day, or something unpleasant) combined with tones of a certain pitch and loudness or a particular environment. We are interested in understanding the mechanisms behind memories set up by unpleasant, even horrific, events as they affect quality of sleep. Our hope is to understand the sleep disturbances in post-traumatic stress disorder.

Rats will have disturbed sleep when presented with the tones alone before their sleep period or when sleeping in the environment associated with the shocks, even many days after the initial training session that incorporated the electric shocks.[40,41] So rats clearly have memories. How those memories are consciously perceived and what the rats might think about them is the big question. Tones or the dangerous environment evoke a memory of "bad" that "upsets" the rat enough that it freezes when awake and sleeps poorly. It is not reflecting on the fact that it is upset, however.

Humans have the unique ability to ruminate about negative events long after they are over. It seems unlikely that rodents have a similar ability, although it would be an interesting question to explore. A human can cause a whole cascade of physiological changes, such as stress hormone release, blood pressure increases, and the like, simply by *thinking* about a negative situation or event.[42] Consider someone going through a painful divorce. The actual stress-inducing events (like court dates) are relatively rare, although constantly thinking about the dramatic changes in one's life can cause changes in the body for months, and even lead to illness. A rat only exhibits these changes during the event itself or to a discrete reminder (cue) of the event. It may be one example of how our highly evolved frontal cortex and its amazing memory capacity do not necessarily always benefit us.

Nevertheless, predators that hunt in packs (or prides in the case of lions) do remarkable things in "organizing" their hunts. Griffin[43] points us to philosopher John Searle regarding lions on the hunt:

> Consider the case of an animal, say a lion, moving in an
> erratic path through the tall grass. The behavior of the lion is

> explicable by saying that it is stalking a wildebeest, its prey.
> The stalking behavior is caused by a set of intentional states:
> it is *hungry,* it *wants* to eat the wildebeest, it *intends* to
> follow the wildebeest with the *aim* of catching, killing, and
> eating it. . . . To be in an "intentional" state is to host a
> mental representation, a brain state that bears a natural
> (causal and teleological) relation to the object represented
> or, in the case of abstract or nonexistent objects, to linguistic
> events that go proxy for them [for "linguistic" read "animal
> calls" here].[44]

In other words, Searle is saying that the brain of the lion is at that moment organized by sensations of hunger and the memory of what eating the wildebeest will do to satisfy its hunger. As a result, the lion is driven to kill. The sounds ("linguistic" events) of other lions feasting on a wildebeest would change the lion's brain state to search out that other kill. Lions hunt in a group that seems organized to hunt down a prey animal by placing themselves in formation in the vicinity of the prey. Remember, though, that these animals are the result of thousands of years of evolutionary honing, so that as successful survivors of the honing process, they must be acutely attuned to the postures and movements of other lions, not to mention their relative distances from the prey they can see and smell. They have memories of rewarding events in the form of pictures (according to Temple Grandin) of successful formations, aided by auditory and olfactory "pictures." Those are their "thoughts" as they operate without reflection on what they are doing, as I conceive of it.

Griffin proposed further that animals could have an imaginary life as we do. "Insofar as animals think and feel, they may fear imaginary predators, imagine unrealistically delicious foods, or think about objects and events that do not actually exist in the world around them."[45] With this last example he went too far, in my view. He suggested that the study of dreams and the pattern of rapid eye movements characteristic of REM sleep might be an avenue into an animal's imaginary life. But despite some early reports of human dreams and their concordance with eye movements, this approach ultimately proved to be fruitless in the study of normal people and certainly would not help in understanding animal thoughts in sleep.[46] Certainly the cats exhibiting REM without atonia do not have very interesting "dreams."

These discussions illustrate quite well the bottom and middle layers of Wynne's sandwich. A horse's perceptual ability at picking up minute visual cues far surpasses ours; that is its evolutionary domain in the bottom layer. Our survival as humans no longer depends on such heightened perception, so we no longer possess that ability; we are not very adept in the bottom layer compared to animals that depend on environmental cues. We are similar, though (this is the middle layer), in that both people and horses can learn, although we learn at vastly different levels of sophistication.

We have all evolved in ways that make it easy for us to learn some things and not others. For example, a dog quickly learns what the rattle in the food bowl means. But just try to teach it how to unravel a leash wrapped around a pole. Leashes were not in its evolving environment until very recently, but odors and the noises prey make were. Dogs as a species are also not likely to evolve such that they can figure out how to untangle their leashes because their survival in the distant past did not depend on being able to do so.

Dennett makes a wise comment on this point:

> People [who recount wonders in their dogs' behavior] are
> less fond of telling tales of draw-dropping stupidity in their
> pets, and often resist the implications of the gaps they find
> in their pets' competences. . . . And dolphins, for all their
> intelligence, are strangely unable to figure out that they
> could easily leap over the surrounding tuna net to safety.
> Leaping out of the water is hardly an unnatural act for them,
> which makes their obtuseness all the more arresting. . . .
> The ability of animals to generalize from their particular
> exploitations of wisdom is severely limited.[47]

When thinking about killing animals, such as for food or at the end of a research project, it is the top layer of Wynne's sandwich, the one that separates our thinking abilities from those of animals, that is relevant. As noted earlier, provided we have made an animal as comfortable as possible during its lifetime (if it is under our control), its death should not present an ethical or moral problem, as long as it cannot contemplate its future.

Contemplation of a future first requires a grasp of the concept of "future." In turn, in order to grasp such concepts, the ability to assign words to them is required, as well as to learn in one way or another what nature has in store. To think about the future; to reflect on it; to think about reflecting on it as I am doing while writing these words all call for language (language and communication not being one and the same). Only humans have such a sophisticated form of communication. Significantly, we are the only species that spontaneously learns a new language if in the company of those speaking it. Nevertheless, the middle layer of Wynne's sandwich, the one that all creatures share, is getting thicker as we learn more about the thinking abilities of animals.[48] Perhaps as work continues the top layer of Wynne's sandwich will become proportionately thinner.

The Great Ape Project

In terms of cognitive ability, what can we say about some of our closer relatives, chimpanzees and the more recently recognized bonobos? Much has been made of their intelligence and rightly so, for they are smart animals. Unfortunately, their intellectual capacities have been introduced to the political arena, in part as evidence of their phylogenetic closeness to humans. In this context high stakes are involved, because any suggestion that humans are not unique in one way or another (other than being members of a single species) could be construed as a victory for the animal rights movement, in their eyes at least, rather than as an appreciation of the wonders of the animal world.

Those interested in such a "victory" may be found among the contributors to *The Great Ape Project*.[49] Edited by Paola Cavalieri and Peter Singer, the book is an eclectic collection of essays ranging from philosophy to science fiction, all arguing on behalf of A Declaration on Great Apes, which mimics the 1948 U.N Declaration on Human Rights.

Before discussing this interesting and provocative idea further, we need to understand the term *great ape*. Great apes, which include chimpanzees, bonobos, gorillas, and orangutans, are members of the family *Hominidae*, subfamily *Ponginae*. Humans are of the same family but are members of the subfamily *Homininae*, although some now try to squeeze us into the "great ape family," clearly for political reasons. But our ancestors parted ways from the *Ponginae* several million years ago.[50] After that subdivision and along our way to becoming modern humans, we left behind quite a few relatives that were more closely related to us then than chimps are now.

Great ape is really a popular term and not a scientific one in the strictest sense—think of dogs, which have the scientific designation, *Canis familiaris*, or cats, *Felis cattus*, in contrast to one that appears throughout the nineteenth century with "great" as an adjective. This usage appeared as far back as 1832 in a bizarre, fanciful tale, *Dennis Read*. A monkey appeared in the story and was also referred to as "the great ape" in passing.[51] In the *New York Times* on March 25, 1883, a discussion of orangutans, chimpanzees, and gorillas referred to these animals as anthropoids and then as "a great ape" as a morphological descriptor.[52]

A famous pair of primatologists, the Yerkes, wrote a magnificent tome called *The Great Apes* in 1929,[53] but throughout the book they used the term *anthropoid* rather than *great ape*, just as I did during my schoolboy years.

Nevertheless, primatologists now quite commonly use *great ape* to distinguish chimps, gorillas, and orangs from lesser apes, such as gibbons. Making humans great apes by fiat, as in the opening sentence of the Declaration on Great Apes ("We demand the extension of the community of equals to include all great apes: human beings, chimpanzees, gorillas and orang-utans")[54] does not make them so.

The Declaration on Great Apes consists of three far-reaching statements. The first is the right to life: "Members of the community of equals may not be killed" except in special circumstances, such as in self-defense. The second provision is "the protection of individual liberty," with all the privileges accorded humans in our Western system of justice. The third prohibits torture, aimed rather obviously at biomedical research, with the assumption that use of animals in biomedical research is torture.

To put it bluntly, I think the Declaration is wrong-headed and even dangerous. Lumping us together with apes is not a scientific claim, of course; the interest here is not scientific but rather political and looks to the future. There is a moral difference between humans and apes that is dismissed by this project. Simply put, we care about the survival of apes; they are incapable of caring about ours. We can take responsibility for them; they cannot reciprocate. In my view, the claim of human rights for animals carries the great danger of diminishing rights for humans, particularly for the weakest among us. The views of the various animal rights and liberation philosophers would result in just that, were they to gain the upper hand. It is much safer to focus on humane care and use of any animal.

Regarding the rights proposed in the Great Ape Project, Franz de Waal has commented that "many of the sentiments and cognitive abilities underlying human morality" are exhibited by other animals, a point discussed earlier. At the same time, however, he explicitly draws the line at animal rights:

> I must express discomfort with attempts to phrase these issues *in terms of rights.* . . . The ultimate result is a call for the abolition of all use of all animals under all circumstances, from hunting to meat consumption, from keeping them in zoos to having them work on the farm. In the process, we sometimes ignore our first obligation, *which is to fellow human beings* (emphases added).[55]

His thoughts second the central theme of this book.

de Waal rightly observed that the proposal is quite condescending. Aren't we really treating apes here as mentally challenged humans? Would we then think of baboons as being like retarded apes? Can we not appreciate them for what they are: magnificent animals with amazing physical and mental abilities? How nice it would be if we could simply admit that we must think seriously about the welfare of the animals, consider carefully to what use they might be put, and do something about it without needing to respond to proposals that go beyond the bounds of reasonableness, as de Waal and I see them. Those sponsoring the project have a political agenda that goes far beyond welfare.

de Waal has studied chimpanzees for many years, respecting them, even loving them, I suspect, and yet he does not buy into *The Great Ape Project*. Jane Goodall, on the other hand, is a signatory. Her strong love for the animals she has studied for so long has led her over the boundary that I believe we should not cross: bringing the great apes into our human moral community. I sympathize with her sentiments, for I am a great admirer of cats, all cats: tigers, lions, cheetahs, house cats. I have studied them for many years and know much about them. Buster has proven to me over and over again that cats can be quite affectionate, not unlike some of the chimps Goodall describes. Yet, unlike Goodall with her chimps, I have (with reluctance) harmed my animals. There was a choice to be made, and I made it in favor of medical progress, on behalf of my fellow humans. In retrospect, it was not an easy choice to make, but one that was justified, in my opinion.

We cannot abandon biomedical research that uses chimpanzees, even while we seek to minimize their use and ensure the best treatment for them. The day we can stop using them in medical research without surrendering the acquisition of important knowledge will be a good day. de Waal has expressed a similar opinion in *Good Natured*.[56] Without question, however, research on primates in general and on chimpanzees in particular is critical to future medical progress, as emphasized by VandeBerg and colleagues in an article in *Nature*. According to these authors, there is a continuing need for chimpanzees in certain types of disease research. They warn that the resource is dwindling, thanks to a moratorium on further breeding because of a fear of overpopulation:

> For example, the need for chimpanzees to test monoclonal-antibody therapies is rapidly increasing as more antibodies are designed. Monoclonal antibodies, genetically engineered to be almost identical to human antibodies, hold great promise for treating cancer; autoimmune diseases, such as rheumatoid arthritis, lupus erythematosis, multiple sclerosis, psoriasis and Chron's disease; asthma, poisoning and septicemia, and virtually any disease caused by viral infection.... Many of the biological receptors targeted by

these antibodies are present only on chimpanzee and
human cells.[57]

The last example is important to me because I have a loved one who has
benefited from just such an antibody in her fight against a form of lymphoma.

The prohibition of torture, the third point in the Declaration on Great Apes,
is problematic, for it assumes that properly conducted research is torture.
Wesley Smith, a lawyer and writer greatly concerned that the animal rights
movement endangers human welfare and human exceptionalism, has made the
following point:

> Of course, such a right would only apply against humans.
> If a pack of chimpanzees attacked another pack, torturing
> and killing, as sometimes happens—no one would suggest
> that they be "punished" for the "crime," since no crime
> would have occurred. If humans did that, it would be
> immoral and criminal, not only because of the pain caused
> to the animals but because the act amounts to lower than
> human action.… Of course, we should punish any human
> who tortures an animal. That is because we are the only
> beings in the known universe who can—and should—be
> held accountable for our actions.[58]

More criticism comes from Jonathan Marks, a biological anthropologist
from the University of North Carolina, who reviewed *The Great Ape Project*
rather negatively. He summed up the project in an essay that was critical on a
number of points: the science presented, the idea that genetic closeness should
dictate the awarding of rights, claims of mistreatment in laboratories based on
conditions from decades ago as if they were today's, and neglect of the moral
imperative of human illness. "Empathetic treatment of apes?" he writes, "Self-
evident! Human rights for apes? An idea born of decadence and misanthropy."[59]

These are strong words. What motivated Marks to write them? Beyond the
poor quality of the science and the misleading claims about current research
practices in *The Great Ape Project*, Marks and his colleague Nora Groce, also an
anthropologist, from Yale, expanded on Marks's recognition of "decadence and
misanthropy" in the book, observing the "ominous undercurrents of eugenics
in action," the subtitle of a recent article. They declare,

> we do not allot rights on the basis of genetic distance. If the
> apes merit "human rights," an obvious question is what is

meant by "human." To the extent that the question is
answerable zoologically as participation in a reproductive
community, gene pool, or evolutionary lineage called *Homo
sapiens*, then the central claim would simply be irrational.
Apes cannot get human rights since they are not human.[60]

An editorial in the *New Scientist* summed up the foolishness of assigning rights
on the basis of genetic closeness to humans:

> Unfortunately, it has become fashionable to stress that
> chimpanzees and humans must have staggeringly similar
> psychologies because they share 98.4 per cent of their DNA.
> But this misses the point: genomes are not cake recipes.
> A few tiny changes in a handful of genes controlling the
> development of the [cerebral] cortex could easily have a
> disproportionate impact. A creature that shares 98.4 per cent
> of its DNA with humans is not 98.4 per cent human, any
> more than a fish that shares, say, 40 per cent of its DNA with
> us is 40 per cent human.[61]

More is at stake in the eyes of Marks and Groce, however: the danger of
loose talk comparing mentally handicapped humans with healthy apes capable
of living unaided lives and (with human help) attaining the achievements of a
child of age 2 or so. After a review of the deplorable actions of the eugenics
movement that reached its apogee with the Nazis, they bring us to the present
with this quote from Singer:

> Once we ask why it should be that all human beings—
> including infants, the intellectually disabled, criminal
> psychopaths, Hitler, Stalin and the rest—have some kind of
> dignity or worth that no elephant, pig or chimpanzee can
> ever achieve, we see the question is as difficult to answer as
> our original request for some relevant fact that justified the
> inequities of humans and other animals.[62]

The lumping together of infants and the mentally impaired with outright
criminals that society would no longer accept as their own is a dangerous step
that Groce and Marks would not take. They end their criticism of *The Great Ape
Project* with these words: "It is a perverse sense of morality, indeed, that seeks

to blur the boundary between apes and people by dehumanizing those for whom rights are often the most precarious."[63]

Wesley Smith sees the same danger, and I agree with him. In a magnificent statement responding to a resolution to follow the tenets of the Great Ape Project, passed by the Spanish parliament, the first government to do so,[64] and which its proponents gleefully predicted would break the "species barrier," Smith affirms the importance of human exceptionalism:

> And why break the species barrier? Why, to destroy the
> unique status of man and thus initiate a wholesale
> transformation of Western civilization. Specifically,
> by including animals in the "community of equals" and in
> effect declaring apes to be persons, the Great Ape Project
> would break the spine of Judeo-Christian moral philosophy,
> which holds that humans enjoy equal and incalculable
> moral worth, regardless of our respective capacities, age, and
> state of health. Once man is demoted to merely another
> animal in the forest, universal human rights will have to be
> tossed out and new criteria devised to determine which
> human/animal lives matter and which individuals can be
> treated like, well, animals.... [I]n the world that would rise
> from the ashes of human exceptionalism, moral value would
> be subjective and rights temporary, depending on the extent
> of each animal's individual capacities at the time of
> measuring.... Thus, if we truly want to make this a better
> and more humane world, the answer is not to think of
> ourselves as inhabiting the same moral plane as animals—
> none of which can even begin to comprehend rights. Rather,
> it is to embrace the unique importance of being human.
> After all, if not our humanity, what gives rise to our duty to
> treat animals properly and to act toward each other in
> accordance with what is—the Great Ape Project
> notwithstanding—our exclusive membership in a
> community of equals?[65]

A final note on *The Great Ape Project*: philosopher Lily-Marlene Russow put an interesting twist on the ethics of the project itself in referring to various essays that depended on linguistic capabilities as a measure of intelligence and, therefore, eligibility for rights. "All of these research projects would be morally very dubious, and virtually all would be judged unacceptable, under the terms of the declaration. This, of course, raises the 'tainted data' problem: Can one legitimately use data from experiments that are judged to be morally despicable?"[66] This ethical question was not raised in the excitement to produce this declaration. In other words, Russow points out that the apes are experimental subjects used without their consent, and they might well prefer being in a compatible group of their peers doing what comes naturally. One can look at it another way, however. Their sympathetic scientist-handlers are giving them an opportunity to enter a more intellectual world, in a sense, to move beyond their species. They can't move them into ours, of course.

Let me hasten to add that in spite of my criticisms of *The Great Ape Project* I am very sympathetic to the plight of endangered apes in the wild and to their treatment when they are in our hands. And as discussed in Chapter 9, there are nuances in the term *animal rights* that I recognize. My concern is that these animals are being used as pawns in a political game that is much bigger than the Great Ape Project, the end move being to prevent the use of animals in research—all animals, not just primates.

Chimpanzee Intelligence

Just how smart are chimpanzees?—as if that were the determining factor that would "allow" them into our moral community, something de Waal and I deny. The issue of community will be addressed in the last chapter; here it is pertinent to discuss another issue that encourages thoughts of bringing apes and humans into one moral community: language.

Early attempts to teach chimps to speak English failed because of the structural features of their throat. So researchers turned ingeniously to American Sign Language to teach a chimp named Washoe to "speak." But claims of impressive results have turned out to be tainted by wishful thinking. One researcher, Herbert Terrace, abandoned his initial belief that he had succeeded with a chimp he whimsically named Nim Chimpsky. Terrace was poking some fun at the very prominent linguist, Noam Chomsky, who argued that language was unique to humans. Nim had learned only 125 words in 3 years to Washoe's 132 in 4 years.[67]

Because Terrace did not have the funds to maintain Nim, he had turned the chimp over to others for study and then sat down to analyze the many hours of videotape he had collected. He found that "Nim often exploited the signs used in the question to formulate his answer. Furthermore, analysis of the tapes uncovered an unconscious tendency on the part of the human signer, while waiting for the response, to offer Nim the signs that he would need for it,"[68] as in the case of Clever Hans. Unlike human children, Nim never showed a spurt of language development typical of a 2-year-old child. The average length of an utterance was a little over one word; longer "sentences" were internally repetitious; and the words expressed wants and were not used to name things spontaneously. This pattern reflects the simpler form of associative learning that Wynne puts in the "similarity middle" of his sandwich. When Terrace and his colleagues analyzed publicly available tapes of the performances of Wahshoe and the gorilla, Koko, they found the same experimental errors and generous interpretations of results that had marred his own study.[69]

Presently, much is being made of the accomplishments of a bonobo named Kanzi. His trainer, Sue Savage-Rumbaugh, uses lexigrams instead of American Sign Language in order to distinguish between use of a symbol and under-standing of its symbolic meaning. Lexigrams are geometric shapes appearing on a computer screen or as plastic tiles. Kanzi actually learned while attending the training sessions of his mother, who did not learn, which is certainly impres-sive. Kanzi works for rewards, though, producing sentences because he wants something. Indeed,

> 96% of Kanzi's utterances take the form of demands for food, toys, tickles, or other activities. . . . [T]hat fact alone implies something fundamentally different about what Kanzi is understanding and what a human child is. . . . Children will say "red" or "plane" or "cat" in circumstances where they show no interest at all in obtaining the object referred to. Uttering the name is the goal in itself. The behavior appears spontaneously at around nine or ten months.[70]

Marc Hauser, on the other hand, is more generous in his assessment of Kanzi's abilities, while recognizing that Kanzi still falls short. He asks, "Why don't bonobos use their capacity for reference and syntax to communicate with each other naturally?"[71] Although he acknowledges that we may not have looked carefully enough, he notes that even Savage-Rumbaugh has yet to come up with a single example.

Wynne really got to the heart of this issue, asking, "Why should evolution have led to nonhumans that can communicate with humans [in any meaning-ful way]?"[72] He argues that banking on genetic relatedness to determine whether a species can talk with us or not misses the point. There has been no evolution-ary pressure for chimps to be able to communicate with us. If anything, it would be dogs, a species that has long lived with us for a very long time, that would have undergone such pressure.[73] We interact with dogs so much that we almost humanize them, bringing them into our fold. No one can pressure cats into anything, of course; Buster goes his own way.

And do we really have to introduce our anthropocentric views into their lives? Why is it so important for animals to be like us (other than to advance an agenda and forestall their use in research)? Why should we expect animals that diverged from our phylogenetic line so many years ago to evolve in an identical, parallel path, rather than adapting to their way of living quite well?

Again, Wynne summarizes the situation beautifully:

> We are not magical beasts but ordinary, mortal beings.
> Our history has led us to the development of certain skills,
> of which language stands out as especially important in
> understanding what makes us different. . . . It is the
> possession of language, self-awareness, and awareness that
> others have minds too that makes it plausible for us to have
> rights and responsibilities. Absent these qualities, arguing
> for animal rights makes as much sense as advocating
> bicycles for fish.[74]

Nevertheless, trying to determine just how well an animal can learn to "talk" is a very human thing to do. We humans desperately want to communicate with the "others," I believe. (We also tend to inflict our own values and beliefs on others—animal and human alike—regardless of that being's level of interest in our way of life.) I mentioned earlier how I wished I knew what was in little Buster's mind as he stood on my chest, staring into my eyes. I can just imagine what it is like to stare into a chimp's eyes. I think it is a fascinating kind of research to pursue. Just keep the innocent apes out of politics and try to take care of them as well as possible when they are under our control. When in the wild, they will decide for themselves how to treat other chimps.

I should note here that research is now revealing a greater ability in animals to surmise what another animal might be intending than was previously thought. This includes remarkable abilities recognized in birds.[75] Two Cambridge ethologists, Nathan Emery and Nicola Clayton, conclude a fascinating article comparing the cognitive abilities of birds with those of primates as follows:

> In this chapter, we have described how some of the
> supposed "uniqueness" of primates in the structure of their
> brains and their advanced cognitive abilities are also present

in a number of bird species, primarily the corvids and parrots. . . . We have also demonstrated that some of the bastions of primate intelligence: tool use, insight, symbolic communication, social learning, mental attribution, and mental time travel, are also present in similar degrees to the primates, and in some cases surpass the available evidence for primates. We suggest that this may largely stem from a lack of research in avian cognition, a primocentric view of animal cognition inherent from the field of anthropology, and a paucity of studies in primate cognition that utilizes EEA, the ecological/ethological approach.[76]

Nevertheless, chimps, gorillas, and orangutans have long been known to be very intelligent animals. What levels of intelligence they achieve, however, is a matter of debate even among experts, as reflected in the introduction to a wonderful but complex book that explores the minds of apes, *Reaching Into Thought: The Minds of the Great Apes,* by two of the editors, Anne Russon and Kim Baird:

> Our contributors do not themselves agree on the intellectual scope of great apes. Some argue that great apes do not attain the highest level abilities except when raised with intensive human tutoring; others, that their most complex abilities are attained in the wild. Neither is the distinction between great ape and monkey intelligence well established.[77]

Daniel Povinelli, a researcher at the University of Louisiana who is pursuing the question of whether other species, apes in particular, can reason about the mental states of others, urges young researchers to always keep an open mind:

> Realize that the scholar who doubts that chimpanzees have a "theory of mind" system, and the scholar who doubts that it is a uniquely human trait, are both skeptics, and that without skepticism there can be no such thing as science. . . . And most of all, do not be afraid of differences if that is where the evidence leads you. Differences among species are real. They're what evolution is all about.[78]

This statement is reminiscent of Gordon Burghardt's generous wish regarding animal mentation in general. Unfortunately, there is a tendency in the politically charged atmosphere in which we find ourselves, thanks to the driving force of the animal rights and liberation movement, to forget just how wonderful animals are in their own right. They have all survived through evolution, and that is something to simply respect and enjoy.

I'll end the subject of apes with my own perspective: to put it bluntly, apes have never done anything for us—delighting us at zoos is an obvious exception —and would not treat us kindly in the wild. But we nonetheless feel a special draw to them beyond our duty to treat animals humanely because of their genetic relatedness to us. We recognize a special duty because of this evolution-ary history and because of the fragility of their actual existence, thanks to a habitat that is diminishing because of us.

Although far removed from us genetically but not socially, dogs are a differ-ent story in terms of their contribution to human welfare. Following the destruction of the twin towers of the World Trade Center in New York by Islamic terrorists on September 11, 2001, search dogs performed heroically in finding living victims and human remains. Many of these animals suffered medical problems as a result. The conjunction of that terrible event and the efforts by those tireless dogs forced a startling question into my mind: is it ethi-cal to continue to use a species that has done so much in the service of human-kind, even in ways that inevitably harm them, in biomedical research? Think of unmatchable guide and helper dogs for the disabled, comforters of the lonely, childhood playmates, and faithful guardians. Should we cease using some of their fellows in research? Should we exempt this special species, related to us by association, not phylogeny? This is a dangerous idea, potentially devastating for some biomedical research, and one that would never have entered my mind as an eager young scientist. At present, I cannot answer these questions.[79]

Justifying Other Uses of Animals | 8

Our humanity demands the humane treatment of animals. In a sense, the "privilege" of calling ourselves or, more to the point, *being* humans requires us to see to the welfare of the animals in our care. Having emerged as the intellectual kings and queens of the planet, we have ruled over our animal cousins, and not always well. We have created roles for animals that suit our purposes— as food and clothing, hunting companions, instruments of war, sources of amusement (both benign and malignant), appeasements to the gods and God, and, from the time of Aristotle, a means for understanding the biological world. Acceptance of the appropriateness of each of these uses has varied over time and across cultures and religions.

Some of the other ways in which we use animals are just as legitimate as their use in research; we should try to put those uses in the context of normal human experience. Biomedical researchers have too often put themselves on a pedestal as a defense in dealing with the current controversy over animal use: "Only the use of animals in biomedical research is truly defensible," some would say, the use of animals in other contexts being somehow less acceptable. In my experience, more than a few scientists are too ready to accept claims made by the animal rights and liberation movement against other animal users, such as hunters, without sufficient knowledge. At the same time they mistakenly assume that all of the (non-animal-rightist) public, including farmers, hunters, and other animal users, will reject criticism of biomedical research and automatically rally to science's defense. This is foolish arrogance, for the public has the right to clear explanations of what scientists do. Failure to speak openly out of fear of retribution from extremists allows seeds of doubt to be sown.

In the following pages I consider a number of different ways in which humans use animals, and state frankly which uses I consider acceptable and which ones I do not. No doubt, these views will find both support and disagreement among various readers. Indeed, Gordon Burghardt and Hal Herzog have thoughtfully analyzed the complexity and inconsistencies of the decision-making processes we each use in making our ethical choices.[1] This has been the most difficult chapter to write because I know that my views will diverge from those of some otherwise sympathetic readers, not to mention the views of those who see no justification for any animal use.

Domestication of Animals

In every case, "animals are perpetual 'others,' doomed to have their interests represented to humans by other humans."[2] But animals have not always been passive instruments in their interactions with us. Early humans did not just march out into the fields and forests saying, "I'll take you and you and you to help me around the house and farm. The rest of you are fair game." Instead, through evolutionary pressures animals insinuated themselves into our lives. Domestication was a two-way street.

According to one view,[3] humans began their interactions with animals by hunting them. Certain animal species developed favorable characteristics, however, that enabled them to be domesticated and used for various purposes. During the last ice age, humans and animals had access to limited and changing resources as the ice cap receded. Those animals most adaptable to these "rapidly" changing harsh conditions survived. Among the survivors were those that tended to retain more of the flexibility of youth—puppyhood, calfhood, and so on. In adapting to varying conditions, these animals matured physically and reproductively before developing behaviors that would have made them fearful of and aggressive toward people. Instead, they became willing to accept intervention and care from familiar humans—an immense benefit for humans, to be sure. Ultimately, domestication ensured survival and good health among the descendents of these animals, so from an evolutionary perspective, domestication was a favorable process. It offered protection for these animals from predators and, in modern times, from injury, disease, and hunger. Thus, they were "rewarded" for following this particular evolutionary trajectory.

The process by which physical and sexual maturation outpaces loss of some infantile behavioral and physical characteristics is termed neotony, and these animals' cuteness draws us to them, as in the case of a human infant, as Konrad Lorenz noted.[4] In selecting for tameness, primitive humans, who probably began to breed specific animals that were most docile, were unknowingly manipulating many genes and rather quickly achieving easily handled animals that retained their juvenile features. For example, the selection for juvenile behavioral features bred dogs, by no means necessarily knowingly, that adapted to perform a herding task with animals born to be their natural prey. Fluffy sheep dogs were bred to be arrested in their development and to retain certain puppy-like physical features and behavioral tendencies, making them playful or nonthreatening around sheep, yet appropriately aggressive when predators tried to penetrate the flock.[5]

This fairly simple, easy-to-follow model of the process of domestication does not tell the whole story though, as Bulliet points out in *Hunters, Herders and Hamburgers: The Past and Future of Human–Animal Relations.*[6] In one interesting example from his highly readable book, he argues that being a predator (such as a cat or dog) may have made animals with little or nothing to fear from other species more approaching or approachable—think also of the very large but herbivorous elephant. These species' reduced fight-or-flight mechanism would make close association with humans easier, even if they did not achieve domestication. Dogs with their "pack instinct" readily fell in line as followers of human will as they gradually developed a more approaching nature.

Even lions and tigers, which remain wild but can be tamed to an extent to perform in circuses by learning small tricks, would fit into the less-fearful category. On the other hand, Bulliet notes, "small prey species like prairie dogs and gazelles can't [be tamed], which is why we don't see gazelle and prairie dog acts under the big-top."[7] They would be too fearful.

We do not see predatory domestic cats doing tricks in circuses, either. I suspect that the size differential between trainer and domestic cat compared with that for a lion or tiger likely explains this: cats are small and easily frightened by large humans, upon whom they cannot prey. Regarding their domestication, a recent genetic study[8] found that the probable origin of the domestic cat was the Near East, around 9000 years ago, coincidently alongside the development of agriculture, instead of much later in Egypt as had previously been believed. Cats were different from animals domesticated for agriculture or transport in that they associated with humans as commensals, that is, feeding on the pests in grain stores without joining human society fully in the same sense as the family dog. Most "owners" of cats recognize their independent spirits; "domestic" may not be a totally accurate description of them.

We humans do not (in the best of circumstances) use domesticated animals as animals in the wild use each other. We think about our treatment of animals and sometimes even worry about it. I believe that we alone of all species can have ethical concerns. This ability to reflect on what we do to animals sets us apart from them. Further, as I will argue later from a secular standpoint, it gives us the right to use animals in certain ways while restricting their use for other purposes. A couple of ways in which we use animals involve harming and often sacrificing them for our own well-being. This is most obvious when killing animals for food. Less obvious to some people, but just as necessary, is using animals in biomedical research. This use can be as difficult for the scientist to undertake as it is for the average layperson to understand.

Various domestic uses of animals that present no ethical problem for some people in one society may be anathema to others. Even pets are an issue these days. Whereas the keeping of pets is an ancient and widely accepted practice for most people, some people regard even this benign practice as "exploitation." Animal rights activists automatically elevate animals to equality with humans when they use this term. In reality, "exploitation" describes a situation whereby one is benefited at the expense of another. This is obviously not the case for most pets, and it can be argued from an individual and a species-population standpoint that it is not completely true for other domesticated animals, including food animals, which would not otherwise exist. Our charge is to keep up our side of the bargain and treat them as well as practicality permits.

Because humans are so powerful, we can decide which species will be pets and which of their fellows within a species might be put to other uses, even eaten.[9] We create animals in the image we wish, to suit our purposes. Pigs, for example, can make wonderful pets for some individuals and equally wonderful food for the same pet owner. Dogs, which are so important in many cultures as pets, are eaten in other cultures and even used for fur. Likewise, horses are ridden in some cultures and eaten in others. The same could be said about cows, as they are perceived differently in various cultures. Such cultural implications for animal use are discussed further below; my point here is that the use of animals by humans is appropriate and natural when viewed within an evolutionary context.

Actually, the various cultural choices of which animals will be eaten, and the reasons behind those choices, are not simple to categorize. Observant Jews and Muslims will not eat pork because of divine command. Many observant Hindus and Buddhists will not eat meat because of their belief in reincarnation, subscription to the doctrine of *ahimsa*, which prohibits harming sentient beings, or, as Bulliet puts it, because "they are told that the cow is their mother and hence not to be harmed, much less eaten."[10] Other preferences go unexplained, such as Americans' avoidance of horse meat, or the lack of chicken and eggs in the diet of the Tuaregs of the southern Sahara.

An increasingly popular animal-related dietary choice is what Bulliet refers to as "elective vegetarianism," a feature of the postdomestic generations. In this case, the current moral debate over the use of animals leads to the conscious decision to avoid the eating of animals that may have been raised inhumanely. This philosophy is also known as ethical vegetarianism, and there are other categories: ovo-vegetarians (who eat eggs), lacto-vegetarians (who drink milk and eat other dairy products), ovo-lacto vegetarians, and vegans, who eat no animal product whatsoever. While the conscious decision to be a vegetarian has existed in some religions for many years, in today's postdomestic culture the choice cuts across religions and cultures. As a society we should respect these choices, and at the same time expect that they will not be forced on others.

Animal Use: Moral and Ethical Issues

Hal Herzog has frequently challenged us in a gentle and, at times, humorous way to think more deeply about how we use animals. For example, in his treatment of the moral status of mice,[11] he points out that mice are vermin, and only a fool puts up with them in his or her house. Yet they have an exalted place in research laboratories and make a tremendous contribution to the understanding of human diseases.

As research animals, mice live in superb quarters. Veterinarians and the institutional animal care and use committees (IACUCs) described earlier oversee their welfare. These are "good" mice, as Herzog puts it. But when these mice escape, their moral status changes dramatically: they become pests and a danger to the health of the colony. They have no protection and may be killed in ways that the IACUC would not approve of for "good" mice at the end of an experiment. Mice may also be raised in laboratories to feed snakes that are the research animals. Snakes are not considered worthy of governmental protection (see Chapter 3), although in my institution their use would still be monitored by the IACUC. Their little living food items would not be regulated either, as far as their mode of "euthanasia" goes. The status of these mice would change dramatically, however, if the experimenter were interested in the defense strategies used by the mice against snakes. In this context, the very same mice would have to be overseen by the IACUC. Nevertheless, Herzog's "bad" mice, no longer protected by law, still present an ethical problem: how should one dispose of them? The mice themselves have not changed from scenario to scenario; instead, our perceptions of them and their purposes have changed dramatically.

Leaving behind the ambiguity of dealing with the mouse kingdom, Herzog then inspires us to consider the ethics of pet food.[12] Some vegetarians argue that we should convert our carnivorous pets to vegetarianism as well, forcing the owners' ethical views on, for instance, a cat, an obligate carnivore requiring a nutrient, taurine, found only in meat. Naturally, the cat would have no say in the matter.[13] To force Buster into becoming a vegetarian would be an unforgivable and foolish denial of his biological and evolutionary identity as a cat. Keeping Buster indoors and depriving him of the opportunity to fulfill his hereditary heritage as a predator presents a related ethical problem.

I know that Buster is inflicting himself on animals within his territory, and it bothers me enough that I have removed our bird feeders since acquiring him. Consequently, we are deprived of watching some beautiful birds and humorous squirrels. Unfortunately, Buster and kin can do quite a bit of damage to surrounding wildlife. Even though well fed, many domestic cats are still avid hunters by nature. As Herzog writes, "Even if each of the pet cats in the United States killed only two mice, chipmunks, or baby birds each year, the number of animals slaughtered by pets would greatly exceed the number of animals used in research."[14] It is a cat's nature to hunt and kill smaller animals (although I don't like it when he doesn't eat them). As the "owner" of a cat, I am well aware that cats represent the closest approximation there is to living with a wild animal.

Community ordinances have drastically reduced the number of dogs running loose (one reason we have too many deer). This is not the case for cats. Because of their solitary wandering habits and some negligent owners who abandon them, they may eventually become feral—domesticated animals that have reverted to wild habits. These animals are unnatural intruders into the environment, exacting a heavy toll on other creatures as predators. Well-meaning people argue that the colonies formed by these cats should be allowed to exist, and that their members should be captured and neutered in order to control the problem they present to local wildlife. Is this the ethical solution, or would it be more responsible to euthanize these feral animals for the sake of those that naturally belong to that environment? Doesn't the wildlife have a right to live unthreatened by cats that are an extension of human encroachment on their habitat? On the other hand, should I keep Buster indoors at the risk of making both of us miserable? It is no easy task, grappling with the ethical dilemmas posed by our interactions with animals, domesticated and otherwise.

Plowing up land in the service of veganism or vegetarianism, thereby sparing some cattle, pigs, and chickens, may nevertheless result in the killing or displacement of small, unseen creatures, such as field mice, ground-nesting birds, or groundhogs. This poses an interesting moral question to one scientist,

S. L. Davis,[15] who has asked if a pig's life is worth more than that of a field mouse. Even our most well-intentioned ethical choices regarding animals may have a hidden cost to the environment or to other animals.

Because we are thinking creatures, we cannot avoid considering what we do with animals; a humane person deliberates. Given our cognitive powers, we have an obligation to use animals as fairly and as compassionately as possible, despite the possibility that the eventual harm that may come to them could be considerable.

For me, no words capture the notion of our obligation to the animals under our control better than a passage I read long ago, as a horse-crazy boy, in the children's book *My Friend Flicka*. I have remembered these words throughout my long career working with animals. In the passage that follows, rancher Rob McLaughlin speaks with one of his sons about a wild mare that had broken loose from their corral with the noose of a lariat around her neck:

> "What if it did choke her?" asked Howard. "You always say she's no use to you." "There's a responsibility we have toward animals," said his father. "We use them. We shut them up, keep their natural food and water from them that means we have to feed and water them. Take their freedom away, rope them, harness them, that means we have to supply a different sort of safety for them. Once I've put a rope on a horse, or taken away its ability to take care of itself, then I've got to take care of it. Do you see that? That noose around her neck is a danger to her, and I put it there, so I have to get it off."[16]

There are situations we simply cannot walk away from. We must act like Rob McLaughlin after we have spilled huge amounts of crude oil in coastal waters; we are obligated to rescue as many marine animals as possible, scrubbing them free of the deadly muck. Likewise, even though we are not obligated to rescue a moose from a pack of wolves, we should seek to remove plastic netting from a marine mammal entangled in it, because we put the netting there.

I acted out Rob's creed before we had centralized veterinary care for our laboratory animals. Fortunately, at that time I was able to hire veterinary students to act as caretakers. Nevertheless, each night before I went home, I made a habit of walking through the quarters to make sure my cats had been fed and watered. This practice started at the beginning of my career 50 years ago, spurred by the memory of that passage I had read as a boy.

In addition to the animal uses already discussed (in biomedical research and as companion animals), what are appropriate uses of animals, and who decides what they are? It all depends on whose ox is being gored, so to speak. Both personal and cultural preferences, and ignorance, of what a particular use actually involves can impact the decision of which use will be condoned and which will be condemned. For example, any use of animals that features *deliberate* harm for casual amusement is abhorrent to me and to most people in our culture. Bear and bull baiting and dog fighting as common amusements were outlawed long ago[17]—and good riddance—although illegal underground dog fighting continues, as the incident described in Chapter 1 demonstrates. On the other hand, if human and beast are both in danger in the context of a particular entertainment enterprise, something of a partnership between human and beast is denoted, and I generally accept that use. Some people will no doubt disagree with me here. Objection to any of the points I make by no means indicates an extreme animal-rights position; instead, differing viewpoints illustrate the range in thinking on what constitutes proper animal welfare and use, based on simple personal preferences and often on cultural background.

Cultural Differences

Different animals mean different things to different groups of people, even within our own Western culture. A conversation with a colleague in the Department of Psychology at the University of Maine vividly brought this fact home to me. He had just attended a forum on animal uses, which also included members of the university's conservation department. Their representative spoke approvingly of hunting and trapping, but was skeptical of what was happening to animals in the psychology department, apparently not understanding the scientific value of the experiments being conducted there. Imagine this same forum at an urban university. Who would be put on the defensive in that setting—the hunter or the biomedical researcher?

Let me begin our discussion of cultural differences with a current controversy. In the United States, horses are beloved, beautiful creatures, in the same iconic category as dogs. Consequently, many people in the United States are horrified by the suggestion of slaughtering them for food. Not so in Belgium, France, and Japan, where horsemeat is sold in special stores, for human consumption. Although I personally have no interest in eating horses, the act in and of itself is not the issue for me. Instead, my concern is how horses are kept while alive and how they are ultimately killed—these are the true welfare issues. Except for my own cultural bias, killing horses for food, to be buried, or to be incinerated are all the same to me, except that the latter two present problems for the environment and are a waste of resources.

But the U.S. Congress has been considering bills in both houses, called the Horse Slaughter Protection Act, which is strongly promoted by the Humane Society of the United States (HSUS), other animal rights groups, and interested parties in the general public. With passage, the act would prevent the annual slaughter of approximately 100,000 horses in the United States and prevent the shipment of them to other countries for that purpose. A number of groups also concerned with the welfare of horses, such as the American Veterinary Medical Association, the American Association of Equine Practitioners, and more than 140 other organizations, oppose the bill, while not necessarily condoning the slaughter of horses for food in the United States. These groups have considered the reality of the situation: if passed, the act would leave about 10 times as many horses as can be accommodated in retirement facilities, roughly 6,000. Those destined for meat can be humanely euthanized by captive bolt in federally regulated facilities, a fate less horrible than lingering with owners who cannot or will not care for them properly.[18] Although there is no federal law yet, political forces have induced states with slaughter houses to pass their own laws, closing the three remaining plants and thereby creating a mess—a surfeit of horses.

Transportation of these animals probably introduces more welfare problems than does any other stage of the process, just as it does for all animals destined for slaughter. So, paradoxically, those working for federal legislation that protects horses may have actually worsened the welfare of many of them. As Dr. Mark Lutschaunig of the American Veterinary Medical Association said in an October 4, 2007, press release, "The reality is, the HSUS has done nothing to address the real issue here, and, in fact, by seeking to ban horse slaughter, they have made things significantly worse. If they really wanted to do something productive to improve the welfare of horses, they would address the issue of unwanted horses in the United States."[19] A statement on the HSUS Web site indicates that the society is opening up some horse sanctuaries and is actively working with horse advocates to find ways to care for unwanted horses. Just what this accomplishes to solve the problem, though, only time will tell. Given the size of their coffers, the HSUS could make a difference if they prove willing to turn out their pockets.

One interesting thought on this issue came recently from Herb Moelis, President of Thoroughbred Charities of America, who reports that USDA statistics point to more than 100,00 unwanted horse in the United States each year. He suggests adding $50 to the $200 Jockey Club registration fee to provide for a foal's later life, a type of Social Security program for horses. Roughly $2 million would be raised from the 40,000 horses registered each year.[20] Whether such actions will be sufficient to care for now-unusable horses remains to be seen.

Another culturally loaded use of animals is bullfighting, approved in some cultures. I do not approve of this practice. The bull is first deliberately exhausted by men who bait him by running around the ring before diving to safety, provoking the bull to chase them. Then the neck muscles of the bull must be disabled by gouging them first with a long spear wielded by a man on horseback, then with heavy darts, placed by several men who race up to the bull to place them there. All of this activity occurs before the matador faces him for the kill. This disablement prevents the bull from making dangerous thrusts of his head, thereby reducing, but not eliminating, the danger that the matador faces. Without doubt all of this activity requires considerable bravery on the part of the men in the ring with the bull, but I disapprove of intentionally inducing such prolonged agony solely for the purpose of entertainment.

Nevertheless, bullfights are Sunday family picnic outings in Mexico. I know this from personal experience, having lived next to the biggest bullring in the world in Mexico City for a few months and attended a fight one Sunday afternoon. A risky, clean kill, the bull in possession of all its powers when confronting the matador (a near disaster for the matador), would be acceptable to me, even though the thought of watching the spectacle is not appealing, because the bull is ultimately used for the kind of food I would eat. Others in our society might disagree, perhaps because the bull is slaughtered in public, or simply because it is slaughtered. In any event, this is fantasy. No one could kill a bull with one clean sword stroke in the face of those slashing horns. I wish they would abandon this cruel sport.

At the same time, I am concerned that an activist segment of one culture may unethically and harmfully interfere with another culture's livelihood. For example, Inuit people of the north used baby seals as a cash crop until several years ago when the outside world intervened to stop this practice, thereby seriously damaging the Inuit economy. The method of killing, a quick blow to the head that causes no prolonged suffering, made for great press coverage because of its seeming brutality and the subsequent sympathetic outpouring from "civilized" society. Photographs of cute baby harp seals provided marvelous fodder for animal rights propaganda. That the activists used films of staged hunts to enhance the semblance of brutality calls into question their own ethical values.[21]

Those who would try to convince the world not to use animals for food, to become vegetarians or vegans, and to discontinue most or all uses of animals are practicing a form of cultural imperialism relative to the less developed areas of the world. Agrarian societies and developing nations and those that rely on fishing for food and income cannot do without animals. In many parts of the world, people would be "hungry, cold, and tired"[22] without their animals. Is it fair, is it moral, to impose wealthy Western political views on peoples that do not have access to the same resources we do?

Another animal-related issue I find troubling involves a subculture of our society, the dog fancy. My own prejudice is that I disapprove of the painful ear cropping of certain breeds of dogs, which thankfully we see less of these days, on the street at least. Likewise, the continued breeding of dogs for structural features grotesque enough to affect normal function is morally questionable. Here the loveable flat-faced English bull dog comes to mind, which has become so compromised in its breathing that it is sleepy all the time because it awakens briefly but often during its sleep period. During sleep its airway is largely blocked by its tongue and soft palate, which are too long relative to the dog's pushed-in face, coupled with the relaxation of the muscles surrounding the airway. Bulldogs suffer from a form of obstructive sleep apnea, a well-known problem in older men.

My colleagues and I determined this by comparing a group of dogs with the standard head shape to that of English bulldogs. Both groups had electrodes attached to their skin for recording the brain waves of sleep and an oximeter (oxygen measuring device) for monitoring levels of oxygen in the blood, which were correlated with each other. Even though the dogs were in a relatively noisy laboratory and had no adaptation time, all the bulldogs fell asleep within 20 minutes, one while being instrumented for recording. The normal dogs never slept during the 150-minute recording period. Furthermore, the blood oxygen levels dropped to levels well below normal during sleep in the bull-dogs.[23] This is not healthy for the cardiopulmonary systems, to say the least. I would like to see a change in what people think of as a proper bulldog, as well as in some other breeds subject to such dramatic manipulation.

Having said this, I want to make clear that I appreciate the interest and love that owners of purebred dogs have for their particular breeds. This love was evident at a breed-rescue conference held by the National Animal Interest Alliance when I was president of that organization. These folks are prolific in their efforts to rescue dogs from pounds and shelters and to find homes for them. Nevertheless, I encourage continued movement toward correction of breed characteristics that interfere with healthy functioning and consideration of altering breed standards that demand practices such as ear cropping.

Before moving on in the discussion here, I want to qualify my conditional acceptance of some of the activities described below. All are subject to abuses, either deliberate or through carelessness, which I do not condone. But nothing in life is risk-free. So when I write that I support a particular use of animals, for example, in rodeos, it is with the understanding that some sort of ethical standard, organizational oversight, or clear set of regulations is in place, such as those of the Professional Rodeo Cowboys' Association. Unfortunately, if we look hard enough we can almost always find abuses for making a case against virtually any human activity. In the early days of the modern animal rights and liberation movement, exposure of abuses or mistakes was thought to be reason enough to halt biomedical research using animals. Now that there are very good controls, the same arguments against animal-based research continue, but the accusations of wrongdoing are usually found to be without merit or are instances of ignorance or abuses carried out by an irregular abusive caretaker or scientist.

Given the broad range of ways in which humans use animals, I could discuss any number of activities without finding one on which public opinion is unanimous. Having already discussed biomedical research, educational uses of animals, and the initial domestication of animals by humans, I next present four additional uses: cockfighting, hunting, rodeo, and modern agriculture. The use of animals in modern agriculture is particularly complex, and a full discussion of them is beyond the scope of this book. It is not easy to put a stamp of approval or disapproval on certain practices without considering the pros and cons of various management techniques as they pertain to animal welfare. Agricultural animal use is further complicated by economic considerations that impact human welfare as well.

Cockfighting

Most people find cockfighting objectionable, myself included. I chose to discuss cockfighting instead of a number of other animal uses because I will use the practice to illustrate a couple of points relevant to biomedical research. I object to cockfighting in particular because it pits bird against bird, without any humans putting themselves in harm's way. The aim seems to be nothing more than the satisfaction of bloodlust, as is the case with dog fighting (both the dogs' and that of human spectators). Yet, for some cultures, such as that of the southern Appalachians, cockfighting is a noble pasttime and wholly consistent with the mores of society. Gamecocks are bred for fighting, and from all reports they are raring to go once in the ring. The sport has a widespread distribution, including essentially all of the Western hemisphere and much of Asia. Within the United States, Cajuns, Delta African Americans, Mexican Americans, and rural whites in the South are drawn to the sport, although it is now outlawed in all 50 states. The sport can also result in big money for those who participate, considering the wagering done on these little fellows in underground contests.[24]

The sport is not without its defenders, who argue from an ethical viewpoint, denying that the sport is "cruel, brutalizing and debasing to humanity."[25] In fact, somewhat unsettlingly, their arguments in favor of cockfighting are strikingly similar to those scientists employ in defending the use of animals in biomedical research (in my view, the purpose of the activity distinguishes one from the other). "Cockers," as they call themselves, argue that aficionados are just average members of the community. One of their points in particular hits uncomfortably close to home: the birds are extremely well cared for and enjoy a life much more comfortable than that of the chickens we eat. Since the birds are worth hundreds of dollars, that is undoubtedly true. I use an analogous argument when defending biomedical research from its detractors, contrasting the first-rate veterinary care that laboratory animals receive with that provided for many pets.

The cocker also argues that for birds with fighting in their blood it would be cruel not to allow this "self-actualization" of sorts. Again, while I think that activity is inhumane, I would make the same type of argument on behalf of dog sledding. Dogs that have spent the previous day racing many miles over rough, forbidding terrain in the great Iditarod Race in Alaska are raring to go the next morning, yelping and jumping as the next stage begins. In this case, however, the driver, or musher, works along with the dogs, which implies a sort of equality of suffering, or partnership, that is similar to the rodeo cowboy and his horse. Dogs and musher are cooperating with each other, struggling against the extremes. Also, the race is a reenactment of the traditional method of transportation in the Arctic regions, honoring this method and the dogs that served.

Hunting

Hunting in the United States is worth discussing here at some length because it also touches on the question of our ethical responsibility to the environment as a whole. To many people, hunting is abhorrent. In my opinion, a fair amount of this abhorrence arises out of ignorance and prejudice. Omnivorous humans who express this disgust also buy their nicely sanitized meat wrapped in plastic from spotless supermarkets—surely there is hypocrisy here. Steven Kellert, author of The Value of Life reminds us that the rural poor kill game as an important protein supplement:

> Hunting for meat may seem anachronistic in modern
> society. But for many rural poor, this activity continues to be
> pragmatically significant, as well as an integral part of a
> lifestyle that focuses on extracting some portion of one's
> living from the land and its creatures.[26]

In modern society, hunters are often depicted by anti-hunting activists as beer-guzzling yahoos participating in a dishonorable sport devoid of moral foundation, for the sheer joy of seeing blood and death. In large measure, the truth is quite different. Although never a hunter myself, I have eaten plenty of game provided by uncles and friends, all good men. I used to keep my water-fowl-hunting friend Dave company during cold days in the Delaware marshes; I was always without a gun, but I participated as much as possible by calling in the geese in return for the enjoyment of Dave's goose dinners. To put a shotgun in my inexperienced hands would have been wrong—not fair to the birds and dangerous for Dave and me. We even spent one New Year's Day morning in a cornfield foxhole near our homes shivering in 12°F weather, attracting not even one goose. I confess that while sitting in the blind with Dave and even when walking in the woods alone I have felt a sense of incompleteness. I do not par-ticipate fully in what I view as an ancient and honorable tradition—honorable, even in today's modern society, if correctly performed.

Hunters are like you and me in many respects, according to Jan Dizard's analysis. He has compared the characteristics and views of hunters and non-hunters using data from the biennial General Social Survey by the National Opinion Research Center, primarily data gathered in 1998.[27] The two groups are amazingly similar. They have comparable income levels, although more non-hunters (28%) have achieved a bachelor's or higher degree than have hunters (17%). In terms of political views, 22% of hunters considered themselves con-servative or extreme conservative, while 18% of the non-hunters classified themselves this way. Hunters were much more likely to favor the death penalty and disapprove of gun control, but both hunters and non-hunters seemed com-parable in their views on gender equality. Also, hunters agreed with the state-ment that "human nature is basically good" slightly more often than did non-hunters (40% versus 36%). Thus, although there are differences between hunters and non-hunters here and there, some of which are due to a gender effect because hunters are predominantly male, there aren't as many as might be expected. The image of hunters portrayed by the survey is certainly not of a group of gun-crazy misfits living on the fringe of civilized society.

Dizard notes that hunting has always been surrounded by traditions and self-imposed rules and has involved only a minority of the U.S. population. Presently, the number stands at 15 to 20 million. The proportion of hunters to non-hunters is, not surprisingly, dropping in the United States.[28] Of course, for conservation purposes the government has stepped in: a hunting license is required, specific to animal type, and there are imposed seasonal and bag limits. Killing an animal is only part of the venture, however. From Dizard's analysis and that of others, such as Kellert, hunters have a strong desire to be one with nature, to participate in an ancient human ritual. Dizard acknowledges that there are some "bad apples," as he puts it, among the hunting fraternity, as there are in any group. But he also argues that "self-restraint is deeply embedded in the culture of sport hunting. It is practiced and reinforced, not as an abstract code practiced for public consumption, but as a deeply held conviction: Self-restraint is what crucially separates hunters from killers."[29] Various hunting organizations, such as the North American Gamebird Association, have strict codes of ethics, reports Dizard.

Dizard frames the hunt as follows. First, the hunter leaves society to enter nature and to adopt a different mindset. This is a world where "rules very different from the rules of society are at work. Most dramatically, the hunter enters nature as one more predator operating in a realm where everything is food for someone or some thing."[30] Dizard argues that "nature is, indeed, a system ruled by predation.... Nature's luxuriant fecundity is matched, must be matched by an equal extravagance of death."[31] Then, there is the obligation to achieve a clean kill. Hunters that Dizard has interviewed "emphasize the lengths to which they go to honor the dignity of the animal they are pursuing." [There is a] "commitment to careful shot selection in hopes of effecting a quick, clean kill"[32] and considerable remorse at failure to accomplish this. Finally, there is the need for restraint and sustainability, taking the clean shot and not being greedy by blazing away at anything that moves.

These are the principles of "fair chase."[33] Good examples of hunters, who strictly apply such principles, are my former barber in northern Idaho, who spends 2 weeks alone in the woods every fall stalking elk in the hopes of bringing one home to fill his freezer; Jan Dizard, flushing pheasants with his pointer; and Dave Marshall, patiently sitting in the middle of a Delaware marsh trying to fool a wily goose into flying low enough for a clean shot.

Thanks to these self-imposed rules, "game species that, 50 years ago, were scarce or nonexistent locally are now abundant."[34] Hunters are conservationists, not only because this represents enlightened self-interest but because they respect, even love, the game they track and the woodlands in which they live.

From early times, hunters have "bonded" with their prey just as the good hunter does today. The good hunter must know his or her quarry intimately to be able to track it down and successfully kill it. With this knowledge comes empathy. Consequently, there is humility, indeed guilt, in taking life. This has been expressed through the ages, from early man (hunters have been primarily men) to present-day societies, such as our own.[35] Some hunters may ultimately so identify with their prey that they lay down their arms and shoot no more. A close friend once told me that he came to a point at which he could not shoot another deer. Similarly, I found I could no longer use cats in my research about 15 years ago, which very likely stems from the same psychological base.

Beyond hunting as a personal, ritual activity, though, hunting may be conducted to redress imbalances in nature due to human interference. The most obvious example is the hunting, or more accurately, the killing by hired sharpshooters of white-tailed deer in various areas where they are overpopulated. Deer cause gross environmental destruction in parks and suburbs where they no longer encounter natural predators. As humans have cleared forests and then provided artificial habitats and food in the form of suburban shrubbery and the borders of fields and forest, whitetail deer have increased from an estimated 500,000 in the United States in 1900 to 33 million today, roughly the same number that greeted the Europeans when they arrived to colonize the continent.

Worse than destroying our shrubbery, deer destroy the habitats of many other creatures. In Pennsylvania, deer destroy $70 million in crops and $75 million in trees each year. A recent 10-year study revealed that more than 20 deer per square mile led to the loss of numerous bird species: eastern wood peewees, indigo buntings, least flycatchers, yellow-billed cuckoos, and cerulean warblers. These are from Audubon's Watchlist, an activity of the Audubon Society and the American Bird Conservancy designed to identify those species that are imperiled so that conservationists can work to save the species from extinction. There is the carnage on the highways as well. Pennsylvania is second in the nation in human fatalities from collisions with deer. Collision damage amounts to thousands of dollars. Finally, as transporters of the deer ticks carrying Lyme disease, deer are a true public health menace. Untreated, the disease can progress to damage to the brain and nerves.[36]

Yet deer are beautiful. They have soulful eyes and graceful movements. Frankly, I could not shoot one. Walt Disney's *Bambi* has reinforced our perception of deer as cute creatures. Consequently, many people work passionately to impede the culling of deer in parks and suburbs, and the hunting of deer elsewhere. These defenders of deer believe that their killing by humans is unethical. When examined carefully, however, this view is revealed as overly simplistic; allowing an overabundance of deer would endanger other species that depend on healthy forest. As humans who instigated their overpopulation, we cannot walk away from the situation created by deer, just as we could not walk away from the devastation caused by an oil spill in a marine ecosystem. Neither can those who object to deer culling dismiss the possibility that their homes may have encroached on the deer's habitat, contributing to the crowding and disruption of the ecological balance.

Deer are remarkably prolific breeders. In many places they lacking natural predators, thus they can literally breed themselves out of an adequate food supply. With few predators available to dispatch them, as would be the case in their natural habitat, the weaker and older deer, teeth worn down to a level that prevents them from grazing efficiently, starve to death. It is not a pleasant fate, but it is one provided by nature for all wild species, unlike the one we provide for our pampered pets:

> Death from malnutrition is an insidious, pathetically slow
> process. Fat depletion and physical weakening progress with
> nearly undetectable signs, until it's too late for recovery.
> In the final stages, however, a deer's coat roughens, its
> hipbones show, and hollows appear in its flanks. The
> starving animal spends most of its time bedded down in a
> curled head to tail position to minimize body surface
> exposure. It adopts a lethargic, uncaring attitude, no longer
> bounding away, flag [tail] waving, as danger nears. Small
> deer, especially, stand hump-backed, their front legs spread
> slightly, back legs close together, [holding] their heads up at
> a 45-degree angle [below horizontal]. . . . At some unknown
> time during starvation, rumen attrition and adrenal
> exhaustion become irreversible. Thereafter, a deer so
> stressed could no longer handle the metabolic stress of
> feeding.[37]

In a particularly poignant passage from *Whitetail Deer: A Year's Cycle*, Curtis Stadtfield further describes the process of starvation: "They are likely to die in March. And they die unmourned, untended, unnoted."[38]

Would not a well-placed shot provide a less agonizing death? The downside here is that shots are not always well placed. The ethical hunter is then enjoined to track the animal down. The suffering of death is obviously prolonged in these cases, but no more, I would think, than in the prolonged suffering of starvation or of nursing a broken leg. The irrefutable fact is that all animals in the wild—all creatures everywhere, in fact—are destined to die. The only question is how.

Those removed from nature by virtue of modern life may not recognize that management of animal populations by humane trapping can actually improve the lot of that species in general. Two very good books describe the complexities of human interactions with animals in the wild and the responsibilities humans have for these animals when natural predators have been removed from the equation. The first is *The Illusions of Animal Rights* by Russ Carman, a farmer, hunter, trapper, and businessman involved in wildlife matters.[39] The second book is entitled *Animal Rights vs. Nature*, by Walter E. Howard, an emeritus professor and wildlife ecologist at the University of California, Davis.[40]

Both authors observe that attempts by animal rights activists to block wildlife management can seriously affect the welfare of numerous species. The harvesting of various species in a government-regulated manner keeps populations at a level that is healthy for them and for their habitat. As Howard observes in a picturesque analogy, "Any gardener knows it is necessary to thin radishes if plump healthy radishes are wanted; similar types of predation of wildlife are equally beneficial to the wellbeing of their populations."[41] He also asks, "Why does the public insist that livestock operators maintain healthy flocks and herds, yet object to proper harvesting of wildlife to keep populations healthy?"[42]

The professional, licensed trapper knows the habits of the species sought and sets traps of appropriate size in optimal spots for trapping that species. Traps for muskrats are set so they drown. Other traps are killer traps, and still others are leg-hold traps appropriately sized for the target species. In this case, the trap holds the animal by the leg, and a well-placed pistol shot ends its life. Of course, we are obligated to continue to devise new and more humane devices for trapping animals. As Howard notes, "We seldom realize that it is actually uncommon for an animal taken by a trapper to die with as much suffering as it would have experienced in a natural death, but more humane traps are needed."[43] There is an important caveat here: trapping by untrained individuals in populated areas brings the real danger of someone's pet being caught. Thus, my discussion and defense of trapping presuppose that this activity is being carried out by professionals or others trained in the proper placement of traps.

A representative from the National Wildlife Federation, Vivian Pryor, testifying against an anti-trapping bill before the House Sub-Committee on Health and the Environment of the Committee on Energy and Commerce (August 3, 1984), had this to say on the issue: "Wildlife research, control of wildlife damage, and harvest of renewable wildlife resources are all frequently accomplished most efficiently and effectively by trapping."[44] She added, "Animals taken in leg-hold traps die in ways that are no more or less severe than when they die naturally. Proper use of leg-hold traps can cause less painful and protracted deaths than those which wild animals might otherwise experience." In her view, concern for animals should focus on protecting habitats, not on trapping. Of course, some trapping does not result in harm or death, and is instead employed to remove a nuisance animal to another area, whether it be a skunk under the back porch or a bear rummaging in trash cans.

As Rob McLaughlin said, "There's a responsibility we have toward animals," and not just domestic animals. One reason that I accept some uses of animals that others do not may be my rural background, even though I am too squeamish to use traps myself. Surprisingly, though, research conducted by the survey firm Responsive Management revealed that about 50% of urban residents surveyed approved of trapping compared with 60% rural folks, according to Mark Duda, Executive Director.[45] Although the difference was statistically significant, the 50% approval by urban and suburban residents is still striking, given that contact with the animal world has become very sanitized for many of these people, and the issues inherent in making a living from animals are remote. Perhaps Bulliet's postdomestic society is not as different as I thought.

The Rodeo and the Cowboy

We leave hunting for a potentially more exhilarating subject: the rodeo. Animal rights activists have focused on rodeos because of the supposed cruelty to animals in rodeos. All rodeo events require incredible skill from both horse and rider, and most demand equally incredible bravery. Registered rodeos follow an explicit set of rules to avoid abuse. The Professional Rodeo Cowboys Association, which sanctions about 30% of the rodeos in the United States, has an impressive set of regulations.[46] The American Association of Equine Practitioners awarded the group their 2003 Equine Welfare Award, which is presented to organizations "that demonstrate exceptional compassion or develop and enforce rules and guidelines for the welfare of the horse."[47] I approve of the concept of the rodeo because it meets my criterion that human and animal share the experience (and the risk to life and limb) on something approaching equal terms; but it should be understood that my approval is contingent upon adherence to the regulations set forth by the Professional Rodeo Cowboys Association. I cannot endorse rodeos that are not regulated (which constitutes the majority, and this needs to change).

For people of the American West, the rodeo embodies the lifestyle and traditions they have upheld, in some cases even to the present.[48] Roping calves was the only way to do some necessary but not-so-nice things (such as branding and castration). On the open range, life was harsh for all. One might squirm at the thought of flipping a calf down at the end of a lariat (thrown with amazing accuracy and incredible skill), but these are not the tiny things one sees gamboling around a mother cow—they are 220- to 280-pound Herefords. The timing and communication between rider and roping horse, which must keep the right tension on the rope so the cowboy can finish tying the calf's legs, is actually a thing of beauty. To me, this communication between human and animal is no different from trying to engage chimpanzees in conversation. As for courage and danger to the human participant, diving from a horse at full gallop in order to grasp the sharp horns of a running steer and then wrestle it to the ground requires considerable bravery and finesse. Otherwise a man could never put a 450- to 650-pound steer on his side.

Bronc riding, also quite dangerous, arose from the need to break wild horses and from the contests between cowboys to see who could stay on a wild horse the longest. Getting off a bucking horse seems worse than trying to stay on, with a good trampling always a possibility. To encourage the bucking of horses, a strap padded with fleece is placed around the flank region with a quick release device. This serves as a cue to go on stage, and the animal will buck more to try to rid itself of the annoyance. Animal rights activists charge that the strap is placed around the genitals, but this is incorrect. Spurs, used to encourage action from the horse and a required part of the ride, must be dull, and are designed to roll over the skin. I acknowledge, though, that those unfamiliar with the tradition might well view the rodeo as I do bull fighting.

Bull riding is a world apart from the activities discussed above. It is the one event that did not naturally grow out of tradition on the range, and I can understand why. I once stood next to a huge Brahman rodeo bull at the museum of the Professional Rodeo Cowboys Association in Colorado Springs. These are very valuable animals, so they are well cared for. I gulped at the thought of trying to remain on one for an 8-second ride, only to face a fair chance of being trampled or gored after being thrown off. The bull rider has to be about the bravest man on earth, often sustaining multiple fractures and worse. Even a broken bone in a cast, or a recently healed broken back—an actual case reported during a rodeo I watched on TV—may not prevent him from taking his next ride. The rodeo clown who lures the bull away from the fallen rider is not far behind in courage, to my mind.

I have some appreciation of the potential for danger when man and large beast come together, even when the relationship is friendly. This may be another reason why rodeos present no ethical problems for me. During my teen years I had a horse named Rocky, who had supposedly been trained as a jumper. But with no formal riding lessons I could never get him to jump, not even across a small stream. That changed one fine day when we went to visit a small herd of horses owned by a Texas cattle dealer who was renting our farmland and that of a neighboring farm. Only a barbed-wire fence with a 4-foot, Western-style barbed-wire gate separated the two farms at the point where a dirt road ran between them. As usual, I was riding bareback, contrary to my father's instructions, being too lazy to saddle up. After a few minutes the herd of semi-wild

Western horses began to gather around us, and Rocky became nervous. Realizing my mistake, I thought it best to leave. Rocky agreed and was by this time trotting, but as a herd of about 10 followed us, we took off at full gallop toward the barbed-wire gate about a quarter of a mile away. One hundred yards from the gate it was time to pull up, but Rocky had other ideas: he was a runaway and fully in charge of the situation. The best thing would have been for me to dive off into the long, soft grass on either side of the road, but when I looked back, I saw to my horror that the galloping herd filled both the road and the verge on either side. With nowhere to go but where Rocky took me, I lowered my head, expecting to be wrapped in barbed wire within a few seconds. Then, not feeling a thing, I realized we had cleared the gate, leaving the herd screeching to a halt on the other side, and me uncut and alive. That will have to suffice as my own version of a bull ride.

Modern Agriculture: Complex Ethical Issues

The use of animals for food presents ethical problems beyond the basic question of whether or not we should eat them. On that score I believe it is natural and acceptable for people to eat animals. I realize that not everyone shares this view.

Discussion of modern agriculture and its effects on animals in this book, however briefly, seems appropriate for a veterinary author; it would be as difficult for me to ignore as the proverbial gorilla in my living room. But to treat the topic as more than a sketch would require a volume or more. I cannot provide a definitive list of deficiencies with my solutions, which would be audacious to say the least. Each species of agricultural animal presents its own welfare problems. Thus I do not discuss all agricultural species or all the issues and challenges they present.[49] Rather, I will touch on some general aspects of modern agriculture, along with a few specific examples to show that solutions to welfare problems are not as obvious as they might seem at first glance. I will restrict myself to dairy cows, poultry, and swine. I feel equipped to write about these species because I have colleagues, food-animal veterinarians and animal scientists, who deal with them regularly.

Experience living on a farm also equips me to discuss agricultural use of animals, but only up to a point, for the same reason presented earlier: modern agriculture has become so big that the issues it presents regarding the welfare of the animals go beyond a section of a chapter. I left farming in simpler times. In the summer of 1953 my family moved from our 52-acre part-time farm in Chadds Ford, Pennsylvania, because my father was transferred by his company to Wisconsin. I was heartbroken because it meant selling Rocky and leaving behind a life I loved. I had willingly spent weekends and summers from the time I was 16 working on a then-large dairy farm. Through the years I had also taken care of our 30 or so laying hens, 2 pigs kept for meat each year, a goat we milked so my father could make cheese, and the 20 or so Plymouth-White Rock Cross capons I raised each year for my 4-H project. I loved the farm, but college and the start of my training as a veterinarian eased the pain of leaving it when I was 17. And, coincidently, the revolution in animal agriculture was just beginning.

Without a doubt, the methods of modern agriculture, those developed in the mid-twentieth century, known as intensive farming or, pejoratively and sensationally, as factory farming, present a major dilemma: animal welfare intertwined with economic sustainability. Animal (and human) welfare and economics have unfortunately clashed in the latter twentieth century, but they can equally be synergistic. Well-managed animals are higher producers.

Debate over modern agriculture is as contentious as it is over biomedical research. But correcting welfare problems is far more challenging in agriculture. Achieving for agriculture the level of regulation that is possible within biomedical research would be a hugely expensive endeavor fraught with political pitfalls in the United States. Advances in agricultural animal welfare in Europe, so touted in *Animal Liberation*, stem from the firmer control of the European Union and not inherently kinder populations, I am sure.

We cannot consider this issue as if we were talking about a herd or flock of little Busters. It would be nice if we could give each of our farm animals the same individual attention that we give our pets, but because of the size of most commercial farms and number of animals in most herds and flocks, that is simply impossible. One of my former veterinary students, John Fetrow, put this point quite clearly and rationally:

> When discussing food animal production technology,
> people often start with the tempting assumption that all
> production techniques should be free of any detriment to
> the animals. This view of the relationship between humans
> and domestic [agricultural] animals may be appealing and
> popular, but it is naïve and not tenable in a rational
> consideration of food production.[50]

What Fetrow is saying here is that in large farm operations, individual animals may be lost in the shuffle because it is just not possible to observe them as closely as one does the family pet. A certain number of deaths in large flocks of chickens, for example, are just a fact of life. Also, anesthesia is not used in castration in some cases, a problem for which we must find a solution. We need to continue to develop ways to maximize welfare in a practical manner. In the agricultural situation, however, food-animal veterinarians are caught in the middle of caring for society's needs as well as the animals'. The Veterinarian's Oath enjoins them to use their "scientific knowledge and skills for the benefit of society through the protection of animal health, the relief of animal suffering, [and] the conservation of livestock resources."

A look at animal welfare on the old family farm reveals that even smaller groups of animals were not treated as pets. For example, the little cockerels I raised were caponized (castrated) by cutting into the flank and extracting the internally placed testes, with no anesthesia. Now, through special breeding, males are raised so rapidly that the removal of testes to promote tenderness is no longer necessary, although caponizing may still be practiced. These birds and their kin nonetheless experience some severe welfare problems, such as lameness from too much weight being added too rapidly to an immature skeleton, as well as those problems associated with crowding during the last half-century.

When I was a boy, dairy cows in cold-winter regions could be confined for long periods in bad weather with their heads held in a stanchion. This structure permitted them to lie down while they ruminated or slept after eating their hay and grain. The cows were milked while in the stanchion, in the early days by hand and then later by milking machines brought to them. These machines eventually developed into ones that hooked to a vacuum line and that could then suck out the milk, sending it to a holding tank. The advent of milking parlors and the housing of the cows loosely in pole barns was a welcome innovation after World War II. Cows could move freely under cover, and the cow marched to the machine that would milk her in the parlor rather than the farmer having to lug the machine to her, a real savings in labor, to which I can personally attest.

When we moved in 1944 to Chadds Ford, Pennsylvania, in the Brandywine Valley, made famous by the painter Andrew Wyeth and his family, my father's dream was to farm with his brother after the war was over. My uncle was killed at the war's end, so that dream never came true, but their plan could only have been a dream anyway. A farm so small, with housing for no more than 20 or 30 cows, would never have been able to compete with larger commercial farms, given that the revolution in agriculture was in full swing. As fewer and fewer farmers began to feed more and more of the U.S. population, production efficiency became an important consideration. Farmers have to make a living, and the world must be fed. Farming is labor intensive as well as hard work, and all societies have tried to minimize that labor. Consequently, in the mid-twentieth century, animals moved from barnyards and pastures to confinement housing where, though deprived of a bucolic atmosphere, they find shelter and protection from predators, diseases, and parasites.[51]

Although everyone enjoys the bucolic sight of black and white cows grazing in a green pasture, bringing the pasture to the cows in the form of harvested grass while they reside in some enclosure is a more efficient use of that pasture for herds of over 400 or so. If put to pasture, this many animals would trample and waste the grass. The question is, do the cows need this pastoral setting for the purposes of their welfare? Other than moving to a new patch of grass to chomp on or to a source of water, cows bred for domestic conditions do little but eat, sleep, and ruminate in order to rechew the grass they have consumed and then regurgitated ("chewing the cud"), which breaks down the fibrous material so that microorganisms in the gut can digest it. Cattle spend about 60% of their day lying down. And when engaged in rumination they are in a drowsy state.[52] Kept dry and at a reasonable temperature, dairy cows can be contented creatures. They lead a rather good life on well-managed farms, all things considered. They have open-side barns, padded stalls, access to feed around the clock, and showers to cool them when the season is hot, as the dairy expert at my school, David Galligan, reports.[53]

Tail-docking, which became popular in the 1980s to help keep the udder clean and the urine-soaked swatch at the end of the tail out of the milker's face, was a practice that caused pain and discomfort to the cows. It is being phased out because trimming just the swatch has proven effective. One study showed that there were no differences in the hygiene of the udder or in milk quality between cows with docked tails and those with tails intact.[54] In this way, science was able to provide farmers with concrete data, which in turn improved the welfare of their animals.

Crowding in confinement housing presents welfare problems that seem to offset the protective advantage of being out of the elements and away from predators. Decreased available manpower (workers can find much easier and higher-paying jobs away from the farm) and increased national demand for food (and at lower prices) have all led to bigger farms and confinement housing that allows greater automation. Obviously, the welfare issues raised by these changes are complex, far more so than most animal rights literature bothers to portray (although claims that all is well in agriculture may also be overstated).[55]

Simply put, then, farms have become larger so that the agriculturalist can stay competitive. By contrst, the Pennsylvania Amish, who live about 40 miles from my home, are relatively self-sufficient on relatively small farms. They have large families that provide labor and can survive with milking a herd of less than 100—or even as few as 60—because they don't have to pay anyone outside the family to do the work. Commercial farmers must milk a bare minimum of 200 cows to eke out a living from dairy farming, and milk them two, even three times a day, *every single day*. It is not surprising, then, that dairy herds have become huge.

If mom-and-pop grocery stores, despite their appeal, are a thing of the past because they can't compete with the big "box" stores, which offer lower prices, is it any wonder that the small family farm can no longer compete in what has become a huge market place? This is not to imply that big is necessarily bad. If farmers manage their farms well and keep the welfare of their animals in mind, then technological improvements, which do require money, can increase the comfort of those animals. Good management, including improved nutrition and adequate veterinary care, is an extremely important part of animal welfare. As I have heard Temple Grandin say, we need good "stockmanship." And small farms are not always examples of good management, simply by virtue of being small. Such farms may not be able to afford the services of a veterinarian, for instance, so the farmer might resort to do-it-yourself doctoring or hire low-paid, substandard help.

In focusing on the "ills" of modern agriculture, remember as well that veterinary and agricultural science has greatly advanced the health of animals. In the twentieth century, a number of diseases of livestock have been eliminated in the United States.[56] Furthermore, although the dairy cattle population fell dramatically from 1924 to the present, there has actually been an increase in milk production. This has significantly reduced the environmental impact of the dairy industry in terms of decreased manure and methane, which contributes to the harmful greenhouse gases currently threatening our climate. In 1924, there were 21.4 million cows producing 4,167 pounds of milk per cow per year, for a total of about 89.2 trillion pounds. In 2006, those numbers stood at 9.1 million cows and 19,951 pounds of milk per cow per year, for a total of *181.8 trillion pounds*. In other words, less than half the number of cows are required today to produce more than twice as much milk as was produced in 1924.[57] We might say that at least the first two of Russell and Burch's 3R's (discussed in Chapter 4), introduced to improve laboratory animal welfare— refinement and reduction—have been achieved by the dairy industry in the United States.

The use of recombinant bovine somatotropin hormone (rBST), administered in the latter portion of a cow's lactation period to sustain production, has been a major contributing factor to this increase in production. It is a myth that it appears in the milk, which would be detrimental to human health. rBST does not appear in milk, for it stimulates production metabolically. There are some welfare considerations concerning the increased risk of mastitis (inflammation and infection of the mammary gland), but proper management with adequate veterinary care can mitigate this problem.[58] The benefits to the environment as a whole in using rBST are remarkable when compared with conventional dairy production systems and organic production, according to a recent analysis published in the *Proceedings of the National Academy of Sciences*.[59] Thanks to the great reduction in the number of cows, the global-warming potential from digestive gas production in a production system employing rBST is far below that of an organic production system, which cannot use rBST. Also, land use is 30% higher in the organic system that requires grazing.

An amazing example of what a forward-thinking farmer can do for his animals and for himself is the 2,000-cow family farm of one of my students, whose grandfather now milks some of his cows using robots. The machines are programmed to attach to a cow identified by computer, thanks to the computer chip in her ear tag as she enters a stall, and to withdraw the appropriate amount of milk during that milking episode. Because she can get milked whenever she feels the need, rather than during the traditional two (or three) times per day, the cow is more comfortable, and the rate of mastitis has been dramatically reduced.

Even the health of agricultural animals is a complex concept with more than one definition. An animal's biological health may not be the same as its economic health. Veterinarians frequently must judge whether it would be more economical to restore an animal to health or to cull it from the herd. Dairy cows produce both milk and meat. The producer must make sure to receive the appropriate return on his or her product, thus the producer is both a dairy and a beef farmer. The need for optimum efficiency requires that an otherwise healthy dairy cow be culled because she is an inefficient producer and is, therefore, not economically "healthy." Killing such an animal may be hard to accept for those who are not acquainted with the business of agriculture. Conversely, this practice may be easier to accept (by meat eaters, at least) given that the cow will not be wasted; instead, it will be turned into meat. Some of my veterinary students without a background in farming feel noble solving biological problems but uneasy solving those presented by economics. One student, obviously not from a rural background (which characterizes most of our students now), wondered why the farmer could not just keep the cow.[60]

Other economic decisions may also be hard for the general public to understand, such as the immediate culling of all male chicks in enterprises producing chickens for egg laying. The separation of calves from their mothers soon after birth, so that milking can begin and the calves can be sent on their paths to become veal, may seem cruel to those who do not earn a farm living, but the alternative would be the bull calves' immediate slaughter. Although female calves can eventually go on to become milking animals, very few males are necessary now, thanks to artificial insemination. Many of the 50% excess must be used in some way. The ethical issue then becomes how the calves are housed for the approximately 5 months they spend on a veal farm.

Peter Singer's book *Animal Liberation,* published in its second edition in 1990, would give the impression that all veal calves spend their lives (no more than 5 months) housed in dark and cramped quarters, and this has often been the case. However, the modern well-managed veal farm is quite different: it is well lit and climate controlled, and calves are provided a nutritious, milk-based diet. The animals are kept in a pre-ruminant state to keep their meat free of the unpleasant flavor that comes from the products of ruminant digestion. (A ruminant is a hoofed animal with a capacious four-chambered stomach that depends on the microorganisms housed there to break down the cellulose in order to obtain nutrients from grass and leaves. It periodically regurgitates some of that ingested in order to re-chew it into finer particles that will be able to pass into the small intestines. The ingesta is the "cud" they chew when relaxed and not eating.) In other words, the calves are kept on a diet of milk supplemented with nutrients and without the fibrous material (like grass) that stimulates changes in the structure and functioning of the stomach. What other economically-feasible action might one take with 50% of the offspring of dairy cattle, besides killing the bull calves at birth? Dairy calves do not have the qualities necessary to provide the meat that comes from the beef breeds.

It is true that calves are not gamboling around green pastures. Of most concern has been the housing of calves in individual stalls. This practice was introduced to monitor the calves individually, to prevent them from the damaging habit of sucking each others' navels, and to keep them away from adult animals. Now that computer monitoring of tagged calves is possible, they can be managed in a group housing system, and in 2007 the American Veal Association adopted this as a standard to be phased in as soon as farms can handle the transition to such housing.

Confinement housing, then, raises many ethical and welfare problems, and Singer describes them in detail in his book's chapter "Down on the Factory Farm."[61] The descriptions he provides, such as veal calves kept in narrow crates in dark conditions because it was thought this would produce the desirable pale meat, were unfortunately accurate in a number of cases in 1975, when the first edition of *Animal Liberation* was published. Poorly treated and unhealthy animals are not as profitable as healthy ones, although this does not mean that there are no welfare problems at all when animals are producing well. Solving these problems, however, can be challenging; and Singer's 1975 book, which ends with vegetarian recipes, pushes the reader hard in one direction without offering realistic solutions.

Indeed, *Animal Liberation* presents a very distorted picture of agriculture in 1990, which Dr. Larry Katz, an associate professor of animal science at Rutgers University, revealed in his review of the chapter, "Down on the Factory Farm... or How to Attack Animal Agriculture with a Pinch of Fact and a Pound of Hyperbole":

> Singer's hyperbole begins in his very first paragraph.
> "It is here, on our dinner table and in our neighborhood
> supermarket or butcher's shop that we are brought into
> direct touch with the most extensive exploitation of other
> species that has ever existed." This patently absurd statement
> sets the tone for many of his descriptions of agricultural
> practices. What non-photsynthetic organism exists without
> exploiting large numbers of other organisms? None, of
> course. "The Peacebable Kingdom" where the lion lies down
> with the lamb has never existed and never will.[62]

Other criticism abounds in Katz's review. For example, contrary to Singer's assertion that corporate agribusiness has largely replaced the family farm, the 1990 Yearbook of Agriculture indicates that [quoting Katz] "of the 2,075 million American farms, they are organized as sole proprietors (87.2%); partnerships (9.6%); family held corporations (2.9%); and other than family corporations (0.3%)." Also, according to Katz, although most of our beef comes from feedlots, "the fact is they spend most of their lives side-by-side with their mothers on pasture and perhaps 100 days in a feedlot, not six to eight months as he [Singer] claims."

Moving away from *Animal Liberation* and on to poultry, it is fair to say that modern poultry practices have borne a huge amount of criticism, particularly for the housing of layers in battery cages, where hens have little room to themselves. Although they can groom, stretch, turn around, and lie down, they cannot dust bathe, flap their wings, nor fly. Indeed, limitations on movement are probably the major welfare problem in caged systems. Many people probably assume that a chicken will be happier and healthier living outside of a cage, and activist organizations push for this without the science to back them up. Yet this claim is not necessarily the case. For example, caged birds are freer of internal and external parasites. From the standpoint of human food safety, eggs in uncaged systems are dirtier because they can be laid outside nesting boxes that are provided. (I found this to be so on a recent visit to an "organic" farm where 12,000 birds were roaming free in a hen house, picking up eggs from the dirty litter as I walked among them).

Also, broken bones are found in fewer of the caged birds than those in the cage-free system. The birds in the cage-free system break their bones, possibly when jumping down from perches. Uncaged birds are also prone to developing open and painful sores on their feet because of infections from perches and litter material contaminated with droppings and infectious material. They are also subjected to more feather picking and cannibalism, a justification for trimming part of the upper beaks in chicks. The immediate pain of the beak trimming and even lingering tenderness must be seen in relation to the pain of being cannibalized by another hen with full armor. Chickens can be nasty critters. The breeding of chickens less prone to feather picking and cannibalism may help eliminate this behavior eventually, and is a recommendation of the United Egg Producers.[63]

Free-range birds are also more vulnerable to both ground predators and predators in the sky—"chicken hawks" as we called them when I was a boy. In any system, though, good management practices are necessary for good welfare. One can find these and other arguments for or against caged or uncaged systems at Feedstuffsfoodlink.com, a Web site maintained by the agricultural magazine *Feedstuffs*.[64] A group of nine well-known animal scientists, members of the Scientific Advisory Committee of the United Egg Producers, concluded the following:

> Research evaluating a variety of systems for housing and managing laying hens shows that each housing system has welfare advantages and disadvantages, but with proper husbandry and selection of equipment, many of these systems can ensure that hens enjoy an acceptable state of welfare.
>
> It is imperative that systems be considered from a holistic perspective; groups or individuals should avoid taking single welfare advantages/disadvantages out of context in an effort to promote a particular system.[65]

To sum up this contentious issue, I defer to a colleague of mine, Eric Gingrich, DVM, a specialist in poultry medicine and management, who, with the aid several members of the Association of Veterinarians in Egg Production (AVEP), made the following statement in May 2007:

> Poultry domestication and the eventual large-scale production for commercial purposes evolved to use confinement. Confinement methods have been improved

and refined over the years to provide a suitable environment for the birds, a safe/ergonomic environment for the workers, and a wholesome and affordable product for consumers. Current egg layer cage systems are the product of this long process and they provide the following welfare advantages.[66]

Dr. Gingrich then lists four advantages that justify modern, well-managed caged systems: safety; freedom from hunger and thirst with less competition from pen mates; improved health: and comfort, being isolated from bad weather and the birds' own droppings. Some would argue, of course, that hens are not able to do all that a hen would like to do. He answers this last concern as follows:

Egg layers have undergone genetic selection by primary breeding companies for more than 50 years to adapt these chickens to cage production. Today's commercial egg layers were bred to perform in cages under exacting requirements for diet, space, temperature, air quality, and disease prevention. Providing these requirements allows for equal or better egg production, egg weights, feed efficiency (converting feed to eggs), and livability when compared to cage-free layers. Modern cage systems and their related efficiencies lead to better use of our land and feedstuffs. Cleaner eggs and improved shell quality lead to improved food safety.[67]

Animal-welfare scientists David Fraser, Joy Mench, and Suzanne Millman[68] have examined various modern farming practices fairly, pointing to areas in need of improvement and the complexities involved in making those improvements. But it was British ethologist Marion Stamp Dawkins, in her brief yet comprehensive book, *Animal Suffering: The Science of Animal Welfare*,[69] who led the way in analyzing how one can scientifically measure the welfare of animals. Dawkins stipulates over and over again that she cannot offer simple solutions. As indicators of animal welfare she lists physical health; comparisons with life in the wild (not always without its own suffering); various physiological measurements, such as heart rate and hormone levels; and behavior, asking how much abnormality has to be shown to justify the statement that the animal is suffering.

Another animal-welfare scientist, one of many who should be mentioned and congratulated here, is John Webster, a professor of animal husbandry at the University of Bristol. Webster wrote a superb book, *Animal Welfare: A Cool Eye Toward Eden*, that considers the nature of animals and our impact on their welfare in every conceivable situation, extending well beyond agricultural animals to our treatment of our cats and dogs. Regarding the welfare of hens in battery cages compared to that of hens in colony situations, he concludes that, overall, "the welfare of laying hens in large commercial colony systems is at least as bad as that of hens in the conventional battery cage."[70] In his opinion the push by ill-informed activist organizations to eliminate the colony system immediately should be ignored in favor of a more measured, scientific approach to improve the welfare in both systems.

In a chapter that updated Dawkins'thinking almost 30 years after her first book, Dawkins examines potential solutions to welfare problems that meet market needs of animal agriculture. She first defines good welfare in simple terms: animals must be healthy and have what they want. For example, laying hens will push a heavily weighted door to reach a place where they can dust bathe, and mink will do the same to reach a pool of water. Working toward providing "furnished cages" that allow such behaviors is a challenge in economic terms; however, Dawkins and others focused on animal-welfare science have conducted scientific studies in commercial settings to find out what works and if it can be profitable. She ends her wonderful chapter with these words:

> We know what it means to talk about animals being healthy
> and having what they want and we can identify the sorts of
> *in context* evidence that we are going to need. Putting good
> welfare into practice and making sure that under
> commercial conditions the welfare of the animals is ensured
> is much, much harder. But if the new contract [that will
> correct the ills of the past] means anything at all, it must
> have clauses that guarantee delivery, not just promises.
> Delivery is the next step.[71]

And there's the rub: matching optimal conditions with the need for people to earn an income. In any case, good science should always lead the way, and good management will ensure the most welfare. As long as an animal is housed in clean, sufficiently large quarters compatible with economic realities, healthy, and well fed, what do we know of its thoughts? Can it suffer in a henhouse or a barn in the sense we people would, pining for the outdoors? It seems doubtful to me, given that for generations that environment would not have been within the animal's experience.

Concerning food animals of today, then, the fundamental question is, how much of their "natural" lives can we deny them in the name of efficiency, knowing that the natural lives of other members of the same or, more accurately,

related species usually end in a lingering death from injury, disease, or malnutrition? How much can we do to animals in the interests of efficiency and profits? Without question, in my mind, we went too far without enough attention to
welfare early in the latter half of the twentieth century, but this does not justify
wholesale abandonment of agricultural practices. Ethical behavior demands
that we seek to correct our errors. Producers, supported by consumers willing
to pay for changes, must strive to balance their economic interests with the
welfare of their animals. And many, in company with animal science specialists
are engaged in this effort.[72] I emphasize that they do so according to scientific
principles and not uninformed prejudices.

Producers are moving in the right direction, but very likely not fast enough
for some indivudals. The pork industry has created the Pork Industry Animal
Care Coalition, which represents producers, processors, retailers, and restaurants and their associations—in other words, each link in the food chain. They
have devised a program so that farms selling pigs to processors that the USDA
inspects will have on-farm animal welfare assessment as part of the new Pork
Quality Assurance Plus (PQA Plus) program.[73] In the dairy and beef industry
there is the Milk and Dairy Beef Quality Assurance Program.[74] And 85% of the
eggs produced in the United States now come from establishments that adhere
to the welfare standards of the United Egg Producers.[75]

These programs are producer generated and not mandated by the government, although I suspect that more and more producers will adopt them as
society changes its view of what is acceptable, and agrees to pay the price. Third-
party audits of welfare practices assuring the public of the welfare of farm animals and the safety of their food supply will be important, of course. Pressures
on producers are also coming from the fast-food chains, such as McDonald's,
which in turn have been pushed by the animal rights organizations and public
perceptions to establish welfare standards and to audit their suppliers. These
companies now employ animal welfare advisors, such as Temple Grandin,
which will ensure that their standards are scientifically based.[76] After all, healthy
animals are better producers.

One of my colleagues, Tom Parsons, who actually worked in my sleep
research laboratory during a portion of his veterinary training, eventually took
over and reinvigorated the school's swine medicine teaching program. He has
been addressing the problem of how to house pregnant sows outside the confinement of the much-maligned gestation crates, which allow little movement
of the sow during the gestation period. While the gestation crate limits movement, it also protects subordinate sows from the ills of a social hierarchy: physical abuse and malnourishment. Success in group housing requires the ability to
control individual nutrition as well as manage aggression and its possible
outcome, trauma.

Much of the aggressive behavior centers around access to food. To manage this behavior, a computer chip is placed on the sow's ear that uniquely identifies her, and triggers the repetitive delivery of a small portion of feed at a time until she receives her allotment of 6 pounds for the day. She then moves forward, away from the eating area, allowing the sow behind her to feed. Those who have eaten their 6 pounds may re-enter the feeding apparatus, but to no avail. (Those who are "repeat offenders" Parsons refers to as "eternal optimists.")

The number of these 400- to 600-pound sows that live together in a large pen is also critical in managing aggression. Whenever pigs are housed together, a social hierarchy forms. The fact that animals pass through the electronic sow feeder in the same order each day provides evidence to social organization that develops within the group. However, as the number of the animals in the pen is increased to upwards of 100, the untoward effects of the social order disappear. Either the pen is large enough that conflict is minimized through avoidance, or perhaps with that many animals in the pen it is simply too hard for the dominant sow to hold particular grudges. In any event, the end result is a dramatic decrease in fighting and subsequent injuries. Also, lactating sows are kept for a week in a farrowing crate that allows newborn piglets to suckle while also protecting them from being crushed (they can reside outside the crate). Then the crate is opened so all can roam about in a 50-foot square pen.

We are proud of this program, but will such programs function as effectively in very large commercial operations? Time will tell, but most producers recognize that society is pushing them away from practices that may negatively impact animal welfare when more humane alternatives are available. To date, over 30,000 sows across the country are now housed in the basic "Penn" gestation system that employs the electronic sow-feeding of group-housed, gestating animals prototyped here at the University of Pennsylvania. Work also continues here on a commercially viable alternative to the farrowing crate so that it can be welfare-friendly to both the sow and piglet.

Three well-known animal scientists and welfare advocates, Stanley Curtis from the University of Illinois, Temple Grandin (discussed in Chapter 7) from Colorado State University, and John McGlone from Texas Tech University, made a joint statement on farm-animal welfare issues on which they had reached common agreement. Concerning the contentious issue of sow gestation stalls, they emphasized once again the need for careful study in addressing welfare problems:

> The scientific evidence shows that sow physiology and
> behavior are essentially equivalent in well-managed stalls
> and group pens. We understand the general public may
> not like gestation stalls. However, we are concerned that,

as pregnant sows are moved from stalls to pens, some sows
may have a reduced state of being due to social stress.
With the only requirement that sows move from stalls to
pens, sow state of being may actually decrease. We urge
caution and a systematic, thorough, ongoing evaluation of
effective group housing systems of pregnant sows bred and
adapted for group housing.[77]

Sows with piglets are big and dangerous animals, so some measure of
confinement is beneficial to piglets that might otherwise be crushed and to
caretakers that might be attacked. Sows allowed to roam free in the field
will not receive the veterinary care they might need because of the dangers of
handling them in this setting. There are always tradeoffs to consider when
demanding a return to the bucolic.

Committed consumers can play a role if they are willing to open up their
pocketbooks to higher-priced food produced under less efficient systems than
those that have become common practice.[78] It may be unrealistic to expect this,
however; a telephone survey of 1,000 individuals across the United States conducted by Oklahoma State University and the American Farm Bureau Federation
revealed that human poverty, the country's health care system, and food safety
were considered to be at least five times more important than farm animal well-
being. The financial well-being of farmers was found to be twice as important as
the well-being of farm animals.[79] Of course, this survey contained a small sample,
and the results could have been skewed depending on the population surveyed.

It is an open question, however, whether nonintensive farming will ever
serve more than the educated, relatively wealthy elite. Feeding the masses will
probably always necessitate large farm operations, so the future of farm-animal
welfare will have to depend on good-faith efforts of farmers themselves and the
various industry associations noted above. Producer, marketer, and consumer
are inextricably intertwined, thus considerable effort will be required to make
changes in modern agriculture that can improve animal welfare. The demands
of upscale markets can create big profits for the middleman, with insufficient
return to the farmer who has tried to respond by moving to a less efficient but
more animal-friendly system. Even organic farming is becoming industrialized
to feed a growing interest; houses containing thousands of birds in one house
are not like the small houses of my youth on the family farm.

To improve animal welfare, producers must be shown that changes in practices will materially affect welfare and that they are not spending hard-earned
money on ideas that do not significantly improve it. To repeat an important
point, scientific inquiry must be the course followed. This is why the studies of

Dawkins and her colleagues that are done in conditions mimicking commercial situations are so important. Change will not occur by relying on uninformed sentiments stemming from uncritical anthropomorphizing. Nor can one walk away from the difficulties by suggesting we become vegetarians. Many people just enjoy the taste of meat and eggs. We need to come up with workable solutions so that welfare and economic viability are not at odds, or we need to at least work toward that goal.

In all of this discussion, remember that the freedom Americans have gained from having only a small proportion of the nation engaged in the production of food has allowed society to pursue to a greater extent other beneficial concerns, such as technological advances, the arts, biomedical research, and education. The United States spends less than 10% of its national income on food, much less then other countries, allowing the remaining 90% to be used for other acquisitions.[80] Less efficient use of animals would mean higher food prices and greater difficulties among poor segments of our population in obtaining proper nutrition. In this sense, the ethical question becomes, how can we balance the equation of welfare versus efficient production of abundant food, and food that the poorer in our society can afford?

I will close this section now by stepping into deep waters: the raising of animals for fur, which can be classified under agriculture. Wearing fur is one of the most damned of human uses of animals, a use that even some of my biomedical friends would probably condemn. In my view, it is a matter of human choice if one believes that animals raised for fur are a renewable resource and are treated humanely, and, contrary to animal rights propaganda, they are. How could a mink farmer convert poorly maintained animals into saleable coats? (Incidentally, of the 836 recorded attacks against animal users recorded by the Foundation forBiomedical Research from 1981 to 2006, those that targeted the fur industry ranked second to those targeting biomedical research establishments and its practitioners, the latter forming more than 90% of those victimized.[81])

Mark Schumacher[82] is one of those victimized. A furrier and a friend of mine, he explained the complexity of this issue in a letter he wrote to a middle-school girl who opposed his profession. He argued that genuine fur is an environmentally sound alternative to artificial furs. Among the points he made were that the extraction of oil, the raw material of artificial fibers, can pollute the waters with oil spills and kill animals directly or by destroying habitat. Processing plants that make artificial fibers can also pollute the air and waters. Also, coats of synthetic fibers fill landfills, while natural furs are biodegradable and return to the earth after 6 months following a lifetime of use. Finally, he argued that abusing the animals would produce a poor product.

Considering ethical behavior, citizens should be greatly concerned about the lawbreaking that goes on as part of the debate over fur, regardless of whether they think fur is ethical. The father of one of my veterinary students was hounded out of business by such behavior; picketing and activists' damage to his store drove away his customers. Many fur farms have been attacked by extremists who have released mink from their cages. These animals are far removed from the wild, so many of them die. Most recently, in Utah 6,000 mink were released by the ALF. Of the 6,000 fragile animals let loose in the wild, 5,500 were recovered, but of them, 500 died of heat exhaustion.[83,84]

The raising of animals for fur is but one of many animal uses discussed in this chapter. Given the wide range of uses covered, there is probably more to disagree with from reader to reader in this chapter than in any other part of the book. Some will consider me too lenient in what I can accept and defend, and others will say I am too considerate of those who would limit or abolish one activity or another. Ultimately, the majority will rule. I only hope that future leaders and law makers will not be too harsh with our rural heritage, forcing a singular lifestyle on all in the belief that they alone are right. All human activity cannot be dictated by animal needs, though we must also recognize that however we use animals, we must use them well.

The Philosophers | 9

N o one can dispute that the publication of Peter Singer's *Animal Liberation* in 1975 was a watershed event for the coming intense debate on human–animal interactions. Tom Regan added his concept of animal rights in 1983 in *The Case for Animal Rights*. A number of other philosophers have weighed in on this issue over the years as well, such as David De Grazia in *Taking Animals Seriously*,[1] Mary Midgley in *Why Animals Matter*,[2] Evelyn Pluhar in *Beyond Prejudice*,[3] James Rachels in *Created from Animals*,[4] and Bernard Rollin in *Animal Rights and Human Morality*.[5] These thinkers vary in their proscriptions against animal use, although all would disagree with my thinking on one or more animal uses. Regarding biomedical research using animals, Regan in his complex and tightly reasoned book concludes (with some others) that animal interests are equal to ours, and that even life-saving research, if it harms an animal, cannot be done ethically (theoretically at least) because it is against the animal's interests. Yet, as the famous ancient Roman orator Cicero is known to have remarked, "One can defend any idea rationally, however that does not make the idea valid or true." Nevertheless, in my view, debates that force us to consider how we can best treat (and use) animals without sacrificing the well-being of our fellow humans are worth engaging in.

Scientists have generally shied away from public discussion of ethical issues. Only a few have directly confronted the philosophical underpinnings of the animal rights and liberation movement. These include Richard Vance,[6] a pathologist at Bowman Gray School of Medicine, with training in philosophy, and the team of Charles Nicoll and Sharon Russell, who have published various essays.[7-9] The general unwillingness of scientists to discuss ethical issues openly, I believe, is largely due to their fear of sacrificing their anonymity by speaking or writing about anything having to do with animal rights. I will risk exposing my naiveté regarding various philosophical issues; there is no way to avoid doing so if I am to explain my professional behavior through the years. Of course, when philosophers step into the realm of science they, too, are in danger of looking naïve.

Some of my colleagues may also feel a sense of guilt, having been convinced that they are engaged in a "necessary evil"—necessary to be sure, but evil nevertheless and, possibly, deep down indefensible philosophically. For my part, I cannot begin to regard as evil an activity that has brought eventual relief from so much pain and disease to so many of my fellow humans and to many animals: carefully performed biomedical research. I cannot consider myself or what I do evil knowing that Nature routinely consigns animals to death by starvation or some quite horrible diseases, and permits predators to disembowel their living prey in order to gain sustenance.

My own confidence in evaluating and countering the ethical positions of those who support animal rights and liberation came after reading the essays by Nicoll, Russell, and Vance. After spending several years reading and mulling over the arguments one finds in Singer's and Reagan's books and, to a lesser extent, the others mentioned, I came to a simple conclusion: one may create any world one wishes with words, but the critical question is whether one would be willing to live in that world. So far, in one important respect, doing without the fruits of future biomedical research, the answer has been "no" from the animal rightist philosophers and their followers.

The discontinuation of the use of animals for various purposes would put unreasonable and, in certain instances, even unthinkable demands on humanity. Biomedical research offers a case in point, if you accept the evidence presented in Chapters 3 and 4 and reject the claims of the various medical professionals put forth in Chapter 5. Bioethicist Lance Stell[10] has challenged those who demand that research not be performed with animals by arguing that they should feel honor bound to refrain from benefiting from the fruits of current biomedical research. That they should do otherwise is unethical in his mind, and in mine. He notes that many devotees of the animal rightsand liberation ideology eschew the eating of meat because they believe that killing animals for food is cruel. But their claim that biomedical research is cruel and useless, even as they continue to benefit from that research by accepting modern medical care, puts animal rights activists in an ethical bind. Stell notes that some religious groups have denied themselves the benefits of medical treatment in accord with their religious teachings, and observes that there is a considerable body of case law documenting this behavior. Then why not the animal rightists, he asks? Where is the proof that they, too, have acted according to their beliefs? Stell would not deny these people the benefits of past research, of course; but integrity demands that they refrain from partaking of the beneficial results of future progress. There seems no way to avoid that ethical decision.

I can hardly do justice to all of the arguments of all the philosophers mentioned above, particularly in just one chapter. My focus will be on Singer and Regan, the two largely uncontested philosophical leaders of the animal rights movement, with examples from writings by a few of the others brought in at appropriate points. Although Singer and Regan represent two schools of moral philosophy, utilitarianism and deontology, or rights philosophy, they reach fairly similar conclusions about animal use. These two contrasting schools of thought have, however unintentionally, spawned a unified movement that Charles Griswold Jr., a philosopher at Howard University, has characterized as follows:

> The animal rights movement illustrates the incoherent
> nature of a moral passion become immoral by virtue of its
> extremism. In the name of the laudable quality of
> humaneness, the use of animals for food, clothing and
> medical experimentation is prohibited. Research that could
> save your child's life, or save you from an excruciating
> disease, is declared unethical. The result is inhumanity
> toward man.[11]

Raimond Gaita, a professor of moral philosophy at King's College in London, argued much the same in an interesting way in his delightful book, *The Philosopher's Dog*, when reflecting on how we would calculate the costs of treating our sick dog with those required for a sick infant:

> People can argue about where to draw the line in a situation
> like that, but I know of no one whose dog would be treated
> as equal to a seriously sick infant. If someone did treat their
> dog like that I would not think of them as a pioneer of
> ethical thought, but as someone whose sentimentality has
> made them wicked.[12]

Peter Singer

With Singer we meet a utilitarian. Utilitarians measure whether the consequences of an action create more or less suffering, stipulating that adherents must always conduct themselves so as to cause the least suffering possible. Singer holds that the balance is negative in the case of most animal use by humans. He views animal rights as only a political construct, although his *Animal Liberation* is often referred to as the "bible" of the movement.

Singer's philosophical views are quite simple and easy to grasp. Consequently, his book has been more influential than Regan's, which is a bit too dense for the average reader in my estimation. *Animal Liberation* is as much exposé as it is a philosophical treatise. In the 1990 edition there are 248 pages of text; of that, 50 and 63 pages are devoted to exposés of biomedical research and modern agriculture, respectively. Only 23 pages are needed to introduce and defend a very simple idea: Pain unites the animal kingdom (including humans). The special qualities that make us human are basically irrelevant and do not elevate us very far from this perspective. The remaining pages of Singer's book are taken up by excoriation of the Judeo-Christian tradition and what it has wrought through the centuries, inflammatory photographs, rebuttals to various challenges to the author's ideas, recording of accomplishments, and recommended choices such as vegetarianism to advance the cause. Although there is much philosophical and interesting historical discussion, the essential thesis is that our most important charge is to consider the interests of animals and humans in equal amounts because we all suffer from pain.

The publication of *Animal Liberation* probably did more to polarize the animal rights–welfare issue since 1975 than any other single event. By discounting the value of biomedical research using animals,[13] the book provided ammunition for attacks on scientists perpetrated by later propagandists. Scientists were subsequently placed in a defensive position and became less and less inclined to fight back against extremist persecution. However, in his review of Kathy Snow Guillermo's book in *Nature* (see Chapter 2) that offered an animal-rightist view of the Silver Spring Monkey case, Singer placed the blame for this polarization squarely on the beleaguered scientists, "with lobby groups funded by the animal research industry opposing every attempt by the animal rights movement to achieve the most moderate gains in animal welfare."[14]

Singer's argument begins with a recounting of past liberation movements (of humans) and how they overcame the prejudice of the nineteenth and twentieth centuries, in which the status quo was sufficient reason to reject any change in thinking. Blacks and women were inferior by society's definition, and if they were given equal rights, the next step would be the bestowal of rights on mere animals. Recall here my earlier comment that the nineteenth-century world extending into the early twentieth century depended extensively on the use of animals so that, in a sense, those in charge may have been expressing a sub-conscious fear that their world would be torn asunder. Singer is seemingly arguing that because these liberation movements were successful, why not animals now?

Animal Liberation works toward Singer's conclusion that the essential fea-ture all of us share somewhere "down" to mollusks is the capacity to suffer as sentient beings. He urges readers to be aware that they, too, could yet be placed at a disadvantage, just as animals are now: (1) in an arbitrarily organized hierarchical society based on IQ, for example; or (2) through some yet-to-be-discovered evidence, that our genetic makeup alone, and not a combination of genes and environment, accounts for our abilities (the potential for marginal-ization of genetically "inferior" people is clear). Singer seems to be using philo-sophical scare tactics here to get the reader to believe that the only sanctuary is the commonality of suffering if some of us are to avoid some fictitious future discrimination. In democratic states, at least, where there is now comprehen-sive civil rights legislation, including the Americans with Disabilities Act, can anyone realistically entertain this hypothetical fear?

Given the fear of the future that he posits, Singer asserts that the only safe (moral) course is to recognize that

> equality is a moral idea, not an assertion of fact. There is no logically compelling reason for assuming that a factual difference in ability between two people justifies any difference in the amount of consideration we give to their needs and interests. *The principle of the equality of human beings is not a description of an alleged actual equality among humans: it is a prescription of how we should treat human beings* [Singer's emphasis].[15]

I agree with him up to this point.

He goes on to say, however, that "if possessing a higher degree of intelli-gence does not entitle one human to use another for his or her own ends, how can it entitle humans to exploit nonhumans for the same purposes?"[16] In Singer's view the moral "glue" that makes all of us a family of equals—humans and animals alike—is the capacity for all of us to suffer (this was the central argument of philosopher Jeremy Bentham).

Thus, having started with a position on behalf of human beings, Singer has added the novel interpretation that has come to drive the animal rights and liberation movement. When Singer writes that humans must give equal consideration to the interests of other individuals, he includes animals as individuals. Failure to include animals, Singer argues, is evidence of "speciesism," a term first introduced by his Oxford colleague, Richard Ryder. This awkward term is, of course, a takeoff of the term *racism*. Singer accords speciesism moral opprobrium equal to that of racism, thereby challenging the primacy of humankind. I certainly think we should do all we reasonably can to alleviate or prevent pain or other suffering in the animals we use, but I feel constrained to consider human needs first. This is the point where solidarity between animals and people breaks down for me.

In his book *Created from Animals: the Moral Implications of Darwinism,* philosopher James Rachels[17] introduced the term "moral individualism," which might be regarded as another way of saying speciesism: one is enjoined by him to treat each individual, animal or human, on a case-by-case basis, not as a class of beings. His reasoning does not differ from Singer's, although his close reliance on Darwinism is more evident. Rachels offers absolutist solutions, such as eliminating all meat eating rather than improving methods of production.

According to Singer, then, suffering is the vital characteristic that gives a being the right to equal consideration. Minimizing or eliminating pain is a good thing, of course, but pain is a part of the everyday world. Following innate drives, animals inflict pain on other animals for "good purpose," in other words, to survive. Wolves that eat an elk while it is still alive are one example. For human beings, this same purpose of survival is served not by ripping apart a living elk but through medical research with animals. Should we deny humanity the ability to survive through this means? Of course not, says Singer, who allows that "if a single experiment could cure a disease like leukemia, that experiment would be justifiable." But, Singer then adds, "since a speciesist bias, like a racist bias, is unjustifiable, an experiment cannot be justifiable unless the experiment is so important *that the use of a retarded human being would also be justifiable* (my emphasis)."[18]

Lest there be any doubt about his position, Singer makes it abundantly clear: "I do not believe it could never be justifiable to experiment on a retarded human. If it were really possible to save many lives by an experiment that would take just one life, and there were no other way those lives could be saved; it might be right to do the experiment. But this would be an extremely rare case."[19] This, of course, is an unrealistic view of how medical science progresses, as discussed in Chapter 4, and is only useful for the purposes of philosophical argument.

Clearly, in this passage, Singer directly challenges the Judeo-Christian precept that all human life is uniquely precious, and he challenges as well Western societies' ancient codes of conduct centered on this idea. Although many adherents and opponents of the animal rights movement may assume that Singer views humans and animals as moral equals, this is actually not the case. The practical result of adhering to his philosophy would, in fact, lead to this consequence: according to Singer, for a human being to be preferred over other animals, he or she must possess certain attributes. Singer explains:

> The preference, in normal cases, for saving a human life over the life of an animal when a choice *has* to be to be made is a preference based on the characteristics that normal humans have, and not on the mere fact that they are members of our own species. This is why when we consider members of our own species who lack the characteristics of normal humans we can no longer say that their lives are always to be preferred to those of other animals [emphasis in original].[20]

Unfortunately, Singer paints a distorted picture of the nature of biomedical research in the service of the thesis in his chapter, "Tools for Research." Russell and Nicoll[21] reviewed the chapter and revealed in an extensive journal article they co-authored a considerable number of distortions that Singer had introduced to favor his claim that using animals for research had not resulted in enough benefit to offset the harm done to them, according to the utilitarian view. Russell and Nicoll's analysis is very harsh, indeed damningly harsh, for a close look at Singer's chapter revealed a high degree of selectivity. And Singer's rebuttal[22] was very weak.[23] Rather than focusing on experiments that have led to various safer anesthetics, or those that resulted in new surgical techniques that made previously impossible operations possible (such as the heart–lung machine that permits prolonged open-heart surgery), or experiments aimed at understanding what causes cells to run wild in cancer, Singer chose to put most of his emphasis on behavioral experiments. These are, without doubt, the hardest experiments for the untutored to conceive as justified. As such, they made the best targets for Singer, whether intentionally or not.

How unbalanced was the chapter? Of those pages devoted strictly to the use of animals in research, half deal with studies on animal behavior and drug addiction. Yet in 1993, when Nicoll and Russell were writing, the National Institutes of Health doled out only 11% of its budget to those institutes funding research on behavior, mental health, and substance abuse, while 37% went to those conducting research on cancer, diabetes, and heart disease. Considering that these percentages would translate roughly to the number of animals used in studying the problems, we might conclude that Singer shied away from picking on targets that the public regards with greater sympathy than mental health and addiction. By ignoring the fact that the experiments he describes out of context were designed to advance understanding that would lead to the alleviation of various kinds of human misery, Singer could glibly dismiss them.

Russell and Nicoll summarized the chapter as follows:

> Some have argued that his book provides "intellectual rigor" to the moral arguments for animals' equality with humans, which had previously been based largely on emotionalism and sentimentality. We have analyzed the contents of the chapter, "Tools for Research," which criticizes the use of animals in biomedical research as well as for drug and product-safety testing.... In addition, Singer mischaracterizes the cited studies in various ways. He quotes selectively and out of context from numerous research projects. He never mentions the objectives of these projects, except occasionally when, in our opinion, he distorts or trivializes them. Singer also cites supposedly damning "evidence" published by other antivivisectionists, even though this "evidence" has been refuted in the literature.[24]

Having voiced these criticisms, it is only fair to acknowledge that at the time when *Animal Liberation* was first published in 1975, biomedical research in the United States was not regulated as it is today (see Chapter 4). Now scientists who use animals are required by law to have oversight from an institutional committee; back in 1975 such oversight was merely a recommendation of the Public Health Service, which funds most of the biomedical research conducted in the United States. Furthermore, the influence of laboratory animal veterinarians in 1975 was not what it is today. This changed with the passage of two laws by Congress in 1985, and the end result was better animal care and, I believe, more thoughtfully conceived and conducted research. Disappointingly, Singer makes no real mention of these improvements in the second edition of *Animal Liberation*, published in 1990, nor in his 2002 paperback edition, which has only a new preface that ignores these advances. The important research monitoring body, the Association for Assessment and Accreditation of Laboratory Animal Care (AAALAC), described in Chapter 4, received no attention either.

One inaccuracy in Singer's book has special relevance to me as a professor in a school of veterinary medicine. In a denial of the claims of institutions that veterinarians are on staff to see to animals' interests, Singer accuses American veterinarians of "conditioned ethical blindness." He writes that "no doubt many veterinarians did go into the field because they cared about animals, but it is difficult for people who really care about animals to go through a course of study in veterinary medicine without having their sensitivity to animal suffering blunted."[25] No survey results support this claim, only a statement from a "veterinary student" who reports being turned off by some incidents in her *pre-veterinary* training that induced her *not* to go to veterinary school. Having taught several thousand future veterinarians for more than 40 years, and having been one myself for decades, I can say with certainty that Singer's unsupported generalization is way off the mark. I might also add that human physicians undergo a certain level of desensitization during their training that is absolutely integral to their ability to perform essential medical procedures without becoming overcome emotionally. Further, Singer glosses over the fact that the vast majority of veterinarians are not biomedical researchers, and are instead the caring individuals who look after the everyday health of our dogs, cats, horses, and other pets.

All but a few (those captured by the extremes of the animal rights and liberation movement) sense a duty to fellow humans that supersedes obligations to other species. Among these duties is the relief of human suffering, an obvious objective of biomedical research employing animals that is clearly acceptable to most. This duty applies to "marginal cases": infants and the brain-damaged of any age. Lewis Petrinovich, a psychologist who authored a trilogy of books examining various human moral concerns, addresses Singer's contention that morality should not be strictly allied with our affections by writing:

> On the contrary, these affections represent an evolved tendency toward emotional bonding in the service of differential reproductive success; they are an essential part of the biological predispositions that promote a cohesive community, and this affectionate basis is highly relevant to morality, conferring the status of a human moral patient on neonates as well as on the cognitively disabled. When matters are cast in terms of evolutionary biology we can meet the test that those humans influenced by our actions have a moral claim not grounded on sentimentality, but on respect for the basic aspects of the human social contract.[26]

It is difficult to ignore the fact that humans have a long evolutionary history that drives us to bind together.

Tom Regan

Coming from the other branch of moral philosophy that focuses on the concept of rights, Regan subscribes to the view that the rights of the being in question are most important. As philosopher Carl Cohen wrote in a published debate with Regan, focusing on Regan's rights argument,

> the use of animals is (for them) intrinsically immoral; it is conduct that violates, always and inevitably, the rights those animals possess. On this account, it does not matter how the advantages and disadvantages of animal experimentation balance out; using animals in science is morally wrong because it violates the rights of conscious beings that we have a compelling moral duty to respect.[27]

People who have then attempted to bring these ideas out of the ivory tower and into the street (non-philosophers, in other words) have tried to change the world dramatically and unrealistically—and cruelly from the human point of view.

Regan believes that animals' lives have an "inherent value" that proscribes use or harm of them. Because animals (warm-blooded animals at least) are conscious and goal oriented, says Regan, they may be regarded as "subjects-of-a-life," a state that gives them inherent value and interests that preclude their exploitation by humans. In response to this proposal, my colleagues and I wrote:

> Certainly, all animals have an inherent interest in survival, in the acquisition of food, and in the avoidance of pain. Are they, however, capable of apprehending interests in the way that human beings do? Can they, for example, understand ethical interests such as justice or autonomy? Can they have any interests in the development of advanced knowledge?[28]

Is there *any* animal that would have *any* interest in taking care of me when I am an enfeebled old man?

Looking at weaknesses in Regan's position that animals are subjects-of-a-life and so have the same inherent value that we do, Tannenbaum[29] notes that humans have "life plans" and are "aware of their history, present and potential futures," while Regan presents no evidence that "a mouse has a certain *perspective* on the world." Tannenbaum also notes that "many people believe that animals with more sophisticated mental capacities and experiences are more valuable and worthy of protection and should be recognized as having moral and legal rights not possessed by other animals." This latter recognition would, of course, introduce the problem of speciesism.

Regan does not assert that animals and humans are equal in every way. Though he argues that animals are equal to humans in their right not to be harmed arbitrarily, in a manner similar to Singer, Regan acknowledges that human beings, at least "normal" human beings, have greater prospects for various satisfactions. Consequently, if a choice has to be made between saving one animal's or one normal human's life (at a time), Regan's nod would go to the human. But perhaps it is reasonable to assume that mentally disabled human beings might fare no better in Regan's scheme than in Singer's.

Ultimately, like the views of Singer, Regan's directly challenge the use of animals in biomedical research. Unlike Singer, Regan is an absolutist and would make that research completely impossible. Concerning biomedical research in particular, Regan has this to say:

> Not even a single rat is to be treated as if the animal's value
> were reducible to his *possible utility* relative to the interests
> of others, which is what we would be doing if we
> intentionally harmed the rat on the grounds that this *just
> might* "prove" something, *just might* "yield" a "new insight,"
> just might produce "benefits" for others [emphases in the
> original].[30]

Regan understands well the destructive implications of his position for biomedical research:

> If that [abandoning animal research] means that there are
> some things we cannot learn, then so be it. We have then no
> right against nature [because nature is not a moral agent]
> not to be harmed by those natural diseases we are heir to.[31]

Regan's thinking would clearly render humanity helpless against the forces of nature, particularly with regard to the conquering of disease and deformity through animal research.

Actually, Singer came up with something quite similar:

> In any case, the ethical question of the justification of animal
> experimentation cannot be settled by pointing to its benefits
> for us, no matter how persuasive the evidence in favor of
> such benefits may be. The ethical principle of equal
> consideration of interests will rule out some means of

> obtaining knowledge. There is nothing sacred about the
> right to pursue knowledge.[32]

The last statement is true, but properly regulated, that pursuit is vital to our well-being and, I would argue, is a consequence of one of humanity's defining characteristics: the thirst for knowledge. We would have wasted a lot of evolutionary "energy" were we to abandon our quests.

Although I disagree with the ideas of Singer, Regan, and others with firm views against human use of animals, I can certainly agree with their wish to better the lot of animals. This is in itself laudable, and has borne fruit through political pressures, as I have already noted in an earlier chapter. We have seen such interest in animal welfare in centuries past, however, so there is nothing new there. The most important difference between Singer and Regan and the animal welfare groups of centuries past is that Singer and Regan now enjoy an audience that has little formal contact with (and, I would venture, understanding of) the animal world. The world that some of these followers would like to see is one that I think the great majority of people would not want to live in—devoid of various interactions with animals. Anarchist segments of the animal rights and liberation movement would be happy, it seems, to live in a world in which the lion would lie down with the lamb (both ultimately starving to death from overpopulation of all animal species lumped together as neither predator nor prey, an unrealistic return to Eden). We humans, along with our domesticated species, would have a better chance of dying some miserable death without modern medicines developed through research that, for the present, must employ animals.

All of this would of necessity follow if Regan's ideas were to be adhered to strictly. Singer, although not an absolutist like Regan, would still tie us up in knots trying to balance suffering on a one-to-one basis. Furthermore, in his last chapter, "Speciesism Today," Singer seems to hope for a return to Eden. We would stop interfering in the lives other species, obviously not eating them. The focus, as a result, is on a return to the issues raised in "Down on the Factory Farm." What negates his argument is his failure to discuss the implications for both human and animal health if we removed ourselves from the animal world. He offers no hope for the sick, only defending himself with the argument that most experiments are "trivial" anyway.

A More Traditional Way of Thinking

An experience I had several years ago sums up my thinking on the subject in rather few words. While walking down Queen Street, the main street of

Lancaster, Pennsylvania, I was musing over the animal rights question and looking down the block to where a group of people waited for the bus. I could see that they were probably Hispanic migrant workers, different in several respects from me—culturally, socially, even by virtue of their language. Unbidden, a question jumped into my mind: why are those people, in various ways not like me, nevertheless recognizable to me as "belonging to me"? Had one of their children and a healthy, exuberant dog—even my dog, or Buster— run out into the street in the middle of traffic, I would have immediately raced for the child, and not the animal. If that child had been obviously seriously impaired mentally, my reaction would certainly have been the same. Why? Because both children would have been human beings.

That answer reveals at least one "prejudice" of mine according to some of the thinking I have just discussed: my choice would have been a severely impaired human over a perfectly healthy animal. I believe most of us would have done the same, because what resides within us (again, most of us, not all of us) is a belief that there is a fundamental difference between animals and human beings. Despite the sense that cruelty toward animals (and humans, for that matter) is wrong,[33] as much for our own moral character as for their sake, most of us recognize a duty to humankind that supersedes other duties. Most of us now recognize that human beings (normal adults, infants, and the mentally impaired) have certain inalienable rights (think of the Declaration of Independence and the Bill of Rights), and that recognition is now accorded to all, if belatedly, in democratic societies at least. Most of us also recognize that animals cannot have rights unless we bestow them out of a sense of stewardship, for rights arise out of a human mental construct.

Carl Cohen, one philosopher who was willing to dispute the animal rightists' ethic very early in the debate, did a nice job of summarizing for laypersons several justifications for the belief that humans have special rights, which the great moral philosophers have struggled to understand without reaching unanimity. There is the theological belief that human rights are a special divine gift, an idea that many thinkers have abandoned in this modern age. Then there is the notion of a human moral community that has developed out of a sense that one's self is part of a reasoning social fabric to which animals cannot contribute, given their inability to reason. Direct intuitive recognition of the rightness of an action within one's community has been put forth by ethical intuitionists and realists: you know you have rights, and no one need instruct you on this point. Finally there is the natural development of self within a human moral community: We, but not animals, are able to reflect on our actions as we develop and recognize where our rights begin and end. Cohen concludes by writing, "However much great thinkers have disagreed about fundamental principles, *the essentially human (or divine) locus of the concept of rights* [Cohen's emphasis] has never been doubted."[34]

According to Cohen, animals lie outside our moral community but are not to be abandoned by us, for we have duties toward them as "moral patients." Infants and the mentally impaired are moral patients because they cannot have the autonomy of normal adults, who are "moral agents." Obviously only we can bestow rights on ourselves and assign certain of them to animals, which provide for their welfare at our hands. As a leading philosopher of our times, Bernard Williams, wrote, "Very significantly, the only question for us is how those animals should be treated. This is not true of our relations to other human beings, and this already shows that we are not dealing with a prejudice like racism or sexism."[35]

Petrinovich takes an evolutionary approach in challenging Regan, Singer, and others with similar views. In the best book written thus far on the arguments for placing our duties to our fellow humans above all else, *Darwinian Dominion: Animal Welfare and Human Interests*, he reasons that we have evolved over thousands and thousands of years into a species that has an innate recognition of its differences from all other species:

> The natural moral sense people have is built on sympathy,
> fairness, self-control, and duty, and is formed out of the
> interaction of innate dispositions with external familial
> experiences. The maternal sentiments on which parental
> affection is based are universal in humans, and are fostered
> by the earliest experiences a neonate has with its caretakers,
> rather than being some late product of evolution. A line is
> crossed when the individual is a member of the human
> species, and these distinctions, too, are graded.[36]

Another philosopher, Michael Leahy, who also marshaled arguments against animal liberation philosophies in *Against Liberation: Putting Animals in Perspective,* suggested a diminishing ordering of obligation that makes sense evolutionarily: "immediate family, relations, friends and colleagues, fellow countrymen, one's racial group, people at large, animals, and natural inanimate objects."[37] Petrinovich directs us to a number of psychological studies that have found that human moral intuitions actually are ordered in just this fashion.

Mary Midgley in *Why Animals Matter,* while applauding Singer's emphasis on sentience rather than species being the more important organizer of our moral thoughts, disagrees with the idea that preference of our own species can be equated with racism. She then adds that Singer refuses to incorporate "a further principle based on nearness or kinship, and dictates a sharp drop in the degree of moral involvement at the species barrier."[38] On this issue, Midgely thinks like Petrinovich and Leahy. She is not one for dismissing species other than humans as unworthy of consideration, however, nor am I. After a fascinating discussion of the complexities of interactions (acceptances and rejections) between humans and other species and among animal species, and the rejection of other human groups by some humans, she concludes with this beautiful, poetic statement:

> It is one of the special powers and graces of our species not to ignore others, but to draw in, domesticate and live with a great variety of other creatures. No other animal does so on anything like so large a scale.[39]

There are other reasons why we should set humans apart from other species without denying an obligation to animals. Michael A. Fox,[40] a Canadian philosopher, put forth clear and sensible examples. Incredibly, however, he soon rejected his own arguments upon re-examination,[41] an act of courage to be sure, but also an indication that words are fragile. In his article, Fox argued away the concept of "human specialness" that he had presented so eloquently in his book. I think much of his original argument still stands, however, and that we can and should set ourselves apart.

Before his change of heart, Fox argued that humans are unique in many obvious ways, such as brain complexity leading to sophisticated use of language (consider Shakespeare's plays in contrast to the human-taught sign language of apes) and use of intricately fashioned tools (e.g., making tools to make other objects, such as automobiles). In my opinion, those who try to draw other species into our fold, the great apes in particular, by emphasizing intellectual abilities that are but shadows of our own, demean these animals. Apes, not to mention other species, cannot come close to us intellectually. Appreciate them in their own right—as wonderful creations of nature.

Fox also claimed that we have a concept of ourselves that goes well beyond a chimp's ability to ape itself in a mirror. We can see ourselves

> as independent individuals with our own integrity, sense of purpose, and worth. We have a concept of our own lives— their origin, duration, self-guided direction, and terminus in death—of world history, and of the limitless reaches of time and space beyond the self. . . . Humans are the beings who because of their acute sense of self experience anxiety, guilt,

> despair, shame, remorse, internal conflict, pride, hope,
> triumph, and so many other emotion-laden states.[42]

We are a species unique in our cognitive abilities: We create beautiful sculptures, write on philosophical issues, and devise equitable laws, to name just a few examples. These laws, as well as religious and philosophical traditions handed down from long ago, bind us together in a moral community. Yet, we are autonomous beings living in that community. Only we, of all species on earth, can be held accountable for our deeds, be judged guilty in a court of law. We are burdened in a way that no other species is, even to the extent of caring for other species. These responsibilities make us special in my view and warrant special consideration and compassion.

This does not necessarily mean that we are more important than animals in a universal sense, but that humans are more important to humans, as Bernard Williams would say.[43] I think what follows from this is that we owe it to other humans to alleviate the pain and misery of disease as best we can, including through biomedical research. Furthermore, events in the past, described in Chapter 6, provide adequate reasons for protecting the specialness of our fellow humans.

None of these arguments as they pertain to biomedical research are enough for certain philosophers. But it is not reasonable to acknowledge that all species strive to stay alive while deliberately threatening our own survival by not trying to understand the biological world around us. I think this is my most powerful argument, one that no philosopher can defeat without being willing to risk personal sacrifice on behalf of animals. To the best of my knowledge, none has yet stepped forward publicly to be the first to take an untested drug or to undergo an untested surgical procedure.

Another critique of animal rights philosophy comes from Rod Preece, author of masterful works on human–animal relationships. He is concerned with the lack of historical accuracy found in the works of some key "animal-rightist" philosophers, which diminishes their efforts, in his eyes. For example, selective interpretations of Judeo-Christian thought as expressed in various editions of the Bible places it as a false foundation for ill treatment of animals in contrast with the supposed generosity of Eastern religions. In *Brute Souls, Happy Beasts and Evolution: The Historical Status of Animals*, Preece states, "Despite the evidence to the contrary, as I have indicated, the purported failure of the Christian tradition to ascribe immortal souls, or even souls of some other kind, to animals has been widely regarded as a symptom of Christianity's supposed failure to recognize the worthiness of other species."[44] (This argument is embedded in many pages discussing a long history of debate about the nature of the soul and the possible presence of animal souls in the early Christian literature.) If one wants to attack one religion or region of the world over another, there is plenty of fodder in the East, Preece tells us. For example, the Jainists of India employ individuals to sweep even insects out of their paths, thereby ensuring more deaths than if they had trod a bit lightly themselves. Cockfighting, outlawed in England in 1835 and now in all states in the United States, continues in Hindu and Muslim India.[45] Also, in North America, Native Americans drove whole herds of buffalo over cliffs in order to kill them "efficiently."[46]

By contrast, Richard Sorabji, Professor of Ancient Philosophy at King's College in London, in an equally scholarly book, *Animal Minds & Human Morals: The Origins of the Western Debate*, is not as generous to Christians and Jews:

> The Aristotelian and Stoic denial of rationality to animals
> proved all too congenial to Christians. . . . I believe it
> accounts for some of our own complacency about animals
> that we are heirs of a Western Christian tradition which
> selected just one side from a much more wide-ranging
> Greek debate [on humans and animals].[47]

Nevertheless, as Griswold wrote, the extremist's "moral passion become(s) immoral by virtue of its extremism." That "immorality" stands out starkly in the mea culpa offered by Michael A. Fox after he rejected the humane views expressed in his book. In reworking his moral stance, Fox recognizes that we are forced to harm other species as we live our own lives. But we can work toward minimizing the harm and recognizing it for what it is—we can minimize the harm by becoming anti-vivisectionists. He acknowledges, however, that giving up animal experimentation immediately might not be possible, but urges that we "commit ourselves to a firm policy of phasing out animal research as rapidly as possible,"[48] always seeking alternatives. I agree with this last statement, but the operative phrase is "as rapidly as possible." For example, as we find more and more defective genes in experimental mice that are the same as those in various human diseases, the number of mice used in medical research will only grow.

Fox then goes on to list in order of unacceptability six classes of experiments for which no alternatives are available, experiments "that *might* [emphasis in the original] be morally justified." The list begins with noninvasive experiments that cause no harm, and ends with experiments that are life saving, "where widespread loss of human life is threatened directly by animals (for instance, as disease carriers)." In the number 5 position, taking precedence over experiments to save human lives, he places "experiments that benefit other animals of the same or different species." Although he thinks that the latter two classes of experiments are "doubtful candidates," Fox's new thinking places the welfare of all animals above that of human beings in his formulation.

We commonly speak of rights when referring to animals, though. Think back to the passage from *My Friend Flicka*. One might say that Rocket, the wild mare with a lariat noose around her neck, had a right to Rob McLaughlin's concern, and there are philosophers, such as Joel Feinberg and Jerry Tannenbaum, who argue forcefully that animals can have rights in this very limited sense.[49, 50] Indeed, Tannenbaum, a lawyer as well as a philosopher, has cogently argued that point of view from a legal standpoint: anti-cruelty laws clearly use rights language. We can be prosecuted for denying an animal food when in our care. It is an animal's "right" to be fed and watered, among other things. Feinberg notes that our animal anti-cruelty laws, which may have been written to protect property purely for the benefit of the human owner, have clearly come to mean something quite different in the twentieth century. They are there to protect the animals.

Feinberg also interjects something that to me seems very important. In a chapter in which he argues forcefully that animals have rights as moral patients, for understanding the difference between humans and animals he states the following:

> In a narrower sense, of course, a human right is a moral
> right held unconditionally and unalterably by all and *only*
> [emphasis in the original] human beings. The right to
> humane treatment is not peculiarly human in this sense, but
> there is at least one kind of absolute and unalterable right for
> which only human beings can qualify, and that is the right
> not to be degraded and exploited even in painless and
> humane ways.... Animals do make some claims against us,
> and by virtue of their capacity to be claimants and rights-
> holders generally, they do qualify for a certain moral respect.
> But the higher kind of dignity that precludes even humane
> use as mere instruments [e.g., humans as beasts of burden
> however humanely treated] requires a level of rational
> awareness that animals cannot achieve.[51]

For Regan it is sufficient that animals are subjects-of-a-life for him to deny a human specialness.

Tannenbaum argues that the animal rights and liberation movement has stolen the concept of animal rights for themselves ; animal users should take it back by admitting that they believe animals do have certain rights. He has cautioned that scientists risk losing the support of a public that is in favor of biomedical research and yet thinks animals have rights in the limited sense just described. He reminds us that "a 1985 Associated Press poll found that 81% of the [United States] population believe that it is necessary to use animals in some applied medical research, and that 76% believe animals have rights."[52] We all bandy around this term, but we need to be clear in defining the term *rights*. Tannenbaum offered sensible advice to an audience of laboratory animal veterinarians and biomedical researchers so that they might avoid losing the respect of a public that understands rights in a way different from the view presented by Regan and his adherents. Tannenbaum observed that the debates would continue, but that the important thing was to distinguish between the terms *animal rights* and the *animal rights movement* and to recognize that not all people who used "rights" language were enemies of science. I certainly learned something from Tannenbaum.

Singer and Regan Together

A fundamental disagreement between Regan and Singer emerged in a bizarre way recently. In an opinion piece in the Raleigh, NC, *The News and Observer,* Regan wrote that "some people think the difference between animal rights and Singer's ideas is just a matter of words. This is not true. Singer's ideas sanction behaviors that both those who believe in animal rights and those who do not must find appalling."[53] What engendered this strong statement? Simply, Singer defended bestiality in a book review in an online sex magazine, *Nerve.*[54] As Regan writes, "Granted, sex involving cruelty to animals is wrong. But, Singer notes, 'sex with animals does not always involve cruelty.' In fact, when done 'in private,' 'mutually satisfying [sexual] activities' involving animals and humans 'may develop.' In these cases, consistent with his utilitarian philosophy, when satisfaction is optimized, Singer can find no wrong." Obviously an animal cannot give informed consent. In that same online book review, seemingly to try to break down the species barrier further, Singer wrote, "But the vehemence with which this prohibition [sex with animals] continues to be held, its persistence while other non-reproductive acts [between humans] have become acceptable, suggests that there is another powerful force at work: our desire to differentiate ourselves, erotically and in every other way, from animals." It is interesting to observe how extreme the viewpoint must be to cause Singer and Regan to diverge politically in addition to philosophically.

Although Sorabji found problems with the attempts by Singer and Regan to encompass the issues of animal use by one unifying principle, in defense of these disagreeing philosophers he wrote, "These are both theories that make us think more deeply, and that is the most important thing in philosophy, not whether one happens to agree, since philosophers are trained to disagree, the most important thing in philosophy."[55] Again, making us think seriously about how we relate to animals is good, but when a certain philosophy becomes a political tool, it can have a profoundly negative effect on people's lives. In this case, the lives of scientists and other legitimate animal users were made miserable by the more radical members of the animal rights and liberation movement. They also impeded the research that is so important for our fight against disease.

Not being an analytical philosopher, indeed, not a philosopher at all, I can only make rational judgments on what makes sense to me. And I have never forgotten a bit of wisdom one of my graduate advisors, a wise, gentle man from Tennessee named Bill Chambers, offered me in the midst of another long-forgotten controversy: "Just because he says it doesn't make it true, Adrian."

Various philosophers and other thoughtful individuals have found Singer's thinking too one-dimensional, ignoring much in our philosophical history that makes a distinction between humans and animals, despite the good intention of improving the lot of animals under our control. As Damon Linker, writing in *Commentary*, notes:

> That animals feel emotions can hardly be doubted; but
> human beings experience life, even at its most "animalistic"
> level, in a way that fundamentally differs from other
> creatures. . . . [H]e [Singer] cannot explain, for example, a
> person's choice to starve himself for a cause . . . choose to
> embrace celibacy for the sake of its noble purity . . . face
> certain death on the battlefield when called upon to do so by
> his country. Still less can he explain why stories of such
> sacrifice sometimes move us to tears.[56]

Charles Darwin himself asserted much the same thing:

> Of all the differences between man and the lower animals,
> the moral sense or conscience is by far the most important. . . .
> [I]t is summed up in that short but imperious word ought,
> so full of high significance. It is the most noble of all the
> attributes of man, leading him without a moment's
> hesitation to risk his life for that of a fellow-creature; or after

due deliberation, impelled simply by the deep feeling of
right or duty, to sacrifice it in some great cause.[57]

Like Singer, James Rachels[58] dispenses with the concept of human dignity
on grounds that his reading of Darwin leads him to the conclusion that we only
differ in degree, and not in "kind," from animals. He is wrong, as is Singer,
in my mind. Although it is the presence of that top layer of Wynne's sandwich
that makes all the difference between humans and animals as far as intellect
goes, more importantly it is the concept of human dignity that protects the
weakest of us. When we abandon it, we are freer to decide arbitrarily that some
humans are not our equals: we lynch; we experiment without consent; and we
condemn other humans to gas chambers.

Regan, who needed only to convince us that animals had rights upon which
we could not trample, crossed an important line in his debate with Cohen by
misrepresenting the value of using animals. He alerted his readers to the fact
that "50% of the FDA approved drugs investigated [by the General Accounting
Office] either had to be taken off the market or relabeled because of their toxic
effects on the people that were using them."[59] In fact, drugs are tested on twice
as many people as animals before the drugs are released to market. Those
adverse reactions showed up after millions of people had used them. Further,
Regan asks a frequently expressed, logically unanswerable question: "How do
you know you had to use animals to develop and test drugs if you never tried?",
referring to the FDA's requirement that animals be used. One could in turn ask
if Regan would agree to volunteer to take the first dose of a drug that had not
yet been tested on a variety of species for possible toxic effects. Furthermore, we
might ask what experiments he would propose for determining the mechanisms of various compounds necessary before one can even develop a life-
saving drug, without using some living being, and without endangering human
beings or animal patients, for that matter.

To conclude this section, I think it fair to assume that had Singer joined me
in that stroll down Queen Street several years ago, spectators would have seen
him dashing for the child, just as I would have, even if that human's future
might have held no prospect "for meaningful relations with others."[60] I wager
that the many thousands of years our species has spent distinguishing itself
from other species[61]— by slowly evolving into communities with rules (laws)
and moral codes, and looking after each other for the good of all (discovering
the Ten Commandments or their equivalent along the way)—would win out.
I think Singer's essential humanity would have taken over his philosophical
mind, at least for the moment. And I think for the same reason that Regan

would have been in hot pursuit with us toward that "defective" child. The point here is that one must ultimately make a choice regarding the use of animals in biomedical research, however much one loves them.

Beyond Biomedical Research

Of course, my views on various uses of animals presented in the preceding chapter make me more vulnerable to criticism than those of some of my fellow researchers who may be convinced that they are "pure" in this debate, because they will have nothing to do with hunting, trapping, wearing furs, or some of the other "crimes" that the animal rights and liberation movement focuses on. That, of course, is their right. But in response, I plead a richness and variety to human life. There are things one can enjoy that others do not and vice versa, as I have discussed. We are human beings living in a complex world. I stand firm on one principle, however, when the issue is biomedical research: human beings must be treated as special, if only to protect the weakest of us.

Regarding other uses, let's use hunting as an example. According to philosopher Lance Stell, who counseled me on this point and should receive full credit for these thoughts, the animal rights position imposes human exceptionalism in a negative way, arguing that we should be above it all, so to speak.[62] What does this mean? Many nonhuman animals are natural predators. So it falls to animal rightists to explain what is wrong with human predation. Animal rightists never argue that nonhuman animal predators are "rights violators," presumably because these animals lack the ability to understand and respect rights. Nevertheless, their predatory behavior inflicts harm on their prey. When a predator kills its prey, the magnitude of what the prey animals loses is unaffected by whether the predator is a moral agent or not. If we ignore the manner in which the prey animal's death is inflicted, from its perspective its loss is the same, irrespective of whether it is inflicted by a lightning strike, flood, or a predator (human or nonhuman). Supposedly, what is morally distinctive about human predation is that human predators violate the prey animal's rights, whereas lightning strikes and nonhuman predation do not.

But this argument presents a problem. Animal rightists commonly believe they have an obligation to prevent sport hunters from killing nonhuman animals. Presumably, this belief rests on the theory that we are as responsible for the harms we can prevent but do not, as we are for the harms we directly inflict (it is what is under our control that matters). If so, then failing to prevent nonhuman predators from killing their prey when it is within our power to do so also wrongs prey animals, because the loss they suffer is just as great as when sport hunting causes their deaths. Both sorts of loss result from an objection-able failure to exercise our power "properly."

To expand on the notion of humans as predators, while respecting anyone's choice to establish another lifestyle of veganism or vegetarianism, I defer to Russ Carman, introduced in Chapter 8. Carman makes a very clear statement on which I cannot improve:

> The physiology of man shows every indication that he is a
> *predator*. The mere fact that we can digest meat; the fact that
> we have teeth capable of tearing and chewing flesh; the fact
> that we have eyes in the front of our heads, as do most
> predators [including chimpanzees], instead of at the sides
> like most prey species; the fact that unlike cattle, sheep,
> rabbits, etc., we actually like the taste of meat provides ample
> proof that we are instinctive meat eaters.[63]

And concerning another form of predator, our cats and dogs, Evelyn Pluhar, in *Beyond Prejudice*, has this to say about the ethical problem that pet food presents:

> Currently pet food is a by-product of the human-oriented
> food industry. If more people became serious about
> respecting the rights of all beings who care about what
> happens to them, they and their companion animals would
> no longer have these sources. Dogs, who are omnivores like
> us, can thrive on vegetarian diets without much trouble,
> but cats need carefully designed diets that include taurine as
> a nutritional supplement.[64]

In my view, forcing cats and dogs to be vegetarians would fall under the category of exploitation. It is a special type of speciesism whereby one imposes personal views on another species that are against that species' very nature.

In the eyes of some, the problem Pluhar raises about the human-oriented food industry extends to nature itself. In *The Omnivore's Dilemma: A Natural History of Four Meals*, Michael Pollan writes:

> The very existence of predation in nature, of animals eating
> animals, is the cause of much anguished hand-wringing in
> the animal rights literature. "It must be admitted," Peter
> Singer writes, "that the existence of carnivorous animals

> does pose one problem for the ethics of *Animal Liberation*, and that is whether we should do anything about it." . . . Mathew Scull in *Dominion*, a Christian-conservative treatment of animal rights, calls predation "the intrinsic evil in nature's design . . . among the hardest of all things to fathom." . . . Scull condemns [referring to gratuitous killing by cats] "the level of moral degradation of which [animals] are capable."[65]

Singer does acknowledge, however, that although we may not be able to keep ourselves from saving a wild animal we see in distress, interference with natural processes in general is not a wise thing to do. It is better to focus on our own behavior in killing animals. In one sense, Scull harkens back to medieval times when animals could be condemned to death in a court of law. What both gentlemen are saying, in fact, is that predatory animals are speciesists too. A "speciesist" weasel slaughters all the inhabitants of a henhouse without stopping to consider them one by one. We cannot turn back the evolutionary clock; predators and prey have evolved together and cannot do without each other. Once more, remember the starving deer alone in March. Better a fairly quick death from a cougar attack, or even a hunter's well-aimed shot, to my thinking.

We humans are not intruders in the world but a part of it, and we have as much right to make our way in it as any other species. At one level we are animals living among animals. We are prolific, omnivorous, and predatory. But we also have the capacity to be responsible predators. This includes the capacity to subordinate our predatory (or other) behaviors toward other animals (as well as toward ourselves) to the governance of moral and legal rules that we propose to each other, and to accept or reject these rules on the basis of their reasonableness. We have also made mistakes that must be corrected. Yet, a pluralistic human society has members that value various things differently. I can enjoy the thrill of a rodeo; you may not. I might buy my wife a fur coat —and did as an act of defiance I must admit—but you may not. In *The Blank Slate: The Modern Denial of Human Nature*, cognitive psychologist Stephen Pinker quotes Harold Laski, a leading British intellectual of the first half of the twentieth century: "Civilization means, above all, an unwillingness to inflict unnecessary pain."[66] The operative word here is "unnecessary." I accept that we humans will have to differ on what is necessary in the richness of human lives while also recognizing the implication from Laski's statement that nature abides by its own rules.

An Enlightening and Amusing Encounter

I have tried to present accurately the views of those with whom I disagree strongly, placing their statements in proper context. If I have erred at any point, it was not deliberate but stemmed from the dangers an amateur faces when entering another academic field, and I offer apology for any offense made. Lest my readers think me too antagonistic toward those who have animal-rightist leanings, in particular those who would eliminate essentially all use of animals, let me close by introducing a friend of mine, an animal rightist and ethical vegetarian who teaches ethics and the philosophy of religion. How we met and some experiences we shared are worth telling, for they further demonstrate that the issues are not simple. I hope they demonstrate that I am not simple either.

In the spring of 1992, while I was serving as director of the Program for Animal Research Issues at the National Institute for Mental Health, a university invited me to participate in a program on animal rights at their annual biotechnology conference. My host told me that an animal rights philosopher—"not the radical, political kind"—would share the podium with me. With no formal training in ethics or philosophy, and only having begun to follow the philosophical aspects of the issue, I was initially leery of the encounter (which I assumed would take a very anti-science tone). However, the nature of the conference meant the audience would not be hostile toward me because it was composed primarily of researchers, and the event was not cast as a debate.

Each of us did what he did best. The philosopher defended his view that genetic engineering of animals for agriculture's needs was ethically wrong, using the arguments of formal ethics. I discussed the necessity of using animals in biomedical research and illustrated how the animal rights and liberation movement had wrongly denigrated research. We did not confront each other's views directly; in one sense, we argued apples and oranges.

Although three nuns in the audience greeted me as one of their prize pupils afterwards (and I was grateful for that support), I did not in any way feel triumphant for two reasons: I knew I had received a good short-course in formal ethics, and I liked my "opponent." His eagerness to meet me and his general friendliness at lunch before our session indicated that this was a person worth knowing, whatever his views. When I learned that many of his relatives were farmers, my respect for him grew. He admitted he knew little about biomedical research, and he has not misrepresented it. Without my realizing it at the time, meeting him has helped me to see more shades of gray in the issue over the years.

This pleasant encounter led directly to a somewhat farcical but enjoyable incident the following fall. At our school we were giving a course for general university freshmen, called "Animals and Society," which featured a variety of experts on animal use as speakers. Although I had been scheduled for two sessions, I thought one would be enough and asked to donate my second session so the students could hear from my new friend. Airfares between his city and Philadelphia are inordinately expensive, especially with last-minute purchases, so that it appeared my idea would have to wait. But a last-minute opportunity suddenly presented itself because of a conference in Washington that he wanted to attend. I made arrangements that same day for a minor expenditure to bring him to Philadelphia.

In my haste, I had forgotten one thing: I was scheduled to talk to the Philadelphia chapter of the Society for Microbiology the evening of my guest's arrival. Not only that, I had invited him to stay at our house. So there I was that evening, revealing the depredations of animal-rights activism against biomedical research, while my wife was serving a vegetarian meal (macaroni and cheese with home-made dill pickles on the side, my invention) to an animal rights philosopher that she had never even met. They got along famously. He loved the meal. Now I have a ready reply to those who might think I am too harsh or narrow in my assessments: *Guess who came to dinner?*

Epilogue

I am coming to the end of a personal odyssey, three odysseys really: that of a lifetime with animals, the one that began in 1981 and culminates with this book, and the actual writing of this book. The first started with pet dogs. Then came the pigeon that fell from its nest in the barn and that I taught to fly. Next was my horse, Rocky, my sole companion during my high school years; then more dogs and cats as my children grew up; and now my simple love for Buster. Between Rocky and Buster have been the dogs I first killed for the anatomy department during veterinary school, the many cats used and killed through the years in my sleep research, and now the rats that I must use for a few more years. Ultimately, my work in the laboratory will come to an end, and then I will finally be like my old friend Jim Sprague and feel glad.

The second odyssey, intellectual in part, began with my agreement to defend Ed Taub in his first court trial in 1981 and ends more than 25 years later, I hope. Too much of my scientific career has been overwhelmed by the animal rights issue and educating the public to the dangers it poses to their health. From simply reacting to the overwhelming attack on biomedical research that began with the Silver Spring Monkey case and then continuing in a militant vein for a number of years out of anger at the attack on me and desperation that few of my colleagues sensed the danger, I have now settled into a more reflective approach. I have learned quite a bit during the past 15 years.

Of course, the act of writing this book has been an odyssey in itself. The initial impetus when I began writing it in 1993 was, frankly, to reveal the depredations of the animal rights adherents who had attacked and tried to intimidate me. After that version went nowhere with a few publishers because it was really too much of a polemic, even if true, a friend read it. He commented, "After saying that the animal rights extremists are a blight on society—and I agree with you—what more is there to say?" Clearly a more reflective, wider-ranging analysis was needed, and my friend warned me that to undertake this would infringe on my scientific work. It has been worth the effort. Looking back to 1981, I see a changed world, and I have changed with it. In addition to increasing my knowledge of new academic fields, I have softened some of my opinions about how we might use animals, and even about some of those individuals who see things differently from me.

While digging back in time to write about my involvement in the pivotal Silver Spring Monkey case, I came across two letters that illustrate my strongly held opinions on the veterinary aspects of the case and my change in attitude toward some in the animal welfare community that I had not appreciated then in the heat of battle. Peter Hand and I[1] had written to *Science* in 1982 to correct a *Science* writer's statements regarding our role in evaluating the situation in Dr. Taub's laboratory. Under the same heading, "Animal Welfare," is a letter from Barbara Orlans,[2] then head of the Scientists Center for Animal Welfare (SCAW), who was reporting on a SCAW conference held in November 1981, just when I was in the process of defending Dr. Taub in court. Dr. Orlans's letter outlined a number of recommendations for improvement of animal welfare that arose from the conference and from her own convictions.[3] The proposals are essentially those in force today, which I described in Chapter 4. Even though I think she was mistaken in her letter regarding veterinary aspects of the Taub case, my hat still goes off to her. At the time, I was too wounded by the Taub experience and too used to doing things in the laboratory on my own—and doing them responsibly—to realize that change had to come. Quite an odyssey it has been!

I still hold strongly to the view that there is a distinct division between animals and humans, created by our evolutionary heritage as well as by our religious heritage in the West, at least. Our heritage enjoins us to give first allegiance to our fellow humans but has also left us with the capacity to recognize duties to our fellow beings: the animals that surround us who will never reciprocate (other than those that are our close, domestic companions, the seeing-eye dog being a splendid example). From this unique capacity arises human dignity. Those who deny this quality pose a real danger to their fellow humans.

There is a fourth odyssey, however, that involves all human beings as we seek to understand the animal world around us and the proper ways to interact with it, as I have tried to sketch in these pages. The subjects I have covered, such as domestication, changing attitudes and understanding of animals over the past couple of millennia, various ethical viewpoints, animal cognition, hunting, agriculture and medical advances, have filled many books. One book, let alone one veterinarian, could not possibly do full justice to all of the topics. But the books by Budiansky, Bulliet, Dawkins, Dennett, Dizard, Grandin, Griffin, Hauser, Nelkin and Jasper, Petrinovich, Preece, Ritvo, Serpell, Sorabji, Sperling, de Waal, Webster, and, of course, Darwin, among others, do this magnificently for one or another of the topics I have discussed. And to give them their due, the books by Tom Regan and Peter Singer, despite my belief that their claims pose a dangerous risk to human welfare, have stimulated us into action in improving the lives of our charge, those of other species.

It is disconcerting to me, therefore, that although I have tried, I have been unable to present all sides of each issue with all their nuances. This would require a book of encyclopedic proportions. I fear that my obvious biases have slanted things in favor of my position. As a scientist I feel uncomfortable with this. But I take heart in yet another bit of wisdom from Darwin, who, writing in a letter to a non-scientist supporter regarding the validity of having a point of view in one's work, opined, "How odd it is that anyone should not see that all observation must be for or against some view if it is to be of any service."[4]

Most of us realize that animals are important to us, have contributed much to our lives in several spheres, and thus deserve thoughtful attention to their welfare. It is their due, and the principle of fair play demands it. The present awareness of our duties toward those under our control—and this more or less extends to every animal on the planet—required centuries to mature. The process continues, as this book makes clear. Our treatment of our fellow humans has evolved as well, and much of the progress for both has occurred in the past two centuries. We can do still better in many instances, and we will, with the aid of science and good will.

Use of animals in biomedical research in the United States saw a big improvement with passage of the two laws administered by the U.S. Department of Agriculture and the Public Health Service in 1985. We pretty much caught up with the United Kingdom, which has long held the lead in management of laboratory animal welfare. Intensive agriculture, which has been so effective in bringing affordable food to the table, clearly went overboard during the second half of the twentieth century in the interests of efficiency and profits. While not objecting to the latter, I think the various industries must look at themselves critically and improve the lot of their animals based on *scientifically acquired information*. And the buying public is ethically bound to share the financial burdens for any changes in agricultural practices. As for hunting, good hunters will always be needed, but any practice that precludes the principle of "fair chase" is despicable in my view, unless, of course, the purpose is to redress harmful imbalances in an ecological system. Finally, I believe it to be a moral obligation for those who object to using animals in biomedical research for philosophical or scientific reasons to volunteer for the many clinical studies searching for human experimental subjects.

Turning to my own profession of veterinary medicine, those on the research side in particular, should take the lead in doing our best to live up to the first sentence of the Veterinarian's Oath: "Being admitted to the profession of veterinary medicine, I solemnly swear to use my scientific knowledge and skills for the benefit of society through the protection of animal health, the relief of animal suffering, the conservation of livestock resources, the promotion of public health, and the advancement of medical knowledge." Note that there is a dynamic tension embodied in that sentence: we must advance "medical knowledge" (one way of promoting "animal" and "public health" as well) and also relieve "animal suffering." In this context, we should minimize the harm done to laboratory and other animals in the name of medical progress, and lead in developing more humane ways of keeping agricultural animals. I think we have a particular duty to find a way, such as an anesthetic that works almost instantly, to eliminate the awful practice of castration without anesthesia, which is done because of economic costs in certain farm situations. Whenever I fantasize about returning to my roots to become a rural veterinarian, often having just read a James Herriot story, the thought of that operation returns me to reality.

Further, the absolutist worlds conceived in the minds of a few philosophers are clearly impractical to my way of thinking. Indeed, ignorance of the natural world has led some followers over the boundary that separates us from animals. The most radical individuals see human life as dispensable; they are willing to kill humans in order to save animal lives. In a sense, they would say, "A rat, is a pig, is a dog, but a boy does not measure up." Essentially, they would separate us from animals and "let nature take its course," even at the expense of human lives. But what would it mean for humanity, domestic animals, and those in the wild, and the environments in which they live, if this extreme view were to prevail? Would benign neglect be the moral course to follow, not to mention the practical course? Obviously I do not think so. As Budiansky wrote, "It is too late in the day to leave nature to its own devices. The world will not stand for it—and nature won't either. Only by active management will the world be fed; only by active management will such goals as preserving biodiversity come even close to being realized."[5]

Our charge is to manage properly, and most especially when working with the animals under our direct control, to adhere to the beautiful ideas expressed by Mary O'Hara through her creation, Rob McLaughlin:

> There's a responsibility we have toward animals. . . . We use them. We shut them up, keep their natural food and water from them that means we have to feed and water them. Take their freedom away, rope them, harness them, that means we have to supply a different sort of safety for them. Once I've put a rope on a horse, or taken away its ability to take care of itself, then I've got to take care of it.[6]

We should do this, above all, because we are humans, the only species capable of assuming such a role: Our humanity depends on it.

Notes

Introduction

1. Rosenberger, 1990, pp. 30–39.
2. Dizard, 1994.
3. Magel, 1989.
4. Singer, 1973, pp. 11–21.
5. Godlovitch et al., 1972, p. 8.
6. Harnack, 1996, p. 240.
7. Lewis, 2005.

Chapter 1

1. Bulliet, 2005.
2. Bulliet, 2005, p. 3.
3. James, 1992, B3.
4. Donovan, 1995, p. 1.
5. Patronek, 1999, pp. 81–87.
6. Herzog 1993, pp. 109, 113.
7. Herzog, 1993, p. 117.
8. McCabe, 1986, p. 115.

9. Venant and Treadwell, 1990.
10. Fox, 1990, p. 98.
11. Americans for Medical Progress, 2005.
12. Vlasek, 2004.
13. Strand and Strand, 1993.
14. Paton 1993, p. 93.
15. Potter, 1970, pp. 127, 153.

Chapter 2

1. Americans for Medical Progress, 2008.
2. Foundation for Biomedical Research, 2008.
3. Pons et al., 1991.
4. Brenner, 2008.
5. Holden, 1981.
6. Taub, 1991, pp. 1–8.
7. Holden, 1981.
8. Taub, 2008.
9. Holden, 1981.
10. Holden, 1981, p. 1219.
11. Brenner, 2008.
12. Taub, 1991.
13. Public Health Service.
14. National Association for Biomedical Research, 1991.
15. National Association for Biomedical Research, 1991.
16. Pons, 1991.
17. Singer, 1994a.
18. Singer, 1994a.
19. Fox, 1994, p. 10.
20. Dantzler et al., 1994, pp. 9–10.
21. Singer, 1994a, p. 523.
22. Singer, 1994a, p. 523.
23. Dantzler et al., 1994, pp. 9–10.
24. Dantzler et al., 1994, pp. 9–10.
25. Singer, 1994a, p. 523.
26. Guillermo, 1993.
27. Orlans, 1993.
28. Taub et al., 1993, pp. 347–354.
29. Liepert et al., 2000, pp. 1210–1216.
30. Taub et al., 1994, pp. 281–293.
31. Kopp et al., 1999, p. 241.
32. Taub, 1980.

33. Levine, 1993, pp. 23–24.
34. Lewin-ICF, 1992.
35. Hand, 1987.
36. Morrison, 1999c.
37. National Institutes of Health, Office for Protection from Research Risks, 1985.
38. Pence, 1990.
39. Hendricks, 1985, pp. 2–4.
40. Pence, 1990, p. 179.
41. Gennarelli, 1983.
42. Torg, 1984, p. A21.
43. Lutherer and Simon, 1992.
44. Lutherer and Simon, 1992, pp. 56–57.
45. National Institutes of Health, Office for Protection from Research Risks, 1990.
46. Lutherer and Simon, 1992.
47. Morrison, 2001b.
48. Singer, 1975.
49. Blankenau, 1995, pp. 56–58.
50. Rosenberger, 1990, p. 33.
51. Report of the School of Arts and Sciences Committee on Academic Freedom and Responsibility, April 30, 1990.
52. Conn and Parker, 2008.
53. Miller, 2007.
54. Henig, 2006.
55. Kennedy, 2006.
56. Miller, 2007.
57. Paddock and LaGarga, 2008.
58. Editorial, 2007.
59. Derbyshire, 2007.
60. Lewis, 2005.
61. Foundation for Biomedical Research, 2006.
62. Alleyne, 2001.
63. Boggan, 2006.
64. Lister, 2002,
65. Tomlinson, 2008.

Chapter 3

1. Miller, 1985a.
2. Morrison, 1999a.
3. Morrison, 1983.
4. Aserinsky and Kleitman, 1953.
5. Dement, 1972.

6. Gottesmann, 2001.
7. Morrison, 1993a.
8. Jouvet and Michel, 1959.
9. Schenck et al., 1986.
10. Jouvet and Delorme, 1965.
11. Henley and Morrison, 1974.
12. Morrison, 1983.
13. Tinbergen, 1971.
14. Singer and Drager, 1972.
15. Bizzi and Brooks, 1963.
16. Brooks and Bizzi, 1963.
17. Morrison and Bowker, 1975.
18. Dement, 1969.
19. Sanford et al., 1993.
20. Ratner, 1967.
21. Singer, 1977.
22. Rosenberger, 1990.
23. Jha et al., 2005.
24. Madan et al., 2008.
25. LeDoux, 1992.
26. Bogusslavsky, 1997.
27. Morrison, 2001a.
28. Young, 1996, p. 451.
29. Ramon y Cajal, 1959, p. 750.
30. Liu and Chambers, 1958.
31. Goldberger et al., 1993.
32. Cheng et al., 1996.
33. Ramon y Cajal, 1959, p. 750.
34. Young, 1996, p. 451.
35. McIntosh et al., 1998.
36. Taub et al., 1998.

Chapter 4

1. Morrison, 2002.
2. Comroe and Dripps, 1976.
3. Thomas, 1974, p. 104.
4. Alberts, 2008, p. 1733.
5. Dudrick, 1977.
6. Dudrick, 1977, p. 27.
7. Dudrick, 1977, p. 27.
8. Festing, 2004.
9. Festing, 2004, p. 736.

10. Festing, 2004, p. 736.
11. Medawar, 1996.
12. Davisson, 2005.
13. Davisson, 2005, p. 342.
14. Seidner et al., 2006.
15. Siegel et al., 2001.
16. Sweeney et al., 1983.
17. Siegel et al., 2001.
18. Siegel et al., 2001.
19. John et al., 2000.
20. Deadwyler et al., 2007.
21. Sly, 2004.
22. Sly, 2004.
23. Ellinwood et al., 2004.
24. Miller, 1985b, p. 425.
25. Thorndike, 1898.
26. Skinner, 1938.
27. Pavlov, 1927.
28. Rollin, 1996.
29. Carroll et al., 2001.
30. For a discussion of the ins and outs of using animals in behavioral research, see the magnificent review by van der Staay (2006).
31. Mowrer and Mowrer, 1938.
32. Miller, 1985b.
33. Taub et al., 1994.
34. Taub et al., 1998.
35. Miller et al., 1985b.
36. Russell and Burch, 1959.
37. Morrison, 1993b.
38. Miller, 2006.
39. Mencken, 1982. p. 12.
40. White, 1995.
41. Tannenbaum, 1995.
42. Tannenbaum, 2000b, p.125.
43. Kulpa-Eddy et al., 2005.
44. Nelson and Mandrell, 2005.
45. Nelson and Mandrell, 2005.
46. Tannenbaum, 2000b, p. 123.
47. Dawkins, 1980.
48. Morrison 1999b.
49. National Association of Biology Teachers, 2009.
50. Orlans, 1991.
51. Trotter, 1992.
52. Texley, 1992.

53. Morrison, 1992.
54. Schrock, 2005, p. 10.
55. Texley, 1992.
56. Schrock, 2005, p. 10.
57. McCormick, 1991, p. 25.
58. Carmichael, 2004.
59. Ra'anan, 2005.
60. Rucker, 2008.
61. Morrison, 1994.

Chapter 5

1. Botting and Morrison, 1997.
2. Morrison, 2002.
3. Van Gijn, 2001.
4. Valenstein, 2005.
5. Carlsson, 2005.
6. Greek and Greek, 2000b.
7. Martin, 1984.
8. Ellingwood, 2004.
9. Cornelius, 1969.
10. Festing, 2001.
11. Botting, 1991, p. 738.
12. Dulbecco, 1986. p. 1055
13. Greek and Greek, 2000b, p. 156.
14. Dulbecco, 1986, p. 1055.
15. Greek and Greek, 200a, pp. 743–744.
16. Beeson, 1980, p. S18.
17. Beeson, 1989, p. 1437.
18. Beeson, 1980, pp. S22–S23.
19. Comroe, 1983.
20. Greek and Greek, 2000b, p. 169.
21. Comroe, 1983, pp. 300–301.
22. Taussig, 1981, p. 162.
23. Greek and Greek, 2000b, p. 180.
24. Nuland, 1988.
25. Blalock and Taussig, 1945, p. 193.
26. Botting and Morrison, 1997.
27. Barnard and Kaufman, 1997.
28. McCormick, 1991.
29. Barnard and Kaufman, 1997.
30. Morrison and Botting, 1997

31. Botting and Morrison, 1998.
32. Wiebers et al., 1990, pp. 1, 3.
33. Barnard and Kaufman, 1997, p. 82.
34. Botting and Morrison, 1998
35. Nuland, 1988.
36. Salsburg, 1997, p. 10.
37. Reines, 1985a, p. 52.
38. Wertenberger, 1980, p. 150.
39. Reines, 1985a, b..
40. Verhetsel, 1986, p. 77
41. Verhetsel, 1986, p. 77
42. Bliss, 1982, p. 11
43. Reines, 1985b.
44. Nicoll and Russell, 1984, pp. 70–71.
45. Verhetsel, 1986, pp. 68–69.
46. Regan and Francione, 1996.

Chapter 6

1. Bulliet, 2005.
2. Turner, 1980, p. 1.
3. Ritvo, 1987, p. 126.
4. Ritvo, 1987, p. 127
5. Ritvo, 1987, p. 128.
6. Ritvo, 1987, p. 131.
7. Worden, 2007.
8. Maehle and Tröhler, 1990.
9. Maehle and Tröhler, 1990, p. 16.
10. Maehle and Tröhler, 1990, pp. 21–22.
11. Preece, 2005.
12. Quoted by Andreas-Holger Maehle and Ulrich Tröhler, from the Institute for the History of Medicine in Göttingen, in a marvelous essay on the attitudes and arguments concerning vivisection from antiquity to the eighteenth century. See Maehle, 1990, p. 23.
13. Editor, 2008a.
14. Ritvo, 1987, p. 157.
15. Ritvo, 1987, p. 162.
16. Turner, 1980, p. 115.
17. Lederer, 1987.
18. Singer, 1994b.
19. Bulliet, 2005.
20. Conniff, 1990, p. 132.

21. Strand and Strand, 1993.
22. Conniff 1990, p. 133
23. Jasper and Nelkin, 1992.
24. Goodwin, 1992, p. 3.
25. Singer, 1975, p. viii.
26. Jasper and Nelkin, 1992 p. 28.
27. Fox, 1986.
28. Jasper and Nelkin, 1992.
29. Parsell, 1989.
30. Morrison, 2006.
31. Maehle and Tröhler, 1990.
32. Tannenbaum, 2006.
33. Cottinham et al., pp. 365–366.
34. Maehle and Tröhler, 1990. pp. 31–32
35. Maehle and Tröhler, 1990, p. 32.
36. Singer, 1990, p. 82.
37. Darwin, 1859.
38. Fox, 1986.
39. Fox, 1990.
40. Midgely, 1983.
41. Rachels, 1991.
42. Singer, 1990.
43. Singer, 1990, p. 206.
44. Lovejoy, 1936.
45. Preece, 2005.
46. Preece, 2005, p. 346.
47. Preece, 2005, p. 347.
48. Preece, 2005, p. 347.
49. Ritvo 1987, p. 1.
50. Finkelstein, 2005.
51. Cavalieri and Singer, 1993.
52. Finkelstein, 2005, p. 18.
53. Finkelstein, 2005, p. 20.
54. Finkelstein, 2005, p. 20.
55. Zawistowski, 2008, p. 2.
56. Arluke and Sax, 1992.
57. Arluke and Saxe, 1992, p. 11.
58. Arluke and Saxe, 1992, p. 11–12.
59. Quoted in Arluke and Saxe's essay from Brady, 1969, p. 12.
60. Arluke and Sax, 1992, p. 14.
61. Arluke and Sax, 1992, p. 28.
62. Lederer, 1995.
63. Quoted in Lederer, 1995, p. 80.
64. Lederer, 1995.

Chapter 7

1. Cornelius, 1969.
2. Dennis, 1983.
3. Meagher, 2001, p. 227.
4. Matta et al., 2008.
5. Meagher, 2001.
6. Wolfle and Liebseskind, 1983.
7. Johnson, 1988.
8. Dennett, 1996, p. 94.
9. Zawistowski, 2008.
10. Storm, 1995, p. 12
11. Schenck, 1993.
12. Morrison, 1993.
13. Morrison, 1993.
14. Wynne, 2004.
15. Budiansky, 1998, p. xiii.
16. de Waal, 2006, p. 65.
17. Darwin, 1883 (1924), p. 619.
18. Darwin, 1883 (1924), p. 610.
19. Seton, 1907.
20. Wickler, 1972.
21. de Waal, 2006.
22. Kitcher, 2006, p. 136.
23. Hauser, 2006, pp. 355–356.
24. Burghardt, 1985, p. 918.
25. Budiansky, 1998.
26. Budiansky, 1998, p. xxxii.
27. Burghardt, 1985.
28. de Waal, 2006, p. 63.
29. Thomas, 1993, p. 68.
30. Pinker, 2005.
31. Keller, 1956.
32. *Webster's Third New International Dictionary*, unabridged edition, 1961.
33. Merker, 2007, pp. 63–64.
34. Grandin and Johnson, 2005.
35. Vallortigara, 2008, p. e42.
36. Vallortigara, 2008, p. e42.
37. Cartwright, 2004.
38. Griffin, 1992, p. 5.
39. Griffin, 1992, p. 25.
40. Jha et al., 2005.
41. Pawlyk et al., 2005.
42. Zoccola et al., 2008.

43. Griffin, 1992, p. 238.
44. Searle, 1984, pp. 14–15.
45. Griffin, 1992, pp. 258–259.
46. Dement, 1972.
47. Dennett, 1996, pp. 115–116.
48. Dawkins, 1993.
49. Cavalieri and Singer, 1993.
50. Benton, 1997.
51. O'Driscoll, 1832.
52. Editor, 1883, p. 12.
53. Yerkes and Yerkes, 1929.
54. Cavalieri and Singer, 1993, p. 4.
55. de Waal, 1996, pp. 214–215.
56. de Waal, 1996.
57. VandeBerg et al., 2005, p. 30.
58. Smith, 2006.
59. Marks, 1994, p. 1117.
60. Groce and Marks, 2001, p. 818.
61. Editorial, 1999, p. 3.
62. Singer, 1990, p. 238.
63. Groce and Marks, 2001, p. 822.
64. La Valle, 2008.
65. Smith, 2008, pp. 15.
66. Russow, 1995, p. 49.
67. Wynne, 2004.
68. Wynne, 2004, pp. 117–118.
69. Terrace et al., 1979.
70. Budiansky, 1998, pp. 156–157.
71. Hauser, 2000, p. 208.
72. Wynne, 2004, pp. 126–127.
73. Dennett, 1996.
74. Wynne, 2004, p. 233.
75. Rogers and Kaplan, 2006.
76. Emery and Clayton, 2004, p. 45.
77. Russon and Bard, 1996, pp. 8–9.
78. Povinelli and Vonk, 2006, p. 405.
79. Morrison, 2009.

Chapter 8

1. Burghardt and Herzog, 1980.
2. Jones, 2003, p. 4.

3. Coppinger and Smith, 1983.
4. Burghardt and Herzog, 1980.
5. Budiansky, 1992.
6. Bulliet, 2005.
7. Bulliet, p. 96.
8. Driscoll et al., 2007.
9. Serpell, 1986.
10. Bulliet, 2005, p. 15.
11. Herzog, 1988.
12. Herzog, 1991.
13. Pluhar, 1995.
14. Herzog, 1991, p. 247.
15. Davis, 2003.
16. O'Hara, 1941, pp. 50–51.
17. Ritvo, 1987.
18. Nolan, 2006.
19. American Veterinary Medical Association, 2007.
20. Moelis, 2008.
21. Herscovici, 1985.
22. Davis, 2008.
23. Hendricks et al., 1987.
24. McCaghy and Neal, 1974.
25. McCaghy and Neal 1974, p. 561.
26. Kellert, 1996, p. 73.
27. Dizard, 2003.
28. Kellert, 1996.
29. Dizard, 2003, p. 169.
30. Dizard, 2003, p. 127.
31. Dizard, 2003, p. 128.
32. Dizard, 2003, p. 129.
33. Posewitz, 1994.
34. Dizard, 2003, p.133.
35. Serpell, 1986.
36. Editor, 2006.
37. Ozoga, 1995, p. 136.
38. Stadtfield, 1975, p. 148
39. Carman, 1990.
40. Howard, 1990.
41. Howard, 1990, p. 150.
42. Howard, 1990, p. 145.
43. Howard, 1990, p. 160.
44. Jasper and Nelkin, 1992, p. 611.
45. Duda, 2008.
46. Professional Rodeo Cowboys Association, 2008.

47. National Animal Interest Alliance, 2008.
48. Lawrence, 1982.
49. For more complete coverage of animal welfare issues in agriculture, see Reynnells and Eastwood, 1997.
50. Fetrow, 2001, p. 1887.
51. Jones, 2003.
52. Ruckebusch, 1971.
53. Galligan, 2006.
54. Schreiner and Ruegg, 2002.
55. Fraser et al., 2001.
56. Steele, 2000.
57. Galligan, 2008.
58. Fetrow, 2001.
59. Capper et al., 2008.
60. Galligan, 2005.
61. Singer, 1975.
62. Katz, 1993, pp. 30–31.
63. Editor, 2008b.
64. Editor, 2008b.
65. Editor, 2008b.
66. Gingerich, 2007.
67. Gingerich, 2007.
68. Fraser et al., 2001.
69. Dawkins, 1980.
70. Webster, 1994, p. 158.
71. Dawkins, 2008, p. 82.
72. Katz, 1993.
73. Editor, 2007.
74. Dairy Quality Assurance, 2008.
75. United Egg Producers, 2008.
76. Barboza, 2003.
77. Curtis et al., 2007.
78. Thompson, 2004.
79. Norwood, 2007.
80. Galligan, 2005.
81. Foundation for Biomedical Research, 2006
82. Schumacher, 1996.
83. House, 2008.
84. Bergreen and Gehrke, 2008.

Chapter 9

1. DeGrazia, 1996.
2. Midgley, 1996.

3. Pluhar, 1995.

4. Rachels, 1991.

5. Rollin, 2006.

6. Vance, 1992.

7. Nicoll and Russell, 1992.

8. Nicoll and Russell, 1994.

9. Russell and Nicoll 1996a,b.

10. Stell, 1995.

11. Griswold, 1986, p. D7.

12. Gaita, 2003, p. 199.

13. Russell and Nicoll, 1996a

14. Singer, 1994a, p. 524.

15. Singer, 1990, pp. 4–5.

16. Singer, 1990, p. 6.

17. Rachels, 1991.

18. Singer, 1990, p. 85.

19. Singer, 1990, p. 85.

20. Singer, 1990, p. 21.

21. Russell and Nicoll, 1996a.

22. Singer, 1996.

23. Russell and Nicoll, 1996b.

24. Russell and Nicoll, 1996a, p. 109.

25. Singer, 1990, p. 71.

26. Petrinovich, 1999, p. 230.

27. Cohen, 1986, p. 7.

28. McInerney et al., 2004, pp. 203–204.

29. Tannenbaum, 2000a.

30. Regan, 1983, p. 384.

31. Regan, 1983, p. 388.

32. Singer, 1990, p. 92.

33. Turner, 1980.

34. Cohen, 1986, pp. 32–34.

35. Williams, 2006, p. 148.

36. Petrinovich, 1999, p. 9.

37. Leahy, 1994, p. 27.

38. Midgley, 1983, p. 96.

39. Midgley, 1983, p. 110.

40. Fox, 1986.

41. Fox, 1987.

42. Fox, 1986, p. 45.

43. Williams, 2006.

44. Preece, 2005, p. 122.

45. Preece and Fraser, 2000.

46. Krech, 1994.

47. Sorabji, 1993, p. 8.

48. Fox, 1987, p. 59.
49. Feinberg, 1978.
50. Tannenbaum, 1995.
51. Feinberg, 1978, p. 60.
52. Tannenbaum, 2000a.
53. Regan, 2001, p. A11.
54. Singer, 2001.
55. Sorabji, 1993, p. 211.
56. Linker, 2001, pp. 41–44.
57. As quoted by Hauser, 2006.
58. Rachels, 1991.
59. Cohen and Regan, 2001, p. 301.
60. Singer, 1990, p. 19.
61. Bulliet, 2005.
62. Stell, 2005.
63. Carman, 1990, p. 87.
64. Pluhar, 1995, p. 348.
65. Pollan, 2006, p. 321.
66. Pinker, 2002, p. 183.

Epilogue

1. Morrison and Hand, 1982.
2. Orlans, 1982.
3. Doddsand Orlans, 1982.
4. Stephen, 1885, pp. 100–101.
5. Budiansky, 1995, 155.
6. O'Hara, 1941, pp. 50–51.

References

Alberts, B. (2008). Shortcuts to medical progress? Science 319: 1733.

Alleyne, R. (2001). Terror tactics that brought a company to its knees. *Telegraph* June 6, 2001. Retrieved December 21, 2007, from http://www.telegraph.co.uk/news/main.jhtml?xml=/news/2001/01/19/ncam119.xml.

Americans for Medical Progress. (2005). Special Report.

Americans for Medical Progress. (2008). Personal communication.

American Veterinary Medical Association. (2007). Press release, October 4, 2007. Retrieved January 23, 2009, from http://www.avma.org/press/releases/071004_unwanted_horses.asp

Arluke, A. and B. Sax (1992). Understanding animal protection and the Holocaust. *Anthrozoos* 5(1): 6–31.

Aserinsky, E. and N. Kleitman (1953). Regularly occurring periods of eye motility, and concomitant phenomena during sleep. *Science* 118: 273–274.

Barboza, D. (2003). Animal welfare's unexpected allies. *New York Times* June 25, 2003. Retrieved August 16, 2008, from http://www.nytimes.com

Barnard, N. and S. Kaufman (1997). Animal research is wasteful and misleading. *Scientific American* 276(2): 80–82.

Beeson, P. B. (1980). How to foster the gain of knowledge about disease. *Perspectives in Biology and Medicine* 23/2 (Part 2): S9–S24.

Beeson, P. B. (1989). Animal experimentation: Context of a quote [Letter]. *Science* 245: 1437.

Benton, M. J. (1997). *Vertebrate Paleontology*. Vol. 2. London: Chapman and Hall.

Bergreen, J. and S. Gehrke (2008). 3 Utahns with animal-rights group claim they freed mink. *The Salt Lake Tribune* September 23, 2008. Retrieved September 30, 2008, http://www.sltrib.com/ci_10534783.

Bizzi, E. and D. C. Brooks (1963). Functional connections between pontine reticular formation and lateral geniculate nucleus during deep sleep. *Archives Italiennes De Biologie* 101: 666–680.

Blalock, A. and H. B. Taussig (1945). The surgical treatment of malformations of the heart in which there is pulmonary atresia. *Journal of the American Medical Association* 128: 189–202.

Blankenau, G. S. (1995). Children and the animal rights agenda. *Field & Stream,* August 4: 56–58.

Bliss, M. (1982). *The Discovery of Insulin.* Chicago: University of Chicago Press.

Boggan, S. (2006). Money talks. *The Guardian,* June 1, 2006. Retrieved December 21, 2007, from http://www.guardian.co.uk/animalrights/story/0,1787250,00.html.

Bogusslavsky, J., ed. (1997). *Acute Stroke Treatment.* London: Martin Dunitz.

Botting, J. (1991). Penicillin: Myth and fact. *RDS News,* June.

Botting, J. and A. R. Morrison (1997). Animal research is vital to medicine. *Scientific American* 276(2): 83–85.

Botting, J. and A. R. Morrison (1998). UnScientific American: Animal rights or wrongs: An op-ed. *HMS Beagle: The BioMedNet Magazine* 25 (Feb. 20): 1–7. Retrieved December 20, 2008, from http://www.aaskolnick.com/morrison/unscian.htm

Brady, R. (1969). *The Spirit and Structure of German Fascism.* New York: Howard Fertig.

Brenner, E. H. (2008). Personal communication.

Brooks, D. C. and E. Bizzi (1963). Brain-stem electrical activity during deep sleep. *Archives Italiennes De Biologie* 101: 648–665.

Budiansky, S. (1992). *The Covenant of the Wild: Why Animals Chose Domestication.* New York: William Morrow.

Budiansky, S. (1995). *Nature's Keepers.* New York: The Free Press.

Budiansky, S. (1998). *If a Lion Could Talk.* New York: The Free Press.

Bulliet, R. W. (2005). *Hunters, Herders and Hamburgers: The Past and Future of Human–Animal Relationships.* New York: Columbia University Press.

Burghardt, G. (1985). Animal awareness: Current perceptions and historical perspectives. *American Psychologist* 40: 905–919.

Burghardt, G. M. and H. A. Herzog Jr. (1980). Beyond conspecifics: Is Brer Rabbit our brother? *Bioscience* 30: 763–768.

Capper, J. L., E. Castaneda-Gutierrez, R. A. Cady, and D. E. Bauman (2008). The environmental impact of recombinant bovine somatotropin (rBST) use in dairy production. *Proceedings of the National Academy of Sciences* 105: 9668–9673.

Carlsson, A. (2005). Nerves as chemical messengers. *Science* 310: 1120–1121.

Carman, R. (1990). *The Illusions of Animal Rights.* Iola, WI: Krause Publications.

Carmichael, M. (2004). Atkins under attack. *Newsweek* (February 23) 143(8): 51. Retrieved November 19, 2008, from http//www.newsweek.com/id/53175

Carroll, M. E., W. K. Bickel, and S. T. Higgins (2001). Non-drug incentives to treat drug abuse: Laboratory and clinical developments. In Carroll, M. E. and J. B. Overmier, eds.

Animal Research and Human Health: Advancing Human Welfare through Behavioral Science. Washington, DC: American Psychological Association, pp. 139–154.

Cartwright, R. (2004). Sleepwalking violence: A sleep disorder, a legal dilemma, and a psychological challenge. *American Journal of Psychiatry* 161(7): 1149–1158.

Cavalieri, P. and P. Singer, eds. (1993). *The Great Ape Project: Equality Beyond Humanity.* New York: St. Martin's Press.

Cheng, H., Y. Cao, and L. Olson (1996). Spinal cord repair in adult paraplegic rats: Partial restoration of hind limb function. *Science* 273: 510–513.

Cohen, C. (1986). The case for the use of animals in biomedical research. *New England Journal of Medicine* 315: 865–870.

Cohen, C. and T. Regan (2001). *The Animal Rights Debate.* Lanham, MD: Rowman and Littlefield.

Comroe, J. (1983). *Exploring the Heart.* New York: W. W. Norton.

Comroe, J. and R. Dripps (1976). Scientific basis for the support of biomedical research. *Science* 192: 105–111.

Conn, P. M. and J. V. Parker (2008). *The Animal Research War.* New York: Palgrave Macmillan.

Conniff, R. (1990). Fuzzy-Wuzzy thinking about animal rights. *Audubon Magazine* November: 121–133.

Coppinger, R. P. and Smith, C. K. (1983). The domestication of evolution. *Environmental Conservation* 10: 283–292.

Cornelius, C. E. (1969). Animal models—a neglected medical resource. *New England Journal of Medicine* 281: 934–944.

Cottingham, J., D. Murdoch, R. Stoothoff, and A. Kenny, eds. (1991). *The Philosophical Writings of Descartes: The Correspondence.* Vol. 3. Cambridge, UK: Cambridge University Press.

Curtis, S., T. Grandin, and J. McGlone (2007). Time for united position on animal welfare. *FeedstuffsFoodLink* July 7, 2007. Retrieved September 30, 2008, from http://www.feedstuffsfoodlink.com/ME2/dirmod.asp?sid=F4A490F89845425D8362C0250A1FE984&nm=&type=news&mod=News&mid=9A02E3B96F2A415ABC72CB5F516B4C10&tier=3&nid=4872BC6D430345B4B210730A62F40D8F

Dairy Quality Assurance (2008). Milk & Dairy Beef Quality Assurance Center. Retrieved September 29, 2008, from http://www.dqacenter.org/

Dantzler, W. H., L. R. Squire, R. G. Petersdorf, J. G. Hardman, D. Johnson, and N. Miller (1994). Humane use of animals. *Nature* 369(6475): 9–19.

Darwin, C. (1859). *The Origin of Species by Means of Natural Selection or the Preservation of Favoured Races in the Struggle for Life,* 6th ed. London: John Murray.

Darwin, C. (1883 [1924]). *The Descent of Man and Selection in Relation to Sex,* 2nd revised and augmented ed. New York: D. Appleton & Co.

Davis, S. L. (2003). The least harm principle may require that humans consume a diet containing large herbivores, not a vegan diet. *Journal of Environmental and Agricultural Ethics* 16: 387–394.

Davis, S. L. (2008). What would the world be like without animals for food, fiber, and labor? Are we morally obligated to do without them? *Poultry Science* 87: 392–394.

Davisson, M. T. (2005). Discovery genetics: Serendipity in basic research. *Institute for Laboratory Resources Journal* 46: 338–345.

Dawkins, M. S. (1980). *Animal Suffering: The Science of Animal Welfare*. London: Chapman and Hall.

Dawkins, M. S. (1993). *Through Our Eyes Only?: The Search for Animal Consciousness*. Oxford: W. H. Freeman.

Dawkins, M. S. (2008). What is good welfare and how can we achieve it? In Dawkins, M. S. and R. Bonney, eds. *The Future of Animal Farming: Renewing the Ancient Contract*. London: Blackwell, pp. 73–82.

Deadwyler, S. A., L. Porrino, J. M. Siegel, and R. E. Hampson (2007). Systemic and nasal delivery of orexin-a (hypocretin-1) reduces the effects of sleep deprivation on cognitive performance in nonhuman primates. *Journal of Neuroscience* 27: 14239–14247.

DeGrazia, D. (1996). *Taking Animals Seriously: Mental Life and Moral Status*. Cambridge, UK: Cambridge University Press.

Dement, W. C. (1969). The biological role of REM sleep (circa 1968). In Kales, A., ed. *Sleep: Physiology and Pathology*. Philadelphia: Lippincott, pp. 245–265.

Dement, W. C. (1972). *Some Must Watch While Some Must Sleep*. Stanford, CA: Stanford Alumni Association.

Dennett, D. C. (1996). *Kinds of Minds: Toward an Understanding of Consciousness*. New York: Basic Books.

Dennis, S. G. and R. Melzack (1983). Perspectives on evolution of pain expression. In Kitchell, R. L., H. H. Erickson, E. Carstens, and L. E. Davis, eds. *Animal Pain: Perception and Alleviation*. Bethesda, MD: American Physiological Society, pp. 151–160.

Derbyshire, D. (2007). Leading scientist denied his knighthood yet again "because of his outspoken support for animal experiment". *Daily Mail,* December 29, 2007. Retrieved January 3, 2008, from http://www.dailymail.co.uk/pages/live/articles/news/news.html?in_article_id=505042&in_page_id=1770.

de Waal, F. (1996). *Good Natured: The Origins of Right and Wrong in Humans and Other Animals*. Cambridge, MA: Harvard University Press.

de Waal, F. (2006). Morally evolved: Primate social instincts, human morality, and the rise and fall of "veneer theory." In Macedo, S. and J. Ober, eds. *Primates and Philosophers: How Morality Evolved*. Princeton, NJ: Princeton University Press, pp. 1–80.

Dizard, J. (1994). *Going Wild: Hunting, Animal Rights, and the Contested Meaning of Nature*. Amherst, MA: University of Massachusetts Press.

Dizard, J. (2003). *Mortal Stakes: Hunters and Hunting in Contemporary America*. Amherst, MA: University of Massachusetts Press.

Dodds, W. J. and F. B. Orlans, eds. (1982). *Scientific Perspectives on Animal Welfare*. Orlando, FL: Academic Press.

Donovan, D. (1995). Trial tomorrow in dalmatian case. *The Philadelphia Inquirer* January 8, 1995: 1.

Driscoll, C. A., M. Menotti-Raymond, A. L. Roca, K. Hupe, W. E. Johnson, E. Geffen, E. H. Harley, et al. (2007). The Near Eastern origin of cat domestication. *Science* 317: 519–523.

Duda, M. (2008). Personal communication.

Dudrick, S. J. (1977). The genesis of intravenous hyperalimentation. *Journal of Parenteral and Enteral Nutrition* 1: 23–29.

Dulbecco, R. A. (1986). Turning point in cancer research: Sequencing the human genome. *Science* 231: 1055–1056.

Editor (1883). The orang, chimpanzee, and gorilla. *The New York Times* March 25, 1883: 12.

Editor (2006). Deer statistics: Can you afford not to go to this forum? *The Swarthmorean* April 12, 2006.

Editor (2007). Animal well-being expert applauds pork industry's PQA plus. *Cattle Network* April 26, 2007. Retrieved September 30, 2008, from http://www.cattlenetwork.com/Swine_Content.asp?contented=125205

Editor (2008a). Bernard, Claude. *Encyclopaedia Britannica.* Encyclopaedia Britannica Online: http://www.britannica.com/eb/article-9078837.

Editor (2008b). Independent committee promotes use of science in animal care guidelines. *FoodstuffsFoodLink* August 8, 2008. Retrieved October 1, 2008, from http://www.feedstuffsfoodlink.com/ME2/dirmod.asp?sid=F4A490F89845425D8362C0250A1FE984&nm=&type=news&mod=News&mid=9A02E3B96F2A415ABC72CB5F516B4C10&tier=3&nid=841985698C0841D8BE15D28CCC6EE27C

Editorial (1999). The great divide? *New Scientist* 13(February): 3.

Editorial (2007). Keeping protests within the law. *Nature Neuroscience* 10: 1501.

Ellinwood, N. M., C. H. Vite, and M. K. Haskins (2004). Gene therapy for lysosomal storage diseases: The lessons and promises of animal models. *Journal of Gene Medicine* 6: 481–506.

Emery, N. J. and N. S. Clayton (2004). Comparing the complex cognition of birds and primates. In Rogers, L. J. and G. Kaplan, eds. *Comparative Vertebrate Cognition: Are Primates Superior to Non-Primates?* New York: Kluwer Academic, pp. 3–55.

Feinberg, J. (1978). Human duties and animal rights. In Morris, R. K. and M. W. Fox, eds. *On the Fifth Day: Animal Rights and Human Ethics.* Washington, DC: Acropolis Books, pp. 45–69.

Festing, M. F. W. (2001). Book review: "Sacred Cows and Golden Geese" by Greek and Greek. *ATLA* 29: 617–620.

Festing, M. F. W. (2004). Is the use of animals in biomedical research still necessary? Unfortunately, "yes". *ATLA* 32(Suppl. 1): 733–739.

Fetrow, J. P. (2001). Food animal welfare and the use of bovine somatotrophin. *Journal of the American Veterinary Medical Association* 218: 1886–1889.

Finkelstein, S. I. (2005). High noon for animal rights law: The coming showdown between pet owners and guardians. *Bellwether* 62 (Summer): 18–21.

Foundation for Biomedical Research (2006). Illegal incidents report: A 25-year history of illegal activities by eco and animal extremists. Available online at: http://www.fbresearch.org/AnimalActivism/IllegalIncidents/IllegalIncidentsReport.pdf.

Foundation for Biomedical Research (2008). Personal communication.

Fox, M. A. (1986). *The Case for Animal Experimentation: An Evolutionary and Ethical Perspective.* Berkeley, CA: University of California Press.

Fox, M. A. (1987). Animal experimentation: A philosopher's changing views. *Between the Species* 3: 55–60.

Fox, M. W. (1990). *Inhumane Society: The American Way of Exploiting Animals.* New York: St. Martin's Press.

Fox, R. E., S. Mineka, and G. H. Bower (1994). Humane use of animals. *Nature* 369: 10.

Fraser, D., J. Mench, and S. Millman (2001). Farm animals and their welfare in 2000. In Salem, D. J. and A. R. Rowan, eds. *The State of the Animals* 2001. Washington, DC: Humane Society Press, pp. 87–99.

Gaita, R (2003). *The Philosopher's Dog.* London: Routledge.

Galligan, D. (2005). Personal communication.

Galligan, D. (2006). Personal communication.

Galligan, D. (2008). Personal communication.

Gennarelli, T. A. (1983). Head injury in man and experimental animals—clinical aspects. *Acta Neurochirurgica Supplement* 32: 1–13.

Gingerich, E. (2007). Statement on the welfare of caged table egg layers. Personal communication.

Godlovitch, S., R. Godlovitch, and J. Harris, eds. (1972). *Animals, Men and Morals: An Inquiry into the Maltreatment of Non-Humans.* New York: Taplinger.

Goldberger, M. M., M. Murray, and A. Tessler (1993). Sprouting and regeneration in the spinal cord: Their roles in recovery of function after spinal injury. In Gorio, A., ed. *Neuroregeneration.* New York: Raven Press, pp. 241–264.

Goodwin, F. K. (1992). Animal research, animal rights and public health. *Conquest* 181: 1–10.

Gottesmann, C. (2001). The golden age of rapid eye movement sleep discoveries: 1. Lucretius—1964. *Progress in Neurobiology* 65: 211–287.

Grandin, T. and C. Johnson (2005). *Animals in Translation; Using the Mysteries of Autism to Decode Animal Behavior.* New York: Harcourt.

Greek, R. and J. Greek (2000a). Animal research and human disease. *Journal of the American Medical Association* 283: 743–744.

Greek, R. and J. Greek (2000b). *Sacred Cows and Golden Geese. The Human Cost of Experiments on Animals.* New York: Continuum.

Griffin, D. R. (1992). *Animal Minds.* Chicago: University of Chicago Press.

Griswold, C., Jr. (1986). The immorality of "animal rights". *Washington Post,* January 5, 1986: D7.

Groce, N. E. and J. Marks (2001). The Great Ape project and disability rights: Ominous undercurrents of eugenics in action. *American Anthropologist* 102(4): 818–822.

Guillermo, K. S. (1993). *Monkey Business: The Disturbing Case that Launched the Animal Rights Movement.* Washington, DC: National Press Books.

Hand, P. J. (1987). Personal communication.

Harnack, A., ed. (1996). *Animal Rights: Opposing Viewpoints.* Opposing Viewpoints Series, edited by D. Bender and B. Leone. San Diego: Greenhaven Press.

Hauser, M. D. (2000). *Wild Minds: What Animals Really Think.* New York: Holt.

Hauser, M. D. (2006). *Moral Minds: How Nature Designed Our Universal Sense of Right and Wrong.* New York: Harper Collins Publishers.

Hendricks, E. (1985). Sensationalism and half-truths cloud Penn lab facts. *Animaldom* 55: 2–4.

Hendricks, J. C., L. R. Kline, R. J. Kowalski, J. A. O'Brien, A. R. Morrison, and A. I. Pack (1987). The English bulldog: A natural model of sleep-disordered breathing. *Journal of Applied Physiology* 63: 1344–1350.

Henig, S. (2006). UCLA professor halts monkey research. *The Chronicle of Higher Education* 53(2): A22.

Henley, K. and A. R. Morrison (1974). A re-evaluation of the effects of lesions of the pontine tegmentum and locus coeruleus on phenomena of paradoxical sleep in the cat. *Acta Neurobiologiae Experimentalis* 34: 215–232.

Herscovici, A. (1985). *Second Nature: The Animal Rights Controversy*. Montreal: CBC Enterprises.

Herzog, H. A., Jr. (1988). The moral status of mice. *American Psychologist* 43: 473–476.

Herzog, H. A., Jr. (1991). Conflicts of interest: Kittens, boa constrictors, pets and research. *American Psychologist* 46: 246–248.

Herzog, H. A., Jr. (1993). The movement is my life: The psychology of animal rights activism. *Journal of Social Issues* 49: 103–119.

Holden, C. (1981). Scientist convicted for monkey neglect. *Science* 214: 1218–1220.

House, D. (2008). Animal Liberation Front frees animals, destroys breeding records in Kaysville and South Jordan. *The Salt Lake Tribune* September 22, 2008. Retrieved September 30, 2008, from http://www.sltrib.com/business/ci_10581217

Howard, W. E. (1990). *Animal Rights vs. Nature*. Davis, CA: W. E. Howard.

Institute for Laboratory Animal Resources (1996). *Guide for the Care and Use of Laboratory Animals*. Washington, D.C.: National Academy Press.

James, G. (1992). Beggar, hit by cab, giving up streets. *New York Times* April 22, 1992: B3.

Jasper, J. M. and D. Nelkin (1992). *The Animal Rights Crusade: The Growth of a Moral Protest*. New York: The Free Press.

Jha, S. K., F. X. Brennan, A. C. Pawlyk, R. J. Ross, and A. R. Morrison (2005). REM sleep: A sensitive index of fear conditioning in rats. *European Journal of Neuroscience* 21(4): 1077–1080.

John, J., M.-F. Wu, and J. M. Siegel (2000). Systemic administration of hypocretin-1 reduces cataplexy and normalizes sleep and waking durations in narcoleptic dogs. *Sleeep Research Online* 3: 23–28.

Johnson, M. (1988). Impending surgery. In Fisher, S. and J. Reason, eds. *Handbook of Life Stress, Cognition and Health*. New York: Wiley, pp. 79–100.

Jones, S. D. (2003). *Valuing Animals*. Baltimore: The John Hopkins University Press.

Jouvet, M. and F. Delorme (1965). Locus coeruleus et sommeil paradoxal. *Comptes Rendus des Séances de la Société dé Biologié et de Ses Filiales* 159: 895–899.

Jouvet, M. and F. Michel (1959). Corrélations électromyographique du sommeil chez le chat décortiqué et mésencéphalique chronique. *Comptes Rendus des Séances de la Société de Biologie et de Ses Filiales* 153: 422–425.

Katz, L. (1993). How to attack animal agriculture with a pinch of fact and a pound of hyperbole (book review). *Coalition for Animals and Animal Research Newsletter* Winter/Spring: 30–31.

Keller, H. (1956). *Teacher: Anne Sullivan Macy*. London: Victor Gollancz.

Kellert, S. R. (1996). *The Value of Life: Biological Diversity and Human Society*. Washington DC: Island Press.

Kennedy, D. (2006). Animal activism: Out of control. *Science* 313: 1541.

Kitcher, P. (2006). Ethics and evolution: How to get there from here. In Macedo, S. and J. Ober, eds. *Primates and Philosophers: How Morality Evolved*. Princeton, NJ: Princeton University Press, pp. 120–139.

Kopp, B., A. Kunkel, W. Muhlnickel, K. Villringer, E. Taub, and H. Flor. (1999). Plasticity in the motor system related to therapy-induced improvement of movement after stroke. *Neuroreport* 10: 807–810.

Krech, S. III. (1994). Ecology and the American Indian. *Ideas: From the National Humanities Center* 30(1): 4–22.

Kulpa-Eddy, J. A., S. Taylor, and K. M. Adams (2005). USDA perspective on environmental enrichment for animals. *Institute for Laboratory Animal Resources Journal* 46(2): 83–94.

La Valle, R. P. (2008). Why they're human rights. *Washington Post* July 27, 2008: B 7.

Lawrence, E. A. (1982) *Rodeo: An Anthropologist Looks at the Wild and the Tame*. Knoxville, TN: University of Tennessee Press.

Leahy, M. P. T. (1994) *Against Liberation: Putting Animals in Perspective*. London: Routledge.

Lederer, S. E. (1987). The controversy over animal experimentation in America, 1880–1914. In Rupke, N. A., ed. *Vivisection in Historical Perspective*. London: Routledge, pp. 236–258.

Lederer, S. E. (1995). *Subjected to Science: Human Experimentation in America before the Second World War*. Baltimore: The Johns Hopkins University Press.

LeDoux, J. E. (1992). Emotion and the amygdala. In Aggleton, J. P., ed. *The Amygdala: Neurobiological Aspects of Emotion, Memory and Mental Dysfunction*. New York: Wiley-Liss, pp. 339–351.

Levine, S. (1993). Fall. *The Philadelphia Inquirer Magazine* February 28, 1993: 23–25, 29, 35.

Lewin-ICF (1992). *The Cost of Disorders of the Brain*. Washington, DC: The National Foundation for Brain Research.

Lewis, J. E. (2005). Congressional testimony. Federal Bureau of Investigation, May 18, 2005. Retrieved November 3, 2008, from http://www.fbi.gov/congress/congress05/lewis051805.htm

Liepert, J., H. Bauder, W. H. R. Miltner, E. Taub, and C. Weiller (2000). Treatment-induced cortical reorganization after stroke in humans. *Stroke* 31: 1210–1216.

Linker, D. (2001). Rights for rodents. *Commentary* 4: 41–44.

Lister, S. (2002). Animal rights bomb maker jailed for attack on lab and abattoir. *The Times* December 13, 2002. Retrieved November 14, 2008, from http://www.timesonline.co.uk/tol/news/uk/article801659.ece

Liu, C. N. and W. W. Chambers (1958). Intraspinal sprouting of dorsal root axons. *Archives of Neurology and Psychiatry* 79: 46–61.

Lovejoy, A. O. (1936). *The Great Chain of Being: A Study of the History of an Idea*. Cambridge, MA: Harvard University Press.

Lutherer, L. O. and M. S. Simon (1992). *Targeted: The Anatomy of an Animal Rights Attack*. Norman, OK: University of Oklahoma.

Madan, V., F. X. Brennan, G. L. Mann, A. A. Horbal, G. A. Dunn, R. J. Ross, and A. R. Morrison (2008). Long-term effect of cued fear conditioning on REM sleep microarchitecture in rats. *Sleep* 31: 498–503.

Maehle, A.-H. and Tröhler, U. (1990). Animal experimentation from antiquity to the end of the eighteenth century: Attitudes and arguments. In Rupke, N. A., ed. *Vivisection in Historical Perspective* London: Routledge, pp. 14–47.

Magel, C. R. (1989). *Keyguide to Information Sources in Animal Rights*. London: McFarland.

Marks, J. (1994). Book review: *The Great Ape Project: Equality Beyond Humanity*, P. Cavalieri and P. Singer, St. Martin's Press: New York, 1993. *Human Biology* 66: 1113–1117.

Martin, J. E. (1984). *A Legacy and A Promise: The First One Hundred Years, 1884–1984*. Philadelphia: University of Pennsylvania.

Matta, J. A., P. M. Cornett, R. L. Miyares, K. Abe, N. Sahibzada, and G. P. Ahern (2008). General anesthetics activate a nociceptive ion channel to enhance pain and inflammation. *Proceedings of the National Academy of Sciences* 105: 8784–8789.

McCabe, K. (1986). Who will live? Who will die? *The Washingtonian* August: 112–116, 118, 153–157.

McCaghy, C. H. and A. G. Neal (1974). The fraternity of cockfighters: Ethical embellishments of an illegal sport. *Journal of Popular Culture* 8: 557–569.

McCormick, B. (1991). AMA challenges "physician" group. *American Medical News* June 17, 1991: 25–26.

McInerney, J. D., A. R. Morrison, and J. R. Schrock (2004). Reaction to "How we treat our relatives". *The American Biology Teacher* 66(4): 253–254.

McIntosh, T., M. Juhler, and T. Wieloch (1998). Novel pharmacologic strategies in the treatment of experimental traumatic brain injury: 1998. *Journal of Trauma* 15: 731–769.

Meagher, M. A. (2001). Clinical implications of animal pain research. In Carroll, M. E. and J. B. Overmier, eds. *Animal Research and Human Health: Advancing Human Welfare through Behavioral Science*. Washington, DC: American Psychological Association, pp. 227–243.

Medawar, P. (1996). *The Strange Case of the Spotted Mice*. Oxford: Oxford University Press.

Mencken, H. L. (1982). *A Mencken Chrystomathy*. New York: Vintage Books.

Merker, B. (2007). Consciousness without a cerebral cortex: A challenge for neuroscience (with commentaries). *Behavioral and Brain Sciences* 30: 61–134.

Midgley, M. (1983). *Animals and Why They Matter*. Athens, GA: University of Georgia Press.

Miller, G. (2007). Science and the public: Animal extremists get personal. *Science* 318: 1856–1858.

Miller, J. (2006). Personal communication.

Miller, N. E. (1985a). Prologue. In Zimbardo, P. G., ed. *Psychology and Life*, 11th ed. Glenview, IL: Scott Foresman, pp. i–vii.

Miller, N. E. (1985b). The value of behavioral research on animals. *American Psychologist* 40: 423–440.

Moelis, H. (2008). Long term care. *Blood Horse.Com Blogs* July 22, 2008. Retrieved September 29, 2008, from http://cs.bloodhorse.com/blogs/finalturn/archive/2008/07/22/Long_2Doo_Term-Care.aspx

Morrison, A. R. (1983). A window on the sleeping brain. *Scientific American* 248: 94–102.

Morrison, A. R. (1992). Speciesism: A perversion of biology, not a principle. *The American Biology Teacher* 54(3): 134–136.

Morrison, A. R. (1993a). Animals' dreams. In Carskadon, M., ed. *Encyclopedia of Sleep and Dreaming*. New York: MacMillan, pp. 37–38.

Morrison, A. R. (1993b). Biomedical research & the animal rights movement: a contrast in values. *The American Biology Teacher* 55: 204–208.

Morrison, A. R. (1994). Understanding (and misunderstanding) the animal rights movement in the United States. In DeDeyn, J. P., ed. *The Ethics of Animal and Human Experimentation*. London: John Libbey.

Morrison, A. R. (1999a). A scientist at work. *The American Biology Teacher* 61: 496–502.

Morrison, A. R. (1999b). Caring about animals and creativity: Pogo revisited. *Lab Animal* 28: 34–37.

Morrison, A. R. (1999c). Choosing to favor animals. Review of *The Human Use of Animals, Case Studies in Ethical Choices*, by F. B. Orlans, T. L. Beauchamp, R. Dresser, D. B. Morton, J. P. Gluck (Oxford Univ. Press, Oxford, 1998). *Science* 283: 181.

Morrison, A. R. (2001a). Making choices in the laboratory. In Paul, E. F. and J. Paul, eds. *Why Animal Experimentation Matters: The Use of Animals in Medical Research*. New Brunswick, NJ: Transaction Press, pp. 49–70.

Morrison, A. R. (2001b). Personal reflections on the "animal-rights" phenomenon. *Perspectives in Biology and Medicine* 44(1): 62–75.

Morrison, A. R. (2002). Perverting medical history in the service of "animal rights". *Perspectives in Biology and Medicine* 45(4): 606–619.

Morrison, A. R. (2006). Thinking about animals: A personal odyssey. *SCAW Newsletter* 28(3): 6–13.

Morrison, A. R. (2009). Ethics, modernity and human–animal relationships. In Ciprut, J., ed. *Ethics, Policy and Democracy: From Primordial Principles to Prospective Practices*. Cambridge, MA: The MIT Press, pp. 83–102.

Morrison, A. R. and J. Botting (1997). Confusion in the ranks. *The American Biology Teacher* 59(7): 388.

Morrison, A. R. and R. M. Bowker (1975). The biological significance of PGO spikes in the sleeping cat. *Acta Neurobiologiae Experimentalis* 35: 821–840.

Morrison, A. R., H. L. Evans, N. A. Ator, and R. K. Nakamura, eds. (2002). *Methods and Welfare Considerations in Behavioral Research with Animals: Report of a National Institutes of Health (National Institute of Mental Health) Workshop*. NIH Publication 02-5083, Washington, DC: U.S. Government Printing Office.

Morrison, A. R. and P. J. Hand (1982). Animal welfare. *Science* 215: 745–746.

Mowrer, O. H. and W. M. Mowrer (1938). Enuresis—a method for its study and treatment. *American Journal of Orthopsychiatry* 8: 436–459.

National Animal Interest Alliance (2008). Rodeo group earns 2003 equine welfare award. Retrieved January 23, 2008, from http://www.naiaonline.org/body/articles/archives/rodeo_award.htm

National Association of Biology Teachers (2009). Position statement -- the use of animals in biology education. January 20, 2009. Retrieved January 20, 2009 from http://www.nabt.org/websites/institution/index.php?p=97

National Association for Biomedical Research (1991). Supreme Court sends latest "Silver Spring Monkey" appeal back to Louisiana State Court. *NABR Update* 12(13).

National Association for Biomedical Research (1994). Animal activist groups fail (again) to gain U.S. Supreme Court attention for primate case. *NABR Update* 15(26).

National Institutes of Health, Office of Protection from Research Risks (1985). Evaluation of Experimental Procedures Conducted at the University of Pennsylvania Experimental Head Injury Laboratory 1981–1984 in Light of the Public Health Service Animal Welfare Policy. Bethesda, MD: National Institutes of Health.

National Institutes of Health, Office for Protection from Research Risks (1990). Report on Investigations of Allegations of Noncompliance with Public Health Service Policy on Humane Care and Use of Animals at Texas Tech University Health Sciences Center, March 16, 1990. Bethesda, MD: National Institutes of Health.

Nelson, R. J. and T. D. Mandrell (2005). Enrichment and nonhuman primates: "First do no harm". *Institute for Laboratory Animal Resources Journal* 46: 171–177.

Nicoll, C. S. and S. M. Russell (1992). Animal rights, animal research, and human obligations. *Molecular Cellular Neuroscience* 3: 271–277.

Nicoll, C. S. and S. M. Russell (1994). Animal rights movement evokes concern. *The American Biology Teacher* 56(2): 70–71.

Nolen, R. S. (2006). Congress holds hearings on horse slaughter ban. *Journal of the American Veterinary Medical Association* 229: 636, 638.

Norwood, B. (2007). Animal welfare survey provides important lessons. *FBNews* 86(22): 4.

Nuland, S. B. (1988). *Doctors—The Biography of Medicine*. New York: Vintage Books, Random House.

O'Driscoll, S. (1832). Dennis Ready: A tale of the Kingdom of Kerry. *Atkinson's Casket* 7(10): 440–443.

O'Hara, M. (1941). *My Friend Flicka*. Philadelphia: Lippincott.

Orlans, B. F. (1982). Animal welfare. *Science* 215: 746.

Orlans, B. F. (1991). The case against dissection. *Science Teacher* 58: 12–14.

Orlans, B. F. (1993). *In the Name of Science: Issues in Responsible Animal Experimentation*. Oxford: Oxford University Press.

Ozoga, J. (1995). *Whitetail Winter*. Minocqua, WI: Willow Creek Press.

Paddock, R. C. and M. L. LaGanga (2008). Officials decry attacks on UC staff; one of two weekend firebombings in Santa Cruz caused a scientist and his family to flee through a window. *Los Angeles Times* August 5, 2008: B1.

Parsell, D. P. (1989). The animal rights movement: It's closed down and stalled research projects, putting scientists on the offensive. *NIDA Notes* Spring/Summer.

Paton, W. (1993). *Man and Mouse: Animals in Medical Research*. Oxford: Oxford University Press.

Patronek, G. J. (1999). Hoarding of animals: An under-recognized public health problem in a difficult-to-study population. *Public Health Reports* 114: 81–87.

Pavlov, I. P. (1927). *Conditioned Reflexes*. London: Oxford University Press.

Pawlyk, A. C., S. K. Jha, F. X. Brennan, A. R. Morrison, and R. J. Ross (2005). A rodent model of sleep disturbances in the anxiety disorders: The role of context following fear conditioning. *Biological Psychiatry* 57: 268–277.

Pence, G. E. (1990). *Classic Cases in Medical Ethics: Accounts of the Cases that Have Shaped Medical Ethics, with Philosophical, Legal and Historical Backgrounds*. New York: McGraw-Hill.

Petrinovich, L. (1999). *Darwinian Dominion: Animal Welfare and Human Interests*. Cambridge, MA: The MIT Press.

Pinker, S. (2002). *The Blank Slate: The Modern Denial of Human Nature*. New York: Viking Press.

Pinker, S. (2005). *The Language Instinct: How the Mind Creates Language*. New York: Harper Collins.

Pluhar, E. S. (1995). *Beyond Prejudice: The Moral Significance of Human and Nonhuman Animals*. Durham, NC: Duke University Press, 1995.

Pollan, M. (2006). *The Omnivore's Dilemma: A Natural History of Four Meals*. New York: Penguin Press.

Pons, T. P., P. E. Garraghty, A. K. Ommaya, J. H. Kaas, E. Taub, and M. Mishkin (1991). Massive cortical reorganization after sensory deafferentation in adult macaques. *Science* 252: 1857–1860.

Posewitz, J. (1994). *Beyond Fair Chase*. Helena, MT: Falcon Press.

Potter, V. (1970). Bioethics, the science of survival. *Perspectives in Biology and Medicine* 14(1): 127–153.

Povinelli, D. and J. Vonk (2006). We don't need a microscope to explore the chimpanzee mind. In Hurley, S. and M. Nudds, eds. *Rational Animals?* Oxford: Oxford University Press, pp. 285–412.

Preece, R. (2005). *Brute Souls, Happy Beasts and Evolution: The Historical Status of Animals*. Vancouver: UBC Press.

Preece, R. and D. Fraser (2000). The status of animals in biblical and Christian thought: A study in colliding values. *Society & Animals* 8: 245–263.

Professional Rodeo Cowboys Association (2008). Animal welfare: The care and treatment of professional rodeo livestock. Retrieved September 29, 2008, from http://www.prorodeo.com/pdfs/AnimalWelfare.pdf

Ra'anan, A. W. (2005). The evolving role of animal laboratories in physiology instruction. *Advances in Physiology Education* 29(3): 144–150.

Rachels, J. (1991). *Created from Animals: The Moral Implications of Darwinism*. Oxford: Oxford University Press.

Ramon y Cajal, S. (1959). *Degeneration and Regeneration of the Central Nervous System*. Translated by R. M. May. Vol. 2. New York: Hafner.

Ratner, S. C. (1967). Comparative aspects of hypnosis. In Gordon, J. E., ed. *Handbook of Clinical and Experimental Hypnosis*. New York: MacMillan, pp. 550–587.

Regan, T. (1983). *The Case for Animal Rights*. Berkeley, CA: The University of California.

Regan, T. (2001). Defending animal rights from a "defender". *The News and Observer (Raleigh, NC)* April 3, 2001:A11.

Regan, T. and G. Francione (1996). The animal rights movement must reject animal welfarism. In Harnack, A., ed. *Animal Rights: Opposing Viewpoints*. San Diego, CA: Greenhaven Press, pp. 194–201.

Reines, B. (1985a). *Heart Research on Animals: A Critique of Animal Models of Cardiovascular Disease*. Jenkintown, PA: The American Anti-Vivisection Society.

Reines, B. (1985b). *The Truth Behind the Discovery of Insulin*. Jenkintown, PA: American Anti-Vivisection Society.

Report of the School of Arts and Sciences Committee on Academic Freedom and Responsibility: Cancellation of the Course on "Animal Welfare and Human Intervention", College of General Studies, University of Pennsylvania, April 30, 1990.

Reynnells, R. D. and B. R. Eastwood. Animal Welfare Issues Compendium. Washington, D.C. Available at: http://www.nal.usda.gov/awic/pubs/97issues.htm

Ritvo, H. (1987). *The Animal Estate: The English and Other Creatures in the Victorian Era*. Cambridge, MA: Harvard University Press.

Rogers, L. J. and G. Kaplan (2006). Think or be damned: The problematic case of higher cognition in animals and legislation for animal welfare. *Animal Law* 12: 151–191.

Rollin, B. E. (1996). The case against animal research in psychology. In Harnack, A., ed. *Animal Research: Opposing Viewpoints*. 98–104. San Diego, CA: Greenhaven Press, 1996.

Rollin, B. E. (2006). *Animal Rights & Human Morality*, 3rd ed. Amherst, NY: Prometheus Books.

Rosenberger, J. (1990). Animal rites. *The Village Voice* March 6, 1990: 30–39.

Ruckebusch, Y. (1971). Comparative aspects of sleep and wakefulness in farm animals. In Chase, M. H., ed. *The Sleeping Brain*. Los Angeles: UCLA Brain Information Service, pp. 23–28.

Rucker, P. (2008). Med school is asked to stop animal use. *Washington Post,* July 2, 2008: B01.

Russell, S. M. and C. S. Nicoll (1996a). A dissection of the chapter "Tools for Research" in Peter Singer's *Animal Liberation. Proceedings of the Society for Experimental Biology and Medicine* 211: 109–138.

Russell, S. M. and C. S. Nicoll (1996b). Reply to Singer's "Blind Hostility". *Proceedings of the Society for Experimental Biology and Medicine* 211: 147–164.

Russell, W. M. S. and R. L. Burch (1959). *The Principles of Humane Experimental Technique*. London: Methuen.

Russon, A. E. and K. A. Bard (1996). Exploring the minds of the Great Apes: Issues and controversies. In Russon, A. E., K. A. Bard, and S. T. Parker, eds. *Reaching into Thought: The Minds of the Great Apes*. Cambridge, UK: Cambridge University Press, pp. 1–20.

Russow, L.-M. (1995). Am I my cousin's keeper? Review of *The Great Ape Project*, Cavalieri, P. and Singer, P. (Eds). *The Hastings Center Report* 25: 49.

Salsburg, D. (1997). Animal experimentation debate, round two. *Scientific American* June: 10.

Sanford, L. D., A. R. Morrison, W. A. Ball, R. J. Ross, and G. L. Mann (1993). The amplitude of elicited PGO waves: A correlate of orienting. *Electroencephalography and Clinical Neurophysiology* 86: 438–445.

Schenck, C. H. (1993). REM sleep behavior disorder. In Carskadon, M. A., ed. *Encyclopedia of Sleep and Dreaming*, New York: MacMillan, pp. 499–505.

Schenck, C. H., S. R. Bundlie, M. G. Ettinger, and M. W. Mahowald (1986). Chronic behavioral disorders of human REM sleep: A new category of parasomnia. *Sleep* 9: 293–308.

Schreiner, D. A. and P. L. Ruegg (2002). Effects of tail docking on milk quality and cow cleanliness. *Journal of Dairy Science* 85: 2503–2511.

Schrock, J. R. (2005). How do you make dissection exciting? ["Ask an Expert" Column]. *National Association of Biology Teachers Newsletter* January, 1, 2005: 10.

Schumacher, M. (1996). Fur is natural and environmentally sound. *National Animal Interest Alliance News* March–April: 14.

Searle, J. R. (1984). *Intentionality: An Essay in the Philosophy of Mind*. New York: Cambridge University Press.

Seidner, G. A., Y. Ye, M. M. Faraday, W. G. Alvord, and M. E. Fortini (2006). Modeling clinically heterogeneous presenilin mutations with transgenic *Drosophila*. *Current Biology* 16: 1026–1033.

Serpell, J. (1986). *In the Company of Animals*. Oxford: Basil Blackwell.

Seton, E. T. (1907). *The Natural History of the Ten Commandments*. New York: Scribners.

Siegel, J. M., R. Moore, T. Thannickal, and B. S. Nienhuis (2001). A brief history of hypocretin/orexin and narcolepsy. *Neuropsychopharmacology* 25: S14–S20.

Singer, P. (1973). Animal liberation. *The New York Review of Books,* April 5, 1973: 11–21.

Singer, P. (1975). *Animal Liberation: A New Ethic for our Treatment of Animals*, 1st ed. New York: The New York Review/Random House.

Singer, P. (1990). *Animal Liberation*, 2nd ed. New York: Random House.

Singer, P. (1994a). License to kill. *Nature* 367: 523–524.

Singer, P. (1994b). *Rethinking Life and Death: The Collapse of our Traditional Ethics*. New York: St. Martin's.

Singer, P. (1996). Blind hostility: A response to Russell and Nicoll. *Proceedings of the Society for Experimental Biology and Medicine* 211: 139–146.

Singer, P. (2001). Heavy petting. *Nerve.com*. Retrieved August 13, 2008, from http://www.nerve.com/opinions/singer/heavypetting/

Singer, W. (1977). Control of thalamic transmission by corticofugal and ascending reticular pathways in the visual system. *Physiological Reviews* 57: 386–420.

Singer, W. and Drager, U. (1972). Postsynaptic potentials in relay neurons of cat lateral geniculate nucleus after stimulation of the mesencephalic reticular formation. *Brain Research* 41: 214–220.

Skinner, B. F. (1938). *The Behavior of Organisms*. New York: Appleton-Century.

Sly, W. S. (2004). Enzyme replacement therapy for lysosomal storage disorders: Successful transition from concept to clinical practice. *Missouri Medicine* 101: 100–104.

Smith, W. J. (2006). Singer: Grant right to life for animals but not babies. *Secondhand Smoke: Your 24/7 Bioethics Seminar* May 26, 2006. Retrieved September 29, 2008, from http://www.wesleyjsmith.com/blog/archive/2006_05_01_archive.html

Smith, W. J. (2008). Spain apes the Declaration of Independence. *The Weekly Standard* 13(42): 15–17.

Sorabji, R (1993). *Animal Minds & Human Morals: The Origins of the Western Debate*. Ithaca: Cornell University Press.

Stadtfield, C. (1975). *Whitetail Deer*. New York: Dial Press.

Steele, J. H. (2000). The history of public health and veterinary public service. *Journal of the American Veterinary Medical Association* 217: 1813–1831.

Stell, L. K. (1995). The blessings of injustice: Animals and the right to accept medical treatment. *Between the Species* 11: 42–53.

Stell, L. K. (2005). Personal communication.

Stephen, L. (1885). *Life of Henry Fawcett*. London: Smith, Elder & Co.

Storm, J. (1995). Among Vietnam's victims: Edison High's class of '65. *The Philadelphia Inquirer* December 17, 1995: G1, 12.

Strand, R. and P. Strand (1993). *The Hijacking of the Humane Movement*. Wilsonville, OR: Doral Publishing.

Sweeney, C. R., J. C. Hendricks, J. Beech, and A. R. Morrison (1983). Narcolepsy in a horse: Case report and review. *Journal of the American Veterinary Medical Association* 183: 126–128.

Tannenbaum, J. (1995). *Veterinary Ethics: Animal Welfare, Client Relations, Competition, and Collegiality*. St. Louis: Mosby.

Tannenbaum, J. (2000a). Animal rights and animal research. In Kraus, A. L. and D. Rehnquist, eds. *Bioethics and the Use of Laboratory Animals*. Dubuque, IA: American College of Laboratory Medicine, pp. 1–46.

Tannenbaum, J. (2000b). The paradigm shift toward animal happiness: What it is, why it is happening, and what it means for medical research. In Paul, E. F. and J. Paul eds., *Why Animal Experimentation Matters: The Use of Animals in Medical Research*. Piscataway, NJ: Transaction Press.

Tannenbaum, J. (2006). Personal communication.

Taub, E. (1980). Somatosensory deafferentation research with monkeys: Implications for rehabilitation medicine. In Ince, L. P., ed. *Behavioral Psychology in Rehabilitation Medicine: Clinical Applications*. Baltimore: Williams and Wilkins, pp. 371–401.

Taub, E. (1991). The Silver Spring monkey incident: The untold story. *Coalition for Animals & Animal Research Newsletter* 4(1): 1–8.

Taub, E. (2008). Personal communication.

Taub, E., J. E. Crago, L. D. Burgio, T. E. Groomes, E. W. Cook III, S. C. DeLuca, and N. E. Miller (1994). An operant approach to rehabilitation medicine overcoming learned nonuse by shaping. *Journal of the Experimental Analysis of Behavior* 61: 281–293.

Taub, E., J. E. Crago, and G. Uswatte (1998). Constraint-induced movement therapy: A new approach to treatment in physical rehabilitation. *Rehabilitation Psychology* 43: 152–170.

Taub, E., N. E. Miller, T. A. Novack, E. W. Cook III, W. C. Fleming, C. S. Nepomuceno, J. S. Connell, and J. E. Crago (1993). Technique to improve chronic motor deficit after stroke. *Archives of Physical Medicine and Rehabilitation* 74: 347–354.

Taussig, H. B. (1981). Personal memories of surgery of tetralogy. In Snellen, H. A., A. J. Dunning, and A. C. Arntzenius, eds. *History and Perspectives of Cardiology, Catheterization, Angiography, Surgery and Concepts of Circular Control*. The Hague, Boston, London: Leiden University Press, pp. 159–163.

Terrace, H. S., L. A. Petitto, R. J. Saunders, and T. G. Bever (1979). Can an ape create a sentence? *Science* 206: 891–902.

Texley, J. (1992). Doing without dissection. *The American School Board Journal* 179 (January): 24–26.

Thomas, E. M. (1993). *The Hidden Life of Dogs*. Boston: Houghton Mifflin.

Thomas, L. (1974). Commentary: The future impact of science and technology on medicine. *BioScience* 24(2): 99–105.

Thompson, P. B. (2004). Getting pragmatic about farm animal welfare. In McKenna, E. and A. Light, eds. *Animal Pragmatism: Rethinking Human–Nonhuman Relationships*. Bloomington, IN: Indiana University Press, pp. 140–159.

Thorndike, E. L. (1898). Animal intelligence: An experimental study of the associative processes in animals. *Psychological Reviews Monograph* 8 (Suppl. 2).

Tinbergen, N. (1971). *The Herring Gull's World*. New York: Basic Books.

Tomlinson, H. Huntigdon delays listing after attacks. *The Guardian* September 8, 2005. Retrieved December 12, 2007, from http://www.guardian.co.uk/business/2005/sep/08/research.animalrights.

Torg, J. S. (1984). Penn work was vital. *The Philadelphia Inquirer* June 8, 1984: A21.

Trotter, A. (1992). Animal rights groups target high school dissection. *The American School Board Journal* January: 21–22.

Turner, J. (1980). *Reckoning with the Beast: Animals, Pain and Humanity in the Victorian Mind*. Baltimore: The Johns Hopkins University Press.

United Egg Producers (2008). United Egg Producers Animal Husbandry Guidelines for U.S. Egg-Laying Flocks. Retrieved September 29, 2008, from http://www.uepcertified.com/media/pdf/UEP-Animal-Welfare-Guidlelines.pdf

Valenstein, E. S. (2005). *The War of the Soups and the Sparks: The Discovery of Neurotransmitters and the Dispute over How Nerves Communicate*. New York: Columbia University Press.

Vallortigara, G., A. Snyder, G. Kaplan, P. Bateson, N. S. Clayton, and L. J. Rogers (2008). Are animals autistic savants? *PLos Biology* 6(2): e42.

van der Staay, F. J. (2006). Animal models of behavioral dysfunctions: Basic concepts and classifications, and an evaluation strategy. *Brain Research Reviews* 52(1): 131–159.

van Gijn, I. (2001). Camillo Golgi (1843–1926). *Journal of Neurology* 248: 541–542.

Vance, R. P. (1992). An introduction to the philosophical presuppositions of the animal liberation/rights movement. *Journal of the American Medical Association* 268: 1715–1719.

VandeBerg, J. L., S. M. Zola, J. Fritz, R. Lee, T. J. Rowell, and W. C. Sutterfield (2005). A unique biomedical resource at risk. *Nature* 437 (September 1): 30–32.

Venant, E. and D. Treadwell (1990). Biting back: Animal researchers, industries go on the offensive against increasingly militant activists. *Los Angeles Times* April 12, 1990: E1, 12, 13.

Verhetsel, E. (1986). *They Threaten Your Health: A Critique of the Antivivisection/Animal Rights Movement*. Tucson: Nutrition Information Centre.

Vlasak, J. (2004). Dr. Jerry Vlasak replies to media libel. *SPEAK* July 24, 2004. Retrieved October 10, 2008, from http://www.indymedia.org.uk/en/2004/07/295293.html.

Webster, J. (1994) *Animal Welfare: A Cool Eye Towards Eden*. Oxford: Blackwell.

Wertenbaker, L. (1980). *To Mend the Heart*. New York: Viking Press.

White, R. J. (1995). Superman's plight and animal paladins. *Washington Times* August 6, 1995: B4.

Wickler, W. (1972). *The Biology of the Ten Commandments*. New York: McGraw-Hill.

Wiebers, D. O., H. P. Adams, and J. P. Whisnant (1990). Animal models of stroke: Are they relevant to human disease? *Stroke* 21: 1–3.

Williams, B. (2006). *Philosophy as a Humanistic Discipline*. Princeton, NJ: Princeton University Press.

Wolfle, T. and J. C. Liebeskind (1983). Stimulation-produced analgesia. In Kitchell, R. L., H. H. Erickson, E. Carstens, and L. E. Davis, eds. *Animal Pain: Perception and Alleviation*. Bethesda, MD: American Physiological Society, pp. 107–115.

Worden, A. (2007). Critics still take aim at PA pigeon shoots. *The Philadelphia Inquirer* December 5, 2007: A1, 18.

Wynne, C. D. L. (2004). *Do Animals Think?* Princeton, NJ: Princeton University Press.

Yerkes, R. and A. W. Yerkes (1929). *The Great Apes: A Study of Anthropoid Life*. New Haven: Yale University Press.

Young, W. (1996). Spinal cord regeneration. *Science* 273: 451.

Zawistowski, S. (2008). *Companion Animals in Society*. Clifton Park, NY: Thompson Delmar Learning.

Zoccola, P. M., S. S. Dickerson, and F. P. Zaldivar (2008). Rumination and cortisol responses to laboratory stressors. *Psychosomatic Medicine* 70: 661–667.

Index

STEFFI

PUBLIC POWER, PRIVATE PAIN

Steffi

Public Power, Private Pain

Sue Heady

First published in Great Britain in 1995 by
Virgin Books
an imprint of Virgin Publishing Ltd
332 Ladbroke Grove
London W10 5AH

ISBN 1 85227 516 2

Typeset by Phoenix Photosetting, Chatham, Kent
Printed and bound in Great Britain by
Mackays of Chatham PLC, Chatham, Kent

Hels Bels – this one's for you!

Contents

Illustrations

Acknowledgements

Lots of people patiently answered my questions while I was researching this book. Many of their names are contained in the text. Those that are not have been excluded according to their wishes. To each and every one of them, huge thanks. Several others helped me in other ways, and I am equally indebted to them. They are: Conny Konzak, Doris Henkel, April Todd, Stella Pearce, Victor Sebestyn, my parents Peter and Janet Heady, and Mal Peachey and Hannah MacDonald at Virgin Publishing.

I am also extremely grateful to all the newspapers and magazines that kindly gave me access to their libraries, in particular: *Serve & Volley*, *The Tennis Times*, *Tennis World*, *Tennis Week*, *Tennis Magazine* in the United States and *Tennis Magazine* in Germany.

1

PUBLIC POWER, PRIVATE PAIN

A S HER FOREHAND sailed several feet over the baseline Steffi Graf bowed her head in defeat. Her opponent Monica Seles, the fast-rising star of the world of women's tennis, raised her arms in celebration.

The year was 1990. The setting was the final of the German Open in Berlin in May. The sixteen-year-old Yugoslav was the proud winner of a title that had begun to look as if it belonged to the German by right, Steffi had won it with such ease in the preceding four years.

Seles's straightforward 6–4, 6–3 win was devastating for Steffi.

The German had failed to defend her title successfully – on home ground. The Yugoslav had ended a 66-match winning streak that had begun almost a year earlier after the final of the 1989 French Open, when Steffi had lost to the Spaniard Arantxa Sanchez-Vicario. Seles had inflicted her first defeat on the German, proving that she was the player most likely to become her principal rival on the women's professional Tour and to launch an assault on Steffi's position at the top of the world rankings. It was the end of an era, and for Steffi, there was a strange sense of déjà-vu. It had been in the final of the German Open four years earlier that Steffi had scored her first victory over the then No.1, the Czech-born American Martina Navratilova. That win had marked the beginning of Steffi's own inexorable rise to the top of women's tennis.

Steffi's ascent had been rapid, but long-lasting. Not for her a short run at the top followed by a speedy fall into 'burn-out' like a couple of other tennis prodigies of the 1980s. Steffi had been primed for the top from an early age. Winning seemed to come

naturally, and after a hugely successful junior career she had turned professional at the tender age of thirteen. A couple of years playing satellite events followed, and from 1984 she had made her mark at the top levels of women's professional tennis.

All this Steffi had achieved essentially with the help of one person – her father. Peter 'Papa' Graf, a part-time tennis teacher, had introduced his daughter to the game at the age of three. It was he who ensured, once he had taught her all he knew, that she received the best training. He had nurtured her career, encouraged her, made enormous sacrifices for her. And when Steffi turned professional he was her coach, her manager, her adviser, her friend.

Without him Steffi would never have reached the No.1 spot in women's tennis, never have achieved an historic Golden Grand Slam in 1988, never have remained in the No.1 spot longer than any other man or woman. And yet the man who had created Steffi now seemed on the point of destroying everything he had worked so hard to attain.

Steffi's loss to Seles capped a terrible week, for far more devastating to the German than her defeat at the hands of the young Yugoslav were the allegations being published in the tabloid press. Steffi's world had been blown apart by revelations that implicated her father in a tangled web of blackmail, extortion, adultery and patrimony.

Although Steffi would deny in the mandatory post-match press conference that off-court events had had any effect on her game, her lacklustre performance on court had indicated otherwise. There had been rumours since the Australian Open in January 1990 that something was amiss in the Graf camp, for Steffi's performances had been less than the perfection that had come to be expected of her.

After Berlin, there were to be more losses on court and many tears off court, and yet Steffi would eventually come through with dignity and grace. The furore caused by the papers strengthened her, her family and her resolve, and she would rise again. But Steffi's relationship with her father, the key to her climb to stardom, had been irrevocably changed by the off-court trauma.

2
A STAR IS BORN

N 1984, GERMAN TELEVISION provided thirteen hours of tennis coverage. In 1993, it provided 2,673 hours. Why the huge increase? Boris Becker and Steffi Graf. Yet their international success was not an overnight phenomenon, and they were by no means the first German tennis champions. Tennis has been an organised sport in Germany since 1902 when the sport's governing body, the Deutscher TennisBund (DTB), was founded.

Cilly Aussem won the ladies' singles at Wimbledon in 1931, defeating her compatriot Hilde Krahwinkel who later – as Mrs Hilde Sperling – walked off with the women's singles at the French Open three years in a row (1935–7). Baron Gottfried von Cramm won the French Open men's title in 1934, was runner-up in the gentlemen's singles at Wimbledon for three consecutive years in the mid-1930s and runner-up at both the French and the US Opens in 1937.

World War II interrupted the flow of tennis champions coming out of Germany. It was not until the late 1960s that the German Tennis Teachers Federation (GTTF) started to develop scientific techniques for tennis training and coaching. These techniques were systematically applied throughout the country, in conjunction with the regional training programmes organised by the DTB. These efforts stimulated interest in the game once more. So did the establishment of a national tennis league, the Bundesliga, in which professionals such as the Romanian characters Ilie Nastase and Ion Tiriac and the Dutchman Tom Okker were to play.

Initially, however, the efforts of the GTTF and of the DTB were relatively small-scale and did not produce a large crop of talented players. But as their activities grew, tennis became less the

exclusive domain of the rich – as it had been worldwide. The reason was that a greater percentage of the population of the then West Germany came to enjoy the fruits of an ever-burgeoning economy – parents had the money to spend on better equipment, club and coaching fees. Youngsters became involved in larger numbers, through an ever increasing spread of clubs, many of which were established at the initiative of the DTB. Every member of a German tennis club automatically became a member of the DTB and the growth in the DTB's membership gives an indication of how quickly the German people were taking up tennis. In 1950, the DTB had 51,000 members. By 1985, it had 1,200,000.

The DTB was well prepared to meet this mushrooming interest in tennis. As with other sports in Germany, its tennis programme was organised into various Bundeslander, each effectively an autonomous region. The regions all held their own tournaments and the youngsters who performed well at these events were selected for special training at the regional tennis centre, under the auspices of the Verbandertrainer, the regional tennis coach. In turn, the Verbandertrainer passed on the names of his best players to the Bundestrainer (national coach) and the really promising youngsters were sponsored by the DTB.

The DTB's well-devised tennis programme and the increasing interest in tennis inevitably led to rising standards of play, and more German players began to emerge on to the international tennis stage. On the men's side, in the late 1970s Rolf Gehring and Uli Pinner were both in the top 25 players. On the women's side, in the 1970s Helga Masthoff was ranked as high as No.3 in the world, and Katia Ebbinghaus was a top-twenty player, while in the early 1980s Sylvia Hanika achieved a top-ten ranking. At Wimbledon 1983 – a year in which Steffi tried and failed to qualify for the event – there were three seeded German players in the ladies' singles event.

It was, however, Boris Becker who would turn the spotlight very firmly on German tennis. In 1985, he achieved worldwide fame when at the age of just seventeen he became the youngest ever – and unseeded – winner of the gentlemen's singles at Wimbledon. The tabloid press named him 'Boom Boom' Becker because of his rocket serve, but this sobriquet could equally have

applied to the impact that his success was to have on the German tennis scene.

Two years later Steffi recorded her first Grand Slam title at the French Open, and in 1988 achieved what no other man or woman has ever accomplished – a Golden Grand Slam (all four Grand Slam titles, plus an Olympic gold medal, in a calendar year). The rise of German tennis was complete. The result, in addition to the huge increase in the number of hours of tennis broadcast on German television, was a substantial rise in the number of tennis courts and a vastly expanded DTB membership which almost doubled from 1.2 million in 1985 to 2.2 million in 1993.

This, then, is the background to the story of Steffi.

Stefanie Maria Graf, now known to millions worldwide simply as Steffi, was born on 14 June 1969 in Neckarau, one of the poorer districts of Mannheim, a grey, bleak city about 75 kilometres south of Frankfurt. Mannheim, the second largest city in the German region of Baden-Wurttemberg, with its grid street system, lacks any great sense of character or historical buildings. It is fairly wealthy, however, thanks to the dominance of heavy industry which includes electrical engineering, car, medical equipment, petrochemicals, paper and glass factories. It was also, incidentally, the birth place some two hundred years earlier of the modern symphony orchestra.

It was here that Steffi's parents Peter and Heidi had lived for many years, and where her father made a living by selling second-hand cars and insurance. In the years prior to the birth of Steffi (the Grafs' first child) Peter had become interested in tennis. He had always been a keen sportsman and had tried to follow in his father's footsteps. Alfons, Peter's father, had played for Friedrichsseld, one of the local football teams in Mannheim that was highly regarded at that time, while following a career in the local sports council.

Peter had been a promising footballer at a young age, but a series of leg injuries forced him to find another sport to play during his free time. As tennis was fast growing in popularity in Germany then, Peter decided that he would give it a go. He might already have been 27 when he took up the game, but being athletic

he took to it easily; within a couple of years he had perfected his baseline game well enough to compete in the upper levels of club tennis. In fact, Peter enjoyed his tennis so much that he decided to train for a tennis teaching certificate, which he secured through the GTTF. It also provided another sideline by which he could earn some extra cash.

Two years after the arrival of Steffi, Heidi gave birth to another child on 4 September 1971, a brother for Steffi, named Michael. A year later, Steffi – still only three years old – started to pester her father. Every time he got home from a hard match he would drop his sports bag on the floor and sit down to enjoy a well-deserved rest. Steffi, however, had other ideas and would toddle over, drag a racket out of his bag and beg him to play with her. Peter found his daughter's habit rather irritating. By the end of the day he was tired, and as he had reached quite a high standard of play by that time he did not think that he would get any satisfaction from teaching a tiny girl.

Steffi persisted. Eventually, Peter took a saw to one of his old, full-size rackets and started to teach his daughter the basics of tennis in the living room of the family home. At first Steffi played for only five or ten minutes at a time, but soon the sessions lengthened. Peter and his young daughter would hit balls to each other over the 'net', a piece of string tied between two chairs. By the time Steffi had broken every light in the chandelier, Peter decided to move the lessons into the basement games room, selling his billiard table so that they would have room to practise. Steffi's enthusiasm never dimmed, and in place of a net Peter stacked some boxes up to the same height as a net on a full-size tennis court, so that practice could begin in earnest.

To encourage Steffi, Peter offered her sweets or a *Salzstange* (a salty stick that Germans eat instead of crisps) every time she hit the ball 25 times in a row. Eventually the stakes went higher. Peter Graf promised that when she was older and better and could hit 50 consecutive balls, Steffi would be given a *Flambage*, a famous German dessert (a combination of vanilla ice-cream, warm raspberries and cream). The very next day on his return from work Steffi was waiting for him. 'Today, I will do it,' she said. And she did.

Steffi, having a sweet tooth, was very keen to get those *Flam-bagen*, and Peter had to start playing impossible shots so that his daughter would not become bloated with ice-cream. The very same eagerness that Steffi showed at an early age is still reflected in the zest she displays for tennis. Steffi was so tennis crazy even aged four that her mother is on record as saying, 'Sometimes I had to force her to do things which other girls of her age usually do, like play with dolls and go to friends' birthday parties.'

It was the strength that Steffi possessed in her right arm – greater than that of a six- or seven-year-old so her father believed – that had convinced Peter it was not too early to start teaching her tennis. Not only that, instinctively Steffi seemed to know how to hold a tennis racket properly, and her concentration was outstanding. The young girl was never distracted, and didn't take her eye off the ball once a rally was in play, even ignoring the ringing telephone or the sound of the door-bell.

At the age of five, Steffi progressed on to a full-size court and soon entered her first competition, although only with the special permission of the tournament organisers. Conny Konzak, the present sports editor of *Bunte* magazine, has known Steffi ever since he helped organise the Sport Scheck Jugend Turnier (Sport Scheck Junior Tournament) in Munich in 1974. He vividly remembers the young Steffi's participation, although it was the car that she arrived in rather than her tennis that immediately grabbed his attention.

Heidi and Steffi Graf swept up to the tournament site in a sparkling version of the latest Porsche 924. 'In those days,' recalls Conny, 'it was one of the very fast sports cars and brand new, and I can still remember Steffi, so very proud to be sitting in the co-driver's seat.' The Graf family might not have had very much money at that time, but due to Peter's fascination with high performance cars and thanks to his connections in the Mannheim motor trade they were able to run some smart cars – usually a Mercedes for Peter and a Porsche for Heidi.

The Sport Scheck Jugend Turnier had over 500 entrants. It was and still is Europe's largest children's tennis tournament. However, children under the age of six were not allowed to compete, so Steffi was too young to play. Ludwig Leuthner, the

tournament director, took pity on the young enthusiastic Steffi because she and her mother had spent three hours travelling from their home to the tournament. Steffi was therefore given special dispensation to play. She lost in the first round and left the court in tears. According to Conny, 'She was so small she could hardly see over the net or hold the racquet, but she wanted to win and that's exactly what she did in the contest the following four years.'

Peter decided that Steffi needed some more coaching and he searched long and hard for the right person to teach her. Eventually he decided to approach the Bundes (Badischen) Leistungszentrum, the DTB's regional tennis centre for Baden-Wurttemberg, which had been established in 1964 in Leimen, some 25 kilometres from Mannheim.

In 1975, Boris Breskvar, an ex-Yugoslav Davis Cup team member and the Verbandertrainer working for the DTB in Leimen at that time, received a phone call from Peter. 'Herr Breskvar,' he said, 'I have a very gifted young daughter. Would you take a look at her, please?' Looking back twenty years later, Breskvar recalls, 'I thought he was mad to think I would play with a six-year-old, but I played with her for twenty minutes and realised she had a lot of talent. She really was special. I had never seen anyone like her before.' As soon as Breskvar stopped playing with her, Steffi burst into floods of tears. 'What's the matter?' asked the coach kindly. Steffi refused to answer, but her father explained that his daughter was upset that Breskvar only wanted to play with her for twenty minutes.

Breskvar was not used to coaching children as young as Steffi, but realising her talent he decided to make an exception. From then on Steffi trained with Breskvar at Leimen. At first, as she was still so young she only attended coaching sessions with the Yugoslav once or twice a week, but she was allowed to use the centre's facilities every day with her father. Says Peter Graf, 'We used to go to the centre, a twenty-five kilometre drive from Mannheim, in the mornings, from seven until eight. Another father probably wouldn't have done that, but I enjoyed motivating this young child.'

At the age of six and now eligible to compete, Steffi returned to Munich's Sport Scheck Jugend Turnier and won the event in her

age group. Two years later, Steffi won the event one age group above her own. By the age of nine, she had won the event four years in a row.

It was a chance meeting in 1977 that led to Steffi receiving her first tennis sponsorship deal. Detlef Grosse was on holiday in Majorca when he met the Graf family. Grosse's son Oliver, a year older than Steffi, was looking for someone with whom to hit and spotted Steffi out on the courts playing some excellent tennis. Grosse approached Peter and asked if the two children could play together. Peter agreed and the youngsters were soon out on the court hitting. Bored of trading strokes, Steffi and Oliver decided to play a game. Oliver won the first game; Steffi took the next twelve to win 6–1, 6–0. Grosse was impressed not only by Steffi's 'extraordinary talent', but also by Peter's determination to ensure that she would be a top tennis player. He was also impressed by the professional methods by which Steffi was then being trained, which were not common in those days, especially at so early an age.

Grosse, who worked for Dunlop-Slazenger in Germany, invited the Grafs to visit him in his office on their return home. Dunlop-Slazenger was very keen at the time to sponsor youngsters, and from 1977 Steffi received all the rackets, tennis balls, clothing and shoes that she needed from the company.

Steffi may have been receiving her equipment free from Dunlop-Slazenger, but she ensured that it was well looked-after. On every white Dunlop Court ball that she received, she proudly inscribed a black 'S', so that just in case the odd ball went flying out of her back garden everyone would know it belonged to her.

In 1978, the Graf family moved from the congested city of Mannheim to the relative peace and quiet of Bruehl, a sleepy dormitory town of about 14,000 inhabitants just ten kilometres or so from Mannheim. To bring in more money on top of what he was still earning from selling cars and insurance, Peter hired three outdoor clay courts just a few hundred metres from the family's new home, where he gave lessons. The courts also provided a perfect place for his daughter to practise. Later, just next to the clay courts, a small indoor facility – the Sportcenter Fuerftenberg Pilsener – housing three tennis courts would be built.

Steffi continued to train at the centre in Leimen, and as she grew older and stronger she started to travel there more often to work with Breskvar. Consequently her progress on the tennis court advanced in leaps and bounds, and by the age of ten Steffi was training with Breskvar every day.

She may have been just one of about twenty children being trained at the centre, but Steffi was always the one that stuck out from the crowd. Wolf-Dieter Spath, then a sports officer and now the President of the Baden Tennis Association, remembers Steffi's professional approach, even at a young age,

> She was very serious, very self-confident and never needed to be forced to play. If she was told to do half-an-hour more of forehands and half-an-hour more of backhands she would do it willingly, and would only cry if she had to finish early.

Breskvar remembers her concentration. 'When she got to the tennis centre, all she thought about was tennis, that was it, just like today, and she enjoyed the hard work.' Even at the tender age of ten, it seems, Steffi knew what she wanted from life. In answer to Spath's question, 'What do you want to be when you grow up?' she replied, 'No.1.' To achieve that aim she worked extremely hard.

Not all the young players visited the centre as frequently as Steffi; it depended how far they lived from Leimen and also on how good they were. 'The best,' relates Breskvar, 'came every day, while we had some students that came only once or twice a week.' Most of them were pretty good.

Leimen in the 1970s and 1980s was a breeding ground for some of the best tennis players to come out of Germany during that period. It was Breskvar who first recognised and harnessed the natural talent of Boris Becker, as well as a host of others including Udo Riglewski, Patrick Baur and Rudiger Haas, all of whom have played on the men's Association of Tennis Professionals (ATP) Tour. Andrea Betsner and Anke Huber, the latter sometimes ranked among the top ten, trained in Leimen and have both played on the Women's Tennis Association (WTA) Tour.

Steffi trained with many of them, even though some were several

years older than her and reluctant to play with the young kid with the huge forehand. Recalls Breskvar,

> It was a difficult time: she was so young and that generation – Becker, Riglewski and Baur – was very strong, and yet nobody wanted to play with Steffi because she was very small and very, very good and she could beat these guys. I remember she and Rudiger Haas won the European Championships under twelves in 1981 and she was better than him that year, she could beat him. It wasn't normal and the guy was crying. After that, I had a lot of trouble trying to find someone to play with Steffi because nobody wanted to play with her. In the end, I had to change them around every thirty minutes. To add to my problems, all the parents wanted their children to play with Steffi all the time because she was the best. It was unbelievable.

Perhaps it was not quite as unbelievable as the fact that two great tennis stars plus a strong supporting cast emerged from a very small area of Germany at the same time. First and foremost, Breskvar says, Steffi and Becker were talented, but then points out that, 'You could be a great skiing talent, but it will not help if you are born in the Sahara.' A case of being in the right place at the right time.

Steffi and Becker were lucky that there was a tennis centre in Leimen. At that time there were not that many tennis facilities in Germany. In addition both lived close by, so they could practise every day. Breskvar also believes it was important that the two did not change coaches while young and so were never confused by the different philosophies, techniques and practice methods of a number of coaches. Breskvar trained Steffi until she was thirteen, and Becker from the ages of six to fifteen.

Andrea Betsner believes Breskvar himself is the reason:

> Breskvar, I think, is the best coach in Germany – and I've practised with a lot of coaches! If he sees someone play at the age of eight, he can tell whether he or she has the talent or not. I do not know how he does it, but he is always right. He has a new player

now, an East German called Jana Kanda. He reckons she is going to be in the top twenty in the next two or three years, we will see if he is right …

Breskvar was certainly right about Steffi. It was as a ten-year-old that Steffi started training with the German national squad. Two years earlier, when the Bundestrainer Richard Schonborn had travelled from his home in Hanover to southern Germany on a talent search, Breskvar had pointed out the eight-year-old Steffi as having potential. Here again, suggests Schonborn, is a reason why Leimen has been successful in producing two great champions. 'Breskvar was a very good friend of mine, and also because it was one of the first regional centres I was very often there, so we developed a very good cooperation between the centre in Baden and the national centre in Hanover.'

Schonborn took note of Breskvar's advice and the following year returned to check on Steffi's progress. It was not until 1979, however, at the age of ten when most children joined the DTB programme, that Steffi started systematic training at the regional and national centres. Up to five times during the winter for a week at a time Steffi, along with all the other outstanding juniors who had been selected, would travel to the national training centre in Hanover.

Steffi's daily training was not restricted to the Leimen centre. It started early in the morning before she went to school, when she would practise for about 45 minutes with her father. Then in the afternoons she would spend a couple of hours or so training with Breskvar at Leimen, and after that she would return home to Bruehl to play an hour or two more with Peter. And just to make sure that he was keeping abreast of her training – and also because he did not have the international experience of Breskvar – Peter would attend her sessions at Leimen and take notes. When that was not possible he would ring the Yugoslav coach to ask what he should be teaching Steffi in the extra hours that he played with her. At weekends, when Steffi was not competing, the two would attend league matches so that they could analyse the strengths and weaknesses of the players that they watched and assess their tactics.

While critics have accused Peter of forcing his daughter out on

to the tennis court from the day she was born, Steffi has frequently denied the notion that she was pushed – at least against her will. This is a claim that friends and journalists who have known Steffi since she was a young girl support.

Estate agent Doris Kollmeier, who was coached by Peter at the courts in Bruehl, clearly remembers Steffi's early tennis career:

> Peter put pressure on Steffi by telling her that she should not lose a single game, she should always win 6–0, 6–0 and if she lost a game he would tell her off, but this worked to Steffi's advantage, because it made her train harder and improved her game.

So did she feel that Peter had ever pushed his daughter? 'Oh no. You can only tell, and demand, so much of children and after that it is up to them whether they respond or not. Steffi did. She wanted to succeed.' This was very unlike the reaction of Doris's sons who also trained with Peter, but who after a year refused to go to lessons, so fed up were they with their coach's demands.

Of course it all depends on one's definition of 'push', but it seems highly unlikely that Steffi was being made to do something that she did not want to do. For sure Peter encouraged and nurtured her talent, dedicating many an hour to the improvement of her game – but it was what Steffi wanted. A major British study into the training of young athletes supports this fact, for it discovered that while a child's initial interest in a particular sport is likely to be fuelled by parents, it is the child who pushes for more training.

The consequences of a father forcing his daughter to play tennis against her will can be extreme. In 1989, German papers reported the story of Klaus Lulling from Dusseldorf, who gave up his job to train his daughter Gabi to become the next Steffi Graf. His training programme included beatings when his daughter played badly. Eventually his wife Ruth, unable to watch her daughter being subjected to a living hell, put six bullets through the body of her husband.

Peter has often wrongly been portrayed as a whip-wielding slave driver. Yet in the early 1970s when he started teaching Steffi the basics of tennis, the women's professional game was very much in

its infancy and was certainly not the huge, money-spinning business that it is today. In 1970, the first year of women's professional tournaments, there was a total of only US$30,000 prize money to be won. In those days, professional tennis players were more likely to make a living than a fortune. Could Peter have foreseen while Steffi was only a few years old that it was worth pushing her because she could one day make a fortune from the game? Those who knew him twenty years ago say quite frankly that he was not smart enough to have thought that way. Perhaps later, however, when it became more obvious just how good Steffi could be, his reasons for encouraging her changed.

During the late 1970s/early 1980s, Steffi was training daily Monday to Friday at Leimen and at home in Bruehl, and occasionally would travel to Hanover for week-long sessions. At weekends, she was playing tournaments. At one of these she reached the final, where she was up against Andrea Betsner. Her opponent remembers,

> I was fourteen and Steffi was eleven when we first played a match. It was the final of the Badischen Tennismeisterschaften, a DTB regional event held in Leimen. I won – I think the score was 6–3, 6–1. Steffi was very upset that she had lost against me and her father turned to my mother, as they stood by the side of the court, and said, 'Next time, Steffi will win' and he was right, she did, not just the next time, but on each of the seven occasions we met after that.

Steffi was not only playing tournaments for herself, she was also playing for the Heidelberg Tennis Club, one of the oldest tennis clubs in Germany. She was recommended to the Club by Breskvar when she was just twelve, and soon started representing the Club in league matches. With Steffi, who was the youngest member of the team playing for them, the women's side registered a series of wins and ended the 1982 season in second position. The following year and for two years after that the Heidelberg Tennis Club's women's team won the national league, mostly on Steffi's strength.

Steffi's progress on the tennis court was phenomenal, and it

persuaded Peter to stop selling second-hand cars and insurance to teach tennis full-time. This meant that he would always be at his courts and could make himself available to train with Steffi for two or three hours a day, or as and when she was free from her other commitments such as school and official DTB training. His decision was vindicated in 1981, when Steffi won the Orange Bowl in Florida, the unofficial world championships for children, and again the following year when Steffi won both the European Championships under twelves and the European Championships under eighteens.

Richard Schonborn was with Steffi when she won the European Championships as a twelve-year-old. He remembers training with her early in the morning before one of her matches:

> She was unhappy because she was hitting balls in the net and out, so I said, 'Come on Steffi, take it easy, we're just warming up, you are good, come on smile, relax, your match is not until the afternoon.' And she came up to me at the net and said, 'What am I to do – smile or play tennis?' It was a typical answer for her. She was so serious, so concentrated, so one hundred per cent focused on tennis.

It was her mental power according to Schonborn, along with her unbelievable footwork, which gave the impression that she was flying rather than running across the court, and her huge forehand, that won matches for Steffi. 'At the age of ten, eleven, twelve, she won all her matches, all her championships, just with her forehand,' he recalls.

While Steffi had been progressing by leaps and bounds on the tennis court, her off-court activities were to suffer somewhat. When the Graf family had left Mannheim for Bruehl in late 1978, they moved to a newly built private estate, and into a nondescript two-up, two-down end-of-terrace house, No.14 Normannenstrasse.

The Grafs' next door neighbours remember her as just another kid, albeit a fairly shy one. 'Steffi would play on the square, as did all the other kids from the neighbourhood. With them, she just played the usual kids games, no tennis.' Probably the only thing

that set Steffi apart were the hard calluses which had already formed on her right, tennis-playing hand.

Having spent two years at school in Vogelstang in Mannheim, Steffi joined seventeen other youngsters in the fourth class of the grundschule, or primary school, in Bruehl where her teacher Gabrielle Geppert remembers Steffi as 'a quiet, friendly girl, who was not arrogant and certainly did not try to grab the centre of attention. She was very disciplined, sensible and rather more mature than the others in her class.'

When she entered the school, Peter had informed Mrs Geppert that Steffi was a very successful tennis player and would have to spend quite a lot of time away from school so that she could compete in junior tournaments. Despite this, Steffi never neglected her school work. 'Steffi was a very good pupil,' stresses Mrs Geppert, 'but she did not have many friends because she had to spend so much time training – she would go straight from school to training.'

Steffi was at the primary school for less than a year and then progressed to the Bruehl-Ketsch Realschule. In Germany, after primary school the children are divided. The more academically gifted children go to the Gymnasium where students take the Abitur, which gives them the constitutional right to go on to university, from where they are expected to take up top positions in the private and public sectors; the not so intelligent go to the Realschule, an intermediate school where children take the Mittlere Reife, which prepares pupils for jobs such as bank clerks and junior executive positions.

There is no doubt that Steffi was an above average Realschule student. Her brother Michael later went to the Gymnasium, and she could have gone there too, but chose instead to go to the Realschule. Explained Mrs Geppert,

Steffi opted for the Realschule so that she could lead the life of a tennis player and would not be burdened with the heavier and more demanding work loads that she would have had if she had taken up a place at the Gymnasium.

At the Realschule Steffi was known – on the days when she did

attend – to fall asleep during classes, exhausted from her exertions on the tennis court. All Fritz Seidel, one of the teachers while Steffi was enrolled there as a student, could remember about the young girl was that, 'While I was at school, Steffi was not at school. She was all over the world playing tennis, but she was not very often at school.'

Steffi's favourite subjects were geography, history and in particular biology, as she was always fascinated by the animal world and plant life. But it was tennis that was her one great love and her schooling certainly suffered. Quite recently Steffi has admitted that when she retires she may go back and study because 'it's something that I have really missed.'

Steffi was never the average student. She would refuse to go to her classmates' birthday parties because they were always in the afternoon, at the very time that she was usually on court practising; it was only when her parents forced her that she attended. Not for Steffi either the usual school-girl crushes and posters of adored pop stars and actors on her bedroom walls. Instead, she had a growing collection of trophies and certificates.

Finally, while still only an eighth-grader, Steffi left the Bruehl-Ketsch Realschule in October 1982. She also left the training centre at Leimen, to turn professional. It may have been the end of her childhood, but Steffi gets angry when people say that she lost her youth. It is, she has declared, what she wanted. She decided she wanted to be No.1 and she did what she had to to achieve that aim.

3
RISING UP

O N 18 OCTOBER 1982, Steffi became the youngest tennis player ever to turn professional. She was just thirteen years and four months old.

It was young, many have said too young, but like numerous players who have turned professional in their teens, Steffi – and her father Peter – felt there was really no other option if she wanted to progress and to carry on playing competitively. Steffi was already winning events in which players up to the age of eighteen were competing. In theory Steffi could have kept on playing these junior events until she was no longer eligible, but in practice that was likely to have resulted in stagnation and possibly loss of confidence. There was always the chance that someone younger and better might come up behind her and start beating her, leaving her a has-been before she had even turned professional.

There was another reason Steffi turned professional. From her point of view as a child, the idea of playing tennis all day was far more appealing than trudging off to school like everybody else of her age. Her parents felt that if Steffi wanted to play tennis then they would back her all the way. After all, why should their young daughter not be given the chance to experience fame and fortune, which would provide her with opportunities that they had not had, coming as they did from a relatively poor background?

So Steffi turned professional, and the very next day on 19 October, she played in her first major match, an indoor event held in Filderstadt, in Germany. Steffi Graf's name was already famous on the German tennis scene, but was little known internationally. Angela Gebhardt, a German journalist who was in Filderstadt for the match, recalls,

For Germany, it was a big event, and the German journalists produced a lot of stories, but there is no way that you can compare it with Jennifer Capriati's premiers or that of Martina Hingis, whom they had been talking about since she was nine years old ... it was nothing, it was quite normal.

There was certainly no sign of the million-dollar contracts associated with Capriati before she turned professional, or the 200 or so representatives of the media from various parts of the globe who gathered to see Hingis's debut in Zurich in October 1994.

A press conference was held before the match, at which Peter expressed pessimism about the outcome. Perhaps it was the start of a superstitious habit – he has frequently had friendly bets against his daughter winning matches – or perhaps he was being realistic. In this her first professional match, Steffi was to play the American teenage sensation Tracy Austin, then ranked among the top five women's players in the world.

Steffi, with her shoulder-length, mousey-blonde hair, braces on her teeth and long gangly legs looked the typical teenager. Tracy, walking out on to the court with her handbag was, at the age of just nineteen, the grown-up, seasoned professional.

Steffi played well, but not well enough, and Tracy won in straight sets 6–4, 6–0. After the match, the German media was anxious to hear what the American thought about their new star. In reply to their questions, Tracy simply said, 'There are hundreds like her back home in the States.'

That was all the incentive Steffi needed to prove otherwise. Playing Futures events, the lower rung of the WTA Tour, Steffi achieved a ranking of 214 by the end of 1982. The following year, she played two events in April and lost in the first round of both. In May, however, she went to play a tournament in Warwickshire in the heart of England and reached the third round. At courtside during that event was a French Open champion, Britain's Shirley Brasher (née Bloomer) and a French Open finalist, Florenta Mihai of Romania, both of whom realised that the 'little kid' from Bruehl had what it took to be a champion. More than anything else, it was her footwork that amazed them – Steffi was so rarely out of position.

From the depths of the English countryside, Steffi travelled to the French Open in Paris. Her ranking was not good enough to allow her direct entry in to the main draw, so she had to go through the qualifying rounds. Steffi battled her way triumphantly past three opponents to qualify. She was into her first Grand Slam event. The youngest player in the tournament, Steffi was still so small that she was mistaken for a ball girl and as she walked on to the court for her first round match, an official gently reminded her that she must stand perfectly still while the players were in action.

Soon news reached the press centre that a ball girl was hitting rather well on one of the outside courts and was definitely worth watching. Always interested in an off-beat story, several journalists made their way to the court and were hugely impressed by the maturity of the young Steffi and the spectacular tennis she was producing.

Steffi caused a stir that day by beating the Scandinavian Carina Karlsson, six years her senior, in straight sets 6–2, 6–1. Grilled by the press after the match, when asked what she had achieved so far Steffi mumbled modestly, 'Nothing yet'. It was left to a German journalist to inform the rest of the world's media that Steffi had, at the age of twelve, won the German and European under-eighteen championships. Steffi was knocked out of the Open in the second round, but the assembled media knew that Steffi Graf was a name to look out for in the future.

Next the young German returned to England to play the qualifying event for Wimbledon, but she was beaten, by the unfamiliar bounce of the ball on grass rather than by a superior opponent. It was her fourteenth birthday, but Steffi was in no mood to celebrate. In frustration she turned to her father at the end of the match and said, 'I don't want to play on grass ever again.'

Steffi played two more Futures tournaments in July and in the second, held in Freiburg, she reached the semi-finals where she was beaten by Catherine Tanvier of France.

In September, at the beginning of the new school year, Steffi gained special permission from the Baden Ministry of Culture to miss school so that she could continue to play on the women's Tour. By the end of the year she had played in another five events, and failed to get past the second round in any of them.

In November, Steffi went to Australia with her mother to play two warm-up events followed by the Australian Open. Unfortunately, the trip ended in tears when Steffi withdrew from her first-round match of the Open when she fell and tore the tendons in her thumb. There would be no trophies for Steffi in 1983, but there was a note of sympathy and encouragement from Martina Navratilova, then the No. 1 player in the world. She wrote:

> Hi Steffi, I heard on TV that your thumb is broken. I hope it doesn't hurt too much. Don't worry, I'm sure you'll be OK soon, your thumb as good as new. At least you will have a chance to catch up at school. All the best, Martina (Navratilova).

It appeared that everyone in the world of tennis, not just the journalists, was keeping an eye on the new kid on the block.

Steffi had not enjoyed great success in 1983, but ten years on when asked about her early days on the Tour she remembered them with affection. Playing satellites and working her way through qualifying tournaments enabled Steffi to see a different side to the Tour that she was soon to leave behind. In stark contrast to the way she now leads her life at the top, Steffi recalled, 'People were not as serious as they are now. It was much more relaxed then, I had more friends and we all used to go out together.' A fact to which Andrea Betsner, who travelled on the Tour with Steffi, will attest. Betsner explained:

> In those days, Steffi travelled with her mother and she was always friendly, playing backgammon, cards, everything, and we had a lot of fun together. It was when her father appeared on the Tour that she was reserved. Her father always said come to the hotel. He never wanted her to have any contact with the other players.

All too quickly, however, 1983 was over and Steffi had a decision to make. When she had turned professional in October 1982, she had come to an agreement with her father that initially she would

only play on the Tour for a year. Once that year was up, they would consider further plans for her future. In December 1983 Steffi was undecided, but it was not altogether surprising that she was leaning towards giving it all up and going back to school.

Having won virtually every tournament she had entered as a junior, Steffi was not used to being beaten. Moreover, tennis was no longer the game it had been. As a junior and amateur, Steffi had in all senses of the word been playing for fun. As a professional, she was playing in a cut-throat world full of pressure, where she was playing for money. In addition, Steffi found playing the WTA Tour a little lonely. She spent more time away from home than she wanted to and she no longer had the tennis friends that she had made during her junior years. While she was leap-frogging ahead into the professional world, they were still progressing slowly but surely in the juniors.

In the end, Steffi – persuaded by her father – decided that she would try the Tour for one more year. Up until this time Peter Graf had not been seen to push Steffi. However, by the early 1980s women's professional tennis had already seen phenomenal change. There was a lot more money in the business and a dozen women had already passed the US$1 million mark in career earnings. Could this have been a reason why Peter was so keen for his daughter to continue?

Peter had to have faith in his daughter's abilities though, for sending Steffi on the Tour was certainly not cheap and the family did not have a lot of cash to spare. In the early 1980s it was estimated that it cost roughly US$25,000 – for air tickets, accommodation, food, coaching fees – to keep a girl on the Tour. The Grafs were lucky in that Peter could act as both Steffi's chaperone and her coach. Even Heidi was a good enough player to provide Steffi with warm-up practice prior to matches, if necessary.

Once Steffi had decided to continue on the Tour, she made good use of the four-month lay-off enforced by her torn tendons and used the time to re-shape her body: 'Steffi's breasts were too large for playing tennis,' her father explained. 'During the break, she took special exercises with weights to reduce the fat from her breasts.'

Once back on court, it looked initially as though father and

daughter had made a mistake. Steffi played three events in April 1984 and lost in the first round of all of them. May proved to be a turning point. At the German Open in Berlin Steffi reached the semi-finals, where she was beaten by her compatriot Claudia Kohde-Kilsch in straight sets. At the French Open later the same month Steffi would lose in the third round, again to Kohde-Kilsch, but this time the match went to three sets. Steffi was closing in.

Steffi returned to Wimbledon the following month, despite the resolution she had made the previous year that she would never play on grass again. After three tough main-draw matches in which she beat American Susan Mascarin, Britain's Sue Barker and Bettina Bunge of Germany, Steffi found herself stepping out on to the hallowed Centre Court opposite the British Jo Durie. Steffi, seemingly unflustered by the fact that she was playing Britain's top-ranked women's player on home ground, put up a terrific fight in what turned out to be a sensational match.

John Barrett, the British BBC commentator and tennis journalist, was watching.

> I think we were all hugely impressed with Steffi's great athletic ability. She looked, as so many teenagers do, like a young colt with long legs and a body not big enough. She had this terrifically aggressive attitude and a huge forehand, which it's true was a little wild at times, but my goodness, she hit some extraordinary winners, and she was obviously very determined – that was the thing that came across.

Having split sets 6–3, 3–6, Steffi eventually lost the match 7–9 in the third. However, rather than the loss, the memory that is far stronger for Steffi today is that once all the tennis was over she forgot to curtsey in the direction of the Royal Box, and had to be pulled back by Durie before she hurriedly left the court with tears of frustration running down her face.

After Wimbledon, Steffi went to the United States to compete in the Los Angeles Olympics, where tennis was to be a demonstration event. As it was an unofficial event, the tennis players were not allowed to march in the opening parade or wear team uniforms.

The competition was only open to those under the age of 21, and only singles – no doubles – were played.

It was not the first time that tennis had been a part of the Olympic Games, but it *was* the first time in 60 years. It had been an event in the 1924 Olympic Games held in Paris, but the tennis had been so badly organised – with unplayable courts, less than basic changing rooms and sub-standard officiating – that the experience had not been repeated, until now.

Played at the Tennis Center of the University of California, Los Angeles, the draw was limited to 32 competitors. Although not a major event, for the two players that came through to win their respective competitions it marked a significant breakthrough. Steffi – once again the youngest competitor – beat Sabrina Goles of Yugoslavia 1–6, 6–3, 6–4 in her final, while the Swede Stefan Edberg – still to make his assault on the top of the men's rankings – took his title with a 6–1, 7–6 win over Francisco Maciel of Mexico.

Steffi played another seven tournaments in 1984, including Filderstadt where she beat well-known names – the Hungarian Andrea Temesvari, Iva Budarova from Czechoslovakia, compatriot Kohde-Kilsch and American Andrea Leand – to reach the final, only to lose in two sets to Sweden's Catarina Lindquist. However, when reviewing the year in 1985 it was the Olympics which stood out in Steffi's mind. 'Everything at the time was a great success but that was the beginning when I was starting to play well and it was my first major tournament – it was great. It was great because there were so many people there – about 10,000 watching,' she explained. 'I remember everything. Almost every good junior was playing there so it was not easy to win. Andrea Jaeger (the American teen sensation) was playing.'

If she had her doubts at the start of the year, by the end of it Steffi was quite sure how she felt about being a professional tennis player. As she explained to John Feinstein in his book *Hard Courts*,

I was winning, and that was nice, but what I loved was *competing*. When I got to No. 1, people asked me about how long I had dreamed about being No. 1. I never really thought about it until

I got to No. 2. Before that, for me, what I liked was competing with the best players, with Chris and Martina and Pam and Hana.

By the end of 1984, Steffi was fast gaining international recognition, thanks to her last sixteen showing at Wimbledon, her Olympic win and her appearance against Catarina Lindquist in the final at Filderstadt. At the age of just fifteen she was already ranked 22nd in the world.

She had not made a huge single splash, but by playing in smaller events Steffi had built strong foundations for the future. By this stage in her career it was Peter who was accompanying Steffi more, partly because he was better qualified on court than Heidi and partly because Heidi was beginning to grow tired of travelling the world, worrying about the younger child that she had to leave behind. Also, now that Steffi had started making money on the Tour Peter could afford to give up his various jobs and travel with his daughter full-time.

Her father did pace Steffi well, there is no doubt of that. At the age of sixteen she was asked why she did not play more exhibitions. Her father replied that it was more important for her to reach the top than to play exhibitions which could exhaust her and frustrate her final aim – to be No. 1, a ranking which she thought it would take her three years to attain.

Steffi was finding that she was not having as much fun as she had enjoyed on the lower rungs of the WTA Tour, though. In 1985, she admitted, 'It's really very difficult to make good friends (on the Tour). You have different schedules from other players, so it's really hard.'

However, 1985 was a breakthrough year for Steffi, and it would have been even better if one of the outstanding players of the old school, the American star Chris Evert, had not stood in her way on numerous occasions. In the first six tournaments that Steffi played that year, she reached the semi-finals or finals of three, where she was consistently beaten by Evert in straight sets. In the fourth round of the French Open she once again met Evert and was yet again solidly beaten.

In June, Steffi was asked what goals she had set herself for

Wimbledon. Without hesitation, she said that she wanted to reach the last eight in 1985 and win the title within three years. She failed in her first goal, losing to the American Pam Shriver in three sets in the fourth round. As time would prove, however, she would win Wimbledon within three years, but only just – in 1988.

Another aim was to be among the top fifteen women's players in the world by the end of the year. Steffi went even better than that. Having reached the final of three major WTA events and despite ending the year without a title, she was ranked No.6 in the world by the year's end. She was, others observed, the best player that year not to win an event.

While Steffi had been progressing in leaps and bounds up the WTA ranking list, another German was zooming up the men's international men's rankings like an express train in a hurry to get to its destination. Boris 'Boom Boom' Becker had at the end of 1983 been ranked at No.563 in the world. A year later he had shot up almost 500 places to end 1984 at No.65. Six months later, of course, Becker had won the Wimbledon men's singles event.

Suddenly Becker was hot. Steffi was not. For years Steffi had been heralded back home as the star of German tennis, the player who was going to make a name for it throughout the world, since she had been winning national junior events for so long. Becker. Who was Becker? He had never been the top ranked player nationally in his age group in juniors, and one DTB coach is even said to have suggested – when Becker was ten or eleven – that he should be withdrawn from the national training programme because he lacked talent and was not worth wasting money on.

Now Becker had blossomed and blasted his way through the men's world rankings. He had, it seemed, come from nowhere to win Wimbledon. Back home in Bruehl a visible sigh of relief ran through the Graf family. They had had so many problems with the media – 'The press has been a nuisance, allowing us no privacy, especially when Steffi comes home,' alleged Heidi – that they were pleased that another German player had taken the spotlight off them.

The Grafs had moved into a new home in Bruehl, just a few hundred metres from No. 14 Normannenstrasse and next to the

indoor tennis facility built by Peter. Despite a high wall, erected to keep journalists and photographers out as well their pet dogs in, the Graf family home was frequently subjected to the paparazzi climbing over it.

With media attention diverted, Steffi was happy to continue her journey to the top of women's tennis with a little less scrutiny and a little less pressure. As a warm-up for the US Open, Steffi played an event in Mahwah in the United States where she reached the final before being beaten by the American Kathy Rinaldi.

A couple of weeks later at the US Open Becker failed to get past the fourth round, where he was beaten by Joakim Nystrom of Sweden 6–3, 6–4, 4–6, 6–4. It was Steffi's turn to make headlines at the US Open 1985 – headlines that focused not only on her tennis. The American journalists had seen Steffi's type before in the form of Andrea Jaeger and Tracy Austin, and they quizzed the young German about the possibility of 'burn-out'. Steffi was ready with her reply. There was no way that she was going to be affected because, 'I don't play too many tournaments. My father is doing it very well. If you have a good timetable, I don't see how you can get burned out.' Steffi had a point. Up until the US Open she had only played in ten tournaments in 1985. By contrast, Gabriela Sabatini, at fifteen a year younger than Steffi, had already played 21.

In the quarter-finals, Steffi and Shriver played a marathon match – the first 39-game, three tie-break match to be played in a women's event – which Steffi won. It was a match that many consider marked the turning point in her rapid ascent to the top. In the semi-finals Steffi lost 2–6, 3–6 to another of the stalwarts of the old school, Martina Navratilova. After the match, Navratilova remarked: 'If she gets any better and hits the ball any harder, I'll quit the game.'

Steffi took her cue. In November the Grafs travelled to Marbella to train at the tennis centre of the German Federation Cup coach, Klaus Hofsass. Once there Steffi concentrated on improving her all-round game, but particularly on strengthening her serve.

If they did not already think so, most tennis observers were totally convinced at the US Open that the German was a serious challenger for the top of the women's rankings. As if to confirm

that sentiment, having seen her train, Hofsass said, 'Steffi has an extraordinarily strong mental approach. If she can change her approach and be more attacking she's in with a chance of making it to No.3, if not No. 1, by next year.'

Following her training trip to Spain Steffi returned to the Tour in February 1986 with renewed vigour and confidence. She had been on the Tour for several years already; she had been working hard and making headway, but she wanted more. Her aim for the year: to win another tournament. She did not have to wait long. And she was aided by another development: her body was changing from that of a seemingly frail, thin child into that of a tall, strong athlete.

Steffi served warning of her improved level of play at the Virginia Slims Championships in March by reaching the semi-finals. Shriver, her beaten opponent in the quarter-finals remarked, 'She's no dummy out there. She also is a better player now. It's been six months [since the US Open and their epic 39-game match], and six months is a lot of time when you are sixteen.'

However, it was in April at Hilton Head in what was Steffi's 47th tournament as a professional that she was to win her first WTA Tour event. She vanquished Evert 6–4, 7–5 in the final to lift the title, and in so doing had beaten the woman who had come to epitomise the classic baseliner at her own game, displaying a further improved forehand which Evert was to describe after the match as 'the best in women's tennis'. The following week Steffi defeated Kohde-Kilsch in the final at Amelia Island, and two weeks later she beat Sabatini in Indianapolis.

She did not have to wait long to beat the then No. 1 player in the world, Navratilova. On her favourite surface, the clay of the German Open in Berlin in May, Steffi was on a roll and swept through the first four rounds without losing more than six games per match. In the final she beat Navratilova for the loss of just five games, 6–2, 6–3. From a position of never having won a professional tournament, Steffi had suddenly acquired four consecutive titles.

Steffi's triumph over Navratilova was the most significant. It was her first win against the No. 1 player in the world – always the hardest to achieve – and would help to strip away any

remaining psychological barriers. Steffi now knew she really was on her way up, and Navratilova surely realised her days as the leading women's player were numbered. The following year, Navratilova missed the German Open. Her reason? 'Officially, I'll tell you that I don't want to listen for a whole hour to Germans rhythmically clapping,' she said, 'but the real reason is that I don't want to be humiliated again. I don't want to go crying off the court again.'

In June, Evert expressed the fears of the top players when she stated, 'Steffi is the one girl to emerge in recent years in the game to win really big events. She is tough, she is fast and she has tremendous ability. Martina and I are having to play better for fear of losing our positions at the top.'

Steffi played the French Open, losing to the Czech Hana Mandlikova in the quarter-finals, and was forced to miss Wimbledon because she had a viral infection – just one of many nagging afflictions that would haunt her during her professional career. However, Steffi fretted so much at being away from the action that her father decided to travel with her to London as a spectator. 'It was bad for me to watch Wimbledon only on television. I was so sad when Martina and Boris were playing in matches that I had to leave the room because I wanted to cry.'

While in London, Steffi felt well enough to put in a little light practice with compatriot Kohde-Kilsch in preparation for the Federation Cup that was to take place in Prague in July. Steffi and the German team went to Czechoslovakia with high hopes of upsetting Navratilova's first visit home in eleven years, but before they had a chance to do that Steffi ran into trouble again. On her way to pick up her bags for a team practice session, a huge gust of wind upended a sunshade and the metal base landed on Steffi's right foot, breaking her big toe. That left Navratilova to pick up her homecoming present – the American team for whom she now played beat Czechoslovakia in the final.

At the 1986 US Open, the centennial of the women's singles event, Steffi once more reached the semi-finals. She was by now the most obvious heir to Navratilova's No. 1 crown, and she was patently not overawed by the thought. She said, 'You can see that Martina Navratilova is not that much better than everyone else. I

think even Chris is not that great any more. I mean she's good, but she's not what she was one or two years ago.'

In the semi-final Steffi faced Navratilova and lost in three sets 1–6, 7–6, 6–7, in what many tennis fans consider to be one of the most memorable women's tennis matches in recent history. In the final set Steffi had three match points – two of them on her favoured forehand flank – and lost them all. Navratilova eventually won the third set tie-break 10–8. Steffi was literally blinded by fury, and so upset at losing the match that she left the National Tennis Center where the US Open is played and was half-way to the airport before she realised that she had left her practice partner behind.

Looking back several years later, out of all the matches that she has played during her career Steffi will never forget that one.

That's the kind of match we're all looking for. The crowd were into it. I felt hot and cold waves through my body. I felt amazingly cold with excitement. What a great feeling. I don't think I'll ever live that kind of emotion again. It's exceptional with me.

Until 1986, Heidi – but far more often Peter – had been travelling with Steffi to every tournament as both chaperone and coach. It was an arrangement that suited Steffi, for as she explained, 'I think it's great that my parents always travel with me. If one of my parents wasn't there, I would get a bit homesick.' She even went as far as to admit a few years later that she had greatly appreciated the protection that Peter provided when she first joined the Tour. It meant that she did not have any friends, and helped her to shut herself off from everything else that was going on around her, which enabled her to perfect her tennis without distraction and to gain the confidence that she needed to defeat her opponents.

In late 1986, however, circumstances changed slightly when Pavel Slozil, the former Czech Davis Cup player who had built up an excellent doubles' reputation on the men's professional Tour, was employed to partner Steffi in practice while Peter retained the title of coach. With Slozil and the rest of the family Steffi went to Gran Canaria to practise before the start of her 1987 campaign. Being on a sun-drenched island enabled Steffi not only to train

outside on the tennis court but also on the sand, where she performed special exercises to improve her footwork and speed.

After Gran Canaria it was apparent that Steffi's serve had greatly improved, her backhand was stronger and more versatile, and her confidence had grown to the point where she could decide when to finish a rally rather than relying on her opponent to make a mistake. Apart from practice there was another reason why Steffi's serve had become stronger – she had grown significantly and had now reached her full height, just about three inches short of six feet.

To the great Ted Tinling, who was involved in various aspects of women's tennis for over 60 years, as Steffi developed she was becoming more and more like the highly successful American of the 1950s, Maureen Connolly. 'They are very similar in manner and mannerisms,' he explained. 'The walk is exactly the same – and the manner in which Steffi dismisses what she has done and moves. She knows exactly where she is going. She also has the same look of disdain for her opponents – and has a miles better service than Maureen had.' And just as Connolly had dominated the women's game in the early 1950s, so too was Steffi to dominate in the late 1980s.

In 1987, for the second year running Steffi missed the Australian Open, justifying her absence by saying that she was still too young to play a full schedule. Perhaps she had foreseen how much she would have to play in the rest of the year, as winning became all too inevitable. The young German fought her way to the final of every event in which she competed, and ended 1987 having lost just two of the 77 matches she had played.

At the Lipton International Players Championships held in Key Biscayne in March, the memory of the three match points she had squandered in her last match against Navratilova at the US Open was still fresh in her mind when Steffi walked on to court to play her semi-final against the American. On the other side of the net, Navratilova – used to bludgeoning her way past others – got a taste of her own medicine. Steffi, determined that victory would be hers, swept past the No. 1 women's player 6–3, 6–2 in 58 minutes to take her place in the final. Two days later Steffi was back on court, where she took two minutes less to defeat Evert 6–1, 6–2 and take the title.

If the tennis world had needed further proof that Steffi had arrived, surely this was it. She had beaten the women's top two players in consecutive matches. A year earlier Steffi admitted, something had been missing from her game. No longer. Steffi had discovered self-belief, and now walked out to face the only two players ranked higher than her knowing that she could win. The twelve years of Navratilova-Evert domination – intermittently threatened by Austin, Jaeger, Mandlikova and Shriver – were over. Steffi provided the WTA Tour with a breath of fresh air – and just in time, for Navratilova and Evert were already in their thirties and heading towards retirement.

In the following two months Steffi won four titles – Hilton Head, Amelia Island, the Italian Open and the German Open – and arrived at Roland Garros for the French Open brimming with confidence. 'Everything's at stake,' Navratilova admitted in an interview prior to the opening of the tournament. 'Once I had an aura of invincibility. Chris had it for a while. Steffi has it right now.'

Almost inevitably it was Navratilova and Steffi, the two top-ranked players, who met in the final. They traded sets and then Navratilova looked as if she would walk away with the title when she was a break up in the third and leading 5–3. Steffi held serve to make it 5–4 in Navratilova's favour and then the American served for the match. Steffi was not going to give up without one hell of a fight, and broke Navratilova to level the match at 5–5. The balance of fortune had changed. Eventually, with Navratilova at 6–7 and serving now to stay in the match, it was the older player who lost her nerve and double-faulted at match point to give Steffi her first Grand Slam title. All that remained for Steffi to do was to run over to her father to give him the customary kiss. Steffi had won 6–4, 4–6, 8–6 in two hours. Navratilova, magnanimous in defeat, said at the press conference after the match, 'She felt sorry for me which I didn't expect. She is a good kid with a good heart – and she is giving women's tennis a shot in the arm.'

Steffi received a huge welcome when she returned home to Bruehl after her French Open victory. Two thousand people lined the streets on Whitsun Monday as Steffi was driven into town, regally accompanied by police outriders. At the town hall 500

invited dignitaries awaited her arrival so that they could toast the star of their town. Steffi, as shy as ever, seemed rather embarrassed by all the fuss that was being made about her, but her eyes lit up when she was presented with a nine-month-old alsatian called Enzo von Descharo.

Steffi was overjoyed to be home, but she did not appreciate the fuss that was being made about her. She had been far happier when Becker had been the focus of attention. 'Now the press are starting to compare us – who's more popular? Who's nicer? I'm not happy about it. What matters is that we both play top-call tennis and I think that's great for German tennis.'

Three days before Wimbledon Steffi celebrated her eighteenth birthday. From now on she was allowed to sign cheques, gain access to the two or three million American dollars that she had already accumulated in savings, sign her own contracts, drive a car and vote in Germany. Her home town of Bruehl presented her with a German driving licence as she had already passed a test in the United States, and Opel gave her a sporty new car filled with 3,000 tennis balls. Dunlop handed Steffi a gold necklace studded with fifteen diamonds – one for every tournament she had won to date – valued at around £150,000. Slozil presented her with a huge portrait of herself that he had specially commissioned.

An offer also came in from actor Don Johnson, then starring in the popular series about smooth talking, tough acting cops, *Miami Vice*, to do a walk-on part on the programme. Pop star George Michael is said to have offered to show her a good time out in London. These were offers most eighteen-year-olds would have jumped at, but Peter Graf was determined that Steffi would concentrate on tennis, and she had to decline them politely.

At Wimbledon it was thought Steffi would have problems playing on grass. She certainly had not had a lot of practice on this type of surface, and had not played in 1986 due to illness. She decided not to play any of the traditional warm-up events. Steffi responded to the sceptics by losing just five games in the first three rounds, and it was not until the quarter-finals when she played Sabatini that she lost a set. As if to prove a point, Steffi rolled over Shriver, considered a grass-court specialist, with the loss of just two games in the penultimate round.

The final was a repeat of the French Open. Steffi faced her old adversary Navratilova. Steffi's inexperience on grass was evident throughout the match, but perhaps it was the thought that she could become the No. 1 player in the world if she beat Navratilova that distracted her, and she lost 5–7, 3–6. But Steffi was far from disappointed, saying,

> After two years of not playing on grass it was an unbelievable thing that I came to the final the way I did. Until the finals I was playing better here than I did in Paris. Here it is a different feeling. It is so green and there is the royalty. Not even Roland Garros is like this.

Three weeks after Wimbledon, Steffi represented Germany in the Federation Cup and helped her team to reach the final, where they met the United States. Steffi's team-mate Kohde-Kilsch lost to Shriver in the first rubber, before Steffi put the Germans back on an even keel by dishing out a comprehensive defeat to Evert, 6–2, 6–1 in less than an hour. It was the crucial doubles rubber, however, which will be remembered for many years to come in the tennis world. Evert and Shriver looked like having an easy win, when they rushed to a 6–1, 4–0 lead. Steffi and Kohde-Kilsch had other ideas and came back to record a 1–6, 7–5, 6–4 win, one of the best women's doubles come-backs ever. Steffi played an important part, running down what lesser players might have considered irretrievable winners and returning serve unbelievably well. It was, as Shriver would say, 'A match made in heaven.'

After the excitement of the Federation Cup Steffi flew to Los Angeles to play in a Virginia Slims event. In the final Steffi met Evert and won, once more in straight sets, 6–3, 6–4. It might have been another routine day's work for all Steffi knew until, running over to give her father a winning kiss, he told her that she had just taken over the No. 1 ranking from Navratilova. Peter and Steffi had discussed the possibility of her grabbing the top spot prior to the match, but in order for her not to feel pressured he had told her that it was not going to be possible.

Steffi's joy was obvious. 'Now that I've taken over the No. 1 spot, I think this means more than anything. It feels great. I can't stop

smiling,' she enthused ecstatically. Evert was complimentary, 'I am surprised it took the computer so long to recognise Steffi as No. 1. After all, she has won eight tournaments this year.' Later Evert added,

Every five or ten years a young player comes along who is really special, really unique. Steffi is one of those special players. You can see it in her eyes, when she's out on the court, she's in a hurry to win. She's obviously a better player than I was at her age, but I can see in her the same intensity, the hunger, the concentration I have had in my career.

Only three other people – Evert, Navratilova and Austin – had held the No. 1 ranking since computer rankings began in 1977. Only two other players – Australian Margaret Court and Billie Jean King – had ever been considered the top-ranked women in the world. Steffi therefore became the first European women's No. 1, Navratilova having already obtained her American citizenship by the time she reached the top spot.

In celebration of her newly won crown at Los Angeles, Steffi, Peter and brother Michael went down to the beach and ran, carefree, into the sea. For a moment a thought passed through Steffi's mind. 'Now that I'm No. 1, what if I stop tomorrow? I could have a nice life on the beach in Los Angeles.' Having achieved what she had set out to do, to be the No. 1 player in the world did not seem such a bad idea. After all, she had already acquired more than enough fame and fortune to last a lifetime. But almost as soon as the thought entered her head, it passed her by. A burning desire to compete and to reach her full potential as a player would ensure that Steffi spent her days on the tennis court, rather than the beach.

The rankings seemed to count for nothing, though, when the tennis circus reached Flushing Meadow for the US Open in September. Steffi made her way through six rounds to the final, losing a single set to Lori McNeil of the United States in the semi-final. In the final – surprise, surprise – Steffi was up against Navratilova, who, none to happy that her No. 1 ranking had been hijacked by some youngster from Germany, was out to draw blood.

After a close first set that went to a tie-break and to Navratilova,

the match was as good as over and the American walked away a 7–6, 6–1 winner. To give Steffi her due, as soon as the final had finished she withdrew from a women's doubles match, complaining that she had another of her niggling illnesses. Flu had set in and she was running a slight temperature.

After the US Open, Billie Jean King was to comment,

> Martina has the great physical talent and Chris has the great mental attitude to make their equation equal, but Steffi will have both going for her as long as she doesn't get hurt. She also has that 'oomph'. You get that feeling only from champions.

Steffi picked up the WTA Player of the Year award and later crowned her year, confirming her status as the world's best woman player, by winning the Virginia Slims Championships in New York's Madison Square Gardens in November. In the final Steffi beat her young rival Sabatini in four sets, 4–6, 6–4, 6–0, 6–4.

Using a culinary metaphor, Steffi surprised everyone with her description of 1987. She summed it up like this:

> If I was a cook, this would be the menu describing my year. The appetizers were Key Biscayne, Boca Raton and Amelia Island, which I won in the spring. The main course was a very tender French Open topped with Berlin and Rome, all of which I won in the summer, with a side dish of Wimbledon and the US Open finals. I just forgot to add the salt and pepper to those. Dessert – and I like dessert very much – was Hamburg, Zurich and now best of all, New York. It's been a very tasty year.

Steffi had not, however, found anyone special with whom to enjoy her 'meal'. The German press in particular seemed to think that it was about time Steffi found herself a boyfriend, but she soon put them straight on that issue. 'Most girls of my age,' she explained, 'think only of boys, boys, boys, but I think only of tennis, tennis, tennis.' There was another issue that was already worrying Steffi. 'I shall,' she admitted, 'find it difficult to find a husband because I shall want to know if he loves me or the tennis player.' Boyfriends were definitely on the back-burner for the time being.

Navratilova – even though she was upset because she had won two Grand Slams, one more than Steffi, and felt that she still deserved the No. 1 ranking – was forced to admit, 'Steffi is No. 1, which is too bad because I had such a good year, but she had an unbelievable year. She won so many events. She had a lot of three-set matches but she won them all.'

At the end of the year, Steffi had won 75 singles matches and lost on only two occasions. 'It's hard for me to realise what I did,' she said. 'It will be very difficult to top this year. In five years, I might say, "How did I do it?"' Unlikely, when Steffi was to play as she did the following year.

1988 was to put an end to Navratilova's murmurings that she should still be the No. 1 ranked player. Steffi would make sure of that.

4
A WINNING STYLE

ATTAINING THE NO. 1 SPOT in the women's rankings is a gargantuan task and to prove it only six players – Martina Navratilova, Chris Evert, Tracy Austin, Monica Seles, Arantxa Sanchez-Vicario and Steffi – have managed it.

There are a great number of factors that affect the creation of a champion, but perhaps the most important is the widely held belief that champions cannot be produced. Certain individuals are quite simply born to be the best. Of course they can be helped along the way and provided with the right environment, but that obsessive perfectionism, that iron will to succeed seen in so many top people in varying fields, must come from within. It is a characteristic that just cannot be taught.

In tennis, almost any player can advance to a certain level through training and the learning of technique, but beyond that good strokes have to be matched by tactical ability, self-confidence and determination, plus the special star quality of a champion.

The charismatic American Richard 'Pancho' Gonzales, who dominated the men's game in the 1950s, expressed his feelings on what it takes to be a champion thus, 'Sacrifice. Giving up enjoyment of life for the sake of practice, and a bloody-minded determination to succeed.' Boris Becker concluded that 'To make it to the top, I believe one needs to be different from the norm.' Steffi herself said in 1988, 'I would not have got where I am today if I wasn't a stable, disciplined, ambitious person. You need a certain type of personality to become No. 1 in world tennis.'

Boris Breskvar in his book *Boris Becker's Tennis* included a

long list of what was needed to be top dog, including physical characteristics, coordination, dexterity, speed, learning ability, motivation, will power, concentration, stability, the willingness to take risks, self-reliance, fighting spirit and footwork. But he suggested that perhaps the most important qualities are agility, coordination and speed in converting thought into action.

So what attributes helped Steffi reach the No. 1 ranking?

According to Breskvar,

A combination of talent and a lot of hard work, because she is not a talent like Navratilova or Sabatini, who have an un-believable feel for the ball, but Steffi is a great athlete and her concentration is unbelievable. I never saw anybody in my life, no girl, no boy, who could concentrate so good at only six or seven years old: Boris (Becker) was nothing, if you compare the concentration of the two. It was unbelievable.

The great American player Billie Jean King confidently predicted that Steffi would win a Grand Slam when she was still in her mid-teens because of her 'quickness, strength and seemingly infallible tennis instincts'.

The Swedish player, Catarina Lindquist, who played Steffi in the young German's first professional final in 1984, said,

I don't think anyone was so focused on being No. 1 in the world before. She didn't talk about it, but you could see it in the way she practised and lived. Tennis seems to be her whole life and she likes it.

For Pam Shriver, another leading player in her day, it is the 'combination of the tangible part – the shot making, power, speed, all the components which make you physically better, and also the intangible part – the mental toughness, the confidence to play the big points better than anyone else'. The tangible parts are Steffi's powerful serve, consistently strong groundstrokes (including the most powerful forehand on the women's Tour) and astonishing speed around the court. The intangible part, in addition to her strong mental powers, is her enthusiasm for playing tennis, which

is seemingly endless – 'I'm addicted to it. I love going on court and hitting the ball.'

That Steffi was hooked on tennis was patently obvious in 1988 when, accidentally bitten on her right hand by one of her dogs, she went to Spain for a few days' break. She was unable to play with her right hand, but insisted on going on court and playing as a left hander instead.

Steffi was fortunate that she had her father to harness and nurture her enthusiasm while she was still young. While many children have their first lessons at the age of about seven, Steffi was learning the basics at just three. That in itself might not have been a good thing, but as her father had a tennis teaching certificate and was a member of the GTTF, he ensured that Steffi was well taught.

As a child Steffi did not model herself on any particular player, but she did take more than a passing interest in both Evert and Navratilova and always wanted to perfect the best of their games – Evert's baseline strength and Navratilova's net play. On the men's professional Tour, Steffi admired American Jimmy Connors for his fighting spirit, and his old foe and fellow American John McEnroe for his touch. All players develop their own individual way of playing, however, and Evert summed up the young German's like this: 'Steffi has that huge forehand and a slice back-hand that give her a style that's all her own.'

Peter willingly spent his free time teaching Steffi as much as he could. When Steffi reached the age of six and he took her to see Breskvar, Breskvar commented that 'she already had a fairly reasonable technique.' From then until Steffi turned professional her coaching was overseen by the DTB, with extra sessions provided by Peter. So not only did she start before most players, but Steffi was also training a lot harder than the other children when they did start playing.

When she first turned professional Peter was very good at working out Steffi's tournament schedule, to ensure that she had enough time to rest between events and did not suffer from burn-out – mental fatigue or physical injury resulting in a player being forced to quit – like so many teenage prodigies. Steffi appreciated this fact, and when at the age of sixteen she was asked whether she

thought it was a good idea to have started on the WTA Tour so young, she said,

> You have to have a coach who knows you really well so that he can say 'Well, now you need a rest' or 'Now you can play one more tournament'. Someone who knows how much you can play. I think that's important because in America most play on hard courts and that's not good for your feet either. Europeans have it better because we only play on clay.

A remark that was surely aimed at the well-publicised burn-outs of the American teenagers Tracy Austin and Andrea Jaeger. As if to confirm this point, when Jennifer Capriati was to have problems in 1993 Steffi refused to support the view that Capriati was a victim of the WTA Tour. She insisted the young American had played too many lucrative exhibition matches, thus implying that Capriati's career had been badly looked after.

When Steffi first turned professional her father was her only coach – as he has always claimed to be. However, when necessary and as Steffi started winning and providing the Grafs with the finances to support them, hitting partners were brought in to practise with her.

When asked in the summer of 1985 how she prepared for matches, Steffi announced, 'I don't really think too much about the match. I just go in and if in the first couple of games you can see already what she does better and what she doesn't do that well – how she is playing at the moment – then you just come into the game like that.' The interviewer sounded surprised, but was assured by Peter that 'this is the best way for young players'.

Perhaps it was this slightly haphazard approach to matches that persuaded Peter that he needed a full-time practice partner for Steffi, someone who would assist her in her final assault on the top of the women's rankings. Perhaps it was also a thrombosis in Peter's right leg which meant that he could no longer practise to the required level with Steffi.

Late in 1986, Peter hired Pavel Slozil to partner Steffi in practice sessions. Peter had reservations about hiring a married man

because he was not convinced that Pavel would be as committed as a single person, but after some thorough questioning Pavel got the job.

Pavel might have found one of Peter's questions, 'Can you play for four hours a day?' fairly insulting. He was after all still competing on the men's Tour when he decided to take up coaching. Although his ranking had fallen to around 70, Pavel was still in good physical shape and was capable of beating the top players on occasion.

He soon understood why Peter had asked the question. He still remembers the very first time that he hit with Steffi – it was 6 November 1986.

I hadn't touched my racket for two weeks, and thought 'It's only a seventeen year old girl ... but then I was really impressed not only by the way she hit the ball, but by her speed and the few breaks that she allowed herself – perhaps a five- or ten-second breather but no drink and no towelling down.

From then on, when she was not playing in a tournament, Pavel spent every day including Saturdays and Sundays hitting four hours a day with Steffi. At the end of their marathon sessions, she was always in better shape than he was. In the beginning he admitted that he found it strenuous work, but he soon got used to it. He had to. He also admitted, 'I sometimes felt Steffi was disappointed with me for not playing better in practice.'

Pavel explained just how intensely the two trained together.

I'm playing much more than I did for myself. We travel much more than I did for myself. Things have changed dramatically for me. I have to really watch what I eat and what I'm doing. Sometimes you go out and have fun, and the next morning you pay for it, because the four hours is very intensive. It's not a matter of staying in a corner and making her run – *you* have to run. You can come down any morning and see how tired I am, how much I am sweating. The quality of tennis is even higher than in her matches, because she's more relaxed and goes for more shots.

Steffi goes to bed at 8.30 or 9 at night. I'm tired, too, in the evening – I just watch television and go to bed.

Together with Peter, Pavel made sure that Steffi stuck to a strict off-court training regime that included running, weightlifting and skipping with weights on her ankles. In addition, Steffi's tournament schedule was carefully planned by Peter and Pavel to try and reduce staleness, to ensure that she suffered no undue jet lag, and to reduce the risk of injuries such as muscle strain caused by frequent changes of playing surface.

One trait of Steffi's character made Pavel's job relatively easy – her dedication.

It's incredible the way you don't have to push her. You don't even have to tell her things like what to eat or when to go to sleep. She was already an intelligent tennis player, and very strong mentally, before I went to work with her. She's one of the best professional athletes I ever met; maybe the best, because since the age of seventeen she's always known what to do.

Pavel encountered Steffi's dedication shortly after they paired up. The only time that the two could practise on the right surface for one of their first tournaments together, an event in Chicago, was from 6 a.m. to 8 a.m. So they had to get up at 4.45 a.m. in temperatures of minus 15 degrees Centigrade every morning to hit. Steffi was on the dot every time.

Steffi's discipline during practice is legendary. She remembers a particular fault from the last match she has played, and works to perfect that shot until she is convinced that she has ironed out all the creases. Just as in a match she is totally focused on her tennis during practice, and is reluctant to talk to her hitting partner or anyone else who might be around the court.

Once asked if there was anything that she would want to change about the Tour, she replied,

I think we need more time in between tournaments. We have one month off a year and I think that's not enough. From my point of view, I don't have the chance any more to practise

something specific because I'm mostly at the end of the tournament having already to prepare for the next one. I don't really have the time to improve any more.

Peter had employed Pavel because he was an excellent doubles player and he wanted the Czech to teach Steffi how to serve and volley. Pavel certainly improved her serve. He made her serve one ball after another until she had developed a more powerful, knee-bending serve, with a slower swing and more snap. It was not unlike and almost as fierce as some of the men's and was a service that was to become one of the most feared on the WTA Tour.

Steffi also started to improve her backhand, considered her weaker side, so that opponents would not be so eager to hit to it. Pavel worked hard to get Steffi to develop a topspin backhand, a stroke with which she had never felt comfortable. Although she was not prepared to start using the shot in matches overnight, at least they ensured that her backhand was more reliable than before. It was not only her weaknesses that were improved upon. Although Pavel did not necessarily notice that her forehand was getting better – because he was playing with her every day – those who played against Steffi knew first-hand that her forehand was going from strength to strength. The change to Steffi's game was evident in 1987 as she made her final assault on the top of the rankings, gaining the No. 1 position on 17 August of that year.

For the next two years – 1988 and 1989 – Pavel seemed to have the unenviable task of trying to improve a game that was so strong that it enabled Steffi not only to retain her No. 1 ranking but ensured that she won her Golden Grand Slam. Always, though, Pavel and Steffi believed that her game could be developed. While encouraging Steffi to be more of an attacking player, he realised that she was far more comfortable playing the modern baseline game. Pavel therefore started teaching her how to use her powerful groundstrokes in a more tactical way, so that she could win points more quickly.

As Steffi commented,

I love to play from the baseline – there's nothing better for me than playing from the baseline, I just love it. I love to play rallies.

I love to play points and go for my shots and I've never really tried to play serve and volley. On a few points and especially at Wimbledon on grass courts, I try to do it and I do it really well, but it's not my natural game and that's why I mostly stick to the baseline.

Two glorious years were followed by two miserable ones. In 1990 and 1991, Steffi – her life thrown into confusion by the tabloids' revelations of her father's alleged affair with a topless model – thought about giving up. These years were not easy for Pavel either, and he too considered quitting. In the end, though, he decided it would be unfair to the rest of Steffi's support team – her family, the family's 'Girl Friday' Horst Schmidt, her masseur Uwe Capellmann, her doctors, her conditioning trainer Erco Pruell, and her left-handed hitting partner Markus Schur. More than improving her actual game, Pavel's job during those difficult times was more one of keeping his charge motivated.

At the end of 1991, Steffi dispensed with his services. Officially Steffi would say, 'We have both grown tired. I'm at the stage when I don't need constant supervision. It's no longer necessary to have a full-time coach.' There had been disagreements, however, over how her game should be developed. While Pavel was still in favour of adopting a serve-and-volley game, Peter wanted to concentrate on the baseline game with which Steffi had been so successful. Ultimately, though, someone had to take the blame for two miserable years, and although they had nothing to do with Pavel, somewhat inevitably it was he who fell from favour.

Coaches or hitting partners are very important to players, but they rarely get the recognition they deserve, except perhaps during Grand Slam events when television crews are likely to angle their cameras at the 'girlfriends' box' (so-called because of the countless number of glamorous women that inhabit it during the men's matches) where the player's friends, family and coach sit. Preparation for matches goes on for weeks, months, even years. And although it is up to the player to perform on court it is the coach who has to train the player, be her baby-sitter, best friend, worst enemy, bag carrier and administrator, plus more – and take the flack when a match does not go according to plan. It is never

an easy relationship, and Pavel's job was certainly not an easy one; not only did he have to please Steffi, but also her father, known as one of the most demanding parents on the women's Tour.

However, Pavel, who spent about 40 weeks a year travelling with Steffi, had obviously enjoyed working with her – 'What more pleasure could I want than working with the best' he would say – and despite the problems of the last two years their partnership was an extremely successful one. Pavel helped Steffi to ten Grand Slam titles as well as 50 other titles, and she lost to only seven players – Sabatini, Navratilova, Seles, Sanchez-Vicario, Shriver, Garrison and Novotna – in the time that they spent working together.

After splitting with Pavel, Steffi went to New York to play in the Virginia Slims Championships, and lost in three sets at the quarter-final stage to Jana Novotna. It had become all too obvious that Steffi needed to take a fresh look at her game. She herself is on record as saying, 'I have to be a little more positive. I also have to try and be a bit looser and enjoy it a little bit more because I take everything a little bit too serious right now.' The Swiss Heinz Guenthardt, another men's doubles specialist who formerly played on the ATP Tour, was brought in to assist. Theirs has been a different relationship from the one she had enjoyed with Pavel, because having gained maturity and vast experience Steffi no longer needs constant supervision. As a result, Heinz travels with her for only about 22 weeks of the year.

Heinz explained his coaching philosophy:

When I took over I did not want to start teaching her backhands and forehands. I just wanted to concentrate on sharpening her mind. I wanted her to think more about her strengths and not the negative aspects. I wanted her to get more pleasure from her tennis and have fun and I could not have asked for more.

By 1992 it was apparent that Steffi was closer to being a complete player, with the help of Heinz. She was using her forehand with more subtlety and was starting to have a better feel for when to approach the net. Steffi still felt, however, that if she had the time to practise specific shots she would be much better at serving and

volleying. 'At the moment,' she said, 'I don't have the time to practise enough to feel comfortable doing it during an important match.'

The following year Heinz was content to see Steffi hitting the ball better, varying her shots and thinking more tactically so that three or four shots in a row made sense and left her opponent five metres from the ball. And he had changed her views on topspin backhands by stressing that her sliced backhand was a great shot that could be used as an attacking rather than a defensive shot. As a result Steffi now uses the slice to move her opponents around, playing it short, hitting it deep and on occasion moving in on it.

Heinz's future with Steffi was questioned when she lost in the first round at Wimbledon 1994, but their working relationship remains intact.

If one dissects Steffi's game clinically, it is initially her serve that puts opponents under real pressure and makes it difficult for them to play aggressively during her service games. Witness what Navratilova had to say having been beaten by Steffi in the final of the year-end Championships in 1989: 'Her serve made the difference. She gets more free points on her first serve than I do on mine. That first serve is awesome.' But her service action also has its down side. Steffi bounces the ball at least three times before serving, often more on big points, and then tosses the ball up high before swinging her racket down to serve. She tosses the ball so high that it can be affected if it is very windy on court, as it was when Steffi lost to Lori McNeil in the first round of Wimbledon in 1994. Generally, though, Steffi's serve is considered a lethal weapon and is one of the fastest on the women's Tour, having been recorded at 105mph.

Steffi's forehand has frequently been credited as being the best and hardest hit in the women's game, although the Yugoslav Monica Seles – when she was playing – and currently both Mary Pierce of France and American Lindsay Davenport, can hit as hard as Steffi. Late in 1986, the great American player John McEnroe watched Steffi playing on television and saw her hitting forehands so hard – with the same tennis racket he was then using – that he phoned the racket maker and asked whether Steffi was actually using a super racket. The reply: 'There's nothing special about her

racket. It's the same one that you're using, just with an extremely high string tension.'

Every time she hits a forehand, using an Eastern grip, Steffi looks as if she's trying to murder the ball and is often successful in killing rallies off with a forehand winner. It is surely with Steffi's help that women's tennis has progressed from the days when an Australian men's player commented on it in jest: 'There's a lob, returned by a lob, followed by a lob ...'

Her forehand stroke is complicated and not the classic stroke that is normally taught to youngsters. Steffi uses topspin, hits the ball a long way in front of her body and as early as possible so that she can utilise the power the ball has received from her opponent's shot and add it to her own, making it a much more powerful stroke. Standing sideways to the net, Steffi transfers her body weight and launches into the shot, providing great power. In addition, her take-back begins much later than most, allowing for and necessitating better acceleration and a faster swing. The take-back is also very high, but she is so fast around the court she can get into position early, and her timing so perfect that she can pull it off. On deep balls she often looks rushed and has to hit the stroke so early that it is almost a half-volley. That is by no means an easy shot to play, but Steffi has so much confidence in the stroke that she makes it look easy and is quite happy to hit away in an uninhibited manner. Instinctively, if necessary she can play the forehand on the run and while jumping.

Steffi's confidence in her forehand stems from the fact that she has played it the same way with only a few minor modifications since she was a young child. When still young, the long, high take-back (common among children when hitting groundstrokes) reduced as she grew, and as special exercises which strengthened her wrist and forearm muscles allowed. Then in 1988, her father realised that Steffi was raising her elbow higher than usual when taking her racket back and as a result was making unforced errors – hence a loss to Gabriela Sabatini in Amelia Island. A few practice sessions soon corrected the problem, as Peter explained: 'I watched Steffi for two hours, then saw what was wrong. I changed her stroke preparation, enabling her to take the ball earlier. The forehand is now the killer shot again. Nobody else in the world can tell Steffi exactly what is wrong, except me.'

Early on, and significantly before 1986 when she had yet to grow into her body and develop a powerful service, Steffi's game was very much dependent upon her forehand; she would run around her backhand so that she could play a forehand at every opportunity. Of course this was also because it was a shot of which she was absolutely sure, and Steffi – with a stubborn streak in her – clung on to any stroke that had given her success in the past. She always needed to be convinced that any change had to be made and she often ended up crying, as she refused to acknowledge that it was in her best interests to alter her technique.

This appears to have happened to her backhand. Ever since 1985, Steffi has been saying that she needs to concentrate on her backhand. At the age of sixteen, she admitted, 'I used to play many slices and I have to play more tops so that's what I am working on, to get it down the line.' And when Pavel was employed in 1986 as Steffi's practice partner, perfecting a topspin backhand was said to be a priority. Yet still Steffi prefers to slice her backhand and rarely uses a topspin backhand in competition, even though – as observers say she does – she plays it with such confidence during practice. There have been occasions, however, when Steffi has used the topspin backhand to great effect, mostly at Wimbledon. A notable illustration of this was against Novotna in the final in 1993, when she hit some superb topspin backhand cross-court passing shots. But still there is room for improvement as Steffi has admitted, even if she does not put thought into action on the court.

Steffi is also a reluctant volleyer, although she regularly claims that she is trying to come to the net more. There is no doubt that she can volley, as she did to secure the winning point of the ladies' final at Wimbledon in 1993, but she does not feel totally at ease at the net. Which is one reason why she does not play doubles regularly.

Steffi has, however, had some notable successes in doubles. In 1987 Steffi and Claudia Kohde-Kilsch won the Federation Cup. Two years later at the Federation Cup the experience was not repeated, and the pair lost to the Czechoslovakian team of Jana Novotna and Helena Sukova in the quarter-finals. Steffi acknowledged then, 'It's not as natural for me to play doubles.' In the late 1980s the two young stars of the WTA Tour, Steffi and Gabriela

Sabatini, teamed up together in a move surely engineered for maximum publicity. Succeed they did, both in attracting huge crowds and in winning the ladies' doubles title at Wimbledon in 1988. They also reached the finals of the French Open three times in the 1980s.

In 1990 Steffi eased up on her doubles' commitments because she wanted to concentrate on retaining her No. 1 position in the singles' rankings – at that time under heavy fire from Monica Seles. Other factors played their part. As Steffi was consistently winning through to the later rounds of tournaments, she increasingly felt the need to lessen her load, especially as the nagging injuries were only likely to worsen the more she played; the easiest way to do this was to stop playing doubles. Steffi, well-known for spending as little time as possible around tournament sites, was even less inclined to hang around waiting for doubles matches which are usually scheduled later in the day.

More recently, however, Steffi has been back on the doubles court, playing the odd event with her close friend on the WTA Tour Australian Rennae Stubbs, who is better known for her doubles successes than any great achievement in singles. Together they won in Hamburg in both 1992 and 1993. Steffi has also been known to play on the odd occasion in the mixed doubles of the Grand Slam events, and usually partners her coach.

But before Steffi even gets out on a court, where she makes tennis look so easy, she has to train hard. Long gone are the days when, as Martina Navratilova described it in the 1970s, training was 'a hit-and-giggle set'. It was Navratilova herself who when she rose to prominence in the late 1970s and early 1980s set new standards of mental and physical training and diet that meant a player could no longer expect to survive on raw talent alone.

Steffi, helped by her father and various practice partners, has by her own admission taken tennis training up to another level. Talking in 1990, she revealed, 'I've changed the game by playing a bit harder and more aggressively than the others. That means that a lot of the younger players are fitter and hitting the ball harder now.'

From her early days at the training centre in Leimen until the early 1990s Steffi worked with a conditioning coach, Pruell. While

she was still a junior, he devised a number of special stretching exercises which were designed to compensate for muscle shortening in the areas of the back, pelvis and thighs. The intensive use of these and other daily stretching routines over the years ensured that Steffi compensated for these weaknesses and also achieved above-average flexibility in the muscle areas concerned.

Pruell also put together a series of exercises for Steffi that included step-ups in order to work her ankle and leg extensor muscles. The benefit of these exercises was obvious when Steffi performed the jump-and-reach test, which involved standing next to a wall and jumping up to see how high she could reach on the wall. At the age of fourteen Steffi could reach no further than 25 centimetres from where her outstretched hand extended while she was stationary. Eighteen months later she could reach 45 centimetres.

Steffi's relatively weak ankle muscles necessitated another special form of training – she used to skip on a soft mat, beginning with six sequences of 30 seconds apiece. Eventually she built up her strength so that she could skip without stopping for two-and-a-half minutes. Try it.

Although Steffi stopped training at the centre in Leimen when she turned professional in 1982 Pruell continued to work with her until 1993, visiting her from time to time when she was at home in Bruehl to go through an hour of conditioning that included stretches for the arms, and exercises for the stomach and back.

On turning professional, Steffi's on-court practice also continued very much as it had while she had attended the centre in Leimen. Her discipline has always been legendary. Steffi has never had to be reminded that she should be practising. On the contrary, her father or coach is more likely to be forced into telling her that she has had enough for one day and really should leave the court. If needs be, she gets up at four or five o'clock in the morning to practise, and is known to have flown into a country for a tournament and been on the practice court within half-an-hour of her plane touching down.

In between tournaments Steffi usually practises for four to five hours per day, gradually reducing the amount of time spent working out on the court as a tournament draws near. In the two or three days before a tournament practice sessions are reduced to

between one-and-a-half and two hours per day, and on match days Steffi practises for only 30 to 45 minutes.

Aside from conditioning and on-court training, Steffi also lifts weights, and runs and skips with weights on her ankles in an effort to improve her foot speed. She enjoys playing basketball, and has in the past practised with the local squad in Heidelberg when at home in Germany; just as often she practises on the court alone, as a way of strengthening her legs.

Steffi's great advantage of course is that she is a natural athlete, probably the greatest athlete ever in women's tennis, although Margaret Court, Billie Jean King and Martina Navratilova were also excellent. Steffi can only play tennis the way she does because she is so fast. Boris Breskvar says about her famous forehand, 'If you taught this shot to someone who is normal fast, they won't have success. It is only good for Steffi because she is so fast.' Speed allows Steffi to reach the ball faster, which means that she hits it earlier, attacks the ball more easily and thus puts her opponent under greater pressure. Speed also increases Steffi's ability to retrieve balls, helping her to win points that others would probably have lost.

In addition to her extraordinary speed Steffi has excellent stamina, and if she had received the necessary training could well have been a very good middle-distance runner. Pavel recounts a story about the time when Steffi took over Navratilova's position at the top of the rankings.

> One of the first thing's on Steffi's mind … was to finish with tennis and try to run in the 800 metres at the Seoul Olympics. It wasn't possible, of course, but the first thing she did in the Olympics, the morning after a twenty-hour flight, was to go out running in the athletics practice stadium with some West German 400 metres men.

Her times over both 800 metres and 3,000 metres are said to be quite astonishing, and Steffi has been known to practise for four hours on court and then do 100-metre sprint intervals. Pavel went on record in 1989 to say that he thinks she has the talent to be a better athlete than a tennis player. Quite something considering she had already won her Golden Grand Slam.

Steffi

Tests done on Steffi in 1989 by the West German tennis team doctor Joseph Keul revealed that she has a 38 per cent greater lung capacity and a 40 per cent larger heart than the normal woman. That means she can inhale five and a half litres of air, while the deepest breath of an average person results in an inhalation of between four and five litres. Although these facts can be attributed in part to her physique some credit must also go to her training programme, which has helped her attain amazing results.

Steffi's diet is naturally a healthy one, although she has always had a weakness for cakes and pastries. Her own special formula on which she sets to work is said to include vitamin B, magnesium, calcium, glucose and carbohydrates. There was certainly no special meal when she prepared for the defence of her title on the second Saturday of Wimbledon 1993. Said Steffi, 'I'll stick to flakes and fruit juice for breakfast, read the paper, practise about 10.30, have lunch, which I'll prepare – mainly salad, potatoes and rice.'

American tennis professional Dennis van der Meer quoted in 1990 talking about women's tennis in the publication *Inside Tennis*, believes that Steffi is setting trends for the future. He said, 'The champions of the future will be in far better condition than today's. Navratilova set the mode. Graf is an example of the speed of foot that women will have, and that will just be average!'

If Steffi has set new levels of physical training for others to follow, she could also teach most of the other players on the women's Tour a thing or two about the mental aspects of the game. Determination, confidence and the ability to concentrate on the job in hand are far more important than having beautiful groundstrokes. A player can have all the talent in the world, but if she is mentally weak she is likely to languish in the lower ranks.

That is what is so special about Steffi. Besides her great physical attributes, she has always been tough mentally and invariably enters a match with fierce ambition. After a win at the Citizen Cup in Hamburg in 1987, Steffi was led to say, 'I am happy with my victory even though it was not as difficult as I had anticipated. I thought I played well throughout the week. I had fun.' Fun it might have been for Steffi, but not for her opponent, compatriot Isabel Cueto, who was comprehensively beaten 6–2, 6–2 in the final.

Not only is Steffi hard mentally, but perhaps more importantly the other players on the Tour know she is very difficult to beat. Chris Evert considered Steffi one of the toughest youngsters, mentally, to have emerged since Tracy Austin. Claudia Kohde-Kilsch in October 1989 made the following point about Steffi's mental strength: 'When Steffi hits a stupid ball and loses a point, she'll stop for a couple of seconds to concentrate. And then you're in trouble. Her next shot will blow you off the court. She is the best.'

When Steffi is really at her peak she is so confident that her opponents walk out on to court not believing that they have a chance to win but rather, thinking, 'OK, how many games can I get?' Inevitably they do not win the match; they rarely win a set, and they are lucky if they get more than a handful of games.

Steffi usually prepares to go on court either by playing cards or backgammon, as she used to when her father travelled with her frequently. Then he used to let her win to ensure that she went on court with a positive frame of mind. Sometimes she just reads.

Once on court Steffi takes on the air of a high-flying executive. She is very focused and shows little or no emotion as she goes about her job in an extremely committed and efficient manner. An outburst would surely be a sign of weakness. The message is clear – the tennis court is her office, in which she strives hard to get her work done in the shortest time possible.

If asked in a job interview for her greatest fault, Steffi would surely reply that she does not suffer fools gladly. And judging by the exasperated look on her face, she would consider herself among the fools on the occasions when she loses a point or a game she feels she should have won, or simply fails to finish a point as early as she would have liked to. There is of course a reason for winning quickly – shorter matches cause less stress to both Steffi's mind and body. 'That is her mentality on the court,' notes her father. 'She is aggressive, likes to make the point quickly. For her body, it's much better.'

Often out on the court long before the chair umpire has called 'time' at change-overs, the Steffi strut to her position on the baseline is legendary. So much so that when asked at the Paris Indoor event in November 1994 about the new rule that sets the time limit between points at Grand Slam events at twenty seconds, American

Jim Courier, the men's former No. 1 ranked player, commented, 'I think what I'm going to do is buy some tapes of Steffi Graf and try to play like her.'

Ted Tinling had his own fascinating way of describing Steffi's fast, efficient way of playing. He said, 'She's what the French call "petite bourgeoise": she plays like she's budgeting the house-keeping money every afternoon.'

Just as she gets on with her job Steffi lets others get on with theirs, and over-rulings by the umpire are often treated with the same indifference whether they are made for or against her. Raging outbursts, once a feature in her youth, are no longer her style; she prefers to stay concentrated and unemotional on court. She seems to be in accord with that other cool customer Stefan Edberg, who avers, 'Tennis is more emotionally draining than people think. Therefore you must not burn all your feelings privately or talk them away publicly.'

So Steffi's physical and mental abilities usually win her matches, but on the rare occasions when she finds herself down she is not averse to superstition to help her cause. At 1–4 down in the third set of the 1993 Wimbledon final against Jana Novotna, Steffi changed her racket. Later, she was asked why. 'I did that once against Martina when I was down 5–7 and 1–2 and I came back to win the match 6–2, 6–1,' she explained. 'So I said to myself "OK, try it" and I tried it and I did well. So probably that was something that was just going for it.'

Usually, though, Steffi Graf's wins have nothing to do with superstition, as 1988 was to prove.

5
'PAPA'

STEFFI CALLS HIM 'PAPA'. Sponsors and DTB officials – in their diplomatic manner – label him 'a difficult man', players on the WTA Tour say simply that he is 'strange' and members of the press usually refer to him in less than complimentary term, although there are the odd few who appreciate his 'wit' and 'character'.

Peter Graf is many things to many people and none more so than to Steffi, to whom he is father, coach, adviser, manager, protector, mentor, friend and tormentor. In some of these roles he has certainly acquitted himself well, but his success rate in others has been dubious. He has built up her confidence, while in other ways he appears, however unwittingly, to have knocked it down.

No one can disparage the frequently maligned Peter for the way he nurtured a tennis champion. He was willing and patient enough to spend hours with his young daughter teaching her the rudiments of tennis. He found her the best coach and facilities in the region when she needed extra training. He made sure she had full medical check-ups twice a year from the age of ten to ensure that she was not doing herself serious damage. And it was he who looked after her best interests in her early years as a professional, severely limiting the number of exhibitions in which she played, and making her take several months' rest at the end of the season so that she did not suffer burn-out.

It was later in his role as Steffi's self-appointed protector that Peter was to flounder. As his daughter moved into the fast lane, heading towards the top of the women's tennis rankings, Peter started gaining a reputation for wanting to be in control. No one – agents, sponsors, officials – could approach Steffi except through

him. On the occasions when interviews were granted he was always nearby so that he could deflect or answer any tricky questions. It was natural. Any father worth his salt would have recognised the need to protect his daughter. After all, Steffi was still only fifteen when she started creating waves.

The problem was that Peter was *not* totally in control of the situation. Here was a classic example of a small-town man who was – albeit through his daughter – thrown into the big time, the very big time. He went from being a big fish in the little pond of Germany where he had been toasted because his daughter was already recognised as a star, to being, at least at the beginning, a small fish in a big pond. Yet he still expected to be feted, still seemed to think he was hugely important. He appeared arrogant, and that grated on people's nerves. In German they call people like Peter *Bauernschlau*, which literally translated means a smart peasant. In English it sounds derogatory, but in German it is simply used to imply that someone is clever but not cosmopolitan – and therein lay Peter's problem.

Peter was clever enough to realise that Steffi was going to be a huge star, but he did not have the experience, nor initially the linguistic ability, to manage her on an international level. Peter might have developed the gift of the gab necessary to make a success of selling second-hand cars and insurance in Mannheim, but top level meetings with sponsors and the like on the WTA Tour were another matter. Conny Konzak, a journalist who has known Steffi since she was five, says, 'It's possible Steffi could have earned fifty per cent more money than she now has, if he (Peter) had more understanding of deals, and contracts.'

As the father of a fast-rising star on the Tour with the potential to be No. 1, Peter knew that he was important and he acted accordingly. He courted and enjoyed the limelight. He used the first person plural as in 'we won', 'we played unbelievably today'. Steffi might have been the one who had triumphed on court, but as far as Peter was concerned this was the culmination of years of hard work and sacrifices on his part, and he was going to share in the glory.

To some, Peter was too like Papa Lenglen, the father of Suzanne, the legendary French tennis player of the 1920s and

1930s. Ted Tinling, who knew both families well, was to observe, 'The similarities between Suzanne and Steffi and their fathers are remarkable. Both fathers built their lives around the daughter. Both daughters adored the father no matter what his flaws.'

Peter's head seemed to be full of fanciful ideas, and there were times when the press were not quite sure of the validity of what he was telling them. There is next to no information about the Grafs' life before they moved to Bruehl in 1978, except that they lived in Mannheim. Not even that is widely known. Most people, including those who followed her career when she was a child, are under the impression that Steffi was born in Bruehl. Even the WTA Tour Media Guide lists Bruehl as Steffi's birth place.

Peter has also told those willing to listen that he has his 'Abitur', the highest educational qualification from a Gymnasium – the top level of school in Germany – which would imply intelligence and status. Investigations reveal, however, that as a child he did not make the grade, and it was only with a lot of hard work at night school when he was in his twenties that he achieved the qualification. Still, Peter's reputation led one member of the media to say, 'Put it this way, I wouldn't have liked to buy a second-hand car from him.'

There are some players on the Tour who think Peter 'strange', partly because he has a habit of placing bets with German journalists against his daughter on big occasions such as Grand Slam finals, and partly because he has often been seen to join journalists on their bench to make odd comments and jokes. Two German journalists recall him once proudly remarking, 'Doesn't she have a great body, my daughter!' He would mix authority and familiarity, confusing people.

From the start Peter maintained that he was there to take the pressure off Steffi, and he certainly did do that. It was he who dealt with tournament officials, arranged practice courts and the scheduling of her matches and so forth, so that she could concentrate solely on her tennis. He also guarded her suspiciously, whispering instructions in her ear and throwing a protective arm around her if others got too close. In 1987, he was nicknamed the 'boo' man, because he quickly sent packing those who got too close.

There is no doubt that Steffi appreciated his dedication to duty

in those early days. She said in 1987, 'It's very important for me to have him at tournaments. We have a very close relationship.' What's more, 'He is the one who takes the pressure off me. People do not get angry with me, they get angry with him.' That is certainly true. At the Seoul Olympics in 1988 Peter was not supposed to arrive until the eve of the tennis programme, but Steffi called him on her arrival in Korea and asked him to get on the next flight to join her. 'I just wanted his presence,' she confided. 'I feel more secure when he is with me, and everything seems much easier.' And again in 1989, she admitted, 'I need my father there. I look up to his seat between every game for inspiration. Papa is so good for me. I feel my tennis improving as he watches.'

Theirs was one of the few father-daughter, coach-player relationships on the Tour that actually worked. Martina Navratilova, who had strong views on the subject, said at Wimbledon in 1990,

I definitely don't think parents should be involved with coaching, because for one thing they are not that good as coaches. OK, they think they're great players and they have read every book, but ... you just can't talk to them. Coaches can be very helpful. Hopefully, the father will stay in the background. Peter Graf was the exception to the rule, where it actually worked with the parent as the coach.

With Peter as coach the two certainly worked well together. Off-court, however, there are signs that Peter protected Steffi to an unnecessary degree. There was the time when at a press conference she told him in German to be quiet so that she could answer questions for herself. And there is a general feeling that the longer Steffi spent on the WTA Tour and the older she became, the more Peter should have loosened his control over her, allowing her room to develop her own personality. As it was, constantly under his protection and separated from others, Steffi remained shy and immature when she should have been growing up.

Even as recently as January 1995, when Steffi made a rare appearance on a German television show, it was apparent that she has still to mature. She is a young adult and yet she seems to have little public personality. Said German journalist Angela Gebhardt,

I haven't really seen her for two years, but it was like two days ago, because she has not changed. She's now twenty-five years old, and she has not changed. That's the terrible thing. She is still very shy and does not want to talk. It really is a strange thing, but it is no wonder.

The last comment was a reference to her father's protective nature.

Sometimes Peter's over-enthusiastic attempts to help his daughter were more obviously destructive than constructive. During the final of an event in Amelia Island, Florida in April 1986, Steffi was serving for the match at 5–4, 15–30 in the third set when she was penalised a point because tournament officials said they had seen Peter coaching her – illegally – from the sidelines for the second time in the match. Steffi subsequently lost the game and the set went to a tie-break which she was lucky to win. Her father of course denied that he had been signalling to Steffi, despite the fact that his hand movements had been caught on film by television cameras. However, he did admit that earlier in the match he had moved seats because he wanted Steffi to come in to the net more.

For an opponent that breach of the regulations was hard to swallow. Chris Evert commented at the time,

It's obvious that he coaches her. He has talked to her in German during matches and given hand signals. The rules say no coaching is allowed. So if you're playing by the rules, that kind of thing can be difficult to accept. It's just not fair.

Peter was unrepentant, saying,

I would go against one hundred people if it is good for Steffi. I am much more aggressive than she is. Sometimes I advise her to do something but she gets embarrassed and refuses – she wants to have good relations with the women on the Tour.

Peter apparently did not care what other people thought of his actions. Everything he did was in his book for the benefit of Steffi, and Steffi alone.

Furthermore, he had an explanation for the penalty point she

had suffered for his illegal coaching. 'There's a prejudice against European players, especially Germans. They don't want them to get to the top.' That was not quite true. Although the WTA did not express as much enthusiasm for Steffi's rise as they could have, it was not only because she was German. It may have had more to do with the fact that they found the controlling Peter rather difficult.

Peter had his own thoughts on what was fair and what was not. He accused the WTA of favouring Navratilova and Evert, and claimed that the Tour revolved around them. Perhaps it did, but then they had dominated women's tennis for over a decade before Steffi began to make her mark and were certainly due a little respect – and like other top players, a few extra privileges. Certainly when Steffi reached the No. 1 position in the rankings and the balance swung in her favour, Peter had no qualms about demanding whatever his daughter needed, be it a practice court to herself or a refusal to play night matches.

He has consistently complained on her behalf. At the International Management Group (IMG), according to John Feinstein's book *Hard Courts*, the agents established their own version of the ATP rankings – the Association of Tennis Parents. The more difficult the parent, the higher the ranking. In the late 1980s, Peter was as dominant at the top of these rankings as his daughter was at the top of the WTA rankings.

It was not only the agents at IMG who complained about Peter. Jurgen Kilsch, Claudia Kohde-Kilsch's step-father and coach, accused Peter of trying to control the DTB; other top players started to complain that Peter wanted not only to exert his control over Steffi but over all the other players as well.

That certainly seemed to be true in late 1988. The WTA announced at the US Open that it was considering a change to the way in which the computer was programmed to calculate world rankings. The Association thought points should be awarded in relation to the size of the prize money offered at tournaments, which would probably have meant that more points would have been available in North America, thus favouring the American players on the Tour. Peter was wholly unamused by this suggestion, and as usual was convinced that the move had been designed specifically to harm Steffi and in this particular case her position at

the top of the rankings. Perhaps it was. There were indications that the WTA did resent Steffi's success, and the animosity towards her was evident in the final of the US Open when a couple of WTA representatives were found in the press box rooting for Sabatini, Steffi's opponent.

Peter accused WTA officials of lying to him and threatened – aside from the fact that he would never speak to them again – that if they went ahead with the changes, *we* will not sign a commitment' for 1989, and that in 1990 he would consider setting up a rival tour to the WTA Tour, based in Europe, The then Executive Director of the WTA, Merrett Stierheim, rejected the accusation of lying, saying he had told Peter that the WTA board would not take any action with regard to the ranking system without first consulting the membership. That had occurred – Steffi had failed to turn up to the meeting – and the membership had agreed unanimously to go ahead with the changes.

Naturally the WTA felt severely pressured, because as their top ranked player Steffi was an important part of the Tour. A month later the rift between the WTA and the Graf family had been healed. The official announcement came through Ana Leaird, WTA Director of Public Relations, who said,

We have managed to find a compromise which the top class and lower ranked players have agreed is acceptable. The situation got out of control for a while during the US Open, but now everyone is satisfied. Steffi is very important to us. She is the world No. 1, the Grand Slam champion, and is going to figure prominently in the women's game for many years. It's important to us that all our players are happy.

Reading between the lines, and through the frank conclusion of Pam Shriver the then WTA vice-president, the WTA was 'intimidated' by Peter and seemingly agreed to his demands. They would not be the first to have been browbeaten by Papa Graf. Says one German journalist,

There are few people who are not afraid of him. You can count them on one hand. Even the ITF has started to do everything

that he wants. He controls everything. He says when she wants to play. No father, and no manager, has that kind of control.

It was strange, though, that Peter should get involved in a heated debate about the WTA ranking system when his daughter was at the US Open trying to win the concluding leg of her Grand Slam. Stranger still was the fact that Peter must have believed he had the popularity and influence to pull off such a feat.

Peter, then, was his usual bluff self when dealing with the WTA. Later, when Merrett Stierheim was succeeded by Gerry Smith as Executive Director of the WTA, Smith requested a meeting with Peter and Steffi to try and iron out any differences that there might have been between the German family and the WTA in the past. They finally sat down together eight months after Smith had first requested an audience.

If ever there is evidence that an inexperienced man has succumbed to the pressures of the big time, then it is through alcohol. Thrown into the limelight, it soon became obvious that Peter had difficulties dealing with the pressures that accompanied his daughter's huge success, and turned to the comfort of alcohol. Coming from a very ordinary background, Peter found it hard to deal with the new-found fame and fortune. Says one who has known the family longer than most,

> Down to his heart, Peter feels that he is not good enough, not cosmopolitan enough to deal with it all, but he is so money eager. He thinks that the more money you make, the better person you are, which is total nonsense, we all know that.

That Peter had a penchant for a drink was well known on the WTA Tour. Steffi was known to have taken glasses out of his hand. While Steffi was out on court, Peter was sometimes to be found propping up the bar. No one, however, dared broach the subject for fear of being subjected to one of Peter's outbursts.

By the French Open of 1989, however, Peter himself had come to terms with the fact that he had a problem. He was unwell, and flew in specially for the final in which Steffi played Arantxa Sanchez-Vicario. After Steffi lost, it is said that Peter was to be

found crying on the shoulder of the late Ted Tinling, sobbing, 'I've ruined my daughter's life, I've got a drinking problem.' Finally Peter had confessed what everybody had long suspected. His illness, after weeks of tests, was revealed to be a stomach ulcer.

Another year, another problem. In 1990 it became obvious that Peter was in trouble again. The writing was on the wall at the Australian Open in January 1990, but the story begins a couple of years earlier.

In the summer of 1988, when Steffi was recovering from a dog bite to her right hand, Peter, Steffi and Pavel Slozil went to Marbella for a few days' rest. During an evening visit to the Navy Club in Puerto Banus Peter was introduced by Klaus Hofsass to a young woman by the name of Nicole Meissner, a good-time girl who at the peak of her career had a set of revealing photos published in the German edition of *Playboy*. Peter is said to have quickly become infatuated and to have started to phone her from around the world.

Nicole joined Peter and Steffi in Monaco, where Steffi was playing in a four-woman exhibition event 'The Ladies Cup' in early 1989. Peter introduced Steffi to Nicole in one of Monaco's famous nightclubs, saying that they were all to be friends. The three of them partied together, and Steffi assumed that Nicole was simply 'a friend of a friend'. Nicole continued to travel with the Grafs, and at Wimbledon 1989 was formally introduced to some German journalists as Steffi's personal assistant.

There seemed to be no problem until the 1990 Australian Open, where Steffi was not playing to her usual high standards, and in her semi-final match against Helena Sukova dropped a set. In the final she appeared bored, lacking motivation, wan and upset, but still survived to beat Mary Joe Fernandez in straight sets. It is a measure of how well Steffi was playing at the time, however, that despite not being in peak form she still won the event. Admittedly several serious contenders who would normally have participated, such as Navratilova, Seles and Sanchez-Vicario, were not playing.

After the final Steffi said: 'Thank God ... it's over ... it's the first Grand Slam this year. It hasn't been the easiest two weeks for me. I didn't play my best but I did win it and that's the most important

thing to me ... it can only get better.' Unfortunately that wasn't to be.

On 9 January, Nicole Meissner had given birth prematurely to a daughter named Tara Tanita. Peter had warned his daughter that there might be a few black clouds ahead.

Still, from Australia Steffi travelled to Japan where she played and won an event in Tokyo the following week, and then headed back to Europe. Unfortunately, while filming a cameo role in a video for the German fashion designer Willi Bogner, Steffi fell while trying to escape the paparazzi and broke her thumb. Away from the game for a couple of months, it was during her two-month recovery period that she seriously considered laying down her racket for ever. 'For the longest time, all I wanted to do was to get away from everything and everyone, including tennis,' she was to say later.

But not being someone who throws in the towel easily, Steffi drew on the inner strength which had taken her to so many victories, and came back with a vengeance. As if to prove something to herself she won an event at Amelia Island in April, defeating Sanchez-Vicario, the last person to beat Steffi (at the French Open in 1989) convincingly 6–1, 6–0 in the final.

Meanwhile, at home in Germany, it soon became apparent that Nicole was trying to arrange an exclusive deal for her story with the German tabloid newspaper, *Bild*. The newspaper approached Peter with Nicole's claims. Soon after Nicole signed a legal document in which she stated that she had never had an intimate relationship with Peter and thus the baby could not possibly be his, despite the fact that his name was on the birth certificate, which is not legally binding proof of paternity in Germany anyway.

Peter presented this sworn affidavit to *Bild* and offered the newspaper money to keep the story under wraps. The story, however, had already made the rounds and a weekly gossip magazine called *Quick* had done its own investigations and printed the story in the week Steffi was playing in Berlin. Peter denied the allegations and said that he had been blackmailed, but there was evidence that Nicole and her partner Eberhard Thust had accepted DM800,000 (£275,000) from Peter. The question was whether this money had been extorted or not.

Thust had persuaded Nicole to go public because the baby would be entitled to a huge inheritance should the child prove to be Peter's daughter. Not only that, but Tara Tanita was a very sick baby, born with three kidneys and in need of major surgery, which Nicole felt should be paid for by Peter. Thust, a colourful character who was arrested as a teenager, described himself as a boxing promoter but found himself promoting Nicole instead. Nicole immediately became a household name in Germany, albeit a hated one for bringing the Graf family into disrepute.

Steffi was in Berlin when news of Peter's alleged affair hit the tabloid headlines. On the day she found out, a telephone call home to her parents failed to console her, and she was driven out of Berlin into the countryside so that she could be on her own. She realised that she had to rise above what was unfolding around her, and yet it was inevitably difficult to concentrate on the job in hand. Just knowing that the crowds seated around the tennis court had read or heard the stories about her father made her feel uneasy. As she said, 'Tennis is played with the mind and mine was on other things.' Peter himself admitted the damage it was doing to his daughter: 'I would understand if she said to me she wanted to pack in her career immediately, although it would be a great pity.' Steffi managed to block the problem from her mind and made it to the final, where she was rolled over by Seles 4–6, 3–6 and then proceeded to smash a hole in the locker room wall with her racket. She would say later, 'I never should have tried to play that final against Seles because really I was not even there.'

The story would continue to haunt her. Observers noticed, not surprisingly, a tension between father and daughter that had not existed before. Without doubt there were family arguments, and Steffi, showing support for her mother, spent time with Heidi in the chic shops of Paris, rather than on the practice court.

At the French Open final, Seles defeated Steffi 7–6, 6–4. Steffi had been 6–2 up in the first set tie-break, but Seles surged back to win the next six points and thus the set. Steffi had choked. She was clearly distracted. She was thinking about what was happening to her and her family off court, rather than what was happening to her on court. Steffi's air of invincibility had been destroyed. She admitted that she was not her 'old self' and that her confidence –

something that can take a long time to build up but can be shattered overnight – had deserted her. Steffi was blunt about who was to blame. 'In Paris and Berlin, I did not just lose against Monica Seles, I was defeated by an opponent who was not even on the court. I lost the two finals to the German press.'

Her 21st birthday, a very private affair celebrated at Mr Chow's in London, usually a high point in a person's life, turned into a very low one. Pavel Slozil said a few days after the French Open, 'Wimbledon is the next big test and we are worried. It could be hell for her. She is under a lot of pressure and needs some peace and quiet at present.'

At one point, she felt under so much pressure that she threatened to move to the United States and not play for Germany if the German newspapers continued to hound her family. Other than the fact that they thought it was a good story – and it was a good story, proved by the fact that *Bild*'s circulation soared to its highest since its establishment – there was another reason why the German journalists picked up on this tale with such glee. For them, it was a case of sweet revenge. Peter was not popular with the German press. He had made their lives difficult and often unpleasant in the past, and now they were going to make sure his life was hell. Their feeling was, 'Why should we help him? He never helped us.'

In the middle of June the Meissner story was still haunting Steffi as she headed for Wimbledon 1990. The terrible thing about this sex scandal was that it was not of her own making, but it was hitting her cruelly. So much so that at press conferences a 'health warning' was issued by the Wimbledon committee which read, 'The committee does not wish the lady champion to be upset and so, if at any time the questions put to her deviate from the subject of tennis, the conference will be ended immediately.' By the quarter-finals the health warning had been abandoned; Steffi was asked whether her tennis was being affected and she replied 'no'. Yet it obviously was.

Not only did Steffi have to contend with questions about her father's affair, she was also sick again, this time with sinus problems and was having difficulty in breathing. She flew to Germany at the weekend, which soon turned out to be a mistake, because she was distressed by the trip and the unpleasant tests that she had

to undergo; she returned in worse shape, with a middle ear infection. Nothing was going right for Steffi. She was miserable as she flew back from Germany, and to make matters worse most of the top women's players such as Navratilova, Seles and Sabatini were attending a fun party held by the WTA Tour's main sponsors that year at the Natural History Museum in London.

In the semi-finals, Steffi met American Zina Garrison. Steffi's performance lacked incisiveness, and when Garrison piled on the pressure Steffi failed to raise her game. It was an upset. The defending champion was out of Wimbledon and heading home where she checked into the Heidelberg University Clinic to have her sinuses operated on. Steffi wasn't happy to be in hospital, but she was happy to be away from the glare of publicity. Before surgery, a sinus specialist did a breathing test with a mirror and on one side no air came out. Said Steffi, 'He couldn't believe I was playing tennis at all.'

Tough as she undoubtedly was, the Meissner affair continued to plague Steffi throughout the rest of 1990 and into 1991, affecting her both as a daughter and as a tennis player. It was, to say the least, a very unhappy period. The emotional and mental strain generated by the revelations about Peter was compounded by her own intermittent health problems, thought to be psychosomatic given the circumstances.

In the autumn of 1990 the Graf family put on an outward display of solidarity when both Heidi and Peter accompanied Steffi to the US Open. And Steffi appeared to have recovered her form on court and was apparently able to concentrate her mind on her tennis – at least up to the final of the women's singles. There she lost in two sets to Sabatini and could only lament, 'Today I had nothing, not the serve or the forehand.' Somewhat uncharacteristically she had been defensive in play. Certainly Sabatini had dominated the match.

In spite of all the disruption to her family life Steffi continued to meet her commitments on the Tour, although she did withdraw from an event in Essen, citing a sinus problem. She played in tournaments abroad, for they at least gave her the chance to escape from the media pressures she was suffering in Germany. At the Brighton tournament in England late in 1990, Steffi was pleased to

be away from Germany while Peter was in court as proceedings in the Meissner case rumbled on. Nevertheless, she is said to have been in constant contact with her father during her absences, to keep his spirits up.

At Brighton, Steffi was to confess that 1990 was not a good year for her: 'It's been a tough year. I'm looking forward to the end of it. There have been many moments that I don't want to remember. Things I didn't want to go through but I had to. There are things that have changed me in quite a few ways.' She added, 'There were times when I was very depressed. There were times when I didn't expect to finish matches, particularly in Paris when I felt dizzy. It was the same at Wimbledon.'

Despite the problems of 1990, Steffi won over US$1 million in on-court earnings, plus US$250,000 from the Virginia Slims Bonus Pool. The American magazine *Forbes* declared her the highest paid female athlete in the world with a total income for 1990 of US$6.1 million, taking into account earnings, bonuses, income from endorsements and appearance fees. The French magazine *Esquire* was moved to name her as one of the 'women we love', while the ITF selected her as the women's world champion.

Steffi only lost five matches in 1990. Unfortunately two of them were in Grand Slam finals – the French and the US – so she ended the year with just one Grand Slam title, the Australian Open. Not bad by anyone's standards other than Steffi's.

Looking back on the year, she remarked,

It was a tough year and I wish I hadn't had it … There are many moments I don't want to remember at all. My concentration and usual feeling was not on the court, but tennis is still what I enjoy doing. There is still so much I am looking for. I am not missing any motivation at all. Last season was very, very long and tough for the mind and body.

There was to be no immediate improvement on either her professional or familial front when 1991 dawned. The black cloud of the paternity suit against Peter darkened. On court Steffi lost to Jana Novotna in the Australian Open and in her next tournament, which was in Tokyo, to Gabriela Sabatini.

Steffi's confidence in her game was seriously undermined by these defeats. Later, she recalled that she had again seriously contemplated quitting after the Tokyo loss, worried that her winning form would not return.

I thought seriously – really seriously – about giving up tennis after being defeated by Gabriela Sabatini in January. I simply felt that whatever I did in training wasn't working. And yet I was working so hard. I told myself I had to spend some time away from tennis. My nerve had gone. I had become weak.

Pavel told her to be patient, she was playing well in practice and her form would come on the court soon enough.

Steffi, however, retreated to the heavily fortressed family home in Bruehl, with its double gates of reinforced steel, a video camera and a surrounding wall which alone had cost as much as the price of a small house to ensure that she would be alone. She was not seen in public for two weeks, preferring to confine herself to her room where she listened to music and decorated her walls.

Eventually blood tests proved conclusively that Peter could not be the father of Nicole's daughter. After the good news Steffi ploughed determinedly on – but worse was to come. Sabatini beat her in the final of the Virginia Slims of Florida, on Steffi's home ground at Boca Raton. The next day she lost her No. 1 ranking to Seles. She had been the No. 1 ranked player since 17 August 1987, a reign of 186 consecutive weeks – far longer than any other man or woman. Only Jimmy Connors comes anywhere close, having been No. 1 for 159 weeks between July 1974 and August 1977.

There were to be ups and downs during the remainder of 1991. She lost her fourth consecutive match to Sabatini, at the WTA event in Amelia Island. Then she won two tournaments in Germany, defeating Seles in one final and Sanchez-Vicario in the other. The next defeat Steffi suffered was at the hands of the Spaniard in the semi-final stage of the French Open in Paris in May. Sanchez-Vicario won 6–0, 6–2.

This result came as something of a shock to observers, not least

because Steffi had swept through earlier rounds without the loss of a set but also because she had never lost a set to love in the nine years that she had been a professional. At the time, there was speculation – and it was purely speculation – that Steffi had smelt alcohol on her father's breath before the start of the match. When she met the press afterwards it was with a vacant stare and worry lines. Sadly she opined, 'I can't remember playing as badly as that. It is a long, long time since it happened and I hope that it's a long, long time until it happens again. I could hardly put the ball in the court.' When asked whether she had been aware that her father had been involved in a scuffle at court-side during her match, Steffi replied that she neither knew, nor cared.

Going into Wimbledon, Steffi had lost six of her 38 matches – more than in the whole of 1990 – but the graph of failure and success was about to take another sharp turn skywards. Steffi pulled herself together to reach the final which she won – but only because Sabatini lost it. It was the longest ladies' singles final for fifteen years and will be remembered for its nail-biting finish, through which Prince William bounced excitedly in the Royal Box. For once everyone seemed to be cheering for Steffi, willing her to win. Steffi's shriek of delight as she realised she had made her winning forehand said it all. And later she admitted, 'This success means so much to me. The tennis was not of the highest standard, but it was important for me to have a big win again. I knew that one day it would turn around.'

Peter as always had something controversial to say. Her victory he claimed had been 'luck', adding, 'Steffi did not play as well as in other finals.' Heidi, however, put the win rather aptly and graciously down to 'fight'. Steffi was just grateful for a win, as she knew people had been writing her off. She had had a point to prove and she had done so. For her it was like a new beginning. It was an emotional return to form for all concerned. Her coach Pavel Slozil, who had seen her through some very rough patches in the previous eighteen months, felt tears well in his eyes when the last point was played.

Steffi's sense of humour even returned, as she joked to compatriot Michael Stich who won the gentlemen's singles that year, 'It's a hard way to become a member of the All England Club, but it's

the best.' A reference to the fact that all winners of Wimbledon are made members of the Club.

Steffi regained the No. 1 ranking, albeit briefly, on two occasions – in August and September of that year. She achieved another landmark in October, when she notched up the 500th single's win of her career in Leipzig. In so doing she became the youngest, at the age of 22 years and three months, ever to do so.

Towards the end of 1991 Steffi's fortunes dipped once more. She lost to Navratilova at the semi-final stage of the US Open and to Novotna in the second round of the Virginia Slims Championships. Most other players would have been content to end the year with a record of 65 matches won to eight lost, but that was not up to the Steffi Graf standard. 'Disappointing,' was how she described the winning of Wimbledon and six other tournaments.

The two years to the end of 1991 had clearly been tough for Steffi. The Meissner case had dragged on for what must have been an interminable time. At one stage, she had – ironically – been subpoenaed by the defence to appear in court in Frankfurt to testify that her father had indeed known Nicole Meissner. This had hardly been a call that would improve her chances of settling her emotional turmoil. Then there had been the delays in carrying out the blood tests on Nicole Meissner's daughter, aimed at determining paternity. These delays were due to the baby's heart problems, which had to be dealt with by surgery and blood transfusions. Peter's blood test was consequently delayed until December 1991. Thus it was not until early 1992 that the judgement in the case was finally delivered in Frankfurt in Peter's favour. He was not the baby's father at wall.

The Meissner affair had taken its toll on Steffi, but it had not overwhelmed her. Peter for his part got off lightly too. He had admitted spending time with the model, but said it was a 'brief affair without much feeling'. It was thought, however, that Nicole was just the tip of the iceberg. As one German journalist asserted, 'He was flirting around all the time. He was always looking. In fact, we talked about women many, many times.'

Steffi did not seem to care. She just greatly appreciated all that her father had done for her during her career and was, despite some

of his known shortcomings, devoted to him. The Meissner affair tested her loyalty to Peter and it did not find her wanting; though that does not mean to say that it did not change her perspective of him. She remained steadfast in the face of all the media exposure, but at the same time she came to a somewhat more objective appraisal of her father. In her efforts to keep the family united, Steffi changed from protected prodigy to its principal defender. She had long been the family's bread winner; now she became its mainstay in other ways, through her strength of character and level-headed approach.

The Meissner affair also changed the relationship between Steffi and Peter. It was noticeable that subsequently Peter did not accompany her as much as he had on her travels. Instead he stayed at home to deal with the administrative side of her affairs, though when she was away they were constantly in touch by telephone.

While distancing herself somewhat from her father and becoming more independent, despite all the problems they have been through together Steffi has still been incredibly loyal to him. 'I just simply don't understand why he hasn't got the respect which should have been due him,' she says.

> Without this man, I would never have become No. 1. Through him I have got to know tennis. He took time to play with me early on and when I now look at the young female tennis players, I think it's amazing that my father made so few mistakes in training me. I think that's remarkable, that's why it's a shame that he doesn't receive the necessary recognition.

Even though Steffi is far more independent these days, her father is still very much in control. If anybody wants Steffi to do an interview, a photo shoot or a promotion, it is still to him that they must go to seek permission. It is a slow process, but Steffi is trying bit by bit to emerge from the shadow of her father.

Rather than for her father, Steffi's hostility over the whole Meissner affair was reserved for the media, 'I shall never understand how the media behaved. It cost me two years of my career. I lost my self-confidence and motivation. I wondered whether to quit. It was almost too much.'

Out of adversity however, Steffi developed new-found character. It was just unfortunate for her that a serious family problem and the associated press coverage which she found so distressing had coincided with the arrival of new and formidable opponents into the top echelon of the rankings – in the form of Monica Seles and Jennifer Capriati.

6

THE GOLDEN GRAND SLAM AND BEYOND

THE GRAF FAMILY spent Christmas 1987 back home in Bruehl and threw a small party to mark Steffi's rise earlier in the year to the top of the women's rankings. Little did Steffi know then, but by the end of 1988 the young tennis star would have good reason to celebrate on a rather more lavish scale. Still, there was a long way to go and a lot of hard work to be done before those festivities could get underway.

Steffi started the year as the No. 1 player in the world – for the first time rather than pursuing, she was going to be pursued. She skipped the traditional warm-up events for the Australian Open, played in Brisbane and Sydney and headed straight for Melbourne – home of the first Grand Slam event of the year – to practise. Steffi's preparation for the tournament was thorough. She chose to spend two weeks in Melbourne prior to the event, not only so that she could acclimatise to the heat that can sometimes reach temperatures of 40 degrees Centigrade on court at that time of year, but also to get the feel for the new Rebound Ace surface that was in use for the first time at the Australian Open.

Previously the Australian Open had been played on the grass courts of the private Kooyong Tennis Club. However, the event had outgrown the quaint clubhouse and its facilities. So in 1988 the tournament was moved to the newly built National Tennis Centre at Flinder's Park, a vast £30 million multi-purpose arena with a 15,000-seater Centre Court and adjoining complex intended primarily for tennis. Grass courts had been ruled out as not being hard-wearing enough, given that the facility was to be available for use all year round by the Australian public. Instead hard courts with a Rebound Ace surface were built.

There was another difference at the National Tennis Centre. The weather in Melbourne can be very unpredictable: in the morning it can be very hot, with beautiful clear blue skies, in the afternoon there can be heavy rain and temperatures 20 to 30 degrees lower. Even more interestingly, as happened during the Australian Open in 1995, play can be stopped on the outside courts by a rain storm while the Centre Court is drenched in sunshine. The Centre Court was built with a retractable roof that could be closed if and when necessary. Steffi, rather astutely with hindsight, but also showing the thoroughness that goes into her preparation for events, practised with the roof drawn shut.

Steffi's tournament preparation paid off. She marched through the first six rounds of the Grand Slam, defeating three seeded players – the Swede Catarina Lindquist, Hana Mandlikova (the Czech-born Australian) and her compatriot Claudia Kohde-Kilsch, with the loss of no more than five games in each round.

Having annihilated the rest of the field on her way to the final, Steffi walked out on to the Centre Court to face Chris Evert. Evert had played in her first Australian Open before Steffi had even reached the age of five, but the fifteen-year age gap certainly did not look as though it was going to affect the quality of the match. As the final got under way the spectators had every reason to believe they would witness a thrilling contest. Chris Evert was playing as brilliantly as she had in her semi-final match, when she had brushed aside the challenge of the second seed Martina Navratilova.

Although Steffi held serve to lead 2–1 in the first set, Evert was making her work extremely hard for every point. At that moment, down came the rain which it had been forecast would last some time. The retractable roof of the Centre Court was closed, but not before the court surface had been soaked. While the surface dried out, Steffi and Chris Evert retired to the players' lounge to watch the infamous Mike Tyson batter Larry Holmes into submission in a world heavyweight title fight beamed in live from Atlantic City.

When play finally resumed, Chris Evert started to miss everything. The parallels with the boxing contest were not lost on Evert, who later compared her own situation with that of Holmes. Completely disorientated by having suddenly to play the final of

an outdoor event indoors, she could not hit a winning ball. A string of double faults, balls flying long and netted shots resulted in her losing the next eight games and in Steffi leading 6–1, 4–0.

The main reason was the Graf forehand. Sensing Evert's vulnerability, Steffi had moved up a gear and was using her notoriously powerful forehand to great effect. When Steffi hit an ace to lead 6–1, 5–1, the crowd showed their embarrassment for the older player by fidgeting nervously in their seats, and could have been forgiven for thinking that the match was all but over.

However Evert, always a fighter herself and perhaps inspired by the attendance of former Australian champions Lew Hoad, Rod Laver, Margaret Court and Evonne Goolagong Cawley who had paraded in front of the crowd during the rain break, refused to give up and clawed her way back into the match. The American's service rhythm returned, and Steffi, perhaps sensing victory a little too early, made a number of unforced errors. Chris Evert won five games in a row, to leave Steffi serving to stay in the set at 5–6. At 30-all, Evert came within two points of taking the set, but Steffi made sure that that was as close as she got. Once the German held serve to force a tie-break the match was as good as over.

The tie-break was all Steffi. Having begun to look desperate during her opponent's incredible come-back, Steffi suddenly displayed the mettle of a champion and regained her fluency. A series of blazing forehands led her to take the tie-break 7–3.

Steffi was delighted with her win in Melbourne. 'It was the best start to the year I could have had. It's very important for the whole year.' When asked how much difference the closing of the roof had made to the outcome of the match, Steffi replied, 'It was the same for both of us. If it hadn't been for the roof, we would still be here watching Holmes fall down a couple more times.'

Chris Evert, who had spent the week before the Australian Open playing outdoors in an exhibition event in Queensland's Sanctuary Cove, obviously didn't see it that way. 'I simply didn't have the feel for an indoor court,' she said. 'The conditions were so different and, unlike Steffi who had regularly practised while the roof was closed in the two weeks before the tournament, I took a long time to adjust.'

The controversial closing of the roof had, however, led Steffi

and Evert to play their part in history – it was the first Grand Slam final to have been contested, at least partially, indoors.

After the Australian Open, Steffi took five weeks off before playing in a hard-court event in the American city of San Antonio, Texas. Once again, she bulldozed her way through the opposition, losing no more than five games in each match, except against the American Lori McNeil to whom she conceded nine games in the semi-finals.

A week later at the Virginia Slims of Florida, played that year in Boca Raton, Steffi was beaten in the finals. Her three-set loss, 2–6, 6–3, 6–1, to Gabriela Sabatini ended a 30-match winning streak that had begun on 21 September 1987 at the Citizen Cup in Hamburg. Following her defeat the critics were out in force, saying that Steffi had lost her confidence. Steffi saw it differently. 'I needed to lose, even though I didn't want to,' she maintained. 'Somehow I think the loss will help me. Winning was getting to be normal and that's not the way it should be.'

As if to prove a point Steffi came back strongly the following week at the Lipton International Players Championships and won through all seven rounds without the loss of a set. In the final Steffi was once again pitted against Chris Evert, who could make only a marginal improvement on the Australian Open final score-line and lost 4–6, 4–6.

Little did she know how wrong she could be, when after the match, Evert made this prediction: 'It's going to be an interesting year. I don't think it's going to be dominated by any one player. Martina is going to do well ... There will be some upsets. Pam Shriver, Gaby and I will do some damage.'

Chris Evert seemed to be on the right track three weeks later, when Gabriela Sabatini beat Steffi in three sets (6–3, 4–6, 7–5) in Amelia Island. However, Steffi came back strongly to win her next tournament, the German Open, played in Berlin in May.

At the French Open later that same month, Steffi seemed very intent on retaining her title and proving her dominance of women's tennis. Up to the semi-finals, Steffi lost just eleven games. Three of her opponents had managed to capture just one game each.

In the semi-finals Steffi was set to play Gabriela Sabatini, and

there were those who believed the German might finally have met her match, the Argentinian having won their previous two encounters. Steffi did not seem unduly concerned, claiming that she was playing on an entirely different level than earlier in the year. 'I'm taking more risks, playing more aggressively and making far fewer mistakes. Also, my attitude is very different in Grand Slam events,' she admitted. Steffi did have to fight harder than she had during the rest of the event – losing nine games in one match compared with eleven games in five previous matches – but she still won through in straight sets 6–3, 7–6.

The final was an entirely different game. Steffi was not prepared to give an inch. The fact that her opponent was the reigning junior world champion and had earlier in the tournament knocked out Martina Navratilova did not intimidate Steffi. She showed no mercy in wiping out the seventeen-year-old Natalia Zvereva 6–0, 6–0 in just 32 minutes.

It was the first time since 1974 when Chris Evert had achieved the feat, that a champion had won the French Open title without conceding a single set. Perhaps more impressively tennis fans would have to look as far back as 1911, when the British player Dorothea Lambert Chambers beat her fellow country woman Dora Boothby at Wimbledon, for the last time that a player had been whitewashed in a major women's championship final.

Steffi's win could be considered the shortest Grand Slam final. At the 1922 Wimbledon, the great Suzanne Lenglen of France swept aside the American Molla Mallory in just 26 minutes, but that was in the days when players did not rest in between games. If seven and a half minutes are subtracted for the time that was spent on change-overs during Steffi's match against Natalia Zvereva, the two players were on court for a mere 24½ minutes.

On accepting the trophy on the Centre Court of the Stade Roland Garros, Steffi felt only the need to apologise. 'I'm sorry it was so fast, but I wanted to play my best here,' she said. All a tearful Zvereva could utter was, 'I haven't lost this bad since I was very little. Steffi is the best.'

A year later Steffi was to admit what a terrible match it had been. 'No sparkle, no rallies, no atmosphere. Zvereva was scared,

tired and not physically strong enough. I didn't feel half the emotion that I had the year before when I won 8–6 in the third set.'

Steffi stayed up until three in the morning celebrating her win in the nightclubs of Paris, but finding someone to dance with was not easy – even if she was the French Open champion. As she complained later,

> I love to dance, but boys seem to back off. Maybe it's because they think I'm famous and that I'll say 'No'. I like men with the guts and courage to ask me for a dance. I was at a disco recently when a boy just stared at me for an hour without saying anything. In the end, I had to ask him for a dance! It's crazy. I like to have fun just like any other girl my age.

From Paris, Steffi headed off to England to start her practice for Wimbledon. She was half-way to completing the Grand Slam, but it was not something that she wanted to think about. Wimbledon, Steffi knew, would be the toughest leg of the Grand Slam, and the person she feared most was Navratilova. 'I'm not thinking about the Grand Slam,' she said before the Championships began. 'Martina is the favourite to win Wimbledon.'

The shortness of the period between the two Grand Slam events in the middle of the year – the French Open and Wimbledon – is always a matter for debate. There are just two weeks separating the two, and players have to make the adjustment from playing on the slow clay of Paris to the fast grass courts of Wimbledon. It is such a difficult adaptation to make that fewer than ten players have managed to win both in the same year.

Steffi had not fallen in love with Wimbledon at first sight. As she explains, 'The first few times I played on grass I found it just so frustrating. The ball didn't bounce, I had to keep playing against people who kept coming to the net and I found adjusting really tough.'

That had been 1983, however. This was 1988, and Steffi had since learnt to love Wimbledon, so much so that she now considered it her favourite tournament. There is no doubt that she was looking forward to the event. 'I love the buzz that Wimbledon produces,' she said. 'I always want to play my best tennis and the drive for success is at its highest level.'

As the oldest of the Grand Slam championships, Wimbledon is certainly considered the most prestigious. The Centre Court, which has been called the Cathedral of Tennis, is steeped in tradition having been built in 1922 and regally overlooked over by the famous Royal Box. 'Centre Court was made for excitement, drama, fun. It seems to create its own energy,' enthused Steffi.

To maximise her chances of winning, Steffi wanted her preparation for Wimbledon to be perfect and so she ignored the traditional women's warm-up events played in Birmingham and Eastbourne, choosing to practise instead. Knowing that Martina Navratilova was going to be her greatest threat at the championships, Steffi employed a left-handed player. For hours on end Markus Schur, a German Bundesliga player, served to the advantage court so that Steffi felt confident at the prospect of hitting backhand returns off Martina's swinging left-hand service. During the tournament itself she practised with the Australian left-hander Mark Woodforde.

As was becoming the norm, Steffi waltzed through the early rounds of the championships as nimbly as a champion dancer picks her way across a crowded dance floor. In the final, as expected she found herself up against the defending champion, Navratilova. Somewhat surprisingly, though, given that the American had won the last six Wimbledon finals and was still considered the better and far more experienced player on grass, Steffi also found herself a winner against Martina Navratilova. No doubt the experience and maturity that Steffi had gained in the year since the two had last played on grass was to help.

At first it looked as though Navratilova's attempt to secure a record ninth Wimbledon singles title would be successful. She took the first set and was a break ahead at 2–0 in the second before Steffi started to play amazing tennis, winning twelve of the next thirteen games. As John Barrett recalls, 'Steffi suddenly hit a stream of winners including several really key topspin backhands, which were just sensational. That was certainly a high point of her career, the games she played from a set and love–two down.'

Pavel Slozil would agree, and still felt a year later that such an incredible match would be hard to reproduce. 'It was the biggest win you can achieve in your whole tennis career,' he stressed.

'Against an eight-time winner who was leading by a set and two–love, on grass, and serving. Steffi came back with unbelievable tennis. You can't make better dreams come true.'

Her attention to detail in her preparation for Wimbledon had paid off, and Steffi won the Wimbledon title in three sets 5–7, 6–2, 6–1. It was one of those rare occasions on which she seemed to be overcome with emotion, and bustling with typical teenage excitement she found it virtually impossible to express her feelings. 'It is a very special feeling – I am very happy and very excited,' was all that she could manage to say delightedly. Even years later, when she had won many more great events, Steffi would remark, 'There have been too many titles to say one stands out, except maybe the first Wimbledon, which is the biggest thrill I got.'

Navratilova was forced to accept that she had been beaten by a better player. 'I played really well that first set and then she started serving better and returning better,' the American explained in her post-match press conference.

I didn't have as much on my serve as I would have liked. I hit some good volleys but she just kept running everything down. She is so fast and got to many balls that others wouldn't have done. She not only got there but she hit winners off them. I didn't succumb to any pressure. I succumbed to a better player. Steffi's No. 1 and has been for over a year. This is the end of a chapter.

Martina Navratilova was a more than gracious loser and presented Steffi with a silver tennis racket charm she had been given by the boxer Sugar Ray Leonard, and which she had worn when she had won at Wimbledon the previous year. And Navratilova had one thing to say about Steffi's chances of winning the Grand Slam: 'Should she win the US Open, I would be the first one to say "Great job". It would be an incredible achievement.'

Her opponent was not the only one to acknowledge Steffi's success. As the first German to win the ladies' championship at Wimbledon since Cilly Aussem in 1931, Steffi was the recipient of a congratulatory note from Helmut Kohl, the German Chancellor. 'You have come a giant step closer to a Grand Slam with your new

success,' he wrote. 'Along with other tennis fans, I fervently hope that you succeed in achieving this goal.'

Steffi's win, alongside that of Sweden's Stefan Edberg in the gentlemen's singles event, vindicated those who had predicted great things for the two youngsters four years earlier at the Los Angeles Olympics. It was also a pleasure for many to see two such mild-mannered players holding the championship trophies once more.

Steffi celebrated at The Hippodrome in London before returning home to Bruehl and a huge civic ceremony where she was presented with a horse. She also had a park named after her, next door to the primary school that she had attended as a child. The local mayor announced that a tree would be planted in the park to mark every tournament that she won. Even today it is barely wooded, so one can only speculate that Steffi carried on winning so many titles that the local authorities decided to give up and retain their park, rather than create a forest. For Steffi, the high point of her victory celebrations was a meeting with a pre-World War II German heavyweight boxer, Max Schmeling, her own sporting hero.

Everyone now thought that Steffi would win the Grand Slam. In fact it was considered a *fait accompli* by the other women on the Tour, who joked that Steffi would only lose the US Open if she had an accident and happened to break a limb – which of course she almost did. Back home in Bruehl Steffi stepped in to break up a fight between one of her beloved dogs, Max, and a neighbour's dog. As she did so Max bit her right hand so hard that Steffi had to have it put in a cast. Luckily it was not a serious injury, and her hand recovered before the US Open began.

As far as the great Australian Margaret Court, the last tennis player of either sex to win a Grand Slam, was concerned, the only thing stopping Steffi achieving a clean sweep of the big four was Steffi herself. Court revealed,

More than anything, winning the Grand Slam is a battle within yourself. It really gets down to how you handle pressure more than how you handle anybody else. Steffi has to forget about the press and the television and not read and listen to what people

say about her. You don't want to let the pressure build within yourself.

In New York, Steffi had a straightforward run through the first five rounds without the loss of a set, and an even easier passage through her semi-final from which Chris Evert was forced to withdraw with stomach flu. In the other half of the draw, second-seeded Martina Navratilova, whom Steffi had expected to be her main obstacle, was knocked out in the quarter-finals by fellow American Zina Garrison. She was subsequently beaten by Gabriela Sabatini in the semi-finals.

In the finals, therefore, Steffi was up against Sabatini, who had already scored two wins over Steffi earlier in the year. It was not a great match by any means, and Steffi made more forehand errors than winners, but she paced herself better than Sabatini and eventually pulled through in three sets, 6–3, 3–6, 6–1. In victory, Peter Graf was critical. 'I cannot understand why Steffi didn't stick to the match plan. She was supposed to attack her forehand. Instead, she hits it all the time to her backhand and that's Gabriela's best shot.' Steffi would admit the following year that she had played a game of Russian roulette during the match. She certainly knew the game plan, and she knew that she was supposed to be playing to Sabatini's forehand, but she did not want to win easily and so she put herself to the test by playing to the Argentinian's strength. And still she won.

It was all over: Steffi had won the Grand Slam. She had pulled off a remarkable feat, but there was no visible show of emotion, no racket flung into the air, no ball hit into the crowd, no net hurdled to embrace her opponent. Rather than feeling a sense of elation, Steffi simply felt the weight of expectation ebb away. 'It's a relief,' she explained. 'Now I've done it. There's no more pressure. Now there's nothing else that people can tell me I have to do.'

The flags of Australia, France, Great Britain and the United States – the countries in which the four Grand Slam events are played – were raised in the National Tennis Center that day. The United States Tennis Association President, Gordon Jorgensen, presented Steffi with a gold bracelet encrusted with four diamonds – one for

each of the four Grand Slam events – as well as the trophy for winning the US Open.

Steffi was only the fifth person in history to achieve the Grand Slam. The American Don Budge had been the first, in 1938, followed by Maureen Connolly in 1953, the Australian Rod Laver (twice) in 1962 and 1969 and Margaret Court in 1970. Of all the Grand Slam winners Steffi was immediately compared with Connolly, for they were both intensely concentrated and almost machine-like on court. Both young women bobbed up and down on their toes during rallies and were extremely fast around the court, and both were precocious young players – Steffi was just nineteen when she completed her Grand Slam, while Connolly had not even turned nineteen when she won hers.

Steffi's Grand Slam was different and more difficult to achieve than for anyone else in the past. All the other Grand Slam winners had played three events on grass and only one, the French Open, on clay. Steffi had won her Grand Slam playing on three different surfaces – hard courts at the Australian and US Opens, clay at the French Open and grass at Wimbledon. And even then the surface of the hard courts was of different composition – asphalt at the US Open and rubberized Rebound Ace at the Australian Open. She had also beaten four different opponents, with very different styles of play.

In October 1994, the No. 1 men's player American Pete Sampras, considered by many to be the only male player then capable of winning the four major tournaments in a calendar year, acknowledged that it is the variety of surfaces on which the Grand Slam events are now played that makes a clean sweep nigh on impossible. The different surfaces present distinct demands.

The Rebound Ace surface can become sticky if it is very hot – Gabriela Sabatini and Mark Woodforde both retired with ankle injuries when the surface impaired their movement during the 1990 Australian Open. (The same year Ivan Lendl started a new fashion by adopting a white Foreign Legion-style hat, and John McEnroe ended up looking like a tribal warrior thanks to the zinc sun-block that covered his nose and lips.) The Open in Paris can be a real endurance test due to the slow red clay of Roland Garros. Then there is the difficult transition in a short space of time to the

fast grass courts of Wimbledon, when players are often tired from the long matches they have usually had to play in Paris. Finally, there is the US Open where players have to overcome not only opponents but also the distraction of jets thundering overhead in their approach to and take-off from La Guardia Airport.

It was all a lot easier when the first Grand Slam was achieved by Budge over 40 years ago. Aside from the matter of surfaces, the Grand Slam was not officially recognised then as it is today, which meant that the players did not have to deal with the great pressure exerted by the media and fans to achieve it.

The title Grand Slam is thought to have been inadvertently coined by the journalist John Kieran of *The Times*. Kieran was reporting in 1933 on the possibility of the popular 25-year-old Australian player Jack Crawford, who had already won the Australian, French and Wimbledon titles that year, also capturing the US Open. In his report, Kieran – a keen bridge player – noted that 'If Crawford wins, that would be something like scoring a grand slam on the courts, doubled and vulnerable.' In the event Crawford lost the final of the US Open to an Englishman, Fred Perry. It was, however, an epic match, Perry winning 6–3, 11–13, 4–6, 6–0, 6–1.

It would be another five years before Don Budge would score the first Grand Slam. When he did, Allison Danzig, a journalist at *The New York Times*, recalled the article written by Kieran that had spawned the title Grand Slam, written in those days in lower case. The occasion was only marked by passing interest at the time, but somehow the title stuck and has survived the passage of time.

In the modern era the Grand Slam is big news, and Steffi collected US$877,724 for her efforts in the four tournaments. Margaret Court eighteen years earlier had made just US$70,000 from her Grand Slam success. Still, Steffi had little time to dwell on her amazing achievement. Just three hours after her US Open victory she was on a plane home to Germany, where she spent two days in Bruehl before flying to South Korea to compete in the Olympic Games. Steffi, tired from all the pressure she had been under in recent months, really only had one wish as she set off on her journey to the other side of the world – to escape to a desert island so that she could be alone and relax. Instead she arrived in

Seoul at Kimpo International Airport and was immediately mobbed by photographers and journalists. It was more than Steffi could bear – she burst into tears.

Once ensconced in the Olympic Village, Steffi took some time to settle down, but when she did she was revitalised by the atmosphere of camaraderie among the competitors. 'Tennis is a lonely sport. Usually it's just you, your coach and perhaps your parents,' she explained. 'But at the Olympics, staying with the German team and eating alongside competitors from other sports, you had a feeling of being all together and supporting one another.'

There were even reports that Steffi had finally found herself a boyfriend, in the form of Arnold Vanderlijde, a Dutch boxer whom she had met in the cereal queue at breakfast. While admitting that she had found him good-looking, Steffi soon scotched the rumours. 'If I speak to a boy for more than five seconds his name and mine are spread across the papers and there is talk of a romance. So far none of it is true.'

Invigorated, Steffi proved to be invincible. She won through four rounds before facing Gabriela Sabatini in the final. Once again, she won. Steffi had clinched a gold medal for Germany, and had in the process become the first tennis player ever to win what her managers would dub a 'Golden Grand Slam'.

As her national anthem was played Steffi watched the familiar red, black and golden shades of the German flag rise slowly to the top of the central flag pole, and with a quick flick of her finger she wiped away a tear of joy. 'I came here really tired, not expecting too much from myself,' she admitted later. 'I was very down somehow, so I'm just amazed that I've done it now. Winning the Grand Slam and then the gold medal – that's amazing. I think it is something not many people after me will achieve.'

A Golden Grand Slam was certainly not a feat that could have been achieved by any players previously but the French. This was because until 1925 the French Open had been closed to all but French nationals, so only they could play in all four major championships plus the Olympics, which included tennis only up until 1924. That is until 1988, when in the 75th anniversary year of the International Tennis Federation (ITF), the game had made its come-back as a full Olympic sport.

Having won her gold medal, Steffi returned to Mannheim, alongside three other Olympic medallists from the region of Baden-Wurttemberg. Thousands of well-wishers gathered to honour their achievements, and their open-top cavalcade took more than two hours to travel just one-and-a-half kilometres through the city.

Steffi played just two more events in 1988. She won the Brighton event in England in October, despite (according to one journalist) the fact that she was not playing at her best. 'She (Steffi) was undoubtedly rusty at Brighton as she lost twelve games in three matches to reach the semi-final,' read his report. The following month she played the end of season Championships in New York and lost for only the third time in the year, to Pam Shriver in the semi-finals.

By the end of 1988 Steffi's success on court meant she had won well in excess of US$1.2 million in prize money. 'It might sound unusual,' she said, 'but I just don't think about the money. The Grand Slam was an objective and I felt fabulous when I finally did it. The Olympic gold was fantastic, too. What is left? Just winning, as usual.'

Steffi's dominance of women's professional tennis was undisputed. It left her with one problem. She had achieved a Golden Grand Slam in 1988 – what could she possibly aspire to in 1989 that would better that feat? Steffi decided that she wanted to reach the end of the year undefeated.

Steffi started 1989 well. She swept through the seven rounds of the Australian Open in Melbourne losing just 24 games, a third of which were won by the Czech Helena Sukova in the final. Not even Sabatini, who had inflicted two of Steffi's three defeats in 1988, had a hope when the two met in the semi-finals. Ted Tinling was watching the match and described it thus: 'It was awesome. I don't believe any woman could have countered the shots that Steffi played, and she had so much in reserve.' Steffi in no uncertain terms had demolished Gabriela Sabatini, 6–3, 6–0, and admitted, 'It was the perfect match.' A rare moment of self-indulgence for a woman known for her highly self-critical approach.

Helena Sukova, ranked No. 8 in the world at the time, had

played extremely well to reach her third Grand Slam final. Against Steffi, however, who was playing with a slight knee injury, Sukova stood next to no chance and Steffi won her sixth Grand Slam title 6–4, 6–4. After her Australian Open victory Pavel Slozil would admit,

> No one else in women's tennis has a heart for the game like Steffi. With her it's work, work, work, run, run, run, work, work, work. Even though she's won another major, she won't want to rest or take a day off. She still loves the game and the practice.

It was at the Australian Open that Steffi was first spotted enjoying quiet evenings *à deux* with the good-looking German Alexander Mronz, despite their attempts at hide-and-seek in order to keep their meetings secret. Steffi had first met Sacha as she affectionately called him four years earlier, but it was not until early 1989 that they became romantically linked.

Peter, far from trying to kill the passion before it had begun (as could have been expected given his desire to control Steffi) seemed to encourage the relationship. Alexander had in his favour the fact that he was also a tennis professional, and so he was well aware of the time that Steffi needed to dedicate to her career.

As Peter himself said,

> This is good for Steffi, good for all of us. It is time for the break. We knew it would be hard on the first boyfriend, but I think Steffi can make good judgements. Alexander is a tennis player. He knows tennis comes No. 1 with Steffi. I think this is a good arrangement. At the end of the day, if she says to him, 'It is nine o'clock now, I have to go to bed,' he says 'Goodnight' and lets her go. I think everything is okay.

Following the Australian Open, Steffi won the next four events she played – in Virginia, Texas, Florida and South Carolina – with the loss of just one set, to Chris Evert in the final of the Virginia Slims of Florida. In the Virginia Slims of Washington, Steffi had scored a double bagel (as a 6–0, 6–0 win is sometimes described) against the former teenage prodigy, Carling Bassett-Seguso. A defeat that

led the Canadian to say, 'Steffi would do very well (in men's events). You can't compare her to one of us because we don't hit the ball nearly as hard. Some of the things she does don't seem human. She is an incredible athlete.'

In April Steffi's goal for the year was shattered by Gabriela Sabatini, who just managed to get revenge for her thrashing at the Australian Open by beating Steffi 3–6, 6–3, 7–5 in the final of the event played at Amelia Island in Florida. Steffi, however, did not seem unduly perturbed and dismissed the defeat, saying 'Losing will definitely help me. It means I'll work harder.'

Steffi certainly swept through her next two events, one in Hamburg the other in Berlin, without the loss of a set in either. Next stop was the French Open, in which both Steffi and Alexander were to play. Since the Australian Open, although both had been busy pursuing their own careers – Alexander, perhaps inspired by their friendship, had won his first professional tournament, the Martinique Challenger, in April – they had certainly not lost touch. Steffi had confirmed that love was very much in the air in April when she admitted, 'Alexander is very, very attractive. We're on the same wavelength. We belong together.'

Although together, Steffi and Alexander stayed in different hotels in Paris. While she was happily ensconced in a top-flight suite he was staying in rather more modest accommodation. For although both play tennis for a living, the difference in their form was blatantly obvious from their earnings the previous year. In 1988 Steffi had earned in excess of US$1 million, while Alexander had taken home less than US$25,000.

Alexander inevitably lost in the first round, but the press were not prepared to let him slip back into the obscurity of the lower end of the men's rankings from where he had come. A post-match press conference was requested, and Alexander was subsequently grilled by the press. To set the record straight, he categorically stated, 'I don't want Steffi's money. I make my own money. What I need is a coach, but I can't afford one.' When asked he also volunteered his view of the women's Tour:

It's a cheek what most of them offer, they are untrained little dumplings who play ping pong. With the exception of a few, the

big money the women make is a scandal. Every man has to fight one hundred per cent in the first round and some girls don't even sweat and they make millions.

Presumably when he mentioned the exceptions, he was including Steffi.

He was right though. Up until the semi-finals, life was a breeze for Steffi. She lost no more than four games in any round and openly agreed with Alexander's views. When asked if she would go and see herself play, she replied, 'I suppose I might go and see her just because everybody seems to be talking about her,' but added that she did not think the women's game was interesting enough for her to pay more than three or four visits.

With hindsight perhaps Steffi wouldn't agree. In the semi-finals for the first time Steffi encountered the might of a young Yugoslav, Monica Seles, whose name had been sending tremors of fear through the WTA Tour long before she had turned professional earlier in the year. Their match was a tremendous struggle, but Steffi's experience eventually pulled her through in three sets 6–3, 3–6, 6–3.

In the final Steffi met Arantxa Sanchez-Vicario, another fast improving youngster from Spain, but there was no reason for Steffi to believe that this would be anything more than a routine match. In three previous meetings, Sanchez-Vicario had managed to win a total of just thirteen games from Steffi.

But Sanchez-Vicario had been doing her homework – she had watched Monica Seles come close to beating Steffi in the previous round, picked up a few useful tips and decided that this time around she was going to win. The teenagers were evenly matched and split the first two sets. In the third Steffi served for the match at 5–3, and the spectators expected her to walk away with the sixth Grand Slam title in a row – but the Spaniard refused to crack. Sanchez-Vicario was in her first Grand Slam final and she was not going to be walked over. In the end it was Steffi who lost her nerve, and the bubbly young girl from Barcelona took the next four games to become the 7–6, 3–6, 7–5 winner of the French Open final.

To give Steffi her due, she had not been feeling well during the

last few days of the tournament. Food poisoning earlier in the week had caused her to lose some seven pounds, she said. On the day of the final itself, when asked by the press why she had felt it necessary to leave the court when she was 5–6 down in the final set, Steffi admitted that she had her period. As if all that was not enough to contend with, Steffi's father had been ill for some time – he had flown in from Germany for the final but left before the last ball was struck – and she was worried about him.

None of that should take anything away from the performance of Arantxa Sanchez-Vicario, who was a deserving winner. Steffi had points to win the first set and had led 5–3 in the third, and still failed to clinch the match. Arantxa had waited long – the match lasted just two minutes shy of three hours – and patiently for her own chances and made the most of them when they were proffered.

Steffi was horribly upset and not even Alexander could comfort her. He had travelled home after his early exit, but had arrived in Paris very early on the morning of the final to support Steffi's bid for the title. When she lost she did not even want to see him. She retired to her room alone, and Alexander was left to spend the evening with Steffi's brother Michael and his girlfriend. There would be no dancing in the discos of Paris until the small hours as there had been in 1988. On the contrary, Steffi went into solitary confinement for three days and wept. The loss, however, focused her – Steffi would not lose another match all year – and it did convince her how much she wanted to win Wimbledon again.

Steffi once again missed the pre-Wimbledon grass court tournaments and settled for a course of private practice at the All England Club. Following the pattern of 1988, her practice partner was Markus Schur. During the tournament itself the young Czech player David Rikl, another left-hander, took over that role, constantly serving swinging deliveries to Steffi.

Unfortunately Alexander could not be by Steffi's side to support her in her quest for another Wimbledon title, because he was in a German hospital bed suffering from torn leg ligaments. However, that did not stop the German press speculating about the relationship between the two tennis players. The tabloid *Bild* ran a story

with the headline: 'Steffi: Will an Engagement Come Within the Year?' Steffi had her own humorous response to that question, 'Haven't you heard? It's all set. I've already picked out a wedding dress.' Perhaps it was that remark which led the newspaper to pursue the story. As Steffi said later,

> Over a ten-day period, the press pushed me from friendship to engagement to getting married to having a baby on the way. Then there was the first crisis of the couple. All in ten days. I said to myself, all that's left is divorce, and I was expecting that too.

While *Bild* was first building up and then demolishing her relationship with Alexander, Steffi was concentrating on destroying her half of the draw at Wimbledon. The line-up of players she defeated on her way to the final was phenomenal. Two young pretenders to her crown, Monica Seles and her French Open victor Arantxa Sanchez-Vicario, were dismissed in straight sets. In the semi-final Steffi played the grand dame of tennis, Chris Evert, who was playing in her last Wimbledon. A sentimental match it might have been, but Steffi showed no mercy and ended Evert's remarkable Wimbledon career with a 6–2, 6–1 thrashing.

Steffi's astute pre-tournament preparation again paid dividends, as almost inevitably she met Martina Navratilova in what turned out to be a fascinating final between the greatest exponents of the baseline and of the serve and volley games respectively then playing.

In the end the younger generation won through, but not before Navratilova had made a strong challenge for that elusive ninth title. It was an ace, hammered down the middle of the court, that not surprisingly gave Steffi her three-set 6–2, 6–7, 6–1 win and her second Wimbledon title. 'She served unbelievably well. Basically,' said Navratilova after the match, 'I got served off the court.'

In an unusual display of emotion, Steffi burst into tears of joy as soon as she had won.

> There was something in my heart that really wanted it so badly and I worked quite a lot for it, especially the last three or four

weeks. There was so much inside of me that I wanted to win and that's why I was giving it everything.

Perhaps it was the ultimatum she had given herself – that if she lost she would cancel a family vacation – that had inspired her to victory.

Steffi was not the only German to win that year, or rather that day, for due to rain both Wimbledon singles' finals were played on the same day for the first time since 1973. Steffi's old friend from the training centre in Leimen, Boris Becker, gave the day a fairy-tale ending by beating Stefan Edberg 6–0, 7–6, 6–4, thus gaining revenge for a four-set defeat inflicted by the Swede in the final the previous year.

After her Wimbledon triumph Steffi took a short break in Spain before continuing her 1989 season. In August, she played two tournaments in the United States before travelling to New York to prepare for the US Open, where she proved to be unbeatable.

In the fourth round, Steffi's psychological stranglehold on the women's Tour was spelt out by the seasoned South African campaigner Ros Fairbank-Nideffer, who lost to the world's No. 1 in the fourth round. 'I didn't believe I could win and Steffi knew I couldn't beat her,' she admitted.

In the quarter- and semi-finals, Steffi played Helena Sukova and Gabriela Sabatini respectively. The Argentinian looked at one point as though she might cause an upset, taking the second set, but in the third Steffi stepped up a gear to win a place in the final against – yet again – Martina Navratilova. Played in temperatures in excess of 40 degrees Centigrade, the match was always going to be an endurance test, and when it went to three sets Steffi could only win as she did, 3–6, 7–5, 6–1.

Just as Steffi was producing some of her best tennis so too was Boris Becker, who bludgeoned his way to the men's singles title and, together with Steffi, into the history books. Never before had two Germans won the world's two oldest championships – Wimbledon and the US Open – in the same year and not since the Americans Bobby Riggs and Alice Marble in 1939 had a pair of compatriots achieved the feat.

In October, Steffi was busy representing Germany in the

Federation Cup and playing in two events, one in Zurich the other in Brighton, both of which she won without any real challenge.

By the end of the year, Steffi's relationship with Alexander was over. Peter was accused of initiating the split, because he had gone on record as saying that Alexander should sort out his career and realise his full potential before he considered a life with Steffi. However, it seems likely that a combination of paternal pressure, media intrusion and the youngsters' commitments to their careers – which meant they spent long periods apart – had resulted in the separation. The two were to remain good friends.

He might have lost Steffi, but Alexander seemed to have gained something from the practice sessions they put in together on the tennis court – his ranking rose more than one hundred places in the time that they were reported to have been going out together.

In 1989, it seemed Steffi's opponents were not so worried about how many games they could take off her but how long they could last on court. Often it was not much longer than 30 minutes, as Steffi during the year succeeded in winning seven matches without the loss of a single game. As she pointed out herself, 'Some of my matches don't last as long as it takes me to sign autographs at the end of a match, or give interviews.'

On the other side of the net, Steffi was just worried about staying awake long enough to win. At the Brighton event she played South African Elna Reinach in the quarter-finals, and waltzed through the match 6–3, 6–1. She admitted later that she had got so bored during the match, 'I was telling myself the only thing I didn't do was to fall asleep.' In the previous round Steffi had played Claudia Kohde-Kilsch and beaten her 6–0, 6–3, but chided herself because, 'When I play against people who are really not so good, I have trouble concentrating.' What would it take to beat Steffi, Kohde-Kilsch was asked? Her reply, 'Hit every serve at 200 miles per hour and then wait.'

Steffi completed the year as she had begun it, by winning a major event – the end of season championships in New York in November. There she beat Martina Navratilova in four sets, 6–4, 7–5, 2–6, 6–2, in a best of five sets final watched by an ecstatic crowd of almost 17,000 people.

Steffi's win/loss record for the year was 86–2 and she was

named as the No. 1 player and No. 1 money earner for the third year running by the WTA. She was also selected as the Professional Athlete of the Year by the Women's Sports Foundation.

Somewhat surprisingly, given Steffi's huge achievement in 1988, there were those, including Pavel Slozil, who believed that Steffi actually performed better in 1989. Said Slozil, 'In my opinion, in 1988 she made sporting history, but in 1989, she played her best tennis ever ...' Certainly the statistics support that conviction, for her 86–2 win/loss record gave her a 97.7 per cent success rate, compared with a 96.1 per cent rate in 1988 when she had won 72 matches and lost three. Steffi also won fourteen titles in 1989, compared with eleven in 1988.

As Steffi had held the top spot throughout 1988 and 1989 it was perhaps not surprising therefore when in 1990 tennis writer Richard Evans named her as his choice for the Woman Player of the 1980s. He cited the 'power, style and grace' with which she won her Grand Slam in 1988 as the reason why she had won over the remarkably consistent Martina Navratilova. Evans also credited Steffi with bringing a new dimension to the women's game, both as an athlete and as a champion, and for producing the forehand that was probably the most feared shot in the history of women's tennis.

In a matter of a few short years, Steffi had entered the superstar league of the sports world.

7

OFF COURT

WHILE STEFFI WAS MAKING a name for herself on court, the reputation she was building for herself off it was not quite as complimentary. It was not all of her own making, and it had not always been that way.

When Steffi had been playing junior events and satellites she had travelled frequently with her mother. There are no doubts that those were happy days and ones that Steffi has recalled with nostalgia. One German player, a contemporary of Steffi's, remembers those early times together at tournaments, 'Her mother and her brother are very friendly and nice, and they always wanted to play games, so we all had a lot of fun together, playing cards, things like that.'

All that became a thing of the past as soon as Steffi started winning and qualifying for events on the main WTA Tour. Suddenly she became far more reserved and shied away from contact with other players. Steffi herself noticed the change and was to suggest later that it was due to the fact that she had joined the top ranks, where rivalries are far greater and more intense than at the satellite level. But it was no coincidence that Steffi was then travelling with her father. Instead of hanging out with the other girls Steffi would, with her father, return to their hotel at the earliest opportunity, presumably so that she could focus on her next match.

It was under Peter's rather stricter tutelage that Steffi started her rapid progression up the women's computer rankings, and at the beginning of 1985 was poised to break into the top ten. In a very short time Steffi had made a quantum leap from satellites to the main Tour, and in the process had left behind her friends, who were still struggling through the lower echelons of the tennis

system. Peter's presence had done wonders for Steffi's tennis, but it had killed her social life. Talking of earlier friends, Steffi admitted later, 'It's been difficult to keep in touch. They've gone their ways and I've gone mine. I've found new friends, but I sometimes regret losing old ones. Those days were a lot of fun.'

That Peter kept his daughter away from the other players is not in question, but it was never likely that the top players were going to be anything more than courteous to Steffi. In 1985, the top ten women were on average eight years older than her. Peter felt that as they were older and had more experience of the Tour, in any off-court contact they should take the initiative. Even so, Navratilova said in 1987, 'I'm not sure her father would let Steffi get close to another player.'

Then again, how many 23-year-olds would go out of their way to make friends with a fifteen-year-old kid? And not just any fifteen-year-old, but one with a ferocious forehand who was threatening the established ranks at the top of women's tennis? Very few, if any. And if they did, Steffi, still a shy teenager, would probably have lacked the confidence to respond. 'I like to laugh but when I'm first around people, I'm more shy. I don't really like to talk too much, so I find it difficult to start a conversation,' she said at the time.

By contrast, Peter would have put a stop to any friendly distraction, for he seems to have taken to heart the advice given to him by Ted Tinling, who said, 'Steffi can have no friends in tennis. You have to understand a star has to be lonely.'

If the young Steffi found herself in the position of an outsider, she was definitely not the first. Chris Evert and Tracy Austin, both in their mid-teens when they joined the Tour, felt just as left out when they made their professional debuts. It probably did not help Steffi's cause that she was a young German who, like most of her young compatriots, was by nature rather less garrulous than their American counterparts, who constituted the largest single group on the Tour.

Yet by talking to the press about her fellow players Steffi did nothing to help her cause. While still on her way to the top, she was reported to have said of Evert, 'She's sneaky, always intriguing. You just don't know where you are with her.' And Steffi seemed none too fond of Hana Mandlikova either, whom she

described as 'too moody'. When later she reached the No. 1 spot, Steffi said she had noticed a gulf forming between her and the other players. 'Every once in a while I ask myself why they're not talking to me. I'm the same as I've always been. Often they seem shy and I have to make the first move.' No doubt some of the other players would laugh at the last statement. Steffi is notorious for walking into the locker room and either not saying a word to anyone or saying 'hello' so quietly that it's barely audible. As soon as she has played her match, she is quick to leave the tournament site – even quicker if she has lost.

A couple of years ago, however, Steffi conceded that the situation had improved, but said,

> Sitting around in players' lounges is not my life, although the atmosphere has become much friendlier over the last two years. There's not such a big age gap as there was with Chris, Martina and Pam. Everyone is a bit more open now, although I don't mix with other players. They can be very single-minded, and I want to hear about different things.

It seems ironic that Steffi should now consider the other players single-minded, for it was surely her own preoccupation with becoming the best that initially annoyed her opponents and distanced her from them. First there was admiration for the way that she set about achieving her aim to be No. 1, then the envy crept in. Finally there was irritation, brought on by her apparent refusal to be one of the crowd, which led to the complaints: Steffi refuses to play evening matches, Steffi always gets her own practice court ... Steffi remained above it all and that just vexed her opponents even more.

Winning tennis matches has a lot to do with mental strength. Like most stars Steffi can be aloof and arrogant, and she cultivates that image whenever she is on or near a tennis court. Exuding the impression that she is far superior to everyone else immediately gives Steffi a mental edge over her opponents. Is it any wonder that she has few friends on the Tour?

Steffi is not alone in this regard, though. As she acknowledges, 'The rivalry among women tennis players is overwhelming – they

respect each other, rather than forming friendships.' That is due in part to the fact that unlike the male professionals, who often get to know each other on the practice courts, the women do not hit together, playing instead with their coaches or practice partners. Steffi never practised with Sabatini, not even when they played doubles together in their early days on the Tour.

The women, particularly in more recent years, tend to stick with their entourages which helps them fight loneliness on the road as well as providing the latest training regime. These entourages vary greatly in size, usually depending on the player's ranking and thus how many people they can afford to keep in tow. An 'entourage' may just be a boyfriend-cum-coach or it might be a small army. Team Navratilova was probably the best known of the latter and could include at any given time a nutritionist, a cook, a conditioning coach, a strategy coach, close friends and a coterie of animals, which included five dogs and a cat at the French Open 1987. One journalist joked in *The New York Times* that the servicing of professional tennis players had become a cottage industry, suggesting that the court-side girlfriends' box where family and friends of the players sit should be fitted with overhead straps in the manner of buses and underground trains, to provide standing room only.

Steffi's own entourage has never been that big. She has always had a number of managers, conditioning coaches, practice partners and specialists at her beck and call, but the number of people accompanying her at events has never stretched to the extent of Navratilova's. In the last few years, she has been travelling with less and less 'human baggage', often turning up with just one person in tow. As a result of being less protected by an immediate coterie Steffi has become more amiable, but still only has one really close friend on the Tour, the Australian Rennae Stubbs.

According to the outgoing Stubbs, the two got together when they played each other in a first-round doubles match at the 1989 Australian Open. Stubbs recalls, 'I said "hello" to Steffi. I was young, naive, totally in awe of her, but I approached Steffi like she was a normal person and that's what she liked about me.' The advantage of having Stubbs as a friend is that she's more successful in doubles, and so it is highly unlikely that Steffi will ever have to face her friend in singles. After all, it is difficult to be

Steffi gets used to trophies, 3 September 1975 *(Werek)*

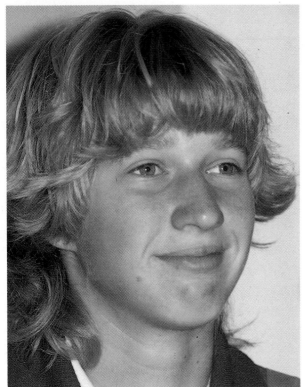

Above Collecting a local club trophy in 1978 *(Werek/Sheck Tennis)*

Left A smiling Steffi faces the press in 1985, her break-through year at Brighton *(Michael Cole)*

Top right Proving a force to be reckoned with, Steffi proudly holds the winner's trophy at Brighton in 1986 *(Michael Cole)*

Bottom right Having beaten her biggest professional rival, Martina Navratilova, Steffi collects the French Open Trophy in 1987 *(Michael Cole)*

Above I wanna be daddy's girl ... a proud father and successful daughter *(Michael Cole)*

Left So young, so troubled. The pain of defeat *(Michael Cole)*

Top right That's my girl ... father and daughter *(Michael Cole)*

Bottom right Always there, always supportive, mother Heidi with the family provider in 1992 *(Michael Cole)*

Left Steffi looks glum but glam during the French Open, 1991 *(Michael Cole)*

Right Not naturally at ease attending social functions, Steffi looks uncomfortable at the Champions' dinner, French Open, 1991 *(Michael Cole)*

Left Even though Steffi was winning consistently, there was still much in her private life to make her sad. US Open, New York, 1992 *(Michael Cole)*

Left Despite battling against injury, Steffi still made off with the US Open Trophy in 1993 *(Michael Cole)*

Left With her current boyfriend, the man many say she will marry, German racing driver Michael Bartels *(All Action Pictures)*

Below Paris, French Open, 1994; with International Tennis Federation President Brian Tobin. Despite playing few tournaments, Steffi is still the queen of the game *(Michael Cole)*

close to someone against whom you are competing on a regular basis – there is too much at stake.

The truth is, though, the time that tennis players get to spend with friends – although it can be greater if the friend also happens to play the Tour – is small compared with the time that friends in the non-tennis world have together. Just take the example of Steffi and Stubbs. During the year they do not necessarily play the same events, so they may go weeks without seeing each other, and then at the end of the season each goes home to opposite sides of the world.

Otherwise, as Steffi has indicated, there are no school friends with whom she keeps in contact. That's not really surprising. She was hardly in school long enough to make lasting friendships and when she was there, it was at the average Realschule from where most students graduate to mundane jobs. Given Steffi's present lifestyle, they are quite likely to have grown apart over the years.

It is no surprise that Steffi was once quoted as saying 'Friends? I have none.' Tennis has been referred to as 'a life of demanding isolation', in which players can depend upon no one but themselves. It can be a sad life. In January 1992, Steffi admitted, 'I often write letters to myself, and when I re-read them I am astounded how depressed and melancholic they are.' A year earlier Seles had said, 'I wouldn't want to be as unhappy as Steffi is.' And Navratilova declared that Steffi 'goes around with the weight of the world on her shoulders'.

Andrea Betsner, an old friend of Steffi's from the Leimen training centre found her to be very friendly when she saw her a few years ago. But when asked whether she thought Steffi was happy Betsner replied, 'Not really. I think she has almost no friends and now she finds it difficult to make friends because she never knows whether they are looking for her money.' Steffi would agree with that. She once said, 'I don't find it easy to trust other people. It seems there are always more people who want things from you than are giving you things.'

If it is hard for Steffi to develop genuine friendships, then it is certainly harder for her to have a boyfriend while she is on Tour. In fact, the difficulty of having a boyfriend on the Tour is one of the complaints most commonly aired by the women players.

Having blossomed into an attractive young woman however, there have been boyfriends. Alexander Mronz in 1989 was said to be the first. There were reports that she had been dating Ken Nahoum, an American photographer based in New York, who had taken shots of her for an advertising campaign. Her most recent male companion has been the good-looking Michael Bartels, a German racing driver, but that relationship appears to have cooled. Generally, these boyfriends have had strong characters, and have not been content simply to follow her around the circuit like a lap dog. Perhaps that's why Steffi is said to have developed a crush on a young English journalist. He was one of the few men who did travel with the Tour and had his own career to follow.

In 1992, Steffi disclosed that she was not particularly interested in having a boyfriend, as tennis was still more important to her. As it always has been. In 1986, in front of members of the press Peter was heard to say, 'In two years, you are going to have a steady boyfriend and then nothing will mean anything to you any more.' Steffi replied, 'Absolutely not.' Then Peter suggested, 'At twenty, you'll be married.' 'No way,' said Steffi. 'Then you'll want children,' added her father. Steffi's response? 'I don't want a boyfriend, I do not want to get married and I do not want any children, definitely not.' In that respect, Steffi is not unlike many modern women who put their career before their personal life.

Sometimes it seems as if her only friends are other celebrities, like German super-model Claudia Schiffer, with whom she was thought to be on good terms – until Peter persuaded his daughter that Claudia came from the weird world of fashion modelling, inhabited by homosexuals, and that they should not spend time together.

The Princess of Wales is said to be another friend. The Princess is certainly a tennis fan, and the two met and then played tennis together at the opening of the WTA's European office in London's Vanderbilt Racquet Club in June 1988. The following year at Wimbledon, Steffi was said to have offered to give the then tennis crazy Prince William, the Princess's elder son, a few lessons. Having just defeated Navratilova in the final, she joked, 'Of course, I shall treat him more gently than I did Martina.' It was the Princess of Wales who is supposed to have recommended to Steffi

that Patrick Demarchelier take the glamorous black and white pictures of the tennis star that appeared in glossy magazines around the world in early 1990.

At the end of the day, though, Steffi likes to be away from tennis and out of the spotlight as fast as possible. 'You need other aspects in life or you'd go mad,' she says, 'particularly when you get older.' So Steffi does what she has to do – plays her matches, attends her mandatory post-match press conferences and then leaves behind the frenzied tennis circus with its troupe of, in many cases, egotistical players, marauding media and bureaucratic officials, for the peace and quiet of her hotel and the constancy of her family. Without the latter, she has admitted, 'I'd never have been No. 1 in the world. We help and support each other in so many ways I don't know where to start or finish.'

She is very close to her brother, Michael, who is a sportsman but not a tennis player. Boris Breskvar, Steffi's coach in Leimen, remembers, 'Peter asked me if I could look at him, to see if I could make something of him. I said I don't think so. He didn't really have the talent, but he's a nice guy.' Michael, when he is not racing for Opel (one of Steffi's main sponsors) in the German Formula 3 Championship often accompanies her to tournaments, especially major events such as Grand Slams. It was Michael who at the French Open in 1993 was the member of the family who was very obviously involved in spurring his sister on to victory. During the final he sat at one end of the court and shouted words of encouragement whenever she was within earshot.

It is with her brother and his friends, from both school and the tennis world – he has been romantically linked with Stephanie Rehe, the American tennis player – that Steffi has been seen enjoying an evening out in Mannheim, not far from the family home in Bruehl. However, since Michael introduced his sister to fellow racing driver Michael Bartels in 1992 Steffi has kept a somewhat lower profile.

It is a pity that Michael is younger than Steffi. Had he been older, Peter might have considered releasing his grip on Steffi and allowed Michael to accompany her to tournaments at an earlier

age, just as both Seles and Sabatini benefited from having older brothers to look after them when travelling.

Naturally, mother Heidi has played a vital role in Steffi's support system too. Neighbours in Bruehl remember Heidi as the practical parent who ran the house, while Peter was always the dreamer, running around with his head in the clouds. Initially, because Peter had work commitments, it was Heidi who accompanied Steffi to tournaments. If Peter was later to encounter critics on the circuit, then it was Heidi who was, in the early days, making friends. Conny Konzak remembers Steffi's mother attending an event in Germany in the early 1980s, and says, 'She was a very lovely person, very happy, not as eager as Steffi's father, but she was proud of her little kid who was the up-and-coming star.'

Later, when Peter took over the constant role of chaperoning Steffi at events, inevitably Heidi complained, 'Sometimes I don't think I see enough of Steffi. Sometimes it is hard for a mother, but Steffi telephones every day, sometimes three times a day.'

Still, Heidi and brother Michael did both travel to support Steffi, particularly at some of the big events. When Steffi lost in the final of the French Open in 1989 she retired to her room alone, leaving her mother and brother to attend the official function. Heidi effectively played Steffi's role – to thank sponsors and those involved in the event organisation – during a special meal that had been laid on to mark the end of the event. The following year at a tournament held in Leipzig Tracy Austin recalls paying a visit to an orphanage with Heidi.

Steffi, it seems, is not into charity work. Her excuse is that she does not have time to help others, but neither does she appear openly to give money to charities. As one regular on the WTA Tour put it,

> Steffi has done nothing for charity in her life, other than maybe hit a few balls on Arthur Ashe Day when she needed to practise on the Stadium Court at the US Open. Her record is disgraceful in that sense. She's not the person that is liable to show up during the Lipton to serve them up for charity in support of the Miami Children's Hospital, or the regular things that happen, like tennis clinics.

Steffi's only claim to a known charitable act occurred in 1992. This is how she told the story:

> Just recently I had an experience that touched me greatly. We were driving to West Palm Beach airport when I saw a badly dressed man standing at the side of the road with a sign saying 'I work anything for food'. This really got to me, so I got out of the car at the next traffic light, ran back and put a US$100 bill into his hand. He started to cry and I cried also.

Still, it hardly bears comparison with the US$1 million that Agassi has given to a children's charity in Las Vegas, or the substantial sum that Sabatini is said to have given to the charity established and run by former teenage tennis phenomenon Andrea Jaeger.

Although it is generally true of the younger players that they do less for charity because they feel they have to stay focused and have yet to prove themselves, surely Steffi no longer has that excuse? She did say back in 1987, 'I want to help the game, but right now, I am only eighteen. When I am older, maybe I can do more things.' Eight years down the line, she appears to have failed to translate words into actions.

It almost seems that Heidi feels she has to do the charity work of two people, to make up for her daughter's shortcomings in this respect. Her acts of kindness vary, from visiting charitable institutions to helping individuals. Once at Wimbledon she met two young fans, Stacy and Stephen Morgan, without tickets. Heidi not only took the children into the Wimbledon complex and gave them tickets to watch Steffi play in the final, she also took them into the players' lounge and introduced them to Steffi.

In more recent years, the wheel has turned full circle. Peter spends less time with Steffi at tournaments, usually only turning up at the semi-final stage (assuming that Steffi is still in the tournament) of the big events, and sometimes is not to be seen at all. He stayed away from Wimbledon 1992 altogether on doctor's orders, suffering from high blood pressure. With Michael leading an increasingly independent life, Heidi is now more often to be seen again at court-side, supporting her daughter. In May 1993, Heidi underwent major back surgery in the United States, and

despite advice from doctors not to travel to Europe for the French Open and Wimbledon, surprised Steffi by turning up. Steffi was reported to be delighted and repaid her mother's devotion by winning both titles.

This change in parental support has come about since the difficult days of 1990, when allegations of Peter's affair with Nicole Meissner and subsequent paternity suit were splashed across the papers. The dignity with which both Heidi and Steffi endured that time can only be admired, and the bond between them has strengthened as a result. Theirs is a close and very trusting relationship. They enjoy sharing a joke together and are happy to spend some of their free hours, like any mother and daughter, shopping.

Not that Steffi is a huge shopper. On the contrary, she is a thrifty multi-millionaire who likes to save rather than spend her money. An illustration of this occurred when she visited Chicago in 1987. Temperatures were well below zero in the Windy City, and Steffi did not possess a warm coat. She rang her father back home in Germany and asked what she should do. 'Go buy one,' he replied. 'But the one I like is too expensive, it costs US$200,' came the reply. Her father ordered her to go and buy the coat plus some sturdy shoes before he lost his daughter to pneumonia. Three hours later the phone rang again in the Graf family home. 'Papa,' said Steffi, 'the shoes cost US$70, should I buy them?'

Even now Steffi rarely carries money with her when she goes shopping, so that she is prevented from making impulse buys that she might regret later. 'I was raised that way,' she has said.

I have been taught to have respect for money. My parents have not had very much. My father had to work hard for it. Therefore it has always been a matter of course to use it sparingly. Besides, I've got almost everything I need and am not the kind of person who buys things I like but wouldn't need. When I go shopping I look around mostly, I rarely buy.

Steffi does however go through phases of buying whole ranges of clothes, but is most often found wearing jeans and T-shirts when she's not on court. Her clothes, when she dresses up for award

ceremonies and official dinners, have bordered on the gauche. Some of the early creations that she wore for the end of tournament Champions Ball at Wimbledon included an unstylish white satin and black creation, and a red lace number which was so low cut that when she arrived at the dinner and lent over to sign an autograph for a fan she fell out of it. In recent years, her dress sense has improved, but she is still happiest wearing a simple combination of jeans and shirts, in which she always looks great – so much so that in 1995 she launched her own line of Steffi Graf jeans.

A shopping splurge, Steffi has said, is buying a new CD. And yet her music collection must be enormous, because whenever she is asked what she spends her money on or what she is buying while she is in a particular town for an event, the reply is inevitably 'CDs'. Her musical taste over the years has varied greatly, and has included Prince, The Cure, Phil Collins, Chris Isaak, Simply Red, Bruce Springsteen, Simple Minds, Roachford, the Stone Roses, the Inspiral Carpets and the Charlatans. Following on from that, one of the few things that Steffi likes to do in the evenings when she is on Tour is attend rock concerts. The list and range of performers she has seen on stage is huge. She has been backstage with Michael Jackson, Foreigner, the Bee Gees and Santana – with whom she jammed for a few brief moments – and has watched Sade, U2 and David Bowie do their thing.

Her love of music has extended in recent years to learning the piano. Steffi has two pianos – one in Germany and one in the United States – but she refuses to allow others to listen to her play. Just as on a tennis court, Steffi is a perfectionist and does not wish to make errors, let alone allow others to witness those errors. 'What I am doing is just Mickey Mouse stuff,' she has said. 'I only want someone to listen to my playing when I am very good.'

Steffi is interested in most types of art, but is particularly keen on the French impressionists such as Monet. She also likes the work of the Swiss sculptor Giacometti because 'he is very subtle and has a vision of people'. Many of the paintings she has collected to date are modern pieces by East Germans which she has bought on visits to Leipzig, but she is also the proud owner of an original work by the Russian-born French painter Chagall. When asked in 1991 whom she would most like to go out to dinner with,

Steffi said that it would have to be the Spanish artist Salvador Dali because 'he was weird, but I loved what he did with his paintings. I always wonder what he was thinking before he painted his pictures and I am fascinated by the little hints he gives about his pictures.'

Steffi paints a little herself and has completed a view from her New York apartment, but she is probably more accomplished as a photographer. She took to photography when she won a camera in a tournament that she played in Japan. Her favourite subject matters were sunsets, people and animals, and for some obscure reason she was particularly keen on holding her camera at an angle so that she ended up with sloping horizons. A good friend, Paul Zimmer, a German photographer who is on hand to snap Steffi's every move on and off the court, was helping her to perfect the art at one point, but Steffi's interest has appeared to wane. She has, however, had just one of her pictures published – a moody shot of Brighton Pier that appeared in *The Times* newspaper.

If she has any free time during the day Steffi enjoys visiting museums and art galleries because she likes to make the most of the trips she makes to the many cities in which she plays during the course of the year. Museums and art galleries are for Steffi of educational value, but they also represent a place where she can enjoy some peace and quiet and where she finds she is rarely approached by the public.

If she is not out and about shopping, sightseeing or taking photographs, Steffi is quite likely to be curled up listening to music and reading. She likes to read the newspapers to keep up with current events, but also enjoys the works of a wide range of authors that includes Stephen King, Frederick Forsyth, Dickens, Kafka, Sartre, the Jack London thrillers when she was much younger, and an all-time favourite, Milan Kundera's *The Unbearable Lightness of Being*. Aside from fiction, Steffi is interested in non-fiction books that help to plug the gaps in her education.

In the evenings, other than attending pop concerts Steffi enjoys watching movies and sometimes goes to the cinema accompanied by her brother Michael as often as three times a week. She does not like multi-million dollar budget action movies, nor is she a great fan of comedies, but prefers more serious, low budget art

movies. She does not, however, watch films just for fun. Steffi likes to analyse them – to think how she would have filmed a certain scene, what lines she would have changed and how she would have lit the various settings.

Usually in bed by 9.30 at night because she likes to be up at first light to practise, Steffi's evening entertainment ends early. A tournament win is rarely celebrated and only on the odd occasion justifies staying up late. 'When I was in juniors,' confesses Steffi, 'there was more ability to get excited over a tournament win than there is now.' The classic illustration of her laconic attitude to success is her failure to do anything other than board a plane when she won the 1988 US Open and thus the Grand Slam. Steffi is even reluctant to observe her birthday, although maybe this has more to do with the timing, for it falls between two of the most important tournaments of the year – the French Open and Wimbledon.

Steffi seldom enjoys going to parties. For one thing, she feels she cannot go out and have a good time, because if she laughs or says something a little too loudly, people will talk about her. For another thing, she's just not a big fan of parties. While still a teenager she went to a party and almost immediately phoned her father to ask him to pick her up, because she did not like the huge amounts of alcohol being consumed and the smokey atmosphere. That was perhaps understandable given that she is a top athlete. Steffi hardly ever drinks alcohol herself, although she has sipped champagne and cognac on special occasions. She does not really like the taste of liquor, she says, favouring instead a mix of Fanta orange and Coke, or alternatively mineral water. She has never smoked a joint and says she has no interest in doing so.

A perfect day, says Steffi, is

doing all the things that I've never done. I would love to go, for example, horse-riding on the beach – that's obviously something beautiful – and anything else exciting that I haven't done, like climbing a mountain, jumping in a lake, things that I can't do every day.

One thing Steffi can't do every day is relax at one of her homes – either in Germany or the United States – because she spends most

of the year travelling on the Tour. But when the opportunity does present itself it is very welcome to her.

The family home in Bruehl is a favourite retreat. There she likes to spend time with her beloved dogs, to whom she talks frequently by phone when she is away from home. If it were possible, she has said that she would like the dogs to be joined by a black panther. As it is not, Steffi is content to play with and walk her dogs in the 60 acres of wilderness that surround her home. The actual house is well tucked away out of sight from prying eyes, and is encircled by a solid brick wall topped with jagged metal that discourages fans from climbing over.

Steffi's spacious home, built after her 1988 Grand Slam success, is found at the end of the road known as Luftschiffring, on which the bungalow that formerly served as the family home stands. The bungalow is still owned by the Graf family, as is No. 14 Normannenstrasse, the terraced house in which they lived when they first moved to Bruehl. Brother Michael now lives in that house and Steffi, when both are in Bruehl, is often seen round there helping her brother clean and wash the dishes.

Steffi has recently acquired another home in Germany, a large apartment in the picturesque old university town of Heidelberg, which is some ten kilometres from Bruehl. When there Steffi is an almost daily visitor to her favourite restaurant, the typically German Wirtshaus Zum Spreisel, to which she was introduced by Boris Becker over ten years ago. There she is most likely to be found munching her way through a salad, although she is also fond of steaks and traditional German dishes such as meat balls wrapped in cabbage, served in soup. Apparently, there is no room in her diet for puddings and traditional German beers.

In the United States, where Steffi spends increasing amounts of time, she divides her time between her home in Boca Raton in Florida and her triplex apartment in New York. Her preference for America stems from her ability to escape the intrusive activities of the German press and to venture out undisturbed by the public, unlike in her own country.

The house in Boca Raton – decorated predominantly in black, because she says she sees enough white on a tennis court – is where she will be found sun-bathing by her own pool or out on the tennis

courts practising under the Florida sunshine. However, when Steffi is based in her apartment in New York – underneath the dome of the former police headquarters building, close to SoHo – she tends to be more active, going to museums, art galleries and the theatre.

Steffi travels so often that a holiday is usually when she gets to be at home, but she does enjoy visiting places she has not been before, such as the Dominican Republic. She has been there 'rough', staying in very basic accommodation without a bathroom, and to several other islands in the Caribbean, all of which are easily accessible from her home in Boca Raton.

This readiness to forego five-star hotel treatment clearly indicates that Steffi is content at times to eschew the millionaire lifestyle that her vast wealth would enable her to follow all the time if she chose, and to do her own thing. It reveals a facet of her character rarely seen by the public, and one that can only be admired. Steffi is obviously not one of these superstars who buys into the whole fame-game lock, stock and barrel.

In fact, so different is the private from the public persona that people who know her well say she has two faces – the tennis player and the young woman – and that they are very different. Claudia Kohde-Kilsch, who shared accommodation with Steffi at the Seoul Olympics in 1988, asserts,

Of course Steffi is very serious on court – everyone is – but she can be very funny. In Seoul we had music on in our room very loud. We would meet and talk with other athletes. Together, we would talk about boys and music. This is normal. But Steffi is very disciplined. She always goes to bed early, no matter what. Steffi has always been very, very ambitious about her tennis.

Others agree. Klaus Hofsass, the German Federation Cup coach and a close friend of the Graf family, says Steffi can be incredibly normal, happy and funny when she is relaxed. A British journalist who knows her well says she is 'a very pleasant, good person, but of course she has the faults that go with being a star. She has her airs and graces, she can be aloof, but still she is a perfectly nice girl, once you get to know her.' The trouble is, few do.

8
LIVING IN THE LIMELIGHT

'YOUR LIFE STOPS being your own. Everyone wants something from you,' Boris Becker was to reflect after his historic win at Wimbledon in 1985.

As her success increased on court, more and more demands were being made on Steffi's time off it, a fact with which she had difficulty dealing and ultimately grew to resent. 'In juniors,' Steffi said in 1986, 'everything was fun. Now much of the fun is on the tennis court. It's not as much fun outside tennis now.' That is where the German was subjected to endless television interviews, photo calls, post-match press conferences, and demands from both sponsors and the public, all of whom wanted their own little piece of this remarkable tennis phenomenon. Time to yourself, as Steffi soon found out, was a very precious commodity indeed.

There are those who remember the days when Steffi was just another unaffected, enthusiastic, albeit quiet youngster, who gave her time quite freely to the press. The first newspaper article ever to be written about Steffi appeared in *Der Schwetzinger Zeitung* when she was just eight years old, and in it she was given the nickname 'the sweet mouse from Germany' because she was so timid.

Even after she turned professional and joined the WTA Tour, Steffi thought nothing of spending her few spare moments shopping with German journalists. And when she played in the Virginia Slims Championships in New York Steffi was more than willing to wake up fifteen minutes earlier than usual specially to do a live interview with a German radio station.

Soon all that was to change. In 1986 Steffi made it into the top

three, and in 1987 she won her first Grand Slam title and became the No. 1 player in the world. Suddenly she was literally running away from the very journalists with whom she had earlier spent many happy hours of her free time. For two weeks immediately after she claimed the No. 1 position, she refused all interview requests.

There were two reasons for her change in attitude.

First and foremost Steffi was young and shy, and she undoubtedly found the sudden glare of the media spotlight too much to bear. It was almost as if the more attention she received the more she clammed up. She had an excuse for not being the natural, cooperative professional that the media had grown used to thanks to articulate top players such as Martina Navratilova and Pam Shriver. Steffi was still a teenager and was, quite typically for a girl of that age, self-conscious.

Going into 1987 the media focus was very intense. As far as the German press were concerned, Becker – who had overshadowed Steffi by winning the gentlemen's singles at Wimbledon in both 1985 and 1986 – was in a slump. The international media meanwhile had switched their attention from Gabriela Sabatini to Steffi, realising that it was the German who was the more serious threat to the era of Navratilova/Evert dominance and the likely successor to the No. 1 spot.

The second reason Steffi started shunning the press was related to the influence of her all-important father. Conny Konzak, at that time working for the German Press Agency, recalls a press conference at the Lipton International Players Championships in Florida's Key Biscayne, when Steffi was just seventeen. 'Her father was standing behind me, in the back row, and he was yelling at her what to say and I remember Steffi saying, in German so only one or two of us could understand, "Why don't you just shut up, I can talk for myself."' While Steffi's father, like many in the same situation, felt that he needed to protect his daughter, it was clear that he rather enjoyed the limelight himself. He was proud of Steffi's achievements, and he wanted the chance to talk to the world's media himself.

Furthermore, Peter controlled all media access to Steffi. Mostly journalists' requests for interviews were turned down. This kind of

behaviour might have been acceptable because Springer Verlag, which publishes the tabloid German newspaper *Bild*, paid the Grafs a substantial amount of money (said to be DM500,000 per year) and could have expected exclusive interviews but Peter was refusing to allow *any* journalists near his daughter in an attempt to protect Steffi, still not out of her teens when she won her Golden Grand Slam. Ultimately this ploy would work against the Graf family. Denied access, the press turned against Steffi, or perhaps more accurately against her father – but still vented their frustration on her. She was labelled the 'Sour Kraut' for her remote, disdainful attitude, as the press interpreted her refusal to talk to them.

Over-protected, and denied the chance to develop her relationship with the media, Steffi remains even today shy and uneasy with journalists. She will sit through press conferences hiding much of her face with her hair and covering her mouth with her hand. She has never regarded the press as much more than a hungry pack of wolves; feed them a scrap and, well satisfied, they will depart in peace. She has never learnt that the press are simply doing their job, just as she does hers. Instead she has maintained her reputation for being a reluctant, moody, bored and sometimes positively rude interviewee. And unlike many of the others, including Monica Seles, Helena Sukova and American Patty Fendick, she is never one to acknowledge or thank the photographers for sending her complimentary pictures of herself.

A few years ago at the Lipton International Players Championships, a television crew were shooting a clip for a tennis programme and were left with their patience severely stretched. The producer gathered together the players then considered the young stars of the women's Tour – Steffi, Sabatini, Jennifer Capriati and Monica Seles. The four were asked to speak in their mother tongue, as the programme was to be distributed internationally. Steffi replied in English that she had been in the United States too long and could not remember how to ... which left the crew tearing their hair out in frustration.

In the inescapable post-match press conferences which Steffi hates – 'The top players do too many and often the journalists have run out of questions to ask' – she will be utterly miserable even if

she has won, and is apt to snap at the most inoffensive query. At the start of her 1994 season a journalist suggested to Steffi that she was looking slimmer and fitter than the last time she had seen her. 'I've never played in this city before,' Steffi shot back. It did not seem to occur to Steffi that the reporter might have seen her play elsewhere. Nor did it occur to Steffi to answer the question.

Steffi's early rise in the world rankings was hardly greeted with enthusiasm by the WTA. First, she was not as at ease with the press as the two former stars Navratilova and Evert. But perhaps more importantly, Sabatini with her beautiful Latin looks was perceived as the ideal heir to the No. 1 crown, the girl who would bring all-out glamour to women's tennis. The WTA was lucky, for the better tennis player, the ugly duckling, eventually grew up to be a beautiful swan.

Unfortunately a pretty young woman does not always make for an engaging interview subject. As one journalist put it,

> She just sits there and looks utterly bored. She can't quite understand why you have to ask all the same questions, time and time again, because she's not going to vary her answers for you. She will not even make the effort to remember a funny incident from her childhood.

If a reporter does remind her of an amusing story from her childhood or refers to something that Steffi has done recently, she will not be drawn on the subject. She will merely assert whether the statements are true or false, a habit which has led the German press to refer to her as 'a blank canvas'. Long gone, obviously, are the days when Steffi told a reporter, 'All the time I am asked the same questions, but I always try to think of different answers.' Nowadays Steffi is so phlegmatic that journalists inevitably end up with mundane articles.

Some of the German journalists who have been following Steffi's career for many years cannot even bear to talk to her any more. Conny Konzak, who had to follow Steffi's every career move in the early days, even considered leaving his job so disenchanted did he become with Steffi. 'As a tennis writer who was

on the Tour for five years, at one stage I would have been so happy to quit the job, travelling with them (the Grafs), because I couldn't get anything new or refreshing out of her any more.' Even German Federation Cup coach Klaus Hofsass, a good friend, admits, 'Steffi should open up more. The barrier between her and the press is just too wide.'

Steffi is not entirely to blame. Just as Hollywood agents wield power over journalists who interview film stars, so too does the coterie of people who protect tennis players. Not only can a parent, an agent, a coach, or the WTA prevent an interview from taking place, but WTA representatives stand in on press conferences – and stand by for interviews – to deflect questions that are deemed inappropriate. The result is that interviews are granted to those who are known not to write hostile pieces. Those who do not have a proven track record are denied interviews, and anyone who produces a critical article is more than likely to be refused further access. As the journalists rely on the tennis players for their livelihood, they cannot afford to be critical. In fact, it can work rather to their advantage if they are compliant, as one British journalist who has consistently written inoffensive articles about Steffi discovered when he was offered a ride on her private jet between tournaments.

This is, quite frankly, ridiculous. The WTA is shooting itself in the foot. The press and public tire quickly of bland articles, and if their support starts to wane then the women's Tour is in for even more trouble. It already has an image problem and has had difficulties in securing a title sponsor thanks to a series of blows in the last few years. These have included the stabbing of Monica Seles, Steffi's subsequent domination, Mary Pierce's paternal problems and Jennifer Capriati's absence and subsequent run-ins with the law (first for allegedly shop-lifting and second for drug possession) not to mention the total lack of characters that have appeared to replace Navratilova and Evert.

With all these negative images winging their way around the world's press, you would think that the WTA would have stopped handling players like Steffi with kid gloves. Steffi is no longer a teenager who needs protecting. She should be advised not to bite the hand that feeds her. Steffi must realise that she has a

responsibility to the press and public, without whom she would not have a career and would not have earned millions of dollars. If players such as Steffi who think they contribute enough simply by turning up and playing do not realise their obligations, then the WTA should take them in hand and set them straight. One regular photographer on the Tour even went as far as to say,

> At some point they (the WTA) should have said 'We're going to fine the hell out of you or throw you out of the Association or whatever, because what you're doing is a detriment to the sport. You're not doing what Billie Jean, or Martina, or Chris, or Tracy did about leaving the situation stronger than you found it.'

And while they are about it, perhaps the WTA should give Steffi some lessons in how to inject a little interest and enthusiasm into her interviews.

Yet the WTA makes it incredibly difficult for the press to gain access to a player. One British journalist, having put in a request to the WTA for an interview with Steffi, was still waiting to meet with her several months later. Eventually, fed up, she approached Steffi's agent, Phil de Picciotto of Advantage International, who was furious when he heard of the long wait, for he had not received the request. The WTA had not dared to approach Steffi and request the interview. The personnel involved had simply gone back to the journalist and informed her that Steffi was not available but would she like Sanchez-Vicario, renowned for her willingness to cooperate, instead? In the end the journalist got her interview with Steffi. It was only in retrospect that she realised her mistake. The 'Barcelona Bumble Bee' as Sanchez-Vicario has been christened by the press, would have made a far more interesting subject for an article. In 1994 Navratilova commented on Steffi's lack of responsibility, when she said, 'Steffi hasn't stepped up to the plate and I don't know why. Maybe she feels that all she owes to the game is just to play but it would be nice for her to give some of it back.' Certainly, the WTA Tour would be better served if Steffi behaved differently.

In her defence Steffi has said,

I never wished to live this life. I didn't want it. I just wanted to play tennis. I never wanted to be a public person, that is why I am sometimes quite bitchy to people. I am not an easy type to handle, but I hate being in the public eye, or even to be followed by paparazzi and press.

It is unfortunate then that Steffi has come to the fore of tennis at a time when professionalism has taken a strong hold on the game, when the top players earn huge amounts of money, are elevated to the level of superstars and are expected to fulfil a role in the media.

As Rod Gilchrist, Deputy Editor of the *Mail on Sunday*, explains,

The print media, and even the broadcast media, have become extremely celebrity and personality led: they are no longer issue led but personality led. Anybody who is a personality will get a big show, and that goes whether they are sports stars, or whether they are show business stars. Sports stars, if they are in a big story, they get married, they get divorced, or they earn a million pounds, or something like that, will get as much prominence in the news pages as a show business star, and in that respect things have changed in the last few years. What were once the preserves of show business and theatrical people, are now inhabited by sports stars.

It is almost as if Steffi would be happier if she had been born 30 or 40 years ago, before playing tennis and being a tennis star commanded such great interest. For her own sanity, it is understandable why Steffi remains a private person, one who is very reluctant to give anything of herself to the public. So many demands are made of her, and some are of a very intrusive nature. Photographers with telephoto lenses appear from nowhere to try and catch that exclusive moment on film, even in helicopters over her Boca Raton house where one of the paparazzi once tried to catch her sunbathing nude. 'Luckily,' said Steffi, 'he only managed to get my back.' Top players are well – even over – rewarded for what they do, but they are mere mortals, too, and are as entitled to their privacy as much as anyone.

In addition to the paparazzi, Steffi has no time for the public who invade her life either. Autograph hunters who hang over railings at the end of a match while the television cameras are rolling may get her signature, but without the cameras fans are unlikely to strike gold. An out-take at the end of a television interview with Steffi that was conducted in a quiet corner of a tournament site revealed that she completely ignored two people who had waited patiently for an autograph. In contrast, Navratilova is known to scold herself if she refuses a young fan an autograph, and will sometimes dwell on her misconduct and the child's disappointment for so long that it will spoil her evening.

Maybe Steffi's actions have more to do with her view of collecting autographs, which she obviously considers a meaningless occupation. 'I would never ask anybody for an autograph. After all, I have often experienced things like this, and I know how it is received. But even in those days when I was still very young, I never had an idol.'

Steffi's indifference does not appear to have affected her popularity with some members of the public. In 1994, there was a report in the newspapers that a fourteen-year-old boy was so desperate to see Steffi play that he took £1,200 from his mother and bought himself a ticket to Orlando in Florida. Once there he avoided customs, booked himself into a hotel, went to Delray Beach to watch his idol in action – and then to the police with a repatriation request.

The German public, however, is no longer as enchanted with Steffi.

In 1985, Becker became a huge star in Germany. He has never been one to do things by halves and winning his first Grand Slam title was no exception. When he won Wimbledon that year, he was the first German, the first unseeded player and the youngest ever winner of the gentlemen's singles. He was younger even than the victor of the Wimbledon boys' singles event that year, Leonardo Lavalle of Mexico. Following Wimbledon he became a super hero in Germany. He was the sporting god for whom his country had been craving, a fact which was much appreciated by the Graf family, for it took the spotlight off Steffi.

However Steffi soon caught up, for if Becker was the sporting

hero Germany had been awaiting, she was the heroine. In 1987, with her blonde, good looks and iron will, plus her first Grand Slam title and the No. 1 ranking, she stole Becker's thunder and overtook him in a German popularity poll. And when the final of the WTA's end of year Championships, which was contested by Steffi and Sabatini, was broadcast on German television, it was watched by 15.7 million people, many more than had watched Becker's singles' victories at Wimbledon.

Steffi's positive image at home was helped by the fact that she has a regal name. '*Die Gräfin*' means the Countess and she is sometimes compared with the '*Mustermaedel*', considered a classic example of perfect young womanhood in Germany. Steffi is loved because she is just like everyone else; the typical girl-next-door, she is straightforward and honest to the point of lacking tact, and she is very loyal, both as a daughter and as a German citizen.

In recent years, however, some think that her once perfect reputation has been tainted by the reflected light of unfortunate incidents such as the allegations of her father's affair and the stabbing of Seles by one of Steffi's deranged 'fans'. The public are also fed up with her refusal to give interviews and her inability to open herself up to the German people, which results in her being labelled boring. As a result, although they still love her they have lost some of their interest in her.

Many Germans were therefore surprised to learn that in 1991 Steffi was still said to be ahead of Becker in the popularity stakes. While both players had a 94 per cent recognition factor – in 1995 it had increased to 100 per cent for both – 43 per cent said they liked Steffi, while only 21 per cent said they admired Becker.

Becker, they say, is far more interesting than Steffi. Becker is loved, not because he is sweet and loyal like Steffi, but because he provides people with talking points. People get worked up about Becker and what he says, something that could hardly be said about Steffi.

Becker lives his life to extremes. With him there are no half measures, and he can be controversial, speaking out about whatever issues interest him. He denounced the neo-Nazis in Germany and he opposed Berlin's bid to stage the Olympic Games, saying that

the money would be better spent on building much needed housing. And he caused a stir when at the 1990 Australian Open he said that if the top players were using drugs he would consider taking them too, as long as it meant being a winner. He has his ups and downs, he has his emotions – which he shows on court and in interviews. People watch his matches on the edge of their seats because it is impossible to foretell whether he will beat or be beaten by his opponent in straight sets, because one day he plays like a dream and the next like a nightmare.

In the last few years there has been a feeling that Steffi is just too much of a winning machine – the results of her matches are all too predictable, and almost without fail she makes it through to the final; and people resent the fact that she does not open up like her compatriot. While Becker appears to enjoy being in the spotlight, Steffi hates it. While he is quite at ease and is willing to talk about any topic under the sun, Steffi is quiet, shy, and ultimately unhelpful in interviews.

Another reason her popularity is down is due to the fact that another, younger star has risen in German sport. In 1993, swimmer Franziska van Alnsick overtook Steffi in the popularity stakes. 'Franzi', a glamorous schoolgirl with Lolita looks, is most famously remembered for her ability to have set a 200 metres freestyle world record in a final for which she had failed to qualify. At the 1994 World Championships in Rome, Franzi did not swim fast enough to qualify for the final, but because one of her team mates fell ill, Franzi was able to take her place in the final. Aside from the fact that she can sometimes swim fast, Franzi's popularity is due to the fact that she hails from Berlin, is good looking, talks openly, is happy to be in the limelight and is likely to add a touch of excitement to any international swimming meet.

There are, of course, other German tennis players, but none has enjoyed quite as much success as Steffi and Becker, and none is as popular. Anke Huber, who was hailed originally as the new Steffi Graf, has never achieved the same kind of success, although she has made it into the top ten. She herself said, 'I am not the next Steffi Graf, I am the first Anke Huber. I think Steffi is such a great person and she's done so much for German tennis, I just don't

want to be the second Steffi. There will never be a second Steffi – she is something special.' Michael Stich, the 1991 Wimbledon champion, is considered boring, lacks charisma, can be moody and obviously has not achieved as much as Becker and Steffi.

If the public has not always been Steffi's No. 1 fan, the sponsors, who fall over themselves to line up endorsement deals with her, definitely are.

Companies will pay well to sign up high profile players who are likely to reach the last three rounds of an event, which are usually televised. The public sees the players using the products, and this enables companies to reach a wider market. Every week a television viewer tunes into tennis and sees Steffi wearing Adidas gear, thus associating Adidas with winning, and it is assumed will automatically select Adidas products when he or she buys tennis equipment.

Players have been endorsing equipment since the beginning of the twentieth century. In 1904, the Slazenger catalogue claimed that the two Doherty brothers, one of whom was in the Wimbledon gentlemen's singles final every year between 1897 and 1906, used Slazenger rackets. There is no record showing whether the brothers simply received free equipment or were paid a fee, but if money did change hands it was a minute amount compared with the figures that top players command these days for endorsing a product. Players really started to benefit in a big way from endorsements with the dawn of Open Tennis in 1968.

The top women's players can now expect to command a fixed fee of between US$250,000 and US$300,000 per year for using a particular racket. On top of that, the player will receive bonuses for reaching certain levels – say the quarter-finals – of tournaments such as Grand Slam events and other top level events. These may seem ridiculous sums to pay somebody to play with a particular racket, but for the racket companies it can be a relatively cheap form of advertising. If a player using one of their rackets wins a Grand Slam, both the player and his racket appear on television and in newspapers and magazines in numerous countries around the world. The spin-off is huge increases in sales of that racket. The cost of running advertisements in all the different media, internationally, would be far greater than the player's endorsement fee.

Thus it seems reasonable that if the racket manufacturer is going to make a fortune, the player should get a percentage.

As an example of how a tennis star can boost a company's sales by association consider the case of Steffi's compatriot, Boris Becker. He helped vastly to improve the sales figures of Puma when the two were associated. Neil Wilson writes in his book, *The Sports Business*,

> In 1984, the year before Becker signed a contract with Puma, a West German sports equipment manufacturer, the company sold 15,000 tennis rackets; the next year, it sold 70,000 and in 1986 300,000. The company believes that Becker's Wimbledon victories generated sales of US$50 million.

At Wimbledon in 1989, a survey revealed that Adidas was by far the most popular clothing brand 'by a substantial margin' – not such a surprise when Steffi won and Stefan Edberg of Sweden made the finals wearing Adidas outfits.

Endorsement deals are not solely dependent upon performance. Some players are far more marketable than others, and 'character' is very attractive to companies seeking to sponsor players on the ATP Tour. The most obvious example is American Andre Agassi who, even when his ranking fell into the twenties in 1993, was still receiving the most money for endorsements because of his popular appeal. Sergei Brugera, the French Open champion from Spain, realised what it means to have character on the ATP Tour when he discovered that the amusing Ukrainian Andrei Medvedev, ranked some way below him, was receiving twice as much in appearance money because as Medvedev so succinctly put it, 'He [Sergei] never says anything in press conferences that makes anyone want to write about him. So the fans don't relate to him and he doesn't sell tickets.'

On the women's Tour, beauty is as much an attraction for sponsors as character is on the men's. Thus Gabriela Sabatini, who rose up through the women's rankings at the same time as Steffi, and was as a youngster far more attractive than the gangly German, made her fortune from endorsements rather than tournament wins, which have tended to be few and far between.

The good looks of a film star are considered so important – if players want to gain endorsement contracts and earn serious money – that in 1987 American marketeers are said to have advised Steffi to have her nose cosmetically reconstructed so that she could increase her earnings. Steffi would not hear of it. She wanted to be judged on her tennis, and her tennis alone – to the extent that when she was asked to pose on the beach in a swimming costume for the WTA Tennis Calendar she refused to have the white sock marks on her ankles covered up. A case of 'I am what I am ...'

Steffi's trump card was her phenomenal talent on the court, and that alone was enough to have sponsors lining up at her door. Ironically, Steffi claims that sometimes she wakes up and wishes she had black – her favourite colour – hair, although she now appreciates that her long blonde hair is an attractive trademark which appeals to sponsors.

Endorsement contracts do not necessarily involve the equipment that tennis players use on court. One of Steffi's earlier sponsors with whom she signed in the middle of 1986 was BASF, a large German chemical producer. Why did BASF sign Steffi? Most probably because their headquarters are in Ludwigshafen, which is joined to Mannheim, the city in which Steffi was born. Another sponsor, in the late 1980s, was KKB, a West German off-shoot of Citibank. Their association came about as a result of an application that she made for a VISA card. The clerk who spotted the application passed it on to his superiors, which resulted in the bank sponsoring Steffi for a year.

By 1987, the year in which Steffi made it to the No. 1 spot, she had a wide range of endorsements that included Granini (a soft drinks company), Adidas tennis clothes, Dunlop rackets, Opel cars, BASF and Gerry Weber clothes, plus the publishers of the tabloid newspaper, *Bild*. Countless other offers had been rejected.

By the following year, when Steffi won her Golden Grand Slam her endorsement contracts exceeded those of any other female tennis player. Usually winning Wimbledon is enough to guarantee a player a substantial income for life. Pat Cash, winner of the gentlemen's singles title in 1987, who has been plagued by injury ever since, still gets lucrative offers to play in exhibition events because of that one win. If winning Wimbledon is enough to line a player's

pocket, imagine how the Golden Grand Slam – in itself a snappy catch phrase invented by Steffi's marketing agent – provided her with a spring board from which to launch herself as one of the richest sportswomen in the world.

Steffi's agent Phil de Picciotto in 1989 called Steffi 'a global commodity'. He explained that, 'She and her family make all the decisions. She only does high quality, long-term lifestyle affiliations that don't cause her to strain her tournament schedule.' As a result Steffi's sponsorship deals tend to portray her as the young, dynamic type, someone who can set an example to both young and old, and someone who gives the impression of being fair and just.

In an attempt to try and repair some of the damage done by the intense press coverage of his alleged affair, Steffi's father arranged a photo session for his daughter with Patrick Demarchelier that appeared in the April 1990 issue of *American Vogue*, and subsequently in a number of other glossy magazines worldwide. The aim was to produce a more feminine image of Steffi that would attract a different type of sponsor. It worked. Peter said he was receiving 300–400 calls a day asking about Steffi's commercial availability after the appearance of the photos. Not all of them were welcome – the offer from *Playboy* to pose nude for almost £500,000 was rejected out of hand. 'They can offer me all the money in the world, but my clothes are staying on,' said Steffi.

Naturally de Picciotto has refused to reveal details of her endorsement contracts, saying only that the earnings from them 'substantially exceed her prize money'. A man of understatement. Some of the top stars earn as much as ten times from endorsements as they do from playing tournaments.

On the same occasion and in the context of his client's friendly professionalism, de Picciotto offered this comment: 'She's intelligent, dedicated, highly successful – and comes from a society that worships success.' Unfortunately the picture he paints of Steffi is not one that is shared by all. She is notorious for not showing up to important sponsors' functions, giving the impression that she takes with one hand while giving little with the other. It is an attitude that has not endeared her to the old school players such as Navratilova and Evert, who gave unselfish support to the promotion of women's tennis and its backers in general.

Steffi's attitude is not, however, dissimilar to that of other young players on the Tour and Navratilova was moved to comment in 1992:

Steffi has been taking a little bit of responsibility and Monica talks a good game, but neither is on our (WTA) board of directors. Neither is Sabatini. These girls came on to the scene when prize money was already big. They didn't have to fight for equality or recognition. They don't stand up and say 'Thank you' to sponsors. They just play, take their cheques and go on their way.

Steffi was certainly showing that kind of attitude when she played in the First Pacific Bank Challenge, a three-day exhibition event in Hong Kong in January 1994. Written into her contract was a twenty-minute appearance at a sponsored lunch in the hotel in which she was staying. When the time came for Steffi to attend, the organisers called up to her suite and asked her to come down. 'OK, I'll be there,' came the reply. Planning a grand entrance, the head of First Pacific Bank took great pride in announcing Steffi's imminent arrival. Then to his embarrassment Steffi was nowhere to be found. The organisers looked high and low, the hotel staff checked every conceivable corner. No Steffi. Thirty minutes late, Steffi – who had decided on a whim to go off and shop – walked into the dining room, took one look and said, 'Oh no, do I have to talk to *everybody*?' Needless to say, she was not invited back in 1995.

Behaviour like that makes comments that Steffi made a couple of years earlier seem rather irrelevant.

The No. 1 player and *all* players have a responsibility to the sport itself and to the fans, sponsors and officials. It is important to keep commitments, always try one's best and take responsibilities as an athlete seriously.

Obviously the kind of attitude she displayed in Hong Kong wins Steffi no friends, but that is unlikely to worry her. So when she did not get invited back in 1995, the loss of the US$100,000 or so that Steffi probably got paid to play in the event in 1994 would have

seemed loose change to a multi-millionairess. And the truth is, Steffi can get away with her attitude problem, because sponsors queue up and are willing to pay millions of American dollars for her to endorse their products.

The fact that Steffi has on various occasions and by assorted bodies been voted the sexiest player of the decade and Miss Luscious Lips, and her legs have been nominated as the sexiest in tennis, only serves to increase her value as far as sponsors are concerned. Even Yannick Noah, probably one of the most alluring and charismatic players ever to compete on the men's Tour, said in 1992 that of the three top women's players, he thought Steffi, thanks to her 'flawless body' had more sex appeal than either Seles or Sabatini.

The strange thing is, sometimes it can help a player's sponsorship appeal if she is derided or starts to lose. In 1988, one of the Italian newspapers, *Corriere della Sera*, wrote that Steffi was 'an ugly potato-faced German'. The article was reproduced in the German newspaper *Bild*; as a result Germans started cancelling holidays to Italy in support of their heroine. The following year Steffi's defeat in the French Open final, although a disaster as far as her tennis was concerned, was a blessing for her finances. Both incidents aroused the public's sympathy and thus increased her marketability, for they showed Steffi to be a mere mortal like the rest of us, rather than a tennis machine. Said de Picciotto after her French Open defeat in 1989, 'The public have seen little of her natural personality but her reaction after a disappointing loss – hugging Arantxa and praising her in her speech – won her a lot of friends, and created even more interest in her.'

That interest does not only come from sponsors. Steffi has attracted attention all over the world, resulting in some unusual associations. She has had a race-horse named after her, although it's obviously not in the same class as Steffi because it usually comes in last. An Italian restaurant in London has named one of its dishes *razza alla Graf*, a fish dish of skate with butter, capers and lemon. Authors such as Martin Amis have written about her. She has received marriage proposals from total strangers. Invitations to dinner from far-flung fans are sent to her home in Bruehl. Poems are written in praise of her performances on court.

A German rock group Die Angefahrene Schulkinder (The Runover Schoolkids) was ordered to pay Steffi roughly £25,000 in damages for writing a song about her that included phrases like 'I wanna make love to Steffi Graf' and suggested that she had had an incestuous relationship with her father. The famous painting by the French artist Manet, which features a woman at the bar of the Folies Bergère in Paris, has been recreated with Steffi in the starring role.

Life at the top certainly does have its bonuses, both big and small. Steffi, like millions of other young people, had always dreamt of flying in a *Top Gun* plane, but being the No. 1 player in the world, she was lucky. Her dream came true. She flew in an F-16 with First Lieutenant Steve Teske from an American air base at Ramstein, close to Wiesbaden in Germany. She flew for an hour and had so much fun that she wanted to do it all over again. On another occasion Steffi was driving through the United States to a tournament when she stopped to try and pick up some medicine from a pharmacy. She knew exactly what she needed, but also knew that it required a prescription. She explained to the pharmacist that her doctor was in Germany so she could not get a prescription and was told that there was no way she could be given the medicine she required. Just as Steffi was walking out of the shop another pharmacist came out of the back store room, saw Steffi, recognised her and asked her what she was doing. She repeated her story and the second pharmacist called a doctor he knew and got the prescription.

For Steffi and the other top players – who must rank among the most spoiled athletes in the world – the perks of the job include private jets between tournaments and having limousines waiting to whisk them away from the courts back to their hotel suite, and from there to wherever they might desire to go. In addition, everybody will make an extra effort to ensure that Steffi, the star, is happy. Getting to go backstage at concerts so that she can meet her favourite rock stars who may happen to be performing locally is another bonus, although Steffi probably does not see it that way. She's leading the life of a rock star anyway, so you can imagine her becoming more than a little blasé about all of it. It always seems

slightly ironic that players such as Steffi, who can afford it, always get to stay in the hotels' finest suites and then have their room bills waived, so honoured are hotels to have a star stay with them.

If fame has its rewards, however, it also has its down side. Steffi has spoken rather pessimistically of her own fame, 'so many bad aspects, so few good'.

A rich, internationally known tennis star who is also an attractive young woman inevitably attracts a number of weirdos and psychos, although it has to be said that Steffi seems to attract more than her fair share. In 1987, on her return from Paris having won the French Open for the first time, Steffi received a jar of poisoned marmalade from a German man in his late twenties, identified only as Frank P., who three years later was to slash his wrists as he walked on to Steffi's practice court. Several men have been arrested for loitering around her homes – both in Germany and the United States – and one even followed her to Wimbledon, in 1993, where he heckled her from the front rows of the Centre Court. She constantly receives demands for money and is subjected to black-mail threats. In January 1989, an anonymous caller threatened to blow up the plane carrying Steffi home after the Australian Open.

Some of the attention she receives is not quite as threatening, but is still distracting and ultimately unwanted. A rich American, Jim Levee, once said, 'I would die for Steffi,' and proceeded to shower her with money and expensive gifts including fur coats and fast cars, before she even knew how to drive. Later, and probably much to Steffi's relief, Levee abruptly switched his focus to the Seles family.

The ultimate loony tune, however, was the German Gunther Parche who stabbed Seles in the back while she was resting in a change-over during a match at the Citizen Cup in Hamburg in the spring of 1993. Parche claimed he was a fan of Steffi's and that he had launched an attack on Seles so that Steffi could return to the No. 1 position in the women's rankings. His crime was more than a traumatic shock for both Seles and Steffi, and it highlighted the very real dangers and attendant pressures to which the leading players in particular are exposed.

9
GREAT RIVALS?

RIVALRIES ARE THE LIFE BLOOD of a one-on-one sport such as tennis. If there were none, the sport would to a degree be reduced to stagnant predictability. As it is rivalries push playing standards higher between the two antagonists, and thus throughout the game, as the rest of the field are forced to improve if they wish to succeed.

Off court, rivalries enhance interest among the public, providing fans with one of two players to root for and provide the inspiration for more members of the public to take up the sport. On the commercial front, well-known and publicised rivalries help boost attendances, which produce increased takings at gates. Electronic media coverage of needle matches in particular boosts promoters earnings, ensures greater listener and viewer figures and, where commercial channels are concerned, enhanced ratings that permit higher advertising rates to be charged.

In her role as President of the WTA Tour Players Association, Martina Navratilova in January 1995 stressed the importance of rivalries, saying,

> We (the WTA) need the rivalries of the top players; the present format does not allow it as the top players play different tournaments all over the world and do not play each other except at the Grand Slams. I would like to see ten Tier 1 (top level) tournaments and everyone would have to play eight of these.

One of the first great rivalries in women's international tennis took place in the 1960s, when the athletic Australian Margaret Court (née Smith) and the balletic Maria Bueno from Brazil dominated

the headlines. Navratilova herself certainly knows a thing or two about rivalries. In the late 1970s and 1980s she and Christ Evert experienced one of the most enduring rivalries of recent times.

Navratilova acknowledged that rivalry with Evert in 1985, when she said,

> I don't think I'm going to be here long enough for a future rival to be as good as Chris is at this point. But of course Gabriela Sabatini is a phenomenal talent and Steffi Graf is very good. Hana (Mandlikova), if she ever gets consistent enough, is a great player. But it will take them longer to get there.

On this point, she was to be proved wrong.

It did not take Steffi long to assert her potential as a contender for the top spot in women's tennis and thus to establish something of a power struggle between herself and Navratilova, the then No. 1. In 1985, Steffi strode into the top ten and the following year in the final of the German Open scored her first win over the Czech-born American. Just over two years later, in August 1987, it was Steffi who knocked Navratilova off the No. 1 pedestal.

Even after Steffi won her Golden Grand Slam in 1988, Navratilova still believed she could regain the No. 1 ranking. They were certainly well-matched, as their final head-to-head record would prove. At the end of 1994, when Navratilova retired, the two had played on eighteen occasions, and both had won nine times.

Claudia Kohde-Kilsch summed up the difference between these two great players when she said in 1989,

> Martina ... has better hands, better shots than Steffi. She can hit drop shots from down here (indicating her feet), play drop shots that Steffi can't do. Steffi, though, is mentally tougher, not as nervous as Martina always seems to be. Steffi's so much more powerful, too, and faster.

The most basic difference of all, of course, was that Navratilova was a natural serve and volleyer, while Steffi is a classic baseline player.

However deadly and serious their contests were on court, Steffi and Navratilova maintained a healthy respect for each other's abilities. At Wimbledon 1993, Steffi was genuinely upset that she did not get to play Navratilova in the final and sent Rennae Stubbs off in search of the American to ask if they could play a few games together for fun. Towards the end of Navratilova's career, as at Wimbledon and the Virginia Slim Championships in 1994, they even took time to practise together.

It was at the 1994 Virginia Slims Championships, which brought Navratilova's singles playing career to an end, that Steffi spoke endearingly about her great rival.

> She (Martina) was always special to me. I have a lot of memories, and a lot of things happened between us and we always had some great matches. I think we had a lot of things that were ... that we liked the same. For example, our passion for Wimbledon, and for competing, just playing tennis, and I think we are similar in this way.

In turn, Navratilova has been quoted as saying, 'I consider the best women's match you could have would be Steffi at her best against me at my best.' Sadly the public never witnessed that match, because the peaks of their careers did not coincide. But their rivalry did produce some memorable encounters, such as the three-set semi-final they played at the US Open in 1986, in which Steffi had three match points and still lost.

It was at Wimbledon, however, that the two consistently produced excellent tennis. They first met on the fabled grass courts in the 1987 final. Steffi, on the rise, had won her previous 45 matches, Martina had not won a single tournament all season. Steffi put up a tremendous fight, but on the big occasion Steffi's nerve failed her and Navratilova took her eighth Wimbledon singles title, thus equalling the record of the American, Helen Wills Moody. Two more great matches followed, in the finals of 1988 and 1989. Steffi won both, but the former will be particularly remembered, for Steffi's victory came in three sets.

With Navratilova's retirement Steffi was the one player left on the women's Tour with a thoroughbred pedigree, backed by a long

and proven record. The other top players had neither the same degree of success nor the consistency, or were too young and had not been on the Tour long enough to have proved themselves.

Looking back however, it is interesting to note that following Wimbledon 1985, when Steffi was starting to make her mark on the Tour, the pundits did not immediately acclaim her as the dominant up-and-coming player. While her credentials were recognised, Gabriela Sabatini, France's Pascale Paradis and the Bulgarian Manuela Maleeva were all being touted as future stars. In fact it was Sabatini, eleven months younger than the German, who initially made more headlines than Steffi. Although that had a lot to do with her Latin looks – dark flowing locks and sparkling brown eyes – it was also because she made an earlier impact on the WTA Tour. While Steffi was knocked out in the fourth round of the French Open in 1985, Sabatini reached the semi-finals, and later that year won her first WTA event in Japan, six months before Steffi was to win hers.

Steffi was not unduly worried by the fact that the media and fans were taking more notice of Sabatini. 'I like it more when the attention is on the other players,' she said. Steffi's father agreed, 'We have a different mentality. We Germans, or maybe just we Grafs, are quiet. We like to have people talk about Boris and Gabriela. Then we can work much better in peace and quiet.'

From 1985 to 1988, Sabatini was Steffi's most obvious contemporary rival. And when they did meet on court it was Steffi who tended to win more often, particularly when it came to the more important matches. The two youngsters' rivalry was not unlike that experienced by Navratilova and Evert in their early days of competition. Evert succeeded in winning eleven of the first thirteen meetings with Navratilova. Steffi won eleven out of her first thirteen encounters with Sabatini. Evert and Navratilova played doubles together, as did Steffi and Sabatini.

At Wimbledon 1986, Ted Tinling, an often very accurate observer of the women's tennis world, commented,

Women's tennis is currently in a far more exciting state of transition than the men's game. Martina and Chrissie's time is just about run, but here we have Graf and Sabatini ready to assume

their roles centre stage plus a whole school-room of wonderfully talented youngsters following along right behind them. And because of Navratilova and Evert, they will all want to be princesses, little divas.

The first major final in which Steffi and Sabatini played was at the Italian Open in 1987. The Foro Italico was packed to the rafters for the occasion, and the whole crowd seemed to be cheering for the *bellissima* Sabatini. The Argentinian's style of play, heavy top-spin on both sides, was well suited to the Italian clay courts. In the end, however, it was Steffi's stamina that won the match – she overcame her opponent and her vocal support in three sets, 7–5, 4–6, 6–0.

Steffi and Sabatini met again at Wimbledon a matter of weeks later, when David Miller in a report published in *The Times* in 1987, drew a delightful comparison between the two.

The sheer elegance of Miss Sabatini compels admiration ... By comparison, Miss Graf at the other end, in what can only be described as looking like an old night-shirt, was appealing in a different way: a strapping, straightforward milkmaid, pleasingly devoid of fuss or self awareness.

Once again, the milkmaid won, but, once again, the match went to three sets.

When in the semi-finals of the Virginia Slims of Los Angeles in August 1987 Sabatini lost to Steffi for the tenth straight time, a reporter asked her how important it was for her to beat Steffi. Sabatini replied, 'It's important, but I think I have a lot of time to beat her. We're both young and have a lot of tournaments ahead of us. I think it would be nice if we developed a rivalry like Navratilova and Evert.' Nice, but not exactly what Steffi had in mind. Steffi, when asked about a rivalry between the two, remarked, 'What rivalry? I've beaten her ten times in a row.'

Although Sabatini had not beaten Steffi in any of their meetings in 1987 she did rather better than most other players in encounters with the German in 1988 and 1989. During those two years, when Steffi held the No. 1 position continuously, Sabatini inflicted

several defeats on Steffi. She was the only player to beat Steffi twice in her Golden Grand Slam year and one of only two players to defeat her in 1989.

Even as late as 1988 some journalists were still maintaining that Steffi and Sabatini would be, in the next decade what Navratilova and Evert had been in previous years. They even suggested that the youngsters' rivalry was more intense because their matches were closer, often going to a third set. Certainly they had deposed the two stalwarts as leaders in the rivalry stakes – if only because Evert had retired in 1989 – and their tussles were set to continue.

In 1990, Steffi and Sabatini met on just four occasions, and won twice each. Sabatini's wins that year were the more significant. She registered perhaps her greatest victory against Steffi in the final of the US Open when the Argentinian, rejuvenated with the help of coach Carlos Kirmayr of Brazil, won 6–2, 7–6. Then at the Virginia Slims Championships in November she upset Steffi at the semi-final stage, again in straight sets.

The following year, Sabatini staked her most serious claim as a legitimate rival to Steffi, by winning their first four meetings. However, when it came to the big event Sabatini was to falter. The 1991 Wimbledon final was a tense affair. Both players had points to prove. Steffi, her tennis having suffered as a result of the allegations levelled at her father, had failed to win a major title that year to date. Sabatini wanted to demonstrate that her victory over Steffi at the US Open in 1990 had not been a one-off. The South American certainly had her chances, but choked – Steffi took the title 6–4, 3–6, 8–6.

It was at Wimbledon that Steffi would say of her rivalry with Sabatini,

We played the first time when I was twelve and she was eleven; that was back in the World Championships, in the Orange Bowl in Miami, and since then we must have played 25 or 30 times, very often anyway. We always have a lot of tough matches, three-setters, close matches, matches that either of us could win and some great ones to remember, so it's always a joy to play her because you know you're going to have a tough competition

and a tough opponent against you and you're always eager to have those matches.

Although she beat Steffi in their first two meetings in 1992, Sabatini was to fade from consideration as a serious rival to Steffi's crown. Although they continued to meet on the Tour (their head-to-head record at the end of 1994 was 27 to eleven in Steffi's favour), there were others who came to provide a greater challenge to Steffi.

Arantxa Sanchez-Vicario, the Spaniard who comes from a family of professional tennis players – her two brothers Emilio and Javier play on the men's ATP Tour – was one such challenge. Sanchez-Vicario's bubbly, exuberant, outgoing personality has won her many fans around the world – as well as the nickname of the Barcelona Bumblebee. On court she is a great all-rounder, whose gifts of speed and thought are matched by a never-say-die spirit.

Whilst they had been on opposite sides of the net on earlier occasions, occasions on which Steffi had trounced the young Spanish girl in straight sets, their first major confrontation was in the final of the 1989 French Open which Sanchez-Vicario won. The victory was her first Grand Slam success and gave a great boost to her confidence to challenge for the very top of the rankings. She was still at that time relatively inexperienced, even though she reached the No. 5 spot that year. It also meant, incidentally, that Steffi's efforts to capture successive Grand Slams were scuppered; and by beating Steffi in Paris she was to be one of just two opponents to vanquish her in 1989.

For the next two years, during a dip in form, Sanchez-Vicario did not provide Steffi with any great challenge, but it was at the French Open once again that she scored a great victory over the German No. 1, beating her 6–0, 6–2 in the semi-finals of the 1991 event. Sanchez-Vicario was evidently on the rise, and matches between the Spaniard and Steffi were noticeably closer, often running to three sets. In the quarter-finals of the 1992 US Open, Sanchez-Vicario scored another memorable upset when she swept Steffi aside in straight sets 7–6, 6–3.

The Barcelona Bumblebee progressed steadily and in six finals

meetings with Steffi in 1993 she won twice – at the Lipton Championships and the Citizen Cup in Hamburg. By the end of that year, Sanchez-Vicario was ranked No. 2 in the world and was pushing for Steffi's top spot. That would take time. In 1994, despite beating the German in consecutive finals at the Canadian and US Opens and also winning the French Open, which meant that she had taken two Grand Slam titles to Steffi's one, Sanchez-Vicario ended the year still at No. 2.

With Steffi's absence from the WTA in much of the latter part of 1994 and the beginning of 1995, the Spaniard was able to steal her crown and assume the No. 1 spot in February. While Sanchez-Vicario began 1995 on a high note, Steffi still holds a significant lead in the head-to-head records. Her victories total 24, to the Spaniard's eight. However, Sanchez-Vicario would be Steffi's main rival on the Tour when she returned from injury.

As the 1990s began, Sanchez-Vicario was not the only young pretender to Steffi's crown. In 1990, amid unprecedented hype and heraldry, the American Jennifer Capriati joined the WTA Tour. On the western side of the Atlantic Ocean, the hope and even the expectation was that Capriati would soon become the natural successor to Evert, who had recently gone into retirement at the end of an illustrious career.

Capriati was well-equipped to make her mark on the professional tennis circuit, despite being a few weeks short of her fourteenth birthday. She was already the holder of two junior Grand Slam titles – the French and the US – and she played in a classic tennis style that was focused, assured and powerful beyond what could reasonably be expected of someone of such tender years.

Capriati soon demonstrated that there was substance behind the hype. In her first tournament, at Boca Raton in March 1990, she reached the final by beating a string of seasoned players before falling to Sabatini. She was soon to set a series of records – youngest player to be ranked in the top ten, youngest Grand Slam semi-finalist, youngest seed in Grand Slam history... Her list of achievements seemed endless, and yet she found it very difficult to beat Steffi. In ten meetings, only once did she manage to record a

defeat against the German and that was in the final of the 1992
Barcelona Olympics, securing the gold medal.

Just over a year before Capriati turned professional, another
youngster, Monica Seles of Novi Sad in Yugoslavia, had made her
debut on the WTA Tour. Her name had been being whispered as
a potential rival to the power of Steffi long before she turned professional in 1989. For two years, she threatened Steffi's top
position, finally in 1991 rising to pre-eminence on the Tour and in
the rankings.

Although Yugoslavian, Monica Seles has since 1985 lived in the
United States. Nick Bolletieri, the tennis guru, had persuaded
Seles's parents to bring her and her brother Zoltan from
Yugoslavia after seeing her play in 1985 in the Orange Bowl, the
junior international age group championships held in Florida. The
whole family then settled into Bolletieri's tennis academy in
Bradenton, Florida. According to Bolletieri, 'In my thirty-odd
years in the game, I've never seen anyone like her. There was only
one thing on her mind even as a tiny tot: to be No. 1 in the world.
No. 2 never meant anything to her.'

Playing as an amateur in 1988, Seles entered the top one hundred after competing in three tournaments, the minimum in which
a player must compete before a ranking can be obtained. Her initial
ranking was No.88. Seles made her professional debut in dramatic
style. Weighing just 99 pounds, the left-hander reached the semi-
finals of the Washington event, upsetting Manuela Maleeva then
the world No. 7 en route. In the semi-finals, Seles had to default with
an ankle sprain, but her ranking still rose to No. 49. 'She's going
to be awesome,' predicted Navratilova. 'She already is awesome!'

Later in 1989, Seles reached the semi-finals in Paris – her earliest visit to the French Open – where she played Steffi for the first
time. It was an enthralling match, which the German managed to
scrape through in three sets 6–3, 3–6, 6–3. It was a remarkable
achievement for Seles. Most observers had thought the match
would be a formality. After all Steffi, coming out of a golden year,
had won the previous 39 matches she had played in Grand Slams
and while she had lots of experience, Seles had very little.

Even Steffi, who weighed in more than 30 pounds heavier than
Seles, was surprised by the amazing display of powerful and steady

hitting produced by the wafer-thin Yugoslav. 'A few can hit harder than me,' remarked Steffi later, 'but they never risk it so consistently.' It was Seles's timing and footwork that compensated for her lack of weight, but eventually Steffi's experience won through. Commented Steffi, 'She [Seles] hit some great winners and is obviously someone to look forward to.' Maybe not.

While Seles had blasted shots low and flat over the net, and had confounded Steffi somewhat, the Yugoslav realised that she needed a stronger serve to beat Steffi – a matter that was soon put to rights. Here finally was someone who could pose a real threat to Steffi's No. 1 ranking. Consistency was a strong point, but Seles was all in all a precocious talent, with an enviable intensity and highly developed competitive instinct, plus excellent natural timing. However, Steffi proved that Seles still had some learning to do when a few weeks later she beat her in the fourth round of Wimbledon, for the loss of just one game.

After that, Seles continued to improve her ranking rapidly. In 1990, she won a string of titles including the Lipton International Players Championships, the US Hardcourt Championships, the Italian Open and the German Open, where she beat Steffi in straight sets in the final. Three weeks later at the French Open, the Yugoslav won her first Grand Slam title by defeating Steffi in two sets 7–6, 6–4.

At the end of 1990 Steffi was still No. 1, but she must have known that her days were numbered, for Seles had climbed to No. 2 in the rankings and had a 2–0 edge on Steffi for their battles that year. In 1991, Steffi tried to hang on to her top ranking for dear life, beating Seles in two finals – in San Antonio and Hamburg – but her gifted, younger rival was winning all the big ones, including the Australian Open. And on 11 March 1991, Steffi inevitably lost her No. 1 crown. Seles went on to prove that she was head and shoulders above the rest by capturing two more Grand Slams, the French and US Opens, leaving Steffi to win the Wimbledon event, at which Seles – mysteriously – did not compete.

In 1992, Seles was once again the dominant force on the women's Tour, winning a string of titles. However, she and Steffi met for the first time in the year in the final of the French Open, and produced a stunning match that resulted in Seles just

managing to scrape through in three sets 6–2, 3–6, 10–8. A month later Steffi gained her revenge and proved that she was still the more dominant force on grass, by beating Seles in straight sets for the Wimbledon title. It was that defeat that ruined Seles's chances of a Grand Slam, for she won the other three major titles that year.

Seles looked set to continue in her winning ways in 1993 and a meeting with Steffi in the final of the Australian Open produced another classic confrontation, which the Yugoslav won 4–6, 6–3, 6–2.

In Hamburg, at the Citizen Cup in April 1993, an unprecedented attack on a player was to occur. Seles, while sitting down during a change-over in her quarter-final match against Magdalena Maleeva of Bulgaria (sister of Manuela), was stabbed in the back by a so-called fan of Steffi's, bent on helping his German heroine to return to the No. 1 ranking. Sadly, that was the last occasion that Seles was to appear on court.

Seles had added a new dimension to the WTA Tour. While her insistence on grunting when she hit the ball was not widely appreciated, she hit the ball double-fisted on both flanks with great ferocity. Her excellent timing enabled her to take balls on the rise and, when she needed, with a delicate touch owing to her complete control of the racket head. Her feeling for the court was intuitive and never had the ball been hit so hard with such pinpoint accuracy on the lines. By 1992, her serve had gained strength too, and was measured at 104mph, compared with Steffi's top service speed of 105mph.

In early 1993, Tracy Austin remarked of Seles,

> So few people have the same intensity level as Monica. She's another ten points beyond Steffi or Arantxa or anybody. In the final of the 1992 US Open, she was beating Arantxa, and when she lost a point, I thought she would die. Her intensity level is unbelievable. She wants to win love and love so badly.

For Ted Tinling, 'No one since Suzanne Lenglen has had such an ability to electrify an audience as Monica.'

When Seles had usurped her place at the top, there were suggestions that Steffi's game had marked time for too long. The

American Mary Joe Fernandez went on record as saying in regard to Steffi's decline, 'When you are No. 1 and you win all the time, it is difficult to change. She dominated for three years or so, but she didn't really improve. Someone new comes along. You can never stop improving.'

While that is undoubtedly true, Steffi was also dealing with family problems off-court that did nothing to help her attempts to maintain her No. 1 position. Seles, however, would never have the chance to realize her full potential; and when she was stabbed in Hamburg, Steffi held a 6–4 lead over Seles in their head-to-head encounters. Theirs would undoubtedly have been a rivalry to challenge the greatness of that enjoyed by Navratilova and Evert, but it was tragically cut short.

10
LIFE WITHOUT MONICA

F THE INCIDENT IN HAMBURG had traumatic results for Monica Seles, the second person that it made life difficult for was Steffi. She had to live with the fact that it had been one of her so-called fans who had attacked Seles, leaving her with the question: is the hitting of a tennis ball across a net really so important that it should lead to this? Obviously upset, she lost the final of the Hamburg event to Arantxa Sanchez-Vicario in straight sets.

After that, Steffi recovered and went on a roll. She won the German Open, defeating Gabriela Sabatini 7–6, 2–6, 6–4 for the title. And then she went to Paris where she gained her third French Open title with a win over Mary Joe Fernandez 4–6, 6–2, 6–4 in the final. In beating Jennifer Capriati at the quarter-final stage, Steffi had regained the No. 1 ranking.

Interviewed prior to Wimbledon, Steffi was asked what still motivated her. 'I want to play better,' she said, placing the greatest emphasis on 'better'. 'I still feel I have got a lot in me – the last few months I've been showing a bit more variety in my game and I'm trying to get it even further than that.' She practised her volleying before the tournament began and said she wanted to come in more on the grass courts. 'I'm not afraid of it any more, I have confidence at the net.'

Ironically, when asked who posed the greatest threat to her at Wimbledon, she prophetically gave just two names, those of Jana Novotna and the American Lori McNeil. They were the two players to give her the most problems at Wimbledon in the next two years.

Steffi was once again in her element at Wimbledon. In the first round she beat Australian Kirrily Sharpe 6–0, 6–0 and in the third

round recorded the same scoreline against Canada's Helen Kelesi. She thus became the first player to win two double bagels in the same year at Wimbledon since Doris Hart in 1953. It was all the more surprising then that after the event she admitted that she had been having injections one minute before the start of every one of her matches and had bravely played through pain, because she wanted so desperately to compete at Wimbledon.

So it was with some ease that the top-seeded Steffi made her way to the final where she met Jana Novotna in a classic duel. Novotna led 4–1, 40–30 in the final set, but failed to pull off the big win. The Czech lost her nerve and Steffi, desperate to hold on to the title that she cherishes above all others, pulled on all her reserves to hang in and win the last five games to score a 7–6, 1–6, 6–4 victory. It was her third consecutive triumph at Wimbledon and her fifth in six years. An excellent win, but perhaps the match will more often be remembered for that touching moment when Novotna was handed her runner's-up prize and collapsed on the shoulder of the Duchess of York, tears flowing freely.

Steffi was to win the US Open in 1993 too. In the final, she played and beat Helena Sukova in two straightforward sets, 6–3, 6–3. Surprisingly, observers felt she was playing better tennis than she had in 1988, her Golden Grand Slam year.

At the Australian Open in 1994, Steffi collected her fifteenth Grand Slam singles title – but still nine fewer than the record holder Margaret Court. It was her fourth Grand Slam title in a row, which means that she is the only player to win four consecutive Grand Slam titles twice in the Open era. Steffi is also the only player – male or female – to win all four Grand Slam titles in the 1990s. To add to all that, in defeating Arantxa Sanchez-Vicario 6–0, 6–2 in less than an hour in the final, Steffi secured the eightieth singles title of her career.

The German No. 1 was thrilled by her performance against Sanchez-Vicario, feeling that she had come as near as she ever has and probably ever will to reaching her ultimate goal: a perfect performance on court. 'It's a great feeling. It's great, it's a great Grand Slam. I don't think there can be many moments when I can say I play like that.' That's about as close as Steffi gets to being excited.

By Steffi's hyper-critical standards, it means she played very well indeed.

Four more titles followed – in Tokyo, Indian Wells, Delray Beach and the Lipton International Players Championships – before Steffi reached Hamburg to play in the Citizen Cup. Just as readers must surely have been starting to get bored by articles stating that Monica Seles's return was desperately needed, Steffi was brought down to size by the determined Sanchez-Vicario.

The Spaniard successfully defended her title, beating Steffi 4–6, 7–6, 7–6 in the final. Steffi was perhaps a little nervous, given the skeletons in her cupboard from the previous year and that there had been threats against her in 1994. Sanchez-Vicario put up a tremendous fight, however, and certainly deserved her win.

It was the beginning of the end, as far as Steffi was concerned. The rest of 1994 was not a great success and her results were worse than in the difficult year of 1990.

Steffi arrived in Paris as hot favourite to win the French Open and a second Grand Slam title in 1994. It was not to be. For the first time in 21 tournaments, she failed to reach the final. France's Mary Pierce used a combination of power, drop shots and looping drives to overpower Steffi in a humiliating straight sets, 6–2, 6–2, defeat. Steffi was gracious, saying, 'It must be a good thing for women's tennis, even though it's difficult for me to say so at this moment.' However, she subsequently announced that she was tired and that she would be unavailable to play for Germany in the Federation Cup.

Despite her failure to win the French Open title, Steffi was still considered to be the only horse in the race to secure the Wimbledon crown. As it happened, the one thoroughbred in the race fell at the first fence, when she was beaten by McNeil, 7–5, 7–6. The hottest favourite had drawn one of the toughest non-seeds, and faltered.

Never before had the defending ladies' champion been knocked out in the first round. It was only the second time since January 1985 that this had happened to Steffi – the other occasion having been at the Virginia Slims Championships in November 1992, when Steffi had lost in straight sets to … McNeil. Gusts of wind, which affected her high service toss, did not help Steffi's chances.

Nor did McNeil's aggressive style of play, as she rushed to the net at every opportunity and chased everything down at the back of the court.

It was the first time for almost ten years that Steffi had lost two consecutive matches. The last time that had happened was when she was beaten in the fourth round of the 1984 Australian Open and then lost the first match she played in 1985, in Key Biscayne, to Jo Durie. Steffi, not surprisingly, just wanted to get away and she immediately retired to her home in Florida.

Some may have suggested that Steffi's losses were due to a lack of motivation, but she would hear none of it. In the post-match press conference, Steffi was asked whether she had lost her hunger for victory. The reply was a terse 'I wouldn't be here if that was so.'

It was possibly the worst upset of Steffi's long and illustrious career and the experienced eye of Pavel Slozil would notice that 'Steffi looked tired, she was nervous, her intensity was gone. I think she will take a break, then work even harder to win the US Open.'

Loss is never easy to accept, especially for those who are so used to winning. Lesser players find an excuse for losing – they complain about the sun getting in their eyes perhaps, as part of their defence mechanism. Great champions such as Steffi strip away those reactions and only consider one option: 'I am the best and I am going to prove it.' Thus when they lose, it is so much harder for them than for lesser mortals. Steffi still gets morose when she loses; that is why she still has the ability to win, because she still feels the pain of defeat.

Steffi hates losing points, let alone matches. The disgust is evident on her face when she loses a point she thinks she had a chance to win during a match. At the Virginia Slims Championships in 1988, she characteristically described losing a set, not the match, to Claudia Kohde-Kilsch as 'disgusting'.

So after defeats at the French Open and Wimbledon, there was talk about how long it would take Steffi to regain her confidence. At the WTA event played in San Diego in the first week of August, Steffi had problems putting away her opponents as her usually reliable forehand started to sail long or wide, amid a loss of concentration.

In the final, however, Steffi proved why she is a great champion. Against Sanchez-Vicario she was back to her winning ways, demolishing the Spaniard 6–2, 6–1. 'Every time she plays me, she's so great. She's got something against me. I don't know what it is,' wailed Arantxa, tongue in cheek. Steffi seemed to miss the joke and dismissed the comment: 'I'm not mad at her, I just played some of my best tennis.' That she did.

Sanchez-Vicario used the Canadian Open final two weeks later to exact her revenge. Although Steffi had four match points she failed to convert them – but there was an explanation. While the Spaniard walked away a 7–5, 1–6, 7–6 winner, Steffi hobbled off court with a back ailment, described by WTA officials as a lower back strain and joint disfunction.

At the US Open in September Steffi demolished her opponents in early rounds. Troubled by a bad back, she obviously saw no reason to hang around. 'I'm not really in a hurry,' Steffi said, but as is her way, underrated her proficiency by adding, 'I guess I'm just playing well.' It was not to be a bed of roses all the way to the title, however. In the final, Steffi lost to Sanchez-Vicario, and then announced that she was taking a long break so that she could recover from a stress fracture in her lower back.

Steffi returned to the Tour two months later to play in the year-end Virginia Slims Championships, but lost in the second round, once again to Mary Pierce, improving only marginally on the French Open scoreline, with the French girl winning 6–4, 6–4.

Although Steffi ended the year still the No. 1 ranked player in the world, Sanchez-Vicario was named the Women's World Champion by the ITF and finished at the top of the Virginia Slims Bonus Pool, having won eight WTA Tour titles, including the French and the US Opens.

The tennis world was already saying 'Steffi is history' before she withdrew from the Australian Open at the beginning of 1995, sidelined once more by injury. Players no longer have the same respect for her on the court, are no longer afraid of her, no longer go out wondering how many games they will be able to secure. Her opponents go out on to court believing they can beat Steffi. Inevitably, it was only a matter of time before Arantxa Sanchez-Vicario took over the No. 1 ranking, as she did in February.

But to write Steffi's career off is premature, even though in the past she has talked about leaving the game at an earlier age than some. She suggested as long ago as the end of the 1987 tennis season that she would not be playing professional tennis after the age of 28. 'Tennis is a lot of fun for me and I will not stop playing for my own fun then. But now I have no time for myself. I'm always running between training and airports, between tournaments to more training, to other engagements.'

In 1990, she confirmed her earlier thoughts, saying,

When Martina began there wasn't the competition there is now, or the same pressure from the outside, from tournaments, sponsors and press. Nowadays you can not go past thirty. You have to be fit for fifteen or sixteen years. There is such a difference.

It definitely has got more difficult for the players. WTA Tour events were played in eleven countries in 1984, while in 1994 they were played in 21, adding to the travelling hours, change of time zones and jet lag that the players have to deal with. On top of this the increased competition between players has resulted in more difficult matches and greater demands for them to be at peak fitness.

As recently as the beginning of 1994, Steffi told the German press, 'I've achieved everything I've wanted. Last year was simply too much. I'm not going to do it again. I need more time for my private life.' There was probably a communal sigh of relief when Steffi uttered those words; Chris Evert once said that the other players, as a way of indicating that the German was unbeatable, all wished Steffi would fall madly in love, get married and get pregnant.

Steffi has certainly shown increasing signs of independence in recent years, most noticeably since the allegations involving her father emerged. In the summer of 1992, Steffi acquired her very own apartment in New York. Later in the year Steffi also gained a serious boyfriend, Michael Bartels. Bartels, described as 'a very, very nice bloke, an absolutely charming guy' is not too bad at his job, either. Back in 1989, he raced and beat compatriot Michael

Schumacher, the current Formula 1 world champion, in the German Formula 3 series.

With her loss of form in the middle of 1994 there were rumours that Steffi had lost her intensity, that it was because she was head over heels in love with Bartels and that tennis was no longer at the top of her priority list. The other explanation put forward was that Steffi felt she had nothing left to achieve, particularly as her great rival, Seles, looked less and less likely to return to the Tour, the longer she stayed away. Steffi has described the rankings as 'meaningless' until Seles returns.

With a series of defeats at the hands of two particular players, Sanchez-Vicario and Pierce, Steffi can no longer believe that there is no one left on the WTA Tour to challenge her. Furthermore, there are a number of good young players emerging such as Croatian Iva Majoli and Lindsay Davenport of the United States who may well challenge for the top in the near future. Steffi might also have realised just how distracting her relationship with Bartels was becoming, for rumours in late 1994 indicated a cooling of their relationship, if not a total break.

Her enforced break away from tennis at the end of 1994 seems to have convinced her how much she loves tennis. To continue to train, play and travel as she has done, for as many as eleven months of the year for the more than twelve years since she turned professional, she herself admits that, 'You have to be dedicated. I love to play, I have won all the tournaments, so there's nothing left but I love the sport, I still enjoy it so much.' And now, at the age of almost 26, she has talked about playing for as long as five more years, if she can regain her health and fitness.

Steffi's change of heart – to carry on playing professional tennis longer than she thought – is not unusual. Evert talked about quitting in 1980 at the age of 26; Navratilova, having thought that she would retire earlier, suddenly found renewed enthusiasm for the game after she had knee surgery and started talking about playing for as long as her knee would hold up. Their re-thinks are really not that surprising.

Take Steffi. She is insecure because she has reached the stage in her life – given that she is approaching 26 and once said that she did not intend to play past the age of 27 or 28 – when she has

started to think about what she should do after tennis. She has no idea what else to do, because tennis has been her life; that is all she knows and so she cannot think of doing anything else.

The story goes that her former coach Pavel Slozil once asked Steffi what she was going to do after tennis. She replied, 'What can I do? I am not qualified to do anything else. I am only a tennis player.' So Pavel sat down and wrote a list of 30 professions that might be suitable for her. Steffi took a quick look at what he had written, screwed up the paper in frustration and said, 'No, it's impossible, I'm not good enough to do any of these things.' That's the conundrum faced by those who have reached the highest level of achievement in their field – trying to re-invent oneself if one is a top class athlete is no easy task.

Of course there are other reasons why Steffi will continue to play tennis, if her health allows her. She is still keen to play perfectly, for that is ultimately what makes her happy. She wants to go out at the top in a blaze of glory, for she enjoys crushing people. Her response to the reporter who asked once whether she ever got bored of easy victories was, 'Do you get bored with caviar?' Steffi certainly does not want to stop playing professional tennis simply because she is injured or no longer has the mental conviction to win matches.

And she still wants to win the big ones. When asked after the Wimbledon 1993 final in which she defeated Novotna what kept her stimulated, she replied,

> Just these few moments that I have after the match, I mean, that gives you a thrill to be out there, and to come back from that match, for example. I mean, these are highlights that you can't have doing something else, at least I feel so.

When Steffi finally does retire from tennis, she does have various interests that she might pursue even if she feels at this stage in her life that she is not qualified for them. She may go back to school, which is one possibility she has considered at different times in her life. At sixteen, she said that she did not think of the future too much, but would perhaps be interested in something that involved animals. Dogs, particularly, are a passion.

Also, when she was younger she said she wanted to run her own hotel, because she had seen so many and spent so much time in them that she would know what it takes to make a perfect one. But she has since gone off the idea.

Several former tennis stars, such as Chris Evert and Tracy Austin, have gone into television commentary, and that is an avenue that Steffi could pursue. However, she has indicated that she does not intend to have anything to do with tennis, because she has already dedicated so much of her life to the sport and wants a change.

Perhaps the area in which she becomes involved is most likely to be influenced by the arts. Steffi has at various times been interested in interior design, art, photography and most recently, fashion. She has had some input into the design of her tennis clothes and has recently launched her own range of jeans.

She has said that she certainly does not want to end up with nothing to do, but perhaps rather than finding a particular job Steffi will use her time to travel to places to which she has been but has not had a chance to investigate or to completely new places such as South America, in which she has expressed an interest. With more than a few million dollars in the bank, the world really is her oyster . . .

EPILOGUE

AT THE BEGINNING OF 1995, Steffi's future as a top player appeared to be in limbo, but in February, after a three-month break due to injury, she made her comeback at the Open Gaz de France in Paris.

She made it quite clear then that she would not undergo surgery to correct what she termed a 'bone spur' in her lower back region. 'The doctors,' she explained, 'have told me that unless I have surgery I'm going to have the problem for the rest of my life. It would put me out for six to eight months and they cannot guarantee that it would be one hundred per cent after, so I've decided against having the operation during my playing career.'

Another consideration, she admitted, which suggested that a family life after tennis might already be playing on her mind, was the fact that 'The doctors also told me they would have to open me up from the front and operate that way, and I feel I am too young for something like that.'

So, still determined to compete on the WTA Tour despite the fact that she is likely to have to play in pain at times, she is modifying her game to reduce stress to the affected area. It is impossible to predict how much longer Steffi's back will stand up to the strain of the professional Tour. As she admitted herself. 'I don't know how much longer I will keep on playing, but right now I am motivated – very motivated.'

Whatever the outcome, her place in the tennis hall of fame is secure. In her time she has been the tops. And in the view of many distinguished observers of the game she is certainly the best to date.

Ted Tinling, tennis observer extraordinaire, imagined a

tournament of the greats that included Suzanne Lenglen, Maureen Connolly, Helen Wills Moody, Martina Navratilova and Steffi Graf. He believed Steffi would reach the final against Connolly and would lose the first set but eventually win on guts, pure strength and 'a dazzling stream of forehand winners'.

Comparing the titans of different eras is always difficult and ultimately subjective, but indubitably Steffi's public success is there for all to see and acclaim.

The only question mark against Steffi's name is whether late in her career – and after – she can enjoy her private life as much as she has quite evidently relished her achievements in her professional career.

CAREER HIGHLIGHTS
AND LOWLIGHTS

Wins/Losses	Injuries/Illnesses
(Losses shown in brackets)	

1982 *Singles*:
European Championships
– Under 12s
European Championships
– Under 18s

1983 *Singles*:
(Australian Open 1st round)   Fell on grass courts during
(French Open 2nd round)   practice in the Australian
Open and tore tendons in
her thumb.

1984 *Singles*:
(Australian Open 3rd round)
(French Open 3rd round)
(Wimbledon 4th round)
(US Open 1st round)

1985 *Singles*:
(French Open 4th round)
(Wimbledon 4th round)
(US Open semi-finals)

1986 *Singles*:
(French Open quarter-finals)   Viral flu led to early exit
(US Open semi finals)   from French Open, and
German Open   withdrawal from
Wimbledon.

Wins/Losses	Injuries/Illnesses

1986 *Singles – contd.*

German Fed. Cup Team
Amelia Island
Hilton Head
US Clay Courts
Pan Pacific
Zurich
Brighton
Mahwah

Forced out of Fed. Cup when sunshade fell and broke her right toe.

Doubles:
German Open, with Sukova
US Clay Courts, with Sabatini
Brighton, with Sukova

1987 *Singles*:
French Open
(Wimbledon finals)
(US Open finals)
Virginia Slims Champ.
Lipton
Los Angeles
European Indoors
Boca Raton
Hamburg
German Open
Italian Open
Hilton Head
Amelia Island

Just before US Open underwent emergency root canal operation, developed an infection, and had a fever during the Championships.

Took a three-week break late in the year, due to sinus trouble.

Doubles:
Amelia Island, with Sabatini

1988 *Singles*:
Australian Open
French Open

Wins/Losses	Injuries/Illnesses
1988 *Singles – contd.*	
Wimbledon	
US Open	
Lipton	Treated for cramps an hour
US Hardcourts	after winning in the Lipton
Hamburg	finals.
German Open	
Mahwah	
Brighton	
Olympics	After the Olympics,
	developed bronchitis.
Doubles:	
Wimbledon, with Sabatini	
Lipton, with Sabatini	
1989 *Singles*:	
Australian Open	During 1989 suffered from a
(French Open finals)	recurring virus.
Wimbledon	
US Open	
Virginia Slims Champ.	
Washington DC	
Boca Raton	
US Hardcourts	
Hilton Head	
Hamburg	
German Open	
San Diego	
Mahwah	
European Indoors	
Brighton	
Doubles:	
Mahwah with Shriver	
1990 *Singles*:	
Australian Open	Broke thumb on the skiing

Wins/Losses	Injuries/Illnesses

1990 *Singles – contd.*
(French Open finals)
(Wimbledon semi-finals)
(US Open finals)
Hamburg
Canadian Open
San Diego
Leipzig
European Indoors
Brighton
New England
Pan Pacific
Amelia Island

slopes in Feb. After the third specialist opinion she had an operation, to avoid jeopardising her chances in the Grand Slam.

Suffered a series of ear, throat and sinus problems through the summer.

1991 *Singles*:
(Australian Open quarter-finals)
(French Open semi-finals)
Wimbledon
(US Open semi-finals)
US Hardcourts
Hamburg
German Open
Leipzig
European Indoors
Brighton

Played with a torn shoulder tendon at Wimbledon, and was treated on court.

1992 *Singles*:
(French Open finals)
Wimbledon
(US Open quarter-finals)
Boca Raton
Hamburg
German Open
Leipzig
Zurich
Brighton

Withdrew from playing in the Hopman Cup with Becker due to ear infection, and from the Australian Open, due to measles. (The press screamed 'Tennis could kill Steffi', and blamed her illness on stress caused by

Wins/Losses   Injuries/Illnesses

1992 *Singles – contd.*
     Philadelphia   blackmail of her father and
     Olympics   the revelation of his affair.)

     Doubles:
     Hamburg, with Stubbs

1993 *Singles*:
     (Australian Open finals)
     French Open   Played the French Open and
     Wimbledon   Wimbledon with painful
     US Open   foot injury, later operated
     Virginia Slims Champ.   on. Administered
     Delray Beach   painkillers throughout
     Hilton Head   Wimbledon.
     German Open
     San Diego
     Canadian Open
     Leipzig

     Doubles:
     Hamburg, with Stubbs

1994 *Singles*:
     Australian Open
     (French Open semi-finals)
     (Wimbledon 1st round)
     (US Open finals)
     Lipton
     Pan Pacific
     Indian Wells
     Delray Beach
     German Open
     San Diego

1995 *Singles*:
     Open Gaz de France

INDEX

DATE DUE

Brodart Co.   Cat. # 55 137 001   Printed in USA

#33407185